Bloom's Shakespeare Through the Ages

Julius Caesar

King Lear

Macbeth

Othello

Bloom's Shakespeare Through the Ages

MACBETH

Edited and with an introduction by
Harold Bloom
Sterling Professor of the Humanities
Yale University

Volume Editor
Janyce Marson

☑Checkmark Books®
An imprint of Infobase Publishing

Bloom's Shakespeare Through the Ages: Macbeth

Copyright © 2008 by Infobase Publishing

Introduction © 2008 by Harold Bloom

Checkmark Books
An imprint of Infobase Publishing
132 West 31st Street
New York NY 10001

Library of Congress Cataloging-in-Publication Data
Macbeth / edited and with an introduction by Harold Bloom ; volume editor, Janyce Marson.
  p. cm. — (Bloom's Shakespeare through the ages)
  Includes bibliographical references and index.
  ISBN 978-0-7910-9842-4 (pbk)
  ISBN 978-0-7910-9594-2 (hc : alk. paper) 1. Shakespeare, William, 1564–1616. Macbeth—Examinations—Study guides. 2. Macbeth, King of Scotland, 11th cent.—In literature. 3. Tragedy—Examinations—Study guides. 4. Regicides in literature. I. Bloom, Harold. II. Marson, Janyce.
  PR2823.M2295 2008
  822.3'3—dc22   2007032378

Series design by Erika K. Arroyo
Cover design by Ben Peterson
Cover photo © The Granger Collection, New York

Printed in the United States of America

Bang EJB 10 9 8 7 6 5 4 3 2 1

This book is printed on acid-free paper.

CONTENTS

SERIES INTRODUCTION
❧

Shakespeare Through the Ages presents not the most current of Shakespeare criticism, but the best of Shakespeare criticism, from the seventeenth century to today. In the process, each volume also charts the flow over time of critical discussion of a particular play. Other useful and fascinating collections of historical Shakespearean criticism exist, but no collection that we know of contains such a range of commentary on each of Shakespeare's greatest plays and at the same time emphasizes the greatest critics in our literary tradition: from John Dryden in the seventeenth century, to Samuel Johnson in the eighteenth century, to William Hazlitt and Samuel Coleridge in the nineteenth century, to A.C. Bradley and William Empson in the twentieth century, to the most perceptive critics of our own day. This canon of Shakespearean criticism emphasizes aesthetic rather than political or social analysis.

Some of the pieces included here are full-length essays; others are excerpts designed to present a key point. Much (but not all) of the earliest criticism consists only of brief mentions of specific plays. In addition to the classics of criticism, some pieces of mainly historical importance have been included, often to provide background for important reactions from future critics.

These volumes are intended for students, particularly those just beginning their explorations of Shakespeare. We have therefore also included basic materials designed to provide a solid grounding in each play: a biography of Shakespeare, a synopsis of the play, a list of characters, and an explication of key passages. In addition, each selection of the criticism of a particular century begins with an introductory essay discussing the general nature of that century's commentary and the particular issues and controversies addressed by critics presented in the volume.

Shakespeare was "not of an age, but for all time," but much Shakespeare criticism is decidedly for its own age, of lasting importance only to the scholar who wrote it. Students today read the criticism most readily available to them, which means essays printed in recent books and journals, especially those journals made available on the Internet. Older criticism is too often buried in out-of-print books on forgotten shelves of libraries or in defunct periodicals. Therefore, many students, particularly younger students, have no way of knowing that some of the most profound criticism of Shakespeare's plays was written decades or centuries ago. We hope this series remedies that problem, and more importantly, we hope it infuses students with the enthusiasm of the critics in these volumes for the beauty and power of Shakespeare's plays.

INTRODUCTION BY
HAROLD BLOOM

Mark Van Doren observed that Shakespeare was an electric field through which we moved our interpretations and that these were lit up (or not) by Shakespeare, considerably more than they illuminated *him*.

Macbeth, always my favorite among the plays, is to me a dramatic poem, which illuminated Romanticism into being, from Milton's Satan on through Byron's Cain to Herman Melville's Ahab and Cormac McCarthy's Judge Holden.

Macbeth's preternatural eloquence is far in excess of his role as a Jacobean villain-hero. A great voice keeps breaking into Macbeth's monologues, the voice of angels coming down:

> Besides, this Duncan
> Hath borne his faculties so meek, hath been
> So clear in his great office, that his virtues
> Will plead like angels, trumpet-tongu'd against
> The deep damnation of his taking-off;
> And Pity, like a naked new-born babe,
> Striding the blast, or heaven's Cherubins, hors'd
> Upon the sightless couriers of the air,
> Shall blow the horrid deed in every eye,
> That tears shall drown the wind.
>
> I. vii. 16-25

Macbeth has been an involuntary mystic since childhood and is "weird" in the Scottish sense, like the "weird sisters" whom we call witches. He is uncanny as they are and a lot more sinister. Since Shakespeare compels us to internalize Macbeth, we also became weird. Of all Shakespeare's dramas, *Macbeth* is the most contaminating in its effect.

The result is that no other literary work is more hurtful. *Macbeth* is a living wound and makes me wonder that even *Hamlet* is less revelatory of Shakespeare's own deep inwardness. Is Macbeth somehow representative of the runaway element in Shakespeare's imagination?

More than ever *Macbeth* seems the dramatic poem of our climate, political and amoral. I come to dread rereading and reteaching the play, because I am less and less able to sever from the usurper. Shadows augment in Macbeth's verbal presence and in the spirit of his solitude.

Do we get what we give or give what we get? Macbeth shows that the two are not the same. No other verbal universe, not even Hamlet's or Lear's, is so labyrinthine a prophecy that, whether in love or in murder, the giving famishes the receiver.

I see that the growing intensity of my responses to *Macbeth* is forcing me into a highly disjunctive style. Years ago, writing about the play, I compared Macbeth's own staccato mode to that of a bad actor ("poor player") perpetually afraid of missing his cues. A temporal frenzy governs Macbeth as he attempts to murder the future, in the massacre of the Macduff children and the vexed endeavor to kill Banquo's son, Fleance.

In spite of recurrent medieval themes, however, the new literature thrives on strangely unexpected rhythms. As Anthony Nuttall puts it in his book on *Timon of Athens*, these rhythms in Shakespeare at least owe much to "the curious way in which Shakespeare's mind continually races ahead of itself." Similarly, Harold Bloom has spoken about Macbeth's "proleptic imagination," an insane drive to accumulate and annihilate the traces of his past, whipping them into his future before he has time to think. When Prince Hal thunders at Falstaff, "What a devil hast thou to do with the time of day?" we feel the stress tearing at an ancient people's way of life, for almost at once the Prince tells us he will redeem the time, "when men think least I will." At that moment he steps into the modern role of Doctor Faustus, who would possess time itself, and he loses Falstaff, who would give it away. The end of an age coincides with the coming of a future whose limits no one can yet foresee, whose changes rush at us before we are ready.

—Angus Fletcher, *Time, Space, and Motion in the Age of Shakespeare*, pp. 53–54.

I will allow Fletcher to conclude my brief observations on *Macbeth* here. As a lifelong Falstaffian, I go on evading time (or trying to), and perhaps that is part of why Macbeth frightens me so much.

BIOGRAPHY OF
WILLIAM SHAKESPEARE
ಇನ್

WILLIAM SHAKESPEARE was born in Stratford-on-Avon in April 1564 into a family of some prominence. His father, John Shakespeare, was a glover and merchant of leather goods who earned enough to marry Mary Arden, the daughter of his father's landlord, in 1557. John Shakespeare was a prominent citizen in Stratford, and at one point, he served as an alderman and bailiff.

Shakespeare presumably attended the Stratford grammar school, where he would have received an education in Latin, but he did not go on to either Oxford or Cambridge universities. Little is recorded about Shakespeare's early life; indeed, the first record of his life after his christening is of his marriage to Anne Hathaway in 1582 in the church at Temple Grafton, near Stratford. He would have been required to obtain a special license from the bishop as security that there was no impediment to the marriage. Peter Alexander states in his book *Shakespeare's Life and Art* that marriage at this time in England required neither a church nor a priest or, for that matter, even a document—only a declaration of the contracting parties in the presence of witnesses. Thus, it was customary, though not mandatory, to follow the marriage with a church ceremony.

Little is known about William and Anne Shakespeare's marriage. Their first child, Susanna, was born in May 1583 and twins, Hamnet and Judith, in 1585. Later on, Susanna married Dr. John Hall, but the younger daughter, Judith, remained unmarried. When Hamnet died in Stratford in 1596, the boy was only 11 years old.

We have no record of Shakespeare's activities for the seven years after the birth of his twins, but by 1592 he was in London working as an actor. He was also apparently well known as a playwright, for reference is made of him by his contemporary Robert Greene, in *A Groatsworth of Wit*, as "an upstart crow."

Several companies of actors were in London at this time. Shakespeare may have had connection with one or more of them before 1592, but we have no record that tells us definitely. However, we do know of his long association with the most famous and successful troupe, the Lord Chamberlain's Men. (When James I came to the throne in 1603, after Elizabeth's death, the troupe's name changed to the King's Men.) In 1599 the Lord Chamberlain's Men provided the financial backing for the construction of their own theater, the Globe.

The Globe was begun by a carpenter named James Burbage and finished by his two sons, Cuthbert and Robert. To escape the jurisdiction of the Corporation of London, which was composed of conservative Puritans who opposed the theater's "licentiousness," James Burbage built the Globe just outside London, in the Liberty of Holywell, beside Finsbury Fields. This also meant that the Globe was safer from the threats that lurked in London's crowded streets, like plague and other diseases, as well as rioting mobs. When James Burbage died in 1597, his sons completed the Globe's construction. Shakespeare played a vital role, financially and otherwise, in the construction of the theater, which was finally occupied sometime before May 16, 1599.

Shakespeare not only acted with the Globe's company of actors; he was also a shareholder and eventually became the troupe's most important playwright. The company included London's most famous actors, who inspired the creation of some of Shakespeare's best-known characters, such as Hamlet and Lear, as well as his clowns and fools.

In his early years, however, Shakespeare did not confine himself to the theater. He also composed some mythological-erotic poetry, such as *Venus and Adonis* and *The Rape of Lucrece*, both of which were dedicated to the earl of Southampton. Shakespeare was successful enough that in 1597 he was able to purchase his own home in Stratford, which he called New Place. He could even call himself a gentleman, for his father had been granted a coat of arms.

By 1598 Shakespeare had written some of his most famous works, *Romeo and Juliet*, *The Comedy of Errors*, *A Midsummer Night's Dream*, *The Merchant of Venice*, *Two Gentlemen of Verona*, and *Love's Labour's Lost*, as well as his historical plays *Richard II*, *Richard III*, *Henry IV*, and *King John*. Somewhere around the turn of the century, Shakespeare wrote his romantic comedies *As You Like It*, *Twelfth Night*, and *Much Ado About Nothing*, as well as *Henry V*, the last of his history plays in the Prince Hal series. During the next 10 years he wrote his great tragedies, *Hamlet*, *Macbeth*, *Othello*, *King Lear*, and *Antony and Cleopatra*.

At this time, the theater was burgeoning in London; the public took an avid interest in drama, the audiences were large, the plays demonstrated an enormous range of subjects, and playwrights competed for approval. By 1613, however, the rising tide of Puritanism had changed the theater. With the desertion of the theaters by the middle classes, the acting companies were compelled to depend more on the aristocracy, which also meant that they now had to cater to a more sophisticated audience.

Perhaps this change in London's artistic atmosphere contributed to Shakespeare's reasons for leaving London after 1612. His retirement from the theater is sometimes thought to be evidence that his artistic skills were waning. During this time, however, he wrote *The Tempest* and *Henry VIII*. He also wrote the "tragicomedies," *Pericles, Cymbeline,* and *The Winter's Tale.* These were thought to be inspired by Shakespeare's personal problems and have sometimes been considered proof of his greatly diminished abilities.

However, so far as biographical facts indicate, the circumstances of his life at this time do not imply any personal problems. He was in good health and financially secure, and he enjoyed an excellent reputation. Indeed, although he was settled in Stratford at this time, he made frequent visits to London, enjoying and participating in events at the royal court, directing rehearsals, and attending to other business matters.

In addition to his brilliant and enormous contributions to the theater, Shakespeare remained a poetic genius throughout the years, publishing a renowned and critically acclaimed sonnet cycle in 1609 (most of the sonnets were written many years earlier). Shakespeare's contribution to this popular poetic genre are all the more amazing in his break with contemporary notions of subject matter. Shakespeare idealized the beauty of man as an object of praise and devotion (rather than the Petrarchan tradition of the idealized, unattainable woman). In the same spirit of breaking with tradition, Shakespeare also treated themes previously considered off limits—the dark, sexual side of a woman as opposed to the Petrarchan ideal of a chaste and remote love object. He also expanded the sonnet's emotional range, including such emotions as delight, pride, shame, disgust, sadness, and fear.

When Shakespeare died in 1616, no collected edition of his works had ever been published, although some of his plays had been printed in separate unauthorized editions. (Some of these were taken from his manuscripts, some from the actors' prompt books, and others were reconstructed from memory by actors or spectators.) In 1623 two members of the King's Men, John Hemings and Henry Condell, published a collection of all the plays they considered to be authentic, the First Folio.

Included in the First Folio is a poem by Shakespeare's contemporary Ben Jonson, an outstanding playwright and critic in his own right. Jonson paid tribute to Shakespeare's genius, proclaiming his superiority to what previously had been held as the models for literary excellence—the Greek and Latin writers. "Triumph, my Britain, thou hast one to show / To whom all scenes of Europe homage owe. / He was not of an age, but for all time!"

Jonson was the first to state what has been said so many times since. Having captured what is permanent and universal to all human beings at all times, Shakespeare's genius continues to inspire us—and the critical debate about his works never ceases.

SUMMARY OF *MACBETH*

Act I

In the brief opening that is scene 1, the audience views a dark and foreboding landscape. Three witches have gathered in an open field during a dark thunderstorm. They agree that at their next gathering they will meet with Macbeth, "when the hurlyburly's done," implying that in the meantime they will toy with his character and entice him to evil. They plan to meet with Macbeth "ere the set of sun," and their haste generates a sense of temporal urgency that persists throughout the play: Impatience for predictions of future glory to become manifest is what prompts Macbeth (and others) to help the future along. The witches' final cackling statement, "Fair is foul, and foul is fair," establishes a central theme of the play: the problem of how to distinguish between appearance and reality and how to interpret contradictory signs and enigmatic statements.

The short scene that follows (scene 2) takes place in King Duncan's camp. An unnamed captain, his battle wounds still bleeding, praises Macbeth's bravery and calls him "valour's minion." The captain describes how Macbeth surged to victory in his battle with Macdonwald and how, when Norway's King Sweno immediately launched a fresh assault, Macbeth defeated Sweno as well. The captain departs to tend his wounds and, shortly after, the Thane of Ross appears. He informs Duncan that the Thane of Cawdor has become a traitor, having joined forces with the king of Norway. Enraged by the report, Duncan resolves to kill this traitor. He bestows the now-vacant title upon Macbeth, making him the new Thane of Cawdor.

Scene 3 returns to a dismal heath and the three witches. One of them resolves to avenge an insult from a sailor's wife by sending tempestuous winds to shake her husband's boat and deprive him of sleep, and the others offer their assistance with this diabolical plot. As they brew their magic potion, the three Weird Sisters join hands and dance around nine times.

A drumroll sounds, and Macbeth and Banquo enter. Macbeth comments on the unpleasant weather on the heath ("So foul and fair a day I have not seen"), unconsciously invoking the words of the three witches in scene 1. Banquo tries to determine what the witches are. He suspects that they are supernatural beings:

With their horrible skinny lips, chappy fingers, and beards—features that make them appear to be men, though they are not—they bear no resemblance to "inhabitants o' the earth," he says. When Macbeth questions the witches, they respond by hailing him three times and greeting him as things he has not yet become—the Thane of Cawdor and the future king. Macbeth is baffled by the witches' riddle. Banquo begs to hear about his own future, and the witches' response is equally incomprehensible: Banquo will be "lesser than Macbeth and greater"; he will be "not so happy, yet much happier"; and he shall beget kings. Macbeth begs to hear more, to know why and how these "imperfect speakers" are able to make their predictions, but the three weird creatures vanish without answering. The men are left to puzzle over their strange encounter, questioning whether their observations are credible or the result of having eaten of some "insane root."

Macbeth and Banquo are soon interrupted by the arrival of Ross and Angus, the Scottish noblemen sent by King Duncan. The messengers convey the king's appreciation for Macbeth's bravery and victory, and they announce that he has been granted the title of Thane of Cawdor. Macbeth and Banquo are shocked by this realization of the witches' prediction. Banquo wonders aloud whether the devil, in the form of these three witches, can speak the truth, while Macbeth asks how he can be given the title already held by another man. Angus explains that the former Thane of Cawdor is to be executed for treasonous acts.

Macbeth is overjoyed with his seeming good luck, but he also is fearful. As Banquo has just warned him, evil speaks in half-truths to "win us with honest trifles," only to deceive by making appearances seem like reality. Lost in thought, Macbeth considers what events would have to unfold to fulfill the witches' final prophecy. The thought makes his heart "knock at [his] ribs," and Macbeth, in an aside, speaks of murdering this unsettling thought. Confounded by the situation ("Nothing is but what is not"), Macbeth declares that the prophecy, if true, will happen without his help: "If chance will have me king, why, chance may crown me, / Without my stir." With this Macbeth finally returns his attention to this companions, and the men set off to see the king.

Scene 4 takes place at King Duncan's palace at Forres, where the king has arrived with his sons, Malcolm and Donaldbain, along with Lennox and other attendants. Malcolm informs Duncan that the former Thane of Cawdor has been executed. Ironically, Duncan comments that it is easy to read someone's character by their physiognomy: "There's no art / To find the mind's construction in the face."

When Macbeth and Banquo arrive with Ross and Angus, Duncan greets the new Thane of Cawdor as "worthiest cousin" and thanks both men for their loyal service. He tells Macbeth that he plans to continue cultivating his career ("I have begun to plant thee, and will labour / To make thee full of growing"), and he promises to reward Banquo in a similar manner. Finally, Duncan names Malcolm as Prince of Cumberland and the heir to the throne. His proclamations made, Duncan announces that he will visit Macbeth at Inverness. Though he responds graciously, Macbeth is disturbed by Duncan's last pronouncement and, in an aside, says that he hopes the light will not reveal his "black and deep desires."

Scene 5 begins with Lady Macbeth reading a letter from her husband, in which he informs her of his encounter with the Weird Sisters, their predictions of political gain, and the immediate fulfillment of their first prophecy: Macbeth is Thane of Cawdor. Elated by the prospect of becoming queen, the ambitious and ruthless Lady Macbeth considers her husband's nature with dissatisfaction. She worries that he is too kindhearted to carry out a decisive plan that would ensure him the throne. Thus, she resolves to take control of their shared destiny and looks forward to his speedy return: "Hie thee hither, / That I may pour my spirits in thine ear." When an attendant informs her of Duncan's imminent arrival, she welcomes his "fatal entrance" and begs the spirits to assist her in her deadly plan by removing all vestiges of feminine weakness: "Unsex me here, / And fill me, from the crown to the toe, top-full / Of direst cruelty!"

When Macbeth enters the scene, she makes her first anticipatory gesture by greeting him as king, referring to his future as the "all-hail hereafter." (The literary term for such anticipation is *prolepsis*, where an effect is assumed before its cause occurs.) Lady Macbeth then immediately shares her murderous plot against Duncan and warns Macbeth not to let any malevolent thoughts show in his face: "Your face, my thane, is as a book, where men / May read strange matters." Macbeth proposes that they discuss the matter further. Lady Macbeth, however, concludes the conversation (and the scene), telling her husband to remain calm and "leave the rest to me."

The next brief scene (scene 6) takes place outside Inverness Castle, where King Duncan has arrived with his sons, Banquo, and other noblemen and attendants. Both Duncan and Banquo admire the castle and regard the small bird they see ("the temple-haunting martlet") as a heaven-sent harbinger of good to come. As they discuss the merits of Inverness, Lady Macbeth graciously comes out to greet them. The scene is packed with dramatic irony. Inverness appears safe and hospitable to Banquo and Duncan, but deadly danger awaits them there. And Lady Macbeth—apparently the perfect hostess, whose sole concern is to serve her guests—has all along been plotting Duncan's murder.

Scene 7 opens with the solitary Macbeth wrestling with his conscience over the plot to murder Duncan. He knows that he owes the king loyalty as his subject, gratitude for the favor he has shown, and protection as his host. Macbeth craves kingship, but he is loath to commit murder and weather its unpredictable outcome. Lady Macbeth enters, and he tells her they must abandon the plot; matters are good enough as they are. His wife responds with derision, attacking Macbeth's masculinity and calling him a coward. When he protests, she belittles his reluctance to act and his anxiety that their plot may fail. Lady Macbeth explains that she plans to place blame for the murder on Duncan's two guards: She will see to it that they get extremely drunk, then smear them with the king's blood as they sleep in ignorant stupor. At last, Macbeth resigns himself to the plan.

Act II

Scene 1 takes place at Inverness around midnight, when Banquo and his son Fleance are conversing before retiring to bed. Banquo comments on the unrelieved darkness of a starless sky. He is tired, but he resists sleep because it would make him vulnerable to "cursed thoughts," or nightmares.

Macbeth enters, briefly startling the men. Banquo, on the king's behalf, praises him and Lady Macbeth for their hospitality and presents a diamond in token of Duncan's gratitude. He reports that the king has gone happily to his bed for the night. Banquo then abruptly tells Macbeth about his dreams of the three Weird Sisters. Macbeth responds, hypocritically, that he "does not think of them," but goes on to suggest a discussion about them later. Throughout this dialogue, Macbeth repeatedly refers to himself as "we," apparently anticipating his royal destiny. When Macbeth obliquely asks for Banquo's loyalty "when 'tis" (when he is king), Banquo gives a noncommittal response.

Banquo and Fleance depart for bed, leaving Macbeth alone to face his fears. He envisions a dagger in front of him, but when he attempts to seize it, nothing is there. Though he blinks his eyes to erase the image, the dagger remains, now dripping blood. Macbeth finally understands that it is only a vision of the "bloody business at hand." His thoughts turn to the dark hour of midnight, when "witchcraft celebrates." The scene ends with the sounding of a bell, ringing Duncan's death knell. Macbeth leaves; there is no more time for procrastination.

Lady Macbeth enters, in scene 2, declaring that the wine that has made the guards drunk "hath made me bold." She has left the guards' daggers out for Macbeth to use and says that if the king had not resembled her own father in his sleep, she probably would have killed him herself. Macbeth returns, visibly shaken, covered in blood, and carrying the two murder weapons. "I have done the deed," he says. Foreshadowing the curse of insomnia that is to come, Macbeth says he heard a voice crying, "Sleep no more! Macbeth does murder sleep." Lady Macbeth interrupts his disturbing thoughts with calculated and practical detachment, instructing him to wash away the evidence and return the daggers to the crime scene. But the tormented Macbeth refuses: "I am afraid to think what I have done; / Look on it again I dare not." Resigned to do it herself, Lady Macbeth departs. Just then begins a loud and insistent knocking, which fills Macbeth with dread. As he begins to panic, Lady Macbeth returns. She criticizes his cowardly anxiety and admonishes him not to be "lost / so poorly in your thoughts." But Macbeth's guilt and anxiety have already taken root: "To know my deed, 'twere best not know myself."

In scene 3, the knocking that began in the prior scene intensifies until one of the drunken porters wakes and comes to the door of the castle. The porter imagines himself opening hell's gate, where a number of sinners are waiting to come in, including a greedy farmer who hanged himself, an equivocator who "committed treason enough for God's sake," and an English tailor who was a thief. It is no coincidence that each one of these sinners possesses one of Macbeth's tragic flaws: The farmer is greedy; the equivocator is full of pretense and lies; and the tailor is a thief, like Macbeth, who has just stolen Duncan's life.

The porter finally opens the door, letting in Macduff and Lennox, who have come to wake the king. In a witty exchange with the visitors, the porter holds forth on the enervating effects of alcohol. Macbeth appears and offers to lead the men to Duncan's room. While Macduff enters the king's chambers, Lennox tells Macbeth the frightening events that disturbed the night in his neighborhood: He heard lamentations, screeching owls, earthquakes, and strange screams of death. Such happenings, he explains, are considered prophesies of "dire combustion and confused events"—a clear political reference to the chaotic status of Scotland. Their conversation is soon interrupted by the wild-eyed Macduff screaming of the king's murder: "Confusion hath made his masterpiece! / Most sacrilegious murder hath broke ope / The Lord's anointed temple." In the midst of this scene of chaos, Lady Macbeth enters and inquires what is going on; she reacts to news of the murder with surprise and horror.

When Macbeth and Lennox return, Macbeth makes an eloquent expression of his grief, which is hypocritical given his direct culpability yet truthful in its analysis of the bloody deeds that have transpired: "Had I but died an hour before this chance, / I had lived a blessed time; for from this instant / There's nothing serious in mortality: / . . . grace is dead." As he concludes this speech, Malcolm and Donaldbain enter and learn of their father's death. Macbeth confesses that in his fury (feigned), he has killed both of Duncan's guards for the crime (which they did not commit). For her part, Lady Macbeth diverts attention by pretending to faint. Banquo tries to establish order by calling a meeting of all the important men in the castle. Malcolm and Donaldbain immediately leave for England and Ireland, respectively, in order to protect themselves from the murderer.

In scene 4, the next morning, Ross and an anonymous old man are outside Macbeth's castle conversing about King Duncan's murder. The old man states that in his seventy years he has never known such dreadful times. Ross believes that heaven is showing its displeasure with mankind; he observes that though it is morning, "darkness does the face of earth entomb, / When living light should kiss it." Macduff enters, saying that he too is in a dark and dismal mood. Ross asks for further news about the murder. Macduff reports that Malcolm and Donaldbain are suspected of foul play, but Ross quickly remarks that it is highly unnatural for a son to kill his father. A wary Macduff then reveals that Macbeth has been chosen as king and is already at Scone for his coronation, while Duncan's body has been taken to Colmekill, "the sacred storehouse of this predecessors," to be buried. Ross plans to go to Scone for the coronation, but Macduff will go home to Fife. Ross takes his leave of the old man, who blesses Ross and Macduff on their way.

Act III

Scene 1 opens at the royal palace at Forres, where Banquo is alone and addressing the absent and highly suspect Macbeth, the newly crowned king. "Thou hast it now, King, Cawdor, Glamis, all / As the weird women promis'd; and, I fear, / Thou play'dst most foully for't." Banquo's thoughts about the witches' prophecy are interrupted by the sound of a trumpet, as King Macbeth and his queen enter with Lennox, Ross, and other lords, ladies, and attendants. The king invites Banquo to the banquet he is holding that evening and then asks Banquo a series of questions about what he plans to do for the rest of the day and with whom.

After he has seen Banquo off for his afternoon ride and the others have left as well, Macbeth delivers a soliloquy in which he states that to be king is nothing unless the king is safe. He does not feel safe because Banquo "hath a wisdom that doth guide his valour / To act in safety; and, under him, / My genius is rebuk'd." Macbeth also reveals his jealous fear that Banquo's sons will someday be kings instead of his own future offspring. "Upon my head they plac'd a fruitless crown, / And put a barren sceptre in my gripe." By the end of the soliloquy, Macbeth concludes that he has no choice but to kill both Banquo and his son, Fleance.

To carry out this plan, Macbeth has fabricated a persuasive story to convince two common murderers that Banquo has treated them poorly. Macbeth has sent for them, and a servant now shows them in. In an approach more typical of his wife, Macbeth goads the men to act on their ill will: "Are you so gospell'd, / To pray for this good man, and for his issue, / Whose heavy hand hath bow'd you to the grave . . . ?" At the end of this manipulative episode, Macbeth requests outright that they murder Banquo and Fleance, urging them to exercise extreme caution to avoid discovery. The murder is to take place on this very night, away from the palace. The men leave, and Macbeth addresses the absent Banquo. "It is concluded: Banquo, thy soul's flight, / If it find Heaven, must find it out tonight."

Scene 2 begins with Lady Macbeth sending a servant to bring her husband to her. While awaiting the king's arrival, she expresses concern for the brooding and fearful Macbeth: "'Tis safer to be that which we destroy, / Than by destruction dwell in doubtful joy." Still the cool and calculating pragmatist, she asks Macbeth why he persists in his pointless anxiety: "Why do you keep alone, / Of sorriest fancies your companions making . . . ? / . . . What's done is done." Macbeth replies that they have only succeeded in wounding the snake, not killing it. So great is his fear of retribution that he declares he would rather be dead than to endure the "torture of mind" that he now suffers.

Surprisingly, Lady Macbeth does not criticize his fears but instead gently reminds him of the need to appear happy before his dinner guests. Macbeth promises to disguise his innermost thoughts and asks her to pay special attention to Banquo during the meal. In his perturbed state Macbeth seems to have forgotten his plan to murder Banquo before dinner, but, soon reminded, he tells his wife that "there shall be done a deed of dreadful note." When Lady Macbeth asks what is to be done, he does not confide in her: "Be innocent of the knowledge . . . / Till thou applaud the deed." Macbeth is in complete charge now as he was not previously, and he is confident that Lady Macbeth will approve of the new murders he has commissioned. Once again Macbeth entreats night to come quickly.

Scene 3 take place in a park outside the palace. The two original murderers have been joined by a third, also sent by Macbeth, and the three wait for Banquo and Fleance to return from their ride in the countryside. As the intended victims enter the park, they are depicted as two medieval travelers approaching an inn at the end of a day's journey, hoping to find safe lodging for the night. The murderers set upon them, stabbing Banquo first. Knowing that he is about to die, Banquo cries out to Fleance, directing his son to flee the palace and avenge his death. Fleance runs away, and Banquo dies. The murderers bemoan Fleance's escape, which leaves their job woefully incomplete: They have not eliminated Macbeth's rival for the throne.

In scene 4, Macbeth enters the banquet hall accompanied by his queen and his lords and attendants. This important scene is consumed with flashbacks, symbolism, imagery, and irony. At first the banquet setting presents a confident Macbeth, assuming his obligation as "the humble host" welcoming the guests, and the hall is a picture of perfect order. He seems a man in absolute control, able to conceal his thoughts and greet his guests. But this guise of self-control quickly dissolves as Macbeth encounters the first murderer. Noting that the murderer has blood on his face, he learns that the blood belonged to Banquo. At the news that Fleance has escaped with his life, Macbeth begins to unravel, and he remains visibly shaken after the murderer leaves.

Lady Macbeth admonishes her husband for neglecting their guests, and Macbeth obliges her by giving the toast. As he does so, Banquo's ghost enters the hall, unnoticed by Macbeth, and sits in his chair. When it is time to seat himself, Macbeth sees no empty place and states, "The table's full." Since the others cannot see Banquo's ghost, they understand that something is terribly wrong with their king. Pointing to the ghost, Macbeth adds to their unease by demanding, "Which of you have done this?" and issuing self-incriminating denials of his guilt. The nobleman Ross, recognizing Macbeth's infirm state of mind, tells everyone to rise to leave, but Lady Macbeth asserts her control.

She directs the guests to remain seated and explains that her husband has often suffered from such "fits" since his youth. Then she privately berates her husband for his loss of courage. He responds by challenging the ghost to speak, and at this the ghost of Banquo disappears.

Macbeth now exerts himself and tries to add credence to his wife's story, telling his guests that he has "a strange infirmity, which is nothing / To those that know me." He even tries to gloss over Banquo's absence by drinking to his health. The ghost then reappears. Abandoning his assumed composure, Macbeth challenges the apparition to take any other shape than that of a ghost, vowing to do battle with it. Banquo's ghost vanishes once more. Lady Macbeth reproaches her husband for spoiling the royal feast. Macbeth, for his part, marvels at her cold and calculating demeanor. She dismisses the guests, directing them to ignore social protocol and instead depart speedily; and thus the well-planned, orderly banquet descends to a scene of chaos.

When the guests have departed, a brief conversation between King and Lady Macbeth reveals the depth of Macbeth's tortured mind: Having committed so many crimes already, he believes he has no recourse but to destroy all remaining threats to his power: "I am in blood / Stepp'd in so far, that, should I wade no more, / Returning were as tedious as go o'er." With Banquo gone, he will turn his attention to Macduff. Macbeth is also desperate to find out his fate, and he plans to consult again with the three witches in whom he has placed his trust. Lady Macbeth, engaging in hopeful self-deception, assures her husband that sleep will cure him.

Scene 5 returns to the heath, with thunder sounding. The Weird Sisters are confronted by their queen, Hecate, the goddess of witchcraft. Hecate is offended by the lack of respect they have shown by their failure to consult with her, a usurpation of her "divine" rights. She voices her complaint in rhymed couplets and instructs the witches to meet her tomorrow morning at the "pit of Acheron" (the gates of hell), where Macbeth will seek them out to learn his future. Hecate considers Macbeth unworthy, a man who "loves for his own ends," and she instructs the Weird Sisters to be ready to conjure up magic spells that will "draw him on to his confusion." Predicting that Macbeth will continue to "spurn fate" and "scorn death," Hecate departs.

Scene 6 presents a guarded conversation between Lennox and an unnamed lord who represents the Scottish citizens. Though the setting is the palace at Forres, this final, brief scene of Act III informs the audience of the state of affairs outside the palace walls. Lennox observes that recent events "have been strangely borne," though it is still generally believed that Malcolm and Donaldbain murdered Duncan and that Fleance likewise killed Banquo and fled. Lennox questions Macduff's similar absence from court, but his companion has a far different report—namely, that Macduff has gone to England to petition King Edward for the services of Northumberland and Siward to restore Scotland to calm and order. Macduff, the lord says, hopes "That by the help of these . . . / . . . we may again / Give to our tables meat, sleep to our nights, / Free from our feasts and banquets bloody knives." It seems that Macbeth's tyranny has spread the curse of insomnia to all of Scotland. The scene concludes with both men praying for the relief of their "suffering country."

Act IV

Scene 1 is the fourth and final witch scene in the play, set in a cavern enclosing a boiling cauldron. The three witches brew their "hell-broth" of "fenny snake," "toe of frog," and a long list of similarly disgusting ingredients while they await Macbeth's arrival. As they concoct their vile magic potion, they chant their famous spell: "Double, double, toil and trouble; / Fire burn, and cauldron bubble." Hecate joins the witches and compliments them on their efforts, and a musical celebration ensues.

Macbeth enters the cavern and demands answers to his questions, no matter what the cost. The witches are eager to oblige and conjure up apparitions to satisfy his queries about the future. Macbeth tries to interrogate each apparition, but the witches tell him he must be content to listen; the spirits know his thoughts and will not be commanded.

The first apparition, a head wearing armor, appears at a clap of thunder; it simply calls out to Macbeth to "beware Macduff" and disappears. The second apparition, again summoned by thunder, is a child covered with blood. It reiterates the witches' original advice: "Be bloody, bold, and resolute; laugh to scorn / The power of man, for none of woman born / Shall harm Macbeth." Macbeth is delighted to hear confirmation of the advice that launched his bloody pursuit of the throne, and his first reaction is to spare Macduff's life, since, apparently, he need not fear him. He quickly changes his mind, however, and resolves to murder Macduff. Thunder sounds again, and the third apparition appears—a crowned child carrying a tree in his hand "that rises like the issue of a king." Macbeth finds this the most threatening apparition of the three because it foretells his replacement by a new king who will restore calm and order. The apparition's final counsel, given in the form of a riddle, tells Macbeth not to worry about conspirators: "Macbeth shall never vanquish'd be, until / Great Birnam Wood to high Dunsinane hill / Shall come against him." This news again reassures Macbeth, because such a feat seems impossible.

But Macbeth is not satisfied. He still wants the answer to one more question: "Shall Banquo's issue ever reign in this kingdom?" Though the witches suggest that he does not want to hear the answer, Macbeth protests and boldly threatens them. Suddenly the cauldron begins to sink, a trumpet sounds, and a procession of eight shadowy kings files through the cavern, the last carrying a mirror that shows Macbeth even more kings. As each king passes, Macbeth recognizes its resemblance to Banquo. Finally, and most horrifying to Macbeth, comes Banquo's ghost following the kings. As the witches and all their trappings vanish, Macbeth is seized with despair that his worst fears will be realized.

Cursing the day, Macbeth summons Lennox, who has been waiting outside. Lennox has not seen the Weird Sisters, but he brings the dread news that Macduff has fled to England. Macbeth is infuriated by this revelation, and he vows to retaliate. He intends to take Macduff's castle by surprise and kill his wife, children, and all other relatives. Macbeth swears that from now on he will, without hesitation, strike down every threat he perceives: "The very firstlings of my heart shall be / The firstlings of my hand."

Scene 2 takes place at Macduff's castle in Fife. Lady Macduff, her young son at her side, is speaking with the noble Ross about her husband's sudden flight from the country. Lonely and afraid, Lady Macduff attributes her husband's desertion to madness, calling him a traitor who acted out of fear. Ross says that it is the times they live in that are traitorous and suggests that Macduff may have shown great wisdom by his action, but he is unable to persuade her.

When the emotionally exhausted Ross leaves, Lady Macduff tells her son that she fears his father is dead. The boy, wise beyond his years, refuses to believe her but asks whether his father is a traitor. She answers that anyone who swears lies is a traitor who should be hanged by honest men. Her son responds astutely that "there are liars and swearers enow to beat the honest men, and hang them up." Their conversation is interrupted by a messenger who warns Lady Macduff that "some danger does approach you nearly." He advises her to take the children and flee Fife. Overcome with astonishment and disbelief, Lady Macduff is too numb to act. In truth, however, there is no time for escape; the murderers are at the door. They enter and demand Macduff. Though her young son bravely defies them, they quickly stab him and he dies. Lady Macduff—screaming, "Murder!"—runs out pursued by the murderers, who are certain to kill her as well.

Scene 3 opens in "desolate shade" before the palace of King Edward in England. Malcolm and Macduff are discussing the dreadful state of affairs in Scotland under Macbeth. While Malcolm says he wants only to weep for his homeland, Macduff professes his longing to take up arms against Macbeth. The two men distrust each other. Macduff assures the prince that he is not treacherous, but Malcolm is not convinced. He proceeds to question Macduff's motives: Why did he leave his wife and children in peril and come to England? Macduff responds that he has lost all hope. When Malcolm replies that he is still concerned for his own safety, Macduff impatiently cries out that there is no hope for Scotland unless he can join forces with Malcolm against Macbeth. Since he knows the prince distrusts him, Macduff feels he must leave.

Malcolm delays him, however. He warns Macduff that the country will also suffer under the next king of Scotland, meaning himself. While Macbeth is bloody, avaricious, deceitful, and malicious, Malcolm says, he himself is far worse and possesses none of the royal graces; he would make "black Macbeth / . . . seem pure as snow." Macduff doubts that hell could produce evil enough to compete with that of Macbeth. But Malcolm insists and expands on this characterization of himself. Finally, Macduff denounces the prince, declaring him unfit to govern Scotland or even to live. He gives up on the fight for his homeland and again bids Malcolm farewell: "These evils thou repeat'st upon thyself / Hath banish'd me from Scotland.—O my breast, / Thy hope ends here!"

Once again Malcolm stops Macduff, praising the latter's integrity of soul and noble passion for Scotland. Malcolm explains that the terrible self-portrait he has painted was only a ploy to test Macduff's trustworthiness, and he professes his own virtue. Macduff is relieved, and he pledges to support Macduff in his attempt to overthrow Macbeth. When Malcolm tells him that Siward and ten thousand English soldiers are at their command, Macduff is struck dumb, confused between appearances and reality. Explaining his silence, Macduff attributes his confusion to the inability to interpret events that have at the same time both benign and malignant appearance—a persistent theme of the play: "Such welcome and unwelcome things at once, / 'Tis hard to reconcile."

A doctor then arrives to say that King Edward is coming; before he leaves, the doctor describes the king's powers of healing. Malcolm explains to Macduff that this holy king also possesses the divine gift of prophecy. This, of course, stands in sharp contrast to the sinister predictions given by the Weird Sisters to the evil King Macbeth. Ross enters, having just arrived from Scotland, and Macduff asks him about the country's state of affairs and the welfare of his wife and children. Ross at first avoids the news of their murder. But when he hears that Malcolm and Macduff are about to lead an attack on Macbeth, he reports the king's latest act of brutality, the "savage slaughter" of Macduff's family. Macduff is overcome with grief at his loss and is tortured with guilt for having left his family defenseless. Malcolm encourages Macduff to put aside his sorrow and take up arms against Macbeth: "Let's make us med'cines of our great revenge, / To cure this deadly grief." Having vented his first shock of grief, Macduff agrees with him. The three set off to meet the king and complete their preparations for battle.

Act V

In scene 1, an unnamed lady-in-waiting in the castle at Dunsinane speaks with a physician about Lady Macbeth's sleepwalking. Having observed the queen for two days, the doctor has seen no incidents like those the gentlewoman has described, and he is beginning to doubt her. Though he asks what Lady Macbeth has said while sleepwalking, the gentlewoman refuses to answer for fear she will not be believed.

Lady Macbeth then enters in a trance, unable to see the others even though her eyes are open. She rubs her hands, as if washing them of some stubborn stain, and speaks: "Out, damned spot! . . . Yet who would have thought the old man to have had so much blood in him." She speaks as though Macbeth were present, and in so doing she incriminates both of them, revealing Macbeth's part in the deaths of Banquo and Macduff's family. Her thoughts, however, are constantly interrupted by the image of blood on her hands: "Will these hands ne'er be clean?" At last she returns to bed, though perhaps not to repose. Having witnessed this spectacle, the doctor declares Lady Macbeth in more need of a priest than a physician. Before departing, he begs the heavens, "God forgive us all!"

It would seem that Lady Macbeth has been reviewing all of the murderous crimes committed in the name of securing the throne. And ironically, given her insistence that she and her husband could not be held accountable for these crimes, thought of them has driven her to insanity. Even more ironically, in her somnambulant state Lady Macbeth has herself become a victim of appearances: She imagines that she sees blood upon her hands. Like her guilt, this bloody evidence stubbornly remains despite her repeated attempts to wash it away. Lady Macbeth once mocked her husband's visions of the dead. Teetering between reality and madness, she now resembles the ghosts of Macbeth's victims that returned to haunt him and expose his guilt.

Scene 2 takes place in the open country near Dunsinane, where the Scottish lords Menteith, Caithness, Angus, and Lennox are reviewing plans for the imminent battle. Drums are beating, flags are flying, and the Scottish soldiers have gathered to prepare for their attack against Macbeth. As Menteith observes, "Revenge burns in them; for their dear causes / Would, to the bleeding and the grim alarm, / Excite the mortified man." The English army, led by Malcolm, Macduff, and Siward, is nearby. Angus announces a rendezvous near Birnam Wood, a place named in the last prophecy of the three witches. From their conversation, the audience learns that Donaldbain has not yet joined his brother Malcolm. The lords also discuss Macbeth's beleaguered state: Although the king has fortified his castle, he is bereft of supporters. It is common knowledge that Macbeth has lost his self-control, and he is generally believed to have gone mad. As the scene closes, the men leave for Birnam Wood, where battle will purge Scotland of its sickness—and fulfill the witches' prophecy.

In scene 3, Macbeth is holed up at the fortified castle at Dunsinane. He is afraid of the approaching army, and he tries to calm his fears by remembering the prophecies of the witches: "Till Birnam Wood to Dunsinane, / I cannot taint with fear." And also, he reminds himself, Macduff was surely born of woman. Finally he lies to himself, denying his fear of the impending assault. But a fearful servant interrupts his thoughts with the news that ten thousand English soldiers are marching toward Dunsinane. Macbeth wants to hear none of it and contemptuously dismisses the servant, then returns to his dismal reflections. "I have lived long enough," he says; he knows that old age will not bring him honor, love, or friendship. Nevertheless, he is determined to fight "till from my bones my flesh be hacked."

As King Macbeth dons his armor, he asks the doctor about his wife. The physician reports that she is "troubled with thick-coming fancies." Macbeth begs the doctor to cure her of the same things he so desperately wants to purge from himself: "Canst thou not minister to a mind diseas'd, / Pluck from the memory a rooted sorrow, / Raze out the written troubles of the brain." By way of response, the doctor articulates the only possible cure, a theme that runs throughout *Macbeth*: "The patient must minister to himself." Macbeth has tragically forfeited this ability in his bloody and obsessive pursuit of the throne. Nevertheless, in a poignant moment, he demonstrates true understanding of the state of affairs in Scotland and almost prayerfully asks the doctor to restore the realm to health: "If thou couldst, Doctor, cast / The water of my land, find her disease, / And purge it to a sound and pristine health." Macbeth's human capital has been pathetically reduced: Only one officer remains to help him. The scene ends with the doctor wishing himself away from the castle of Macbeth, saying that no amount of money would draw him back.

Scene 4 takes place in the country near Birnam Wood. As they had planned, the Scottish rebels have joined forces with Malcolm, Macduff, and the English soldiers. Malcolm enters and encourages those around him: "I hope the days are near at hand that chambers will be safe" (to sleep in peace again). He reports that many have deserted Macbeth, and only "constrained things whose hearts are absent" still serve him. Finally, he advises the soldiers to cut boughs off the trees to use as camouflage in their approach to Dunsinane. Then they are off to war. Unlike those in the previous scene, these soldiers under the calm encouragement of Malcolm are both eager and prepared for battle. There is hope that goodness will prevail and a healed Scotland will result.

Scene 5 returns to the castle at Dunsinane, where Macbeth is talking to Seyton and his soldiers. He is still deceiving himself as he boasts to the others about their defensive position: "Our castle's strength will laugh a siege to scorn." But his empty words are soon interrupted by the jarring sounds of wailing women. Macbeth claims that he is unaffected by the sounds, having become inured to "slaughterhouse thoughts." He nonetheless asks Seyton why they are crying and at that point learns that they are lamenting his dead queen. Though he expresses no grief at his loss, Macbeth comments on the total emptiness of life in his most famous soliloquy: "Tomorrow, and tomorrow, and tomorrow, / Creeps in this petty pace from day to day, / To the last syllable of recorded time; / And all our yesterdays have lighted fools / The way to dusty death." It is here that Macbeth so eloquently expresses the consequences of his proleptic vision. In his relentless effort to secure his future as king of Scotland, Macbeth has been negligent; and in his refusal to live in the present, he has assured himself an empty life that will lead him to a dusty death, devoid of purpose and meaning, with no admirable record to be remembered by. Instead, his will be "a tale / . . . signifying nothing."

When a messenger does interrupt the king's thoughts, it is to inform him that Birnam Wood is in fact approaching Dunsinane: "I looked toward Birnam, and anon methought the wood began to move." Remembering the prophecy of the three witches, Macbeth curses "the fiend that lies like truth." If the woods are truly approaching Dunsinane, he understands, he is a doomed man. Macbeth ends the scene with a death wish: "I 'gin to be aweary of the sun." Nevertheless, he decides to fight and die in his armor like a man.

In scene 6, the rebel forces, approaching under cover of tree branches, have nearly reached the castle gate of Dunsinane. The soldiers have thus fulfilled the witches' prophecy of Birnam Wood coming to Dunsinane. Like other events in the play, the army's approach has succeeded by appearing to be something it is not. Malcolm instructs his troops to throw down their branches, as they no longer need camouflage; he has assumed the leadership he rightfully deserves and is clearly in control of his forces. Malcolm orders Siward and his son to lead the first charge, while he and Macduff follow. Siward sets off, indicating he is well prepared for the fight, and Macduff displays the same eagerness, telling his troops to sound the trumpets.

Scene 7 is fast-paced, filled with military action and the sounds of war. Macbeth enters the battlefield, wondering aloud what kind of man would not be born of woman, when Young Siward arrives and demands his name. At Macbeth's response, the young soldier challenges him to combat. They fight and Macbeth kills Young Siward, then leaves for another part of the field. Macduff enters in pursuit of the king, determined to deliver his personal revenge for his family. As Macduff continues his search, Siward tells him the state of the conflict: The castle has surrendered without a struggle, and many of Macbeth's men have deserted him. It appears the battle is almost over.

As he enters in scene 8, Macbeth admits that he has contemplated falling on his own sword to end the torture of his mind. But he has decided to continue the fight. Macduff spies his enemy and calls out, "Turn, hell-hound, turn!" Macbeth, troubled by his bloody crimes against the man's family, tells Macduff to retreat and save himself. Ignoring this, Macduff advances and challenges the king to fight. As they clash, Macbeth brags that he is invulnerable: "I bear a charmed life which must not yield / To one of woman born." Macduff then delivers news that dispels the charm: "Macduff was from his mother's womb untimely ripped." Macbeth suddenly grasps that he is doomed, and he curses the witches' trickery. Nevertheless, he decides to fight Macduff because the alternative of surrender would be far worse. "I will not yield, / To kiss the ground before young Malcolm's feet." There are still some vestiges of the heroic warrior in the king. Macbeth raises his shield, and they go off fighting.

Malcolm, the elder Siward, and Ross enter the scene in solemn conversation. Malcolm is concerned for their friends who are missing in action. Siward, the veteran soldier, reminds him that there will be deaths in any battle but observes that, fortunately, their losses seem small. Malcolm then specifically mentions that Macduff and Young Siward are missing. Ross, again assuming the role of messenger, delivers the bad news that Siward's son "has paid a soldier's debt." The young man died fighting, like a true soldier, and Siward says that with this knowledge he can release his son peacefully to God. Macduff then approaches, carrying Macbeth's severed head and saluting Malcolm, "Hail, king! for so thou art." The noble thanes join in the acclaim, and trumpets sound. Malcolm now addresses the crowd. He immediately elevates the thanes to earls and announces that they should call home their exiled friends, steps that seem sure to return sanity to his country and destroy the fear and turmoil. The chaos of Macbeth has passed, and a dream of peace in Scotland seems possible once again.

KEY PASSAGES IN
MACBETH

※⊖

Act I, i, 11–12

All: Fair is foul, and foul is fair.
Hover through the fog and filthy air.

These final lines of the witches' first ritual, chanted at the very beginning of *Macbeth*, introduce key themes of the play: first, the problem of how to interpret conflicting statements; and second, the infectiousness of evil.

The first line of the pair is an example of a rhetorical device called chiasmus, in which the order of words in one clause is inverted in the next: "Fair is foul, and foul is fair." As this line demonstrates, chiasmus can be used to create an inconclusive statement, which casts doubt on its own meaning and raises anxiety in the listener or reader. Indeed, a multitude of messages throughout the play are received with anxiety and uncertainty; prophecy, letters, facial expressions, gestures—all are endlessly questioned. The problem of how to interpret information troubles Macbeth till the very end.

In the second line quoted here, the witches cast a spell over the kingdom. This ominous yet undisclosed circumstance will "hover" and spread its poison throughout Scotland, creating a diseased kingdom that infects all who dwell within its confines.

—⟋⟍⟋— —⟋⟍⟋— —⟋⟍⟋—

Act I, iii, 1–24

First Witch: Where hast thou been, sister?
Second Witch: Killing swine.
Third Witch: Sister, where thou?
First Witch: A sailor's wife had chestnuts in her lap,

And munch'd, and munch'd, and munch'd: 'Give me,' quoth I.
'Aroynt thee, witch!' the rump-fed ronyon cries.
Her husband's to Aleppo gone, master o'th' *Tiger*:
But in a sieve I'll thither sail,
And like a rat without a tail;
I'll do, I'll do, and I'll do.
Second Witch: I'll give thee a wind.
First Witch: Thou'rt kind.
Third Witch: And I another.
First Witch: I myself have all the other,
And the very ports they blow,
All the quarters that they know
I'th' shipman's card.
I will drain him dry as hay:
Sleep shall neither night nor day
Hang upon his pent-house lid;
He shall live a man forbid:
Weary sennights nine times nine,
Shall he dwindle, peak and pine:
Though his bark cannot be lost,
Yet it shall be tempest-toss'd.

This second witches' scene presents their obsession with numbers and repetition, which becomes an important theme in *Macbeth*. The witches' obsession foreshadows both the obsessive nature of Macbeth's relentless pursuit of power and the excess of murder and violence that result.

It also depicts the capricious, menacing nature of the witches. When the sailor's wife refuses the first witch's demand, she incurs the wrath of the witch, who is resolved to assault her husband in a most cruel manner. The witch proclaims that she will sail on a "sieve" and try to blow the ship to pieces with strong winds. In the mythology of witches it was common for the hags to travel in a bottomless boat. Describing herself in this exploit as "like a rat without a tail," the witch refers to another article of contemporary superstition: The Jacobeans believed that a witch could assume the form of any animal but could not produce the tail because no existing part of a woman's body was comparable to a tail.

When the witch curses the sailor with an attack of relentless insomnia, she is condemning him to the worst fate available in the world of *Macbeth*. This terrible fate will deny her victim the healing balm of sleep and force him to lose track of time and place. Indeed, the play portrays insomnia and other sleeping disorders as dreadful predicaments with fatal consequences; Lady Macbeth's sleepwalking is perhaps the most striking example. The witch's curse foreshadows the plague of insomnia that later strikes the murderous King Macbeth and infects all of Scotland, as his subjects become afraid to close their watchful eyes.

———— ———— ————

Act I, iii, 39–46

Banquo: What are these
So wither'd and so wild in their attire,
That look not like th'inhabitants o' th'earth,
And yet are on't? Live you? or are you aught
That man may question? You seem to understand me,
By each at once her choppy finger laying
Upon her skinny lips: you should be women,
And yet your beards forbid me to interpret
That you are so.

Here Banquo questions the nature of the Weird Sisters. His interrogation presents an instance of uncertain interpretation: He cannot be certain what they are because their outward appearance gives contradictory signs of what they are. They live on the earth but look so wild as to suggest that they are supernatural beings.

Banquo is furthermore unable to tell whether the beings are male or female because they have women's bodies but beards like men. Banquo's inability to recognize the witches' sexual identity introduces another question that the play explores: What are the patterns of behavior and thought that differentiate men from women?

———— ———— ————

Act I, iii, 65–85

First Witch: Lesser than Macbeth, and greater.
Second Witch: Not so happy, yet much happier.
Third Witch: Thou shalt get kings, though thou be none:
So all hail, Macbeth and Banquo!
First Witch: Banquo and Macbeth, all hail!
Macbeth: Stay, you imperfect speakers, tell me more.
By Sinel's death I know I am Thane of Glamis;

But how of Cawdor? the Thane of Cawdor lives,
A prosperous gentleman; and to be King
Stands not within the prospect of belief,
No more than to be Cawdor. Say from whence
You owe this strange intelligence?

This scene presents a series of riddles regarding the nature of Macbeth's future status and happiness. Macbeth is both seduced and frightened by the witches' enigmatic statements. He is correct is his assessment that to be king is "not within the prospect of belief": Not only does he have anything but a commanding view of the future, but (in a pun on the word) he has no future prospects.

What is most important about this conference with the witches, however, is that it marks the beginning of Macbeth's rapid downfall. He will act on their prophesies despite his disturbing doubts about their statements. It is at this point that Macbeth embarks upon an uncertain journey, fraught with anxiety and paranoia, and these symptoms appear only a few lines later within the same scene.

Act I, iii, 126–140

Macbeth: [*Aside*]   Two truths are told,
As happy prologues to the swelling act
Of the imperial theme.—I thank you, gentlemen.—
[*Aside*] This supernatural soliciting
Cannot be ill, cannot be good;—
If ill, why hath it given me earnest of success,
Commencing in a truth? I am Thane of Cawdor.
If good, why do I yield to that suggestion
Whose horrid image doth unfix my hair
And make my seated heart knock at my ribs,
Against the use of nature? Present fears
Are less than horrible imaginings:
My thought, whose murder yet is but fantastical,
Shakes so my single state of man, that function
Is smother'd in surmise, and nothing is,
But what is not.

This speech reveals Macbeth's impulse to dismiss the negative side of every tentative prediction and act in spite of his severe doubts. He believes that he has received an "earnest of success," a pledge of an abundant future reward. He thus shows that he is willing to dismiss the supernatural source of these predictions. When he contemplates the reality of what he must do in order to achieve the throne, Macbeth tries to mitigate his anxiety of regicide, dismissing "present fears" as less important than the workings of his "horrible" imagination. Throughout the play, Macbeth proves unable to shake his present disquiet and apprehensions. He nonetheless proceeds to pursue a life "smother'd in surmise" and all that this term implies, including an ever-escalating paranoia.

The speech also shows how, in choosing to believe the predictions of three supernatural beings, Macbeth gives way to obsession with his royal destiny. Macbeth's relationship with the future can be expressed through a rhetorical device called prolepsis, in which an anticipated event is represented as having already taken place. Prolepsis functions as both a figure of speech and a figure of thought.

Prolepsis is used as a figure of speech in which the speaker anticipates and answers arguments from an opponent in order to prevent the opponent from using them. By answering an interlocutor's argument in this way, the orator gets ahead of himself and, if successful, gains control of the debate, thereby precluding an unfavorable outcome. A proleptic argument can take place within an individual; thus, proleptic thinking becomes a means of self-persuasion and a way to dismiss troublesome thoughts. Macbeth convinces himself in just this manner.

As a figure of thought, prolepsis describes Macbeth's total preoccupation with future reward. Through his relentless pursuit of what he is not entitled to, Macbeth condemns himself to live in an imagined world beyond the present. This status has disastrous implications. Perhaps the most significant consequence of Macbeth's living in the future is that, except for a few isolated moments when he suffers the pangs of conscience, he can never be present to himself. In this speech, as he grasps at the rewards of the future, Macbeth never pauses to reflect upon the terrible price he will pay.

Ironically, Macbeth is without hope for the future. He relies on wishful thinking, a state of mind in which relevant facts are subconsciously ignored or distorted. Hope, by contrast, requires an abiding faith in the future.

⟞⟝⟝⟞ ⟞⟝⟝⟞ ⟞⟝⟝⟞

Act I, v, 15–24

Lady Macbeth: Glamis thou art, and Cawdor; and shalt be
What thou art promis'd: yet do I fear thy nature;
It is too full o' the milk of human kindness,
To catch the nearest way. Thou wouldst be great;

Art not without ambition, but without
The illness should attend it: what thou wouldst highly,
That wouldst thou holily; wouldst not play false,
And yet wouldst wrongly win: thou'ldst have, great
    Glamis,
That which cries 'Thus thou must do,' if thou have it;
And that which rather thou dost fear to do
Than wishest should be undone. Hie thee hither,
That I may pour my spirits in thine ear,
And chastise with the valour of my tongue
All that impedes thee from the golden round,
Which fate and metaphysical aid doth seem
To have thee crown'd withal.

After reading her husband's letter, Lady Macbeth invokes the malice required to commit murder that she finds her husband so lacking in. She believes that Macbeth has too much compassion to secure the crown through this expedient. Convinced that she is the stronger of the two, Lady Macbeth declares herself willing to act without fear or doubt and whatever is necessary.

To Lady Macbeth, the doubts and fears expressed by her husband are a waste of time; she receives his misgivings as a challenge to embolden him. She plans to do this by playing on his masculinity, using "the valour of [her] tongue" to banish any feelings that stand between Macbeth and the murder of King Duncan. Indeed, her desire for power is so great that she does not pause to question the reliability of the witches' prediction. Rather, she responds as swiftly, deceptively, and violently as necessary to fulfill a supernatural prophecy.

Act I, v, 38–48

Lady Macbeth: The raven himself is hoarse,
That croaks the fatal entrance of Duncan
Under my battlements. Come, you Spirits
That tend on mortal thoughts, unsex me here,
And fill me, from the crown to the toe, top-full
Of direst cruelty! Make thick my blood,
Stop up th'access and passage to remorse;
That no compunctious visitings of Nature
Shake my fell purpose, nor keep peace between

Th'effect and it! Come to my woman's breasts,
And take my milk for gall, you murd'ring ministers . . .

Even as she resolves to commit murder in order to make her husband king, Lady Macbeth learns that the very man who stands between Macbeth and the throne is to be under her protection that night. She regards his death as a foregone conclusion. She declares that the raven, a carrion bird whose appearance signals grief and sorrow, has lost his voice in expectation of King Duncan's "fatal" arrival.

Lady Macbeth now raises her murderous plans to a much higher level. Her desire for a state of emotional abnormality, which was merely suggested a few lines back, has now taken on a diabolical fervor expressed through a series of images of a diseased body with thick blood and stopped passages. Likewise, in the prior passage, she planned to manipulate her husband by playing on his masculinity; now she wishes to assume a masculine identity herself: Appealing for courage, she invokes the presiding spirits to "unsex me here" so that she can carry out the regicide of King Duncan.

Act I, vi, 11–20

Duncan: See, see! our honour'd hostess,—
The love that follows us sometime is our trouble,
Which still we thank as love. Herein I teach you,
How you shall bid God yield us for your pains,
And thank us for your trouble.
Lady Macbeth: All our service
In every point twice done, and then done double,
Were poor and single business, to contend
Against those honours deep and broad, wherewith
Your Majesty loads our house: for those of old,
And the late dignities heap'd up to them,
We rest your hermits.

This scene, which immediately follows Lady Macbeth's murderous pledge, is brief but important. It highlights the bonds of hospitality as practiced in the time of the play's action. Here, Duncan presents himself as a guest who is humble in his thanks and gracious toward his hostess, although he is king. For her part, Lady Macbeth conducts herself as the perfect hostess.

Duncan's behavior demonstrates both a strong religious faith and his deep trust that his subjects will return the love he bestows upon them. Both qualities, of course, are lacking in his host and hostess. Here Lady Macbeth pays lip service to her responsibility, outwardly showing respect and concern for her guests' well-being. Her convincing performance testifies to her deep hypocrisy. This scene is an early example of how Lady Macbeth and her husband subvert the obligations they are bound by in their quest for gain.

———————————

Act I, vii, 1–16

Macbeth: If it were done when 'tis done, then 'twere well
It were done quickly: if th'assassination
Could trammel up the consequence, and catch
With his surcease success; that but this blow
Might be the be-all and the end-all here,
But here, upon this bank and shoal of time,
We'ld jump the life to come. But in these cases
We still have judgment here; that we but teach
Bloody instructions, which, being taught, return
To plague th'inventor: this even-handed justice
Commends the ingredients of our poison'd chalice
To our own lips. He's here in double trust;
First, as I am his kinsman and his subject,
Strong both against the deed; then, as his host,
Who should against his murderer shut the door,
Not bear the knife myself.

As Macbeth contemplates the murder he is about to commit, he wishes that it could be quickly done and thoroughly put behind him. He does not want to think about or pay a price for his bloody act: "That but this blow / Might be the be-all and the end-all here." Using the common metaphor of time as a river, Macbeth says he would leap from its flow to strike such a deed without consequences—to "jump the life to come." This figurative transcendence from all the consequences of one's own actions is, of course, thoroughly impossible. It is also an instance of proleptic thinking. Macbeth wants to think about the serene reward of the future, not the evil deed contemplated in the present. The metaphor of a "shoal of time" serves to underscore not only the shallow and meaningless life that Macbeth is determined to live but also the small amount of time that is still left to him as well.

In spite of his murderous scheme, Macbeth exhibits an ability to reflect momentarily on his ethical responsibility toward Duncan, to whom he is doubly bound as both subject and host. He is aware that his plans are especially depraved given the hospitality he is obligated to extend. As host Macbeth owes his guest protection from the very crime he is about to perpetrate.

Many critics have commented on the status of hospitality in *Macbeth*. The importance of hospitality as a means of political and communal stability is such that it was codified from its earliest time. From the Latin *hospitalias*, hospitality refers to the practice of receiving and entertaining guests. As well as the provision of food and safe lodging, hospitality requires generosity and goodwill. The Jacobean concept of hospitality encompassed ethical, political, and religious duties inherited from classical and medieval interpretations. Most importantly for *Macbeth*, it also included early seventeenth-century interpretations of the social obligations incumbent upon king and court.

The Senecan perspective on hospitality is a particularly relevant classical interpretation, because Seneca (4 B.C.–A.D. 65) has been identified as an influence for Shakespeare and his contemporaries and for *Macbeth* in particular. A philosopher of the Stoic school of ancient Rome, Seneca was interested in the fulfillment of an individual's ethical obligations. In *De Beneficiis*, Seneca emphasized the role of the giver of hospitality over the object given or the reaction of the recipient. External actions were intended to help the host achieve inner virtue or peace of mind. When *Macbeth* is examined against this definition, the absence of virtue and well-being, in both the court and in the hearts of its host and hostess, is immediately clear. Macbeth and his queen are so consumed with greed that they are incapable of manifesting anything but self-serving gestures and bloody deeds.

Macbeth has also been characterized as a medieval play, and thus the monastic tradition of hospitality is relevant as well. Hospitality was considered part of Christian charity and was practiced as a way of fulfilling one's obligation to perform good deeds. The most important manifestation of a code of hospitality is found in the religious orders. For instance, the Rule of St. Benedict stated that adherence to the tenets of hospitality was crucial to the formation of Christian character. The Benedictine Rule obliged monasteries to welcome all travelers, especially pilgrims, and to guarantee their comfort and safety. Like its classical forerunner—but framed in a spiritual context—the monastic tradition saw hospitality and its constituent ethical responsibilities as necessary for the maintenance of law and order, both within the monastery and in the larger outside community. The hosts of *Macbeth* fail this measure of hospitality as well. Macbeth presides over a chaotic world that guests must escape in order to save their lives; his realm provides no safe haven.

By the reign of King James I in the early seventeenth century, hospitality had acquired a more secular and political agenda: namely, to preserve the privileges of the noble and royal class. The rules of hospitality in the banquet hall, for example, promote public and private interests. Each party to the banquet receives something in the arrangement. For the guests, the benefit was sumptuous food and entertainment. For the host, it was the distinction of having provided the feast for important people, who then owed him a degree of loyalty. The rules of hospitality thus preserved the status quo for the privileged class in Jacobean England. And the need to preserve class distinction really was compelling, as a series of proclamations issued during the reigns of Elizabeth, James, and Charles (1590s through late 1630s) helps to show. These laws forbade the gentry to live in or about the city except when Parliament was in session, and they mandated the landholders' return to the country during times of harvest failure to stabilize rural relationships and thereby avoid the problems created by an absentee nobility.

Macbeth provides numerous examples of a subversive practice of hospitality at the royal household at Dunsinane: The guests are in mortal danger once they enter the gates of the castle; and the host and hostess are so preoccupied that, at best, they neglect their obligation to entertain their guests, and at worst, they display an unseemly loss of emotional control for all to see. The banquet itself is transformed from a celebration of good food and fellowship into a living nightmare where guests are murdered in their chambers, and the aristocratic society in attendance must leave with great haste, abandoning all rules of protocol and social privilege.

Recently, another paradigm for the status of hospitality in *Macbeth* has been offered in which Macbeth's tragedy is characterized as a self-imposed exile from home. Through his insistence upon living in the future, Macbeth can neither live in the present nor be present to himself; he is exiled from himself. Living in a state of self-imposed exile, Macbeth is rendered incapable of extending a gracious and hospitable welcoming to anyone, even himself.

By any definition, numerous obligations incumbent upon host and hostess are subverted in the dark and violent tragedy of *Macbeth*.

Act II, i, 33–56

Macbeth: Is this a dagger which I see before me,
The handle toward my hand? Come, let me clutch thee.
I have thee not, and yet I see thee still.
Art thou not, fatal vision, sensible
To feeling as to sight? or art thou but
A dagger of the mind, a false creation,
Proceeding from the heat-oppressed brain?

I see thee yet, in form as palpable
As this which now I draw.
Thou marshall'st me the way that I was going;
And such an instrument I was to use.
Mine eyes are made the fools o' the other senses,
Or else worth all the rest; I see thee still,
And on thy blade and dudgeon gouts of blood,
Which was not so before. There's no such thing:
It is the bloody business which informs
Thus to mine eyes. Now o'er the one halfworld
Nature seems dead, and wicked dreams abuse
The curtain'd sleep; witchcraft celebrates
Pale Hecate's offerings, and wither'd murder,
Alarum'd by his sentinel, the wolf,
Whose howl's his watch, thus with his stealthy pace.
With Tarquin's ravishing strides, towards his design
Moves like a ghost.

This speech shows another instance where Macbeth cannot distinguish illusion from reality. He sees a dagger and he desperately wants to clutch it, but it has no tactile presence. He is forced to dismiss his vision as a figment of his proleptic imagination, conjured because he knows that he will soon kill Duncan. Macbeth quickly interprets his vision of a dagger with "gouts of blood" as a harbinger of the bloody business he is about to embark upon. Macbeth has no powers of introspection, so it is ironic that he frames this illusionary weapon as a "dagger of the mind, a false creation." It demonstrates once again that there is a constant undercurrent of self-doubt, that he is tormented on a deep and unconscious level.

Act II, iii, 1–17

[*Knocking within. Enter a Porter.*]
Porter: Here's a knocking indeed! If a man were porter of hell-gate,
he should have old turning the key. [*Knocking.*] Knock, knock, knock!
Who's there, i' the name of Beelzebub? Here's a farmer, that hanged
himself on the expectation of plenty: come in time; have napkins enow
about you; here you'll sweat for't. [*Knocking.*] Knock, knock! Who's
there, in the other devil's name? Faith, here's an equivocator, that could
swear in both the scales against either scale; who committed treason
enough for God's sake, yet could not equivocate to heaven: O, come in,

equivocator. [*Knocking.*] Knock, knock, knock! Who's there? Faith, here's an English tailor come hither, for stealing out of a French hose: come in, tailor; here you may roast your goose. [*Knocking.*] Knock, knock; never at quiet! What are you? But this place is too cold for hell. I'll devil-porter it no further: I had thought to have let in some of all professions that go the primrose way to the everlasting bonfire. [*Knocking.*] Anon, anon! I pray you, remember the porter.

In a play in which one bloody deed follows close on the heels of the last, the porter offers the only comic relief to be found. Here, he is clearly quite drunk and loose-tongued. But there is a frightening truthfulness in what he says. He is truly the "guardian" at the entrance to "hell-gate" of Macbeth's castle, a nightmare world created by Macbeth and his wife. But what is most important about the porter's speech is its mention of equivocation.

To equivocate is to speak ambiguously—to mean one thing while implying something else, to deliberately mislead and avoid making statements that are in good faith. The play is laden with equivocal language. In particular, Macbeth is led down the "primrose path" to his own destruction thanks to misleading double messages that he fails to evaluate fully. Macbeth becomes an equivocator himself after committing his bloody murders.

To Shakespeare's contemporaries, however, the porter's reference to an equivocator "who committed treason enough for God's sake" would have brought to mind one specific equivocator: Henry Garnett. In 1606, he was convicted of participating in the Gunpowder Plot, a treasonous conspiracy to kill the king.

On the morning of November 5, 1605, James I learned that a plan to explode the Houses of Parliament had been prevented just hours before he was due to attend the parliamentary session. Guy Fawkes was found lurking in a cellar under the Houses of Parliament with some twenty barrels of gunpowder. Under torture, Fawkes confessed to his part in a conspiracy to destroy England's Protestant government and replace it with Catholic leadership. It was organized by Robert Catesby, an English Catholic whose father had been persecuted by Queen Elizabeth I for refusing to conform to the Church of England.

During the next few weeks, English authorities killed or captured all the plotters. Among those arrested and executed was the Rev. Henry Garnett, a Jesuit priest who had advocated equivocation as a way to deflect questions if the authorities asked what religion one practiced. Garnett was the author of a secret document titled *A Treatise of Equivocation*, which was published around 1595, when it was a capital offense for a Roman Catholic priest to enter England. To the Protestant establishment that dominated Shakespeare's audience, equivocation had a very bad reputation indeed.

Act V, v, 16–27

Seyton: The queen, my lord, is dead.
Macbeth: She should have died hereafter;
There would have been a time for such a word.
To-morrow, and to-morrow, and to-morrow,
Creeps in this petty pace from day to day
To the last syllable of recorded time,
And all our yesterdays have lighted fools
The way to dusty death. Out, out, brief candle!
Life's but a walking shadow, a poor player
That struts and frets his hour upon the stage
And then is heard no more: it is a tale
Told by an idiot, full of sound and fury,
Signifying nothing.

Hearing that Lady Macbeth has killed herself, Macbeth states that the timing is all wrong: "She should have died hereafter," at some point in the future; consequently, there is nothing to be said. He lacks the ability to grieve even for his own wife.

In this famous soliloquy, Macbeth broods on the subject of time. Finally forced to look back at what he has done to fulfill the dubious prophecy of power, he recognizes that all the bloody acts he committed were for naught. His earlier, proleptic metaphors are replaced with a wearisome account of human mortality. He now refers to the future at a plodding tempo emphasized by the hyphenated spelling of Shakespeare's day: "To-morrow, and to-morrow, and to-morrow / Creeps in this petty pace from day to day. . . ." His reckless pride has been reduced to a servile crawl as he recognizes that he is, after all, merely a slave to time and self-delusion.

Macbeth now understands that he was seduced by delusions of grandeur. His belief that he had an eternity to reap the rewards of his actions was misguided. He says that his life is as brief as a candle's and his actions as trivial as those of a loud but insignificant actor who soon leaves the stage. Macbeth concludes that the story of his life, despite all its bluster, will be a short tale "signifying nothing."

List of Characters in *Macbeth*

Macbeth is the Scottish nobleman who treacherously steals the throne by murdering King Duncan. Initially a man of much virtue and honor, Macbeth undertakes progressively fouler crimes and sinks to moral bankruptcy, throwing Scotland into a state of chaos. His evil acts finally lead to his demise when rebel forces lead an attack against him.

Lady Macbeth is the wife of Macbeth. Even more driven by greed and power than her husband, she is the manipulative force behind the murder of Duncan. Like her husband, she also becomes tortured by her bloody deeds, and she ultimately succumbs to madness and kills herself.

The three witches, also called the Weird Sisters, are the personification of evil in the play. They prophesy that Macbeth will become the king of Scotland, and their enigmatic predictions plant the seed of greed in his mind. Tragically, Macbeth does not understand that he is being fed with riddles.

Hecate is the queen of the witches.

Duncan is the king of Scotland. He is a generous ruler who rewards Macbeth for his martial success.

Banquo is a general in Duncan's army. The three witches prophesy that his descendents will someday be kings. He is Macbeth's close friend at the outset, but after seizing the throne Macbeth begins to fear Banquo and finally has him murdered. Banquo's ghost returns to haunt Macbeth.

Fleance is Banquo's son, who accompanies his father to court functions. Macbeth sends murderers to kill both father and son, but Fleance escapes with his life, thus thwarting Macbeth's effort to cut off the family line.

Macduff is a general in Duncan's army who suspects Macbeth of murdering Duncan. He flees to England where he urges Malcolm to overthrow Macbeth and seize his rightful crown. While he is away, Macbeth murders his entire family. Macduff vows personal revenge and succeeds in beheading Macbeth in the final battle.

Malcolm is King Duncan's oldest son, rightful heir to the throne of Scotland. He flees to England after his father's murder and later returns to lead a successful attack against Macbeth.

Donaldbain is Duncan's younger son, who flees to Ireland after his father's murder and does not return.

Lennox is one of Duncan's nobles who accompanies Macbeth to Duncan's chambers after his murder. Lennox is suspicious of Macbeth and fearful for Scotland.

Ross is a Scottish nobleman and cousin to Macduff. He brings the good news that Macbeth has been named Thane of Cawdor and the bad news about Macduff's murdered family.

Angus is a Scottish nobleman who, with Ross, announces Macbeth's rise to Thane of Cawdor. He later opposes Macbeth.

Menteith is a Scottish nobleman opposed to Macbeth.

Caithness is another Scottish nobleman opposed to Macbeth.

Siward is the earl of Northumberland and a veteran military officer. He becomes an ally of Malcolm and Macduff and leads the first attack against Macbeth's forces.

Young Siward is the son of Siward, who follows his father to fight against Macbeth in Scotland. He is killed in single combat with Macbeth.

The **captain** describes Macbeth's heroism in his victorious battle against a Scottish traitor and the king of Norway. Based on his report King Duncan bestows the vacant title Thane of Cawdor upon Macbeth.

The **old man** is an ordinary Scottish citizen who has never before seen such menacing omens as those attending King Duncan's murder.

An unnamed **lord** indicates that public opinion has turned against Macbeth after Banquo's death, though no one yet speaks it openly.

Lady Macduff is Macduff's wife. Her concern for the immediate well-being of her husband and young son stands in contrast to the Macbeths' relentless pursuit of future greatness. She and her entire household are murdered at Macbeth's command.

The **porter** is the drunken servant who attends the door of Macbeth's castle. He answers the relentless knocking that starts up just as Duncan is murdered.

The **murderers** are desperate men whom Macbeth persuades to kill Banquo and Fleance.

Seyton is the only officer in Macbeth's army who remains loyal to him as the Scots rise up in rebellion. Significantly, his name is pronounced "Satan."

A **waiting-gentlewoman**, or lady-in-waiting, ensures that the physician witnesses Lady Macbeth's sleepwalking and murderous talk.

The **physician** witnesses Lady Macbeth's sleepwalking but declares he cannot cure her malady of conscience.

A **servant** unnerves Macbeth with his evident fear and unwelcome news of ten thousand English soldiers on the horizon.

A **messenger** in Macbeth's service reports, to his master's dismay, that Birnam Wood is moving toward Dunsinane hill.

CRITICISM
THROUGH THE AGES

MACBETH
IN THE SEVENTEENTH CENTURY
꙼ᩚ

Although scholars and editors are not absolutely certain regarding the dates of the composition and first performance of *Macbeth*, the general consensus places it sometime between 1599 and 1606. Indeed, many scholars opt for 1606, as there is evidence that *Macbeth* was written by command as one of the plays to be given before King James I and the king of Denmark during the latter's visit to England in the summer of 1606. Adding further support for the 1606 date, scholars cite the existence of several topical references in *Macbeth* to the events of that year, namely the execution of the Rev. Henry Garnett for his alleged complicity in the Gunpowder Plot of 1605, as referenced in the porter's scene. At that time, Shakespeare's company was renamed the King's Men (it was previously known as The Lord Chamberlain's men) following the accession of James I in 1603. The title role was created by the great Richard Burbage and the role of the infamous queen by the boy-actress Edmans.

William Warner's contemporary historical poem provides a brief commentary on the character of the historical "Makebeth" and the calamitous events precipitated by his unrelentingly guilty conscience. Referring to "Makebeth" as a monster, Warner's poem highlights the irremediable suffering borne of a tortured imagination that is compelled to dwell unremittingly upon the bloody acts he has committed. "Whose guiltie Conscience did it selfe so feelingly accuse, / As nothing not applide by him, against himselfe he vewes."

The first printed text of *Macbeth* was the 1623 Folio edition of Shakespeare by John Heminge and Henry Condell and was, in all likelihood, an adapted version based upon a promptbook, exhibiting signs of alteration. The lyrical episodes of Hecate and the witches (III. v and IV. i) are often thought to have been added by another playwright. The second Folio edition of Shakespeare was published nine years later.

Given the scarcity of printed texts in general, and specifically the uncertainty of when the play, as Shakespeare wrote it, actually became available, criticism as we know it today simply does not exist for *Macbeth* in the early seventeenth century. However, we do possess two interesting eyewitness accounts of and comment on early productions of the play, as well as a popular revised version of the play, which itself is a sort of commentary on Shakespeare's original.

The first eyewitness account comes from Simon Forman, a prominent English occultist, astrologist, and herbalist active in London who set up a medical practice in Billingsgate, providing astrologically based remedies. Among Forman's manuscripts is a small document titled "Bocke of Plaies," which records Forman's descriptions of four plays he attended for the period 1610 to 1611 and his interpretation of the morality contained within them. Among the four was a performance of *Macbeth* at the Globe Theatre on April 20, 1610. There are a few problems with the account: Apparently, April 20, 1610, did not fall on a Saturday, and Forman's mentioning of characters riding on horseback in *Macbeth* is doubtful, given that circumstances of Jacobean dramaturgy and stagecraft would not be able to accommodate such a performance. Nevertheless, despite the confusion, it is clear that Forman did attend some of the earliest performances of *Macbeth,* and his commentary provides us with a rare perspective on the early productions of Shakespeare.

During the reign of the Puritans, from 1642 to 1660, the British theaters were closed for political and ideological reasons. However, following the death of Oliver Cromwell and the accession of Charles II to the throne, the theaters reopened and flourished once again. *Macbeth* likewise made a comeback, but through the radically altered version of Sir William Davenant, which was first performed around 1664 and later published in 1674. Davenant, who claimed to be Shakespeare's illegitimate son, was a very successful playwright, theater manager, and poet who enjoyed the enthusiastic support of Charles II. He was even appointed poet laureate in 1638. Davenant did not hesitate to alter, cut and amend Shakespeare's text, even borrowing from another work, Thomas Middleton's *The Witch*. His version of *Macbeth* became a musical spectacular, replete with witches portrayed in a series of comic turns as they flew, danced, and sang in ever increasing numbers. This more lighthearted portrayal of Shakespeare's foreboding witches was meant to please audiences, though scholar Bernice Kliman explains that even then some critics "found the dancing and singing witches too silly to countenance."

Davenant also removed the porter and the doctors, had the character Seyton change sides at the end, and altered the language so as not to offend the gentry. He also added several scenes, including one in which Lady Macbeth is confronted by the ghost of Duncan and advises Macbeth to forfeit his ill-gotten crown and restore the kingdom to peace. This striking reversal on Lady Macbeth's part represents Davenant's concern with supporting morality onstage; in 1653, he wrote a pamphlet titled "A Proposition for Advancement of Moralitie by a New Way of Entertainment of the People." He was clearly concerned with civic instruction and knew that his audience, which had experienced the Interregnum and the Restoration, was far different from the playgoers of Shakespeare's time.

An eyewitness account of this version was made by Samuel Pepys, an English naval administrator and member of Parliament, who kept a diary from 1660 to 1669. Today his diary is considered an invaluable primary source for the English Restoration period. Pepys saw Davenant's *Macbeth* on at least four occasions in the 1660s and thought it an excellent work, both highly entertaining and profoundly tragic. Davenant's production replaced the Folio version of the play until 1744, when David Garrick, a celebrated eighteenth-century actor, presented a play closer to the Folio text.

1606—William Warner.
From *A Continuance of Albions England*

William Warner (1558–1609) was an English poet who was popular in Shakespeare's day. His best-known work is *Albion's England* (1586), a compendium of history, myth, and biblical stories in 14-syllabled verse. Warner continued to add to it over the years.

... One *Makebeth*, who had traitrously his sometimes Souereigne slaine,
And like a Monster not a Man vsurpt in *Scotland* raigne,
Whose guiltie Conscience did it selfe so feelingly accuse,
As nothing not applide by him against himselfe he vewes,
No whispring but of him, gainst him all weapons feares he borne,
All Beings jointly to reuenge his Murthres thinks he sworne,
Wherefore (for such are euer such in selfe-tormenting mind)
But to proceed in bloud he thought no safetie to find.
All Greatnesse therefore, saue his owne, his driftings did infest (. . .)
One *Banquho*, powrefulst of the Peers, in popular affection
And prowesse great, was murthred by his tyrannous direction.
Fleance therefore this *Banquhos* sonne fled thence to *Wales* for feare,
Whome *Gruffyth* kindly did receiue, and cherisht nobly there.

c. 1611—Simon Forman. From *The Bocke of Plaies and Notes thereof per Formans for Common Pollicie*

Simon Forman (1552–1611) was an Elizabethan occultist, astrologist, and herbalist who provided astrologically based remedies from his medical practice in Billingsgate, in London. In 1594 Forman survived the plague outbreak in London, but following the death of one of his patients, he was jailed. After his death, Forman was implicated in the murder of Thomas Overbury through his association with his two patients, Lady Frances Howard and Anne Turner. Forman's texts have proved to be a treasure trove of rare, odd, and unusual data on one of the most studied periods of cultural history. His intimate knowledge of Shakespeare's circle makes him especially attractive to literary historians.

In Mackbeth at the Glob, 1610, the 20 of Aprill [Sat], ther was to be obserued, firste, how Mackbeth and Bancko, 2 noble men of Scotland, Ridinge thorowe a wod, the[r] stode before them 3 women feiries or Nimphes, And saluted Mackbeth, sayinge 3 tyms vnto him, haille Mackbeth, King of Codon; for thou shalt be a kinge, but shall beget No kinges, & c. then said Bancko, what all to mackbeth And nothing to me Yes, said the nimphes, haille to thee, Bancko, thou shalt beget kings, yet be no kinge. And so they departed & cam to the Courte of Scotland to Dunkin king of Scots, and yt was in the dais of Edward the Confessor. And Dunkin bad them both kindly wellcome. And made Mackbeth forth with Prince of Northumberland, and sent him hom to his own castell, and appointed mackbeth to prouid for him, for he wold Sup with him the next dai at night, & did soe. And mackbeth Contrived to kill Dunkin, & thorowe the persuasion of his wife did that night Murder the kinge in his own Castell, beinge his gueste. And ther were many prodigies seen that night & the dai before. And when Mackbeth had murdred the kinge, the blod on his hands could not be washed off by Any means, nor from his wiues handes, which handed the bloddi daggers in hiding them, By which by means they became moch amazed and Affronted, the murder being knowen, Dunkins 2 sonns fled, the on to England, the other to Walles, to saue themselues. They being fled, they were supposed guilty of the murder of their father, which was nothinge so. Then was Mackbeth crowned kinge; and then he for feare of Banko, his old companion, that he should beget kings but be no kinge him self, he contriued the death of Banko, and caused him to be Murdred on the way as he Rode. The next night, being at supper with his noble men whom he had to bid to a feaste to the whiche also Banco should haue com, he began to speake of Noble Banco, and to wish that he wer there. And as he thus did, standing vp to drincke a Carouse to him, the ghoste of Banco came and sate down in his cheier behind him. And he turninge About to sit down Again sawe the goste of banco, which fronted him so, that he fell into a great passion of fear and fury, vttering many wordes about his murder, by which, when they hard that Banco was Murdred they Suspected Mackbet.

Then Mack dove fled to England to the kings sonn, And soe they Raised an Army, And cam to scotland, and at dunston Anyse ouerthru Mackbet. In the mean tyme whille macdouee was in England, Mackbet slewe Mackdoues wife & children, and after in the battelle mackdoue slewe mackbet.

Obserue Also howe mackbets quen did Rise in the night in her slepe, and walke and talked and confessed all, & the doctor noted her wordes.

―――⁓⁓⁓― ―⁓⁓⁓― ―⁓⁓⁓―

1664—William Davenant. Excerpts from his adaptation of *Macbeth* (performed 1664, published 1672)

William Davenant (1606–1668) was an English poet and dramatist with close political ties to the royal court as well as the renowned poet John Milton. During the Restoration, Davenant became a prominent theater manager. At Lincoln's Inn Fields, he set up an acting troupe, which he called the Duke of York's Players, and produced some lavish productions, including *Macbeth* in 1664.

[The scenes included here are Davenant's additions to Shakespeare's text. In the first, Lady Macbeth is confronted by the ghost of Duncan and advises Macbeth to forfeit his ill-gotten crown; in the second, Davenant invents a scene in which the witches exult lightheartedly in the rarified atmosphere to which they are about to ascend, behaving much differently from Shakespeare's foreboding creatures.]

Macb: How does my gentle love?
Lady Macb: Duncan is dead
Macb: No words of that.
Lady Macb: And yet to me he lives.
   His fatal ghost is now my shadow, and pursues me
   Where e'er I go.
Macb: It cannot be, my dear;
   Your fears have misinformed my eyes.

[Enter DUNCAN'S GHOST.]

Lady Macb: See there! Believe your own!
   [*To the Ghost*] Why do you follow me? I did not do it.
Macb: Methinks there's nothing.
Lady Macb: If you have valor, force him hence!

[Exit GHOST.]

   Hold, hold, he's gone. Now you look strangely.
Macb: 'Tis the strange error of your eyes.

Lady Macb: But the strange error of my eyes
  Proceeds from the strange action of your hands.
  Distraction does by fits possess my head
  Because a crown unjustly covers it.
  I stand so high that I am giddy grown.
  A mist does cover me, as clouds the tops
  Of hills. Let us get down apace.
Macb: If by your high ascent you giddy grow,
  'Tis when you cast your eyes on things below.
Lady Macb: You may in peace resign the ill-gained crown.
  Why should you labor still to be unjust?
  There has been too much blood already spilt.
  Make not the subjects victims to your guilt.
Macb: Can you think that a crime, which you did once
  Provoke me to commit? Had not your breath
  Blown my ambition up into a flame,
  Duncan had yet been living.
Lady Macb: You were a man.
  And by the charter of your sex you should
  Have governed me; there was more crime in you
  When you obeyed my counsels than I contracted
  By my giving it. Resign your kingdom now,
  And with your crown put off your guilt.
Macb: Resign the crown, and with it both our lives.
  I must have better counselors.
Lady Macb: What, your witches?
  Curse on your messengers of hell! Their breath
  Infected first my breast. See me no more.
  As king your crown sits heavy on your head.
  But heavier on my heart. I have had too much
  Of kings already.

[DUNCAN'S GHOST appears.]

  See, the ghost again!
Macb: Now she relapses.
Lady Macb   [*To Macbeth*] Speak to him if thou canst.
  [*To the Ghost*] Thou lookst upon me, and showst thy wounded breast.
  Show it the murderer!
[Exit GHOST.]

        * * *

[Enter HECATE and three WITCHES.] *Music and Song.*

[*Spirits within*]   Hecate, Hecate, Hecate, oh come away!
[*Hecate*] Hark, I am called. My little spirit, see.
   Sits in a foggy cloud and stays for me.
[*Spirits within*]   ·   Come away, Hecate, Hecate, oh, come away!

[*Machine descends carrying* SPIRITS.]

Hecate: I come, I come, with all the speed I may.
   With all the speed I may. Where's Stadling?
Second Spirit: Here.
Hecate: Where's Puckle?
Third Spirit: Here, and Hopper too, and Hellway too.
First Spirit: We want but you, we want but you!
   Come away, make up the count.
Hecate: I will but 'noint, and then I mount;
   I will but 'noint, and then I mount.
First Spirit: Here comes down one to fetch his due,
   A kiss, a coll, a sip of blood;
   And why thou stayst so long I muse,
   Since the air's so sweet and good.
Hecate: Oh, art thou come? What news?
Second Spirit: All goes fair for our delight.
   Either come, or else refuse.
Hecate: Now I'm furnished for the flight;
   Now I go, and now I fly,
   Malkin, my sweet spirit, and I.
Third Spirit: Oh, what a dainty pleasure's this,
   To sail I'th'air while the moon shines fair,
   To sing, to toy, to dance and kiss.
   Over woods, high rocks, and mountains,
   Over hills and misty fountains,
   Over steeples, towers and turrets.
   We fly by night 'mongst troops of spirits!
   No ring of bells to our ears sounds,
   No howls of wolves nor yelps of hounds,
   No, nor the noise of water's breach,
   Nor cannons' throats our height can reach.

[*Exit* HECATE and the spirits.]

1664–1668—Samuel Pepys.
From the *Diary of Samuel Pepys*

Samuel Pepys (1633–1703) was an English naval administrator and member of Parliament, famous chiefly for his comprehensive diary. The detailed private diary that he kept during 1660–1669 was published after his death and is one of the most important primary sources for the English Restoration period. It provides a fascinating combination of personal revelation and eyewitness accounts of great events, such as the Great Plague of London, the Second Dutch War, and the Great Fire of London.

[November 5, 1664]

Up and to the office, where all the morning, at noon to the 'Change, and thence home to dinner, and so with my wife to the Duke's house to a play, "Macbeth," a pretty good play, but admirably acted. Thence home; the coach being forced to go round by London Wall home, because of the bonefires; the day being mightily observed in the City. To my office late at business, and then home to supper, and to bed.

[December 28, 1666]

To the Duke's house, and there saw Mackbeth most excellently acted, and a most excellent play for variety.

[January 7, 1667]

. . . thence to the Duke's house and saw Macbeth; which though I saw it lately, yet appears a most excellent play in all respects, but especially in divertisement, though it be a deep tragedy; which is a strange perfection in a tragedy, it being most proper here and suitable.

[December 21, 1668]

To the Duke's playhouse, and saw "Macbeth." The king and court there, and we sat just under them and my Lady Castlemaine. And my wife, by my troth, appeared, I think, as pretty as any of them; I never thought so much before, and so did Talbot and W. Hewer. The king and Duke of York minded me, and smiled upon me; but it vexed me to see Moll Davis in the box over the king and my Lady Castlemaine, look down upon the king, and he up to her. And so did my Lady Castlemaine once; but when she saw Moll Davis she looked like fire, which troubled me.

MACBETH
IN THE EIGHTEENTH CENTURY
❧

The eighteenth century marked both the beginning and the burgeoning of Shakespeare studies and criticism. The first standard collected edition of Shakespeare's plays was produced by Nicholas Rowe (1709). This was followed by the editions of Alexander Pope (1725), Lewis Theobald (1734), Samuel Johnson (1765–1768), George Steevens (1773 and 1778), and many others. Rowe's edition is also significant in that it provided a biography of Shakespeare, using the scant information (some of dubious reliability) available concerning Shakespeare's life.

The eighteenth century has been commonly referred to as the neo-classical age, a description which is true only in the general sense that it was dominated by a reverence for and observance of the rules for dramatic writing as set forth by ancient writers, in particular Aristotle. Aristotle's so-called "unities," as interpreted by eighteenth-century critics, decreed that plays should observe the unities of time (take place within a single day), place (happen in one particular place, not several), and action (have one plot and no subplots). Nevertheless, while classical authority was considered paramount, literary criticism exercised a great deal of latitude within this established criteria. Consequently, though much of the century's critical evaluation of Shakespeare in general and of *Macbeth* in particular discusses Shakespeare in the context of Aristotle's precepts, it also encompasses a wide range of view and topics, from Shakespeare's violation of the unities and the use of elevated language to his achievement in general. Admiration for Shakespeare is evidenced by the numerous books and essays which sought to identify and define the essence of Shakespeare's genius. In his introduction to the fifth volume of *Shakespeare: The Critical Heritage*, Brian Vickers attributes the beginning of Shakespearean idolatry to the critics of the 1740s and 1750s. (It is interesting to note that, before this time, William Davenant's musical version of *Macbeth* held the London stage and continued to be widely praised by writers such as John Downes). Indeed, while Shakespeare's work was subject to a wide range of opinions, the eighteenth century firmly established his reputation as a uniquely gifted poet and playwright.

Samuel Johnson, the preeminent literary critic of the age, admired Shakespeare for his powers of invention, lauding him as one who "effused so much novelty upon his age or country." Johnson's *Notes on Shakespeare's Plays* contain observations on *Macbeth* that are remarkable in their scholarly approach to both the historical and psychological context in which the play must be understood, as well as in his understanding of key passages of the play. Johnson's critique is especially important for his appreciation of Shakespeare's psychological insight. For example, he observes that "the arguments by which lady Macbeth persuades her husband to commit the murder, afford a proof of Shakespeare's knowledge of human nature." However, Johnson also had some judgments that few critics today would agree with; for example, he complained that the play "has no nice discriminations of character."

Elizabeth Montagu's essay on *Macbeth* celebrates Shakespeare's imaginative powers, finding the character of Macbeth to be much more sympathetic than the traditional Greek chorus.

> The self-condemnation of a murderer makes a very deep impression upon us when we are told by Macbeth himself, that hearing, while he was killing Duncan, one of the grooms cry *God bless us*, and *Amen* the other, he durst not say *Amen*. Had a formal chorus observed, that a man in such a guilty moment, durst not implore that mercy of which he stood so much in need, it would have had but a slight effect.

Montagu also defends Shakespeare's use of supernatural beings to demonstrate Macbeth's vulnerability to their prophecies of future political power and continues with a discussion of the healing powers of the pity and terror in *Macbeth*: "If the mind is to be medicated . . . surely no means are so well adapted to that end, as a strong and lively representation of the agonizing struggles that precede, and the terrible horrors that follow wicked actions."

Francis Gentleman maintains that Shakespeare intended to present Macbeth as a "detestable monster," while discounting those brief moments of conscience that Macbeth exhibits. Gentleman concludes that *Macbeth* is a "first-rate tragedy."

William Richardson's essay "On the Character of Macbeth" is essentially a psychological discussion of Macbeth's deteriorating character. Richardson charts his "extraordinary change" from "ambitious without guilt" to "false, perfidious, barbarous, and vindictive."

Finally, Thomas Whately paid tribute to Shakespeare's imaginative powers in his posthumously published discussion of the similarities between the characters of Richard III and Macbeth, both of whom are driven to seize the throne based on a supernatural agency. Whately focuses on Shakespeare's ability to take the fables surrounding each historical figure and fashion these fictions into a plausible story.

1708—John Downes.
From *Roscius Anglicanus*

John Downes (d. 1712) was a bookkeeper and prompter for Davenant's theater at Lincoln's Inn Fields from June 1661 through October 1706. Upon his retirement in 1706, Downes recorded his experience at the theater along with some impressions of the great actors with whom he worked. His work, *Roscius Anglicanus; or, an historical review of the stage from 1660 to 1706*, was first published in 1708. It is thought that he may be the John Downes recorded as buried in St. Paul's, Covent Garden, in June 1712.

The tragedy of *Macbeth*, alter'd by *Sir William Davenant*; being drest in all its Finery, as New Cloath's, new Scenes, Machines, as flying for the Witches; with all the Singing and Dancing in it: THE first Compos'd by Mr. Lock, the other by *Mr. Channell* and *Mr. Joseph Priest*; it being all Excellently perform'd, being in the nature of an Opera, it Recompenc'd double the Expence; it proves still a lasting Play.

1745—Samuel Johnson.
"Macbeth," from *Notes on Shakespeare's Plays*

Samuel Johnson (1709–1784), often referred to simply as Dr. Johnson, was one of England's greatest literary figures: a poet, essayist, biographer, lexicographer, and often considered the finest critic of English literature. He was also a great wit and prose stylist and is still frequently quoted.

[Johnson's General Observation on Macbeth*]*
This play is deservedly celebrated for the propriety of its fictions, and solemnity, grandeur, and variety of its action; but it has no nice discriminations of character, the events are too great to admit the influence of particular dispositions, and the course of the action necessarily determines the conduct of the agents.

The danger of ambition is well described; and I know not whether it may not be said in defence of some parts which now seem improbable, that, in Shakespeare's time, it was necessary to warn credulity against vain and illusive predictions.

The passions are directed to their true end. Lady Macbeth is merely detested; and though the courage of Macbeth preserves some esteem, yet every reader rejoices at his fall.

[Note on the first scene of the play]

In order to make a true estimate of the abilities and merit of a writer, it it always necessary to examine the genius of his age, and the opinions of his contemporaries. A poet who should now make the whole action of his tragedy depend upon enchantment, and produce the chief events by the assistance of supernatural agents, would be censured as transgressing the bounds of probability, be banished from the theatre to the nursery, and condemned to write fairy tales instead of tragedies; but a survey of the notions that prevailed at the time when this play was written, will prove that Shakespeare was in no danger of such censures, since he only turned the system that was then universally admitted, to his advantage, and was far from overburthening the credulity of his audience.

The reality of witchcraft or enchantment, which, though not strictly the same, are confounded in this play, has in all ages and countries been credited by the common people, and in most, by the learned themselves. These phantoms have indeed appeared more frequently, in proportion as the darkness of ignorance has been more gross; but it cannot be shown, that the brightest gleams of knowledge have at any time been sufficient to drive them out of the world. The time in which this kind of credulity was at its height, seems to have been that of the holy war, in which the Christians imputed all their defeats to enchantments or diabolical opposition, as they ascribed their success to the assistance of their military saints; and the learned Dr. Warburton appears to believe (*Suppl. to the Introduction to Don Quixote*) that the first accounts of enchantments were brought into this part of the world by those who returned from their eastern expeditions. But there is always some distance between the birth and maturity of folly as of wickedness: this opinion had long existed, though perhaps the application of it had in no foregoing age been so frequent, nor the reception so general. Olympiodorus, in Photius's extracts, tells us of one Libanius, who practised this kind of military magic, and having promised [Greek: choris opliton kata barbaron energein] "to perform great things against the barbarians without soldiers," was, at the instances of the Emperess Placidia, put to death, when he was about to have given proofs of his abilities. The Emperess shewed some kindness in her anger by cutting him off at a time so convenient for his reputation.

But a more remarkable proof of the antiquity of this notion may be found in St. Chrysostom's book *De Sacerdotio*, which exhibits a scene of enchantments not exceeded by any romance of the middle age: he supposes a spectator overlooking a field of battle attended by one that points out all the various objects of horror, the engines of destruction, and the arts of slaughter. [Greek: Deichnuto de eti para tois enantiois kai petomenous hippous dia tinos magganeias, kai oplitas di' aeros pheromenous, kai pasaen goaeteias dunomin kai idean.] "Let him then proceed to shew him in the opposite armies horses flying by enchantment, armed men transported through the air, and every power and form of magic." Whether St. Chrysostom believed that such performances were really to be seen in a day of battle, or only endeavoured to enliven his description, by adopting the notions of the vulgar, it is equally certain, that such notions were in his time received, and that therefore they were not imported from the Saracens in a later age; the wars with the Saracens however gave occasion to their propagation, not only as bigotry naturally discovers prodigies, but as the scene of action was removed to a great distance.

The Reformation did not immediately arrive at its meridian, and tho' day was gradually encreasing upon us, the goblins of witchcraft still continued to hover in the twilight. In the time of Queen Elizabeth was the remarkable trial of the witches of Warbois, whose conviction is still commemorated in an annual sermon at Huntingdon. But in the reign of King James, in which this tragedy was written, many circumstances concurred to propagate and confirm this opinion. The King, who was much celebrated for his knowledge, had, before his arrival in England, not only examined in person a woman accused of witchcraft, but had given a very formal account of the practices and illusions of evil spirits, the compacts of witches, the ceremonies used by them, the manner of detecting them, and the justice of punishing them, in his Dialogues of *Daemonologie*, written in the Scottish dialect, and published at Edinburgh. This book was, soon after his accession, reprinted at London, and as the ready way to gain King James's favour was to flatter his speculations, the system of *Daemonologie* was immediately adopted by all who desired either to gain preferment or not to lose it. Thus the doctrine of witchcraft was very powerfully inculcated; and as the greatest part of mankind have no other reason for their opinions than that they are in fashion, it cannot be doubted but this persuasion made a rapid progress, since vanity and credulity co-operated in its favour. The infection soon reached the Parliament, who, in the first year of King James, made a law, by which it was enacted, chap. xii. "That if any person shall use any invocation or conjuration of any evil or wicked spirit; 2. or shall consult, covenant with, entertain, employ, feed or reward any evil or cursed spirit to or for any intent or purpose; 3. or take up any dead man, woman or child out of the grave,—or the skin, bone, or any part of the dead person, to be employed or used in any manner of witchcraft, sorcery, charm, or enchantment; 4. or shall use, practise or exercise any sort of witchcraft, sorcery, charm, or enchantment; 5. whereby any person shall be destroyed, killed, wasted, consumed, pined, or lamed in any part of the body; 6. That every such person being convicted shall suffer death." This law was repealed in our own time.

Thus, in the time of Shakespeare, was the doctrine of witchcraft at once established by law and by the fashion, and it became not only unpolite, but criminal, to doubt it; and as prodigies are always seen in proportion as they are expected, witches were every day discovered, and multiplied as fast in some places, that Bishop Hall mentions a village in Lancashire, where their number was greater than that of the houses. The Jesuits and sectaries took advantage of this universal error, and endeavoured to promote the interest of their parties by pretended cures of persons afflicted by evil spirits; but they were detected and exposed by the clergy of the established church.

Upon this general infatuation Shakespeare might be easily allowed to found a play, especially since he has followed with great exactness such histories as were then thought true; nor can it be doubted that the scenes of enchantment, however they may now be ridiculed, were both by himself and his audience thought awful and affecting.

[Note on Act I, vii]

The arguments by which Lady Macbeth persuades her husband to commit the murder, afford a proof of Shakespeare's knowledge of human nature. She urges the excellence and dignity of courage, a glittering idea which has dazzled mankind from age to age, and animated sometimes the house-breaker, and sometimes the conqueror; but this sophism Macbeth has for ever destroyed, by distinguishing true from false fortitude, in a line and a half; of which it may almost be said, that they ought to bestow immortality on the author, though all his other productions had been lost:

> *I dare do all that become a man,*
> *Who dares do more, is none.*

This topic, which has been always employed with too much success, is used in this scene with peculiar propriety, to a soldier by a woman. Courage is the distinguishing virtue of a soldier, and the reproach of cowardice cannot be borne by any man from a woman, without great impatience.

She then urges the oaths by which he had bound himself to murder Duncan, another art of sophistry by which men have sometimes deluded their consciences, and persuaded themselves that what would be criminal in others is virtuous in them; this argument Shakespeare, whose plan obliged him to make Macbeth yield, has not confuted, though he might easily have shewn that a former obligation could not be vacated by a latter: that obligations laid on us by a higher power, could not be over-ruled by obligations which we lay upon ourselves.

[Note on Act IV, i]

As this is the chief scene of enchantment in the play, it is proper in this place to observe, with how much judgment Shakespeare has selected all the circumstances of his infernal ceremonies, and how exactly he has conformed to common opinions and traditions:

> *Thrice the brinded cat hath mew'd.*

The usual form in which familiar spirits are reported to converse with witches, is that of a cat. A witch, who was tried about half a century before the time of Shakespeare, had a cat named Rutterkin, as the spirit of one of these witches was Grimalkin; and when any mischief was to be done she used to bid Rutterkin *go and fly,* but once when she would have sent Rutterkin to torment a daughter of the countess of Rutland, instead of *going* or *flying,* he only cried *mew,* from whence she discovered that the lady was out of his power, the power of witches being not universal, but limited, as Shakespeare has taken care to inculcate:

> *Though his bark cannot be lost,*
> *Yet it shall be tempest-tost.*

The common afflictions which the malice of witches produced were melancholy, fits, and loss of flesh, which are threatened by one of Shakespeare's witches:

> *Weary sev'n nights, nine times nine,*
> *Shall he dwindle, peak, and pine.*

It was likewise their practice to destroy the cattle of their neighbours, and the farmers have to this day many ceremonies to secure their cows and other cattle from witchcraft; but they seem to have been most suspected of malice against swine. Shakespeare has accordingly made one of his witches declare that she has been *killing swine,* and Dr. Harsenet observes, that about that time, *a sow could not be ill of the measles, nor a girl of the sullens, but some old woman was charged with witchcraft.*

> *Toad, that under the cold stone,*
> *Days and night has, thirty-one,*
> *Swelter'd venom sleeping got;*
> *Boil thou first i'the charm'd pot.*

Toads have likewise long lain under the reproach of being by some means accessory to witchcraft, for which reason Shakespeare, in the first scene of this play, calls one of the spirits Padocke or Toad, and now takes care to put a toad first into the pot. When Vaninus was seized at Theleuse, there was found at his lodgings *ingens Bufo Vitro inclusus, a great toad shut in a vial,* upon which those that prosecuted him, *Veneficium exprebrabent, charged him,* I suppose, *with witchcraft.*

> *Fillet of fenny snake,*
> *In the cauldron boil and bakae:*

Eye of newt, and toe of frog;—
For a charm, &c.

The propriety of these ingredients may be known by consulting the books *de Viribus Animalium* and *de Mirabilibus Mundi*, ascribed to Albertus Magnus, in which the reader, who has time and credulity, may discover very wonderful secrets.

Finger of birth-strangled babe,
Ditch deliver'd by a drab;—

It has been already mentioned in the law against witches, that they are supposed to take up dead bodies to use in enchantments, which was confessed by the woman whom King James examined, and who had of a dead body that was divided in one of their assemblies, two fingers for her share. It is observable that Shakespeare, on this great occasion, which involves the fate of a king, multiplies all the circumstances of horror. The babe, whose finger is used, must be strangled in its birth; the grease must not only be human, but must have dropped from a gibbet, the gibbet of a murderer; and even the sow, whose blood is used, must have offended nature by devouring her own farrow. These are touches of judgment and genius.

And now about the cauldron sing—
Black spirits and white,
Blue spirits and grey,
Mingle, mingle, mingle,
You that mingle say.

And in a former part,

—weyward sisters, hand in hand,—
Thus do go about, about.
Thrice to thine, and thrice to mine.
And thrice again to make up nine!

These two passages I have brought together, because they both seem subject to the objection of too much levity for the solemnity of enchantment, and may both be shewn, by one quotation from Camden's account of Ireland, to be founded upon a practice really observed by the uncivilised natives of that country: "When any one gets a fall, *says the informer of Camden*, he starts up, and, *turning three times to the right*, digs a hole in the earth; for they imagine that there is a spirit in the ground, and if he falls sick in two or three days, they send one of their women that is skilled in that way to the place, where she says, I call thee from the east, west, north, and south, from the groves, the woods, the rivers, and the fens, from the fairies *red, black, white*." There was likewise a book written before the time of Shakespeare, describing, amongst other properties, the *colours* of spirits.

Many other circumstances might be particularised, in which Shakespeare has shown his judgment and his knowledge.

⎯⁓⁓⎯ ⎯⁓⁓⎯ ⎯⁓⁓⎯

1769—Elizabeth Montagu. "The Tragedy of *Macbeth*," from *An Essay on the Writings and Genius of Shakespeare*

Elizabeth Montagu (1720–1800) was a writer and an intellectual host-ess in London who established "conversation parties," during which lit-erature was usually a topic. She was a close friend of Horace Walpole, Samuel Johnson, David Garrick, Hannah More, Fanny Burney, and many others.

This piece is perhaps one of the greatest exertions of the tragic and poetic powers, that any age, or any country has produced. Here are opened new sources of terror, new creations of fancy. The agency of Witches and Spirits excites a species of terror, that cannot be effected by the operation of human agency, or by any form or disposition of human things. For the known limits of their powers and capacities set certain bounds to our apprehensions; mysterious horrors, undefined terrors, are raised by the intervention of beings, whose nature we do not understand, whose actions we cannot control, and whose influence we know not how to escape. Here we feel through all the faculties of the soul, and to the utmost extent of her capacity. The dread of the interposition of such agents is the most salutary of all fears. It keeps up in our minds a sense of our connection with awful and invisible spirits, to whom our most secret actions are apparent, and from whose chastisement, innocence alone can defend us. From many dangers power will protect; many crimes may be concealed by art and hypocrisy; but when supernatural beings arise, to reveal, and to avenge, guilt blushes through her mask, and trembles behind her bulwarks.

Shakspeare has been sufficiently justified by the best critics, for availing himself of the popular faith in witchcraft; and he is certainly as defensible in this point, as Euripides, and other Greek tragedians, for introducing Jupiter, Diana, Minerva, &c. whose personal intervention, in the events exhibited on their stage, had not obtained more credit, with the thinking and the philosophical part of the spectators, than tales of witchcraft among the wise and learned here. Much later than the age in which Macbeth lived, even in Shakspeare's own time, there were severe statutes extant against witchcraft.

Some objections have been made to the Hecate of the Greeks being joined to the witches of our country.

Milton, a more correct writer, has often mixed the pagan deities, even with the most sacred characters of our religion. Our witches' power was supposed to be exerted only in little and low mischief this therefore being the only example where their interposition is recorded, in the revolutions of a kingdom, the poet thought, perhaps, that the story would pass off better, with the learned at least, if he added the celebrated Hecate to the weird sisters; and she is introduced, chiding their presumption, for trading in prophecies and affairs of death. The dexterity is admirable, with which the predictions of the witches (as Macbeth observes) prove true to the ear, but false to the hope, according to the general condition of all vain oracles. And it is with great judgment the poet has given to Macbeth the very temper to be wrought upon by such suggestions. The bad man is his own tempter. Richard III. had a heart that prompted him to do all, that the worst demon could have suggested, so that the witches would have been only an idle wonder in his story; nor did he want such a counsellor as Lady Macbeth: a ready instrument like Buckingham, to adopt his projects, and execute his orders, was sufficient. But Macbeth, of a generous disposition, and good propensities, but with vehement passions and aspiring wishes, was a subject liable to be seduced by splendid prospects, and ambitious counsels. This appears from the following character given of him by his wife:

> Yet do I fear thy nature;
> It is too full o'th' milk of human kindness
> To catch the nearest way. Thou would'st be great;
> Art not without ambition; but without
> The illness should attend it. What thou would'st highly
> That wouldst thou holily; would'st not play false,
> And yet would'st wrongly win.

So much inherent ambition in a character, without any other vice, and full of the milk of human kindness, though obnoxious to temptation, yet would have great struggles before it yielded, and as violent fits of subsequent remorse.

If the mind is to be medicated by the operations of pity and terror, surely no means are so well adapted to that end, as a strong and lively representation of the agonizing struggles that precede, and the terrible horrors that follow wicked actions. Other poets thought they had sufficiently attended to the moral purpose of the Drama, by making the furies pursue the perpetrated crime. Our author waves their bloody daggers in the road to guilt, and demonstrates, that so soon as a man begins to hearken to ill suggestions, terrors environ, and fears distract him. Tenderness and conjugal love combat in the breasts of a Medea and a Herod, in their purposed vengeance. Personal affection often weeps on the theatre, while jealousy or revenge whet the bloody knife: but Macbeth's emotions are the struggles of conscience; his agonies are the agonies of remorse. They are lessons of justice, and warnings to innocence. I do not know that any dramatic writer, except Shakspeare, has set forth the pangs of guilt separate from the fear of punishment. Clytemnestra is represented by Euripides, as under great terrors, on account of the murder of Agamemnon; but they arise from fear of punishment, not repentance. It is not the memory of the assassinated husband, which haunts and terrifies her, but an apprehension of vengeance from his surviving son: when she is told Orestes is dead, her mind is again at ease. It must be allowed, that on the Grecian stage, it is the office of the chorus to moralize, and to point out, on every occasion, the advantages of virtue over vice. But how much less affecting are their animadversions than the testimony of the person concerned! Whatever belongs to the part of the chorus, has hardly the force of dramatic imitation. The chorus is in a manner without personal character, or interest, and no way an agent in the drama. We cannot sympathize with the cool reflections of these idle spectators, as we do with the sentiments of the persons, in whose circumstances and situation we are interested.

The heart of man, like iron and other metal, is hard, and of firm resistance, when cold, but, warmed, it becomes malleable and ductile: It is by touching the passions, and exciting sympathetic emotions, not by sentences, that the tragedian must make his impressions on the spectator. I will appeal to any person of taste, whether the following speeches of Wolsey, in another play of Shakspeare, the first a soliloquy, the second addressed to his servant Cromwell, in which he gives the testimony of his experience, and the result of his own feelings, would make the same impression, if uttered by a set of speculative sages in the episode of a chorus.

> *Wolsey.* So farewell to the little good you bear me!
> Farewell, a long farewell to all my greatness!
> This is the state of man: to-day he puts forth
> The tender leaves of hope; to-morrow blossoms,
> And bears his blushing honours thick upon him;
> The third day comes a frost, a killing frost,
> And, when he thinks, good easy man, full surely
> His greatness is a ripening, nips his root;
> And then he falls, as I do—I have ventur'd,
> Like little wanton boys that swim on bladders,
> These many summers in a sea of glory,

But far beyond my depth; my high-blown pride
At length broke under me, and now has left me,
Weary and old with service, to the mercy
Of a rude stream, that must for ever hide me.
Vain pomp and glory of this world! I hate ye;
I feel my heart new open'd. Oh, how wretched
Is that poor man, that hangs on princes' favours!
There is, betwixt that smile we would aspire to,
That sweet aspect of princes, and our ruin,
More pangs and fears than war or women have:
And when he falls, he falls like Lucifer,
Never to hope again.

And in another place,

Let's dry our eyes, and thus far hear me, Cromwell,
And when I am forgotten, as I shall be,
And sleep in dull cold marble, where no mention
Of me must more be heard, say then, I taught thee;
Say, Wolsey, that once trod the ways of glory,
And sounded all the depths and shoals of honour,
Found thee a way, out of his wreck, to rise in;
A sure and safe one, though thy master miss'd it.
Mark but my fall, and that which ruin'd me;
Cromwell, I charge thee, fling away ambition,
By that sin fell the angels; how can man then,
The image of his Maker, hope to win by't?
Love thyself last; cherish those hearts, that hate thee;
Corruption wins not more than honesty.
Still in thy right-hand carry gentle peace,
To silence envious tongues; be just, and fear not.
Let all the ends, thou aim'st at, be thy country's,
Thy God's, and truth's; then, if thou fall'st, O Cromwell,
Thou fall'st a blessed martyr. Serve the king;
And pr'ythee, lead me in;
There take an inventory of all I have,
To the last penny, 'tis the king's. My robe,
And my integrity to heav'n, is all
I dare now call mine own. O Cromwell, Cromwell,
Had I but serv'd my God with half the zeal
I serv'd my king, he would not in mine age
Have left me naked to mine enemies.

I select these two passages as containing reflections of such a general kind, as might be with least impropriety transferred to the chorus; but if even these would lose much of their force and pathos, if not spoken by the fallen statesman, how much more would those do, which are the expressions of some instantaneous emotion, occasioned by the peculiar situation of the person by whom they are uttered! The self-condemnation of a murderer makes a very deep impression upon us when we are told by Macbeth himself, that hearing, while he was killing Duncan, one of the grooms cry *God bless us*, and *Amen* the other, he durst not say *Amen*. Had a formal chorus observed, that a man in such a guilty moment, durst not implore that mercy of which he stood so much in need, it would have had but a slight effect. All know the detestation, with which virtuous men behold a bad action. A much more salutary admonition is given, when we are shewn the terrors that are combined with guilt in the breast of the offender.

Our Author has so tempered the constitutional character of Macbeth, by infusing into it the milk of human kindness, and a strong tincture of honour, as to make the most violent perturbation, and pungent remorse, naturally attend on those steps to which he is led by the force of temptation. Here we must commend the poet's judgment, and his invariable attention to consistency of character, but more amazing still is the art with which he exhibits the movement of the human mind, and renders audible the silent march of thought; traces its modes of operation in the course of deliberating, the pauses of hesitation, and the final act of decision; shews how reason checks, and how the passions impel; and displays to us the trepidations that precede, and the horrors that pursue, acts of blood. No species of dialogue, but that which a man holds with himself, could effect this. The soliloquy has been permitted to all dramatic writers; but its true use seems to be understood only by our Author, who alone has attained to a just imitation of nature, in this kind of self-conference.

It is certain, that men do not tell themselves who they are, and whence they came; they neither narrate nor declaim in the solitude of the closet, as Greek and French writers represent. Here then is added to the drama an imitation of the most difficult and delicate kind, that of representing the internal process of the mind in reasoning and reflecting; and it is not only a difficult, but a very useful art, as it best assists the poet to expose the anguish of remorse, to repeat every whisper of the internal monitor, conscience, and, upon occasion, to lend her a voice *to amaze the guilty and appal the free*. As a man is averse to expose his crimes, and discover the turpitude of his actions, even to the faithful friend, and trusty confident, it is more natural for him to breathe in soliloquy the dark and heavy secrets of the soul, than to utter them to the most intimate associate. The conflicts in the bosom of Macbeth, before he commits the murder, *could not*, by any other means, have been so well exposed. He entertains the prophecy of his future greatness with complacency; but the very idea of the means by which he is to attain it, shocks him to the highest degree.

> This supernatural soliciting
> Cannot be ill, cannot be good. If ill,
> Why hath it giv'n me the earnest of success,
> Commencing in a truth? I'm Thane of Cawdor.
> If good, why do I yield to that suggestion,
> Whose horrid image doth unfix my hair,
> And make my seated heart knock at my ribs,
> Against the use of nature?

There is an obscurity and stiffness in part of these soliloquies, which I wish could be charged entirely to the confusion of Macbeth's mind from the horror he feels, at the thought of the murder; but our Author is too much addicted to the obscure bombast, much affected by all sorts of writers in that age. The abhorrence Macbeth feels at the suggestion of assassinating his King, brings him back to this determination;

> If chance will have me king, why, chance may crown me,
> Without my stir.

After a pause, in which we may suppose the ambitious desire of a crown to return, so far as to make him undetermined what he shall do, and leave the decision to future time and unborn events, he concludes,

> Come what come may,
> Time and the hour runs thro' the roughest day.

By which, I confess, I do not, with his two last commentators, imagine it meant either the tautology of time and the hour, or an allusion to time painted with an hour-glass, or an exhortation to time to hasten forward; but I rather apprehend the meaning to be, *tempus et hora*, time and occasion, will carry the thing through, and bring it to some determined point and end, let its nature be what it will.

In the next soliloquy, he agitates this great question concerning the proposed murder. One argument against it is, that such deeds must be supported by others of like nature:

> But, in these cases,
> We still have judgment here; that we but teach
> Bloody instructions, which, being taught, return
> To plague th' inventor; this even-handed justice
> Commends th' ingredients of our poison'd chalice
> To our own lips.

He proceeds next to consider the peculiar relations, in which he stands to Duncan:

> He's here in double trust:
> First, as I am his kinsman and his subject,
> Strong both against the deed; then, as his host,
> Who should against his murd'rer shut the door;
> Not bear the knife myself.

Then follow his arguments against the deed, from the admirable qualities of the King:

> Besides, this Duncan
> Hath borne his faculties so meekly, hath been
> So clear in his great office, that his virtues
> Will plead, like angels, trumpet-tongu'd, against
> The deep damnation of his taking off.

So, says he, with many reasons to dissuade, I have none to urge me to this act, but a vaulting ambition; which, by a daring leap, often procures itself a fall. And thus having determined, he tells Lady Macbeth;

> We will proceed no further in this business.
> He hath honour'd me of late; and I have bought
> Golden opinions from all sorts of people,
> Which would be worn, now in their newest gloss,
> Not cast aside so soon.

Macbeth, in debating with himself, chiefly dwells upon the guilt, yet touches something on the danger, of assassinating the King. When he argues with Lady Macbeth, knowing her too wicked to be affected by the one, and too daring to he deterred by the other, he urges, with great propriety, what he thinks may have more weight with one of her disposition; the favour he is in with the King, and the esteem he has lately acquired of the people. In answer to her charge of cowardice, he finely distinguishes between manly courage and brutal ferocity.

> *Macbeth.* I dare do all that may become a man;
> Who dares do more, is none.

At length, overcome, rather than persuaded, he determines on the bloody deed

I am settled, and bend up
Each corp'ral agent to this terrible feat.

How terrible to him, how repugnant to his nature, we plainly perceive, when, even in the moment that he summons up the resolution needful to perform it, horrid phantasms present themselves: murder alarmed by his sentinel the wolf stealing towards his design; witchcraft celebrating pale Hecate's offerings; the midnight ravisher invading sleeping innocence, seem his associates; and bloody daggers lead him to the very chamber of the King. At his return thence, the sense of the crime he has committed appears suitable to his repugnance at undertaking it. He tells Lady Macbeth, that, of the grooms who slept in Duncan's chamber,—

Macbeth. There's one did laugh in's sleep, and one cry'd, Murder!
They wak'd each other; and I stood and heard them;
But they did say their prayers, and address them
Again to sleep.
Lady. There are two lodg'd together.
Macbeth. One cry'd, God bless us! and, Amen! the other;
As they had seen me with these hangman's hands.
Listening their fear, I could not say, Amen,
When they did say, God bless us!
Lady. Consider it not so deeply.
Macbeth. But wherefore could not I pronounce, Amen?
I had most need of blessings, and Amen
Stuck in my throat.
Macbeth. Methought, I heard a voice cry, Sleep no more!
Macbeth doth murder sleep; the innocent sleep.

Then he replies, when his Lady bids him carry back the daggers;

Macbeth. I'll go no more.
I am afraid to think what I have done
Look on't again I dare not.

How natural is the exclamation of a person, who, from the fearless state of unsuspecting innocence, is fallen into the suspicious condition of guilt, when, upon hearing a knocking at the gate, he cries out;

Macbeth. How is it with me, when every noise appals me?

The Poet has contrived to throw a tincture of remorse even into Macbeth's resolution to murder Banquo.—He does not proceed in it like a man who, impenitent in crimes, and wanton in success, gaily goes forward in his violent career; but seems impelled onward, and stimulated to this additional villainy, by an apprehension, that, if Banquo's posterity should inherit the crown, he has sacrificed his virtue, and defiled his own soul in vain.

> *Macbeth.* If 'tis so,
> For Banquo's issue have I 'fil'd my mind;
> For them, the gracious Duncan have I murder'd;
> Put rancours in the vessel of my peace
> Only for them; and mine eternal jewel
> Giv'n to the common enemy of man,
> To make them kings, the seed of Banquo kings.

His desire to keep Lady Macbeth innocent of this intended murder, and yet, from the fulness of a throbbing heart, uttering what may render suspected the very thing he wishes to conceal, shews how deeply the Author enters into human nature in general, and in every circumstance preserves the consistency of the character he exhibits.

How strongly is expressed the great truth, that to a man of courage, the most terrible object is the person he has injured, in the following address to Banquo's ghost!

> *Macbeth.* What man dare, I dare.
> Approach thou like the rugged Russian bear,
> The arm'd rhinoceros, or Hyrcan tyger
> Take any shape but that, and my firm nerves
> Shall never tremble: or, be alive again,
> And dare me to the desart with thy sword;
> If trembling I evade it, then protest me
> The baby of a girl. Hence, terrible shadow
> Unreal mock'ry, hence!

It is impossible not to sympathize with the terrors Macbeth expresses in his disordered speech:

> *Macbeth.* It will have blood.—They say, blood will have blood.
> Stones have been known to move, and trees to speak;
> Augurs, that understand relations, have,

By magpies, and by choughs, and rooks, brought forth
The secret'st man of blood.

The perturbation, with which Macbeth again resorts to the Witches, and
the tone of resentment and abhorrence with which he addresses them, rather
expresses his sense of the crimes, to which their promises excited him, than any
satisfaction in the regal condition, those crimes had procured.

Macbeth. How now, you secret, black, and midnight hags!
What is't you do?

The unhappy and disconsolate state of the most triumphant villainy, from a
consciousness of men's internal detestation of that flagitious greatness, to which
they are forced to pay external homage, is finely expressed in the following
words:

Macbeth. I have liv'd long enough: my way of life
Is fall'n into the sear, the yellow leaf:
And that which should accompany old age,
As honour, love, obedience, troops of friends,
I must not look to have; but in their stead,
Curses not loud but deep, mouth-honour, breath,
Which the poor heart would fain deny, and dare not.

Toward the conclusion of the piece, his mind seems to sink under its load of
guilt; despair and melancholy hang on his words. By his address to the physician,
we perceive he has griefs that press harder on him than his enemies:

Macbeth. Canst thou not minister to a mind diseas'd,
Pluck from the memory a rooted sorrow;
Raze out the written troubles of the brain;
And, with some sweet oblivious antidote,
Cleanse the stuff'd bosom of that perilous stuff
Which weighs upon the heart?

The alacrity with which he attacks young Siward, and his reluctance to engage
with Macduff, of whose blood he says he has already had too much, complete a
character uniformly preserved from the opening of the fable, to its conclusion.—
We find him ever answering to the first idea we were made to conceive of him.
    The man of honour pierces through the traitor and the assassin. His mind
loses its tranquillity by guilt, but never its fortitude in danger. His crimes
presented to him, even in the unreal mockery of a vision, or the harmless form of

sleeping innocence, terrify him more than all his foes in arms.—It has been very justly observed by a late commentator, that this piece does not abound with those nice discriminations of character, usual in the plays of our Author, the events being too great to admit the influence of particular dispositions. It appears to me, that the character of Macbeth is also represented less particular and special, that his example may be of more universal utility. He has therefore placed him on that line, on which the major part of mankind may be ranked, just between the extremes of good and bad; a station assailable by various temptations, and standing in need of the guard of cautionary admonition. The supernatural agents, in some measure, take off our attention from the other characters, especially as they are, throughout the piece, what they have a right to be, predominant in the events. They should not interfere, but to weave the fatal web, or to unravel it; they ought ever to be the regents of the fable and artificers of the catastrophe, as the Witches are in this piece. To preserve in Macbeth a just consistency of character; to make that character naturally susceptible of those desires, that were to be communicated to it; to render it interesting to the spectator, by some amiable qualities; to make it exemplify the dangers of ambition, and the terrors of remorse; was all that could be required of the tragedian and the moralist. With all the powers of poetry he elevates a legendary tale, without carrying it beyond the limits of vulgar faith and tradition. The solemn character of the infernal rites would be very striking, if the scene was not made ludicrous by a mob of old women, which the players have added to the three weird sisters. The incantation is so consonant with the doctrine of enchantments, and receives such power by the help of those potent ministers of direful superstition, the Terrible and the Mysterious, that it has not the air of poetical fiction so much as of a discovery of magical secrets; and thus it seizes the heart of the ignorant, and communicates an irresistible horror to the imagination even of the more informed spectator...

1770—Francis Gentleman. "Macbeth," from *The Dramatic Censor; or, Critical Companion*

Francis Gentleman (1728–1784) was an eighteenth-century actor and drama critic. He wrote several plays and supplied the introduction and notes to *Bell's Acting Edition of Shakespeare* in 1774.

There are many circumstances and events to bring about the most unthought of changes in human affairs, wherefore that man who premeditated the worst means at first, must have by nature a deep depravation of heart; and such Macbeth will appear infected with, from the whole of that speech which begins

"Two truths are told," &c. notwithstanding some what like palliation is offered in two or three lines; indeed his conclusion seems to banish what he beautifully stiles *fantastical murther*; but cannot banish from spectators his barbarous ideas so suddenly conceived; we have dwelt upon this circumstance to strengthen our opinion, that the author meant to draw him a detestable monster, which some critics have rather disputed, allowing him a generous disposition, which we find no instance of; even the conscientious struggles which we shall presently find him engaged with, might arise in the most villainous nature—he who does a bad action precipitately, or without knowing it to be such, may stand in some measure excusable; but when a man has scrupulously weighed every relative circumstance in the nicest scale of reflection; and after all determines upon what nature, gratitude, and justice, would avoid, he must be composed of the worst materials. . .

Macbeth, for its boldness of sentiment, strength of versification, variety of passions and preternatural beings, deserves to be esteemed a first-rate tragedy, containing a number of beauties never exceeded, with many blemishes very censurable; dangerous in representation, as has been said, to weak minds; unintelligible to moderate conceptions in several places, upon perusal; therefore chiefly calculated for found understanding, and established resolution of principles, either on the stage or in the study.

/

1780—William Richardson. "On The Character of Macbeth," from *A Philosophical Analysis and Illustration of Some of Shakespeare's Remarkable Characters*

William Richardson (1743-1814) was a poet, playwright, and professor at Glasgow University.

In the character of Macbeth, we have an instance of a very extraordinary change. (. . .) He is exhibited to us valiant, dutiful to his sovereign, mild, gentle, and ambitious: but ambitious without guilt. Soon after, we find him false, perfidious, barbarous, and vindictive. All the principles in his constitution seem to have undergone a violent and total change. Some appear to be altogether reduced or extirpated; others monstrously overgrown. Ferocity is substituted instead of mildness, treasonable intentions instead of a sense of duty. His ambition, however, has suffered no diminution: on the contrary, by having become exceedingly powerful, and by rising to undue pretentions, it seems to have vanquished and suppressed every amiable and virtuous principle. But, in a conflict so important, and where the opposing powers were naturally vigorous, and invested with high authority, violent must have been the struggle, and obstinate the resistance. Nor could the prevailing passion have been enabled to contend with virtue, without having gained, at some former period, an unlawful ascendancy. Therefore, in treating the history of this revolution, we shall consider how the usurping principle became so powerful; how its powers were exerted in its conflict with opposing principles; and what were the consequences of its victory.

(. . .) Ambition grown habitual and inveterate in the soul of Macbeth, suggests the idea of assassination. The sense of virtue, compassion, and other kindred principles, are alarmed, and oppose. His ruling passion is repulsed, but not enfeebled. Resigning himself to the hope of profiting by some future emergency, he renounces the idea of violence. A difficulty appears: it renews, rouses, and inflames his ambition. The principles of virtue again oppose; but, by exercise and repetition, they are, for a time enfeebled. They excite no abhorrence; and he reflects, with composure, on his design. But, in reflecting, the apprehension of danger, and the fear of retribution alarm him. He abandons his purpose; is deemed irresolute: not less innocent for not daring to execute what he dares to desire, he is charged with cowardice. Impatient of the charge, and indignant; harrassed by fear, by the consciousness of guilt, and by humanity struggling to resume her influence, he rushes headlong on his bane.

1785—Thomas Whately. "Remarks," from *Remarks on Some of the Characters of Shakespere*

Thomas Whately (d. 1772) was a member of Parliament from 1761 until his death and held various political posts. He was best known during his life as the author of *Observations on Modern Gardening* (1770). In his book *Remarks on Some Characters of Shakespere* (1785), Whately had intended to present eight or ten of Shakespeare's characters, but he could not complete the project and the book was published after his death. Whately's book attracted the attention of Charles Knight in 1811, which led to his edition of Shakespeare. He also won the acclaim of Horace Walpole who, in 1786, declared Whately to have provided the best commentary on Shakespeare's genius.

Every play of Shakespere abounds with instances of his excellence in distinguishing characters. It would be difficult to determine which is the most striking of all that he drew; but his merit will appear most conspicuously by comparing two opposite characters, who happen to be placed in similar circumstances:—not that on such occasions he marks them more strongly than on others, but because the contrast makes the distinction more apparent; and of these none seem to agree so much in situation, and to differ so much in disposition, as RICHARD THE THIRD and MACBETH. Both are soldiers, both usurpers; both attain the throne by the same means, by treason and murder; and both lose it too in the same manner, in battle against the person claiming it as lawful heir. Perfidy, violence and tyranny are common to both; and those only, their obvious qualities, would have been attributed indiscriminately to both by an ordinary dramatic writer. But Shakespere, in conformity to the truth of history, as far as it led him, and by improving upon the fables which have been blended with it, has ascribed opposite principles and motives to the same designs and actions, and various effects to the operation of the same events upon different tempers. Richard and Macbeth, as represented by him, agree in nothing but their fortunes.

The periods of history, from which the subjects are taken, are such as at the best can be depended on only for some principal facts; but not for the minute detail, by which characters are unravelled. That of Macbeth is too distant to be particular; that of Richard, too full of discord and animosity to be true: and antiquity has not feigned more circumstances of horror in the one, than party violence has given credit to in the other. Fiction has even gone so far as to introduce supernatural fables into both stories: the usurpation of Macbeth is said to have been foretold by some witches; and the tyranny of Richard by omens attending his birth. From these fables, Shakespere, unrestrained and indeed uninformed by history, seems to have taken the hint of their several characters; and he has adapted their dispositions so as to give to such fictions, in the days he wrote, a show of probability. The first thought of acceding to the throne is suggested, and success in the attempt is promised, to Macbeth by the witches: he is therefore represented as a man, whose natural temper would have deterred him from such a design, if he had not been immediately tempted, and strongly impelled to it. Richard, on the other hand, brought with him into the world the signs of ambition and cruelty: his disposition, therefore, is suited to those symptoms; and he is not discouraged from indulging it by the improbability of succeeding, or by any difficulties and dangers which obstruct his way.

Agreeable to these ideas, Macbeth appears to be a man not destitute of the feelings of humanity. His lady gives him that character.

> —I fear thy nature;
> It is too full o' the milk of human kindness,
> To catch the nearest way.[1]—

Which apprehension was well founded; for his reluctance to commit the murder is owing in a great measure to reflections which arise from sensibility:

—He's here in double trust
First, as I am his kinsman and his subject;
Strong both against the deed; then as his host,
Who should against his murderer shut the door,
Not bear the knife myself.[2]—

Immediately after he tells Lady Macbeth,—

We will proceed no further in this business;
He hath honoured me of late.[3]

And thus giving way to his natural feelings of kindred, hospitality, and gratitude, he for a while lays aside his purpose. A man of such a disposition will esteem, as they ought to be esteemed, all gentle and amiable qualities in another: and therefore Macbeth is affected by the mild virtues of Duncan; and reveres them in his sovereign when he stifles them in himself. That

—This Duncan
Hath borne his faculties so meekly; hath been
So clear in his great office,[4]—

is one of his reasons against the murder: and when he is tortured with the thought of Banquo's issue succeeding him in the throne, he aggravates his misery by observing, that,

For them the gracious Duncan have I murder'd;[5]

which epithet of *gracious* would not have occurred to one who was not struck with the particular merit it expresses.

The frequent references to the prophecy in favour of Banquo's issue, is another symptom of the same disposition: for it is not always from fear, but sometimes from envy, that he alludes to it: and being himself very susceptible of those domestic affections, which raise a desire and love of posterity, he repines at the succession assured to the family of his rival, and which in his estimation seems more valuable than his own actual possession. He therefore reproaches the sisters for their partiality, when

Upon my head they plac'd a fruitless crown,
And put a barren sceptre in my gripe,
Thence to be wrench'd with an unlineal hand,
No son of mine succeeding. If 'tis so,
For Banquo's issue have I 'fil'd my mind,

For them the gracious Duncan have I murder'd;
Put rancours in the vessel of my peace
Only for them; and mine eternal jewel
Given to the common enemy of man,
To make them kings, the seed of Banquo kings!
Rather than so, come, Fate, into the list,
And champion me to the utterance.[6]—

Thus, in a variety of instances, does the tenderness in his character shew itself; and one who has these feelings, though he may have no principles, cannot easily be induced to commit a murder. The intervention of a supernatural cause accounts for his acting so contrary to his disposition. But that alone is not sufficient to prevail entirely over his nature: the instigations of his wife are also necessary to keep him to his purpose; and she, knowing his temper, not only stimulates his courage to the deed, but, sensible that, besides a backwardness in daring, he had a degree of softness which wanted hardening, endeavours to remove all remains of humanity from his breast, by the horrid comparison she makes between him and herself:

—I have given suck, and know
How tender 'tis to love the babe that milks me:
I would, while it was smiling in my face,
Have pluck'd my nipple from his boneless gums,
And dash'd the brains out, had I but so sworn
As you have done to this.[7]—

The argument is, that the strongest and most natural affections are to be stifled upon so great an occasion: and such an argument is proper to persuade one who is liable to be swayed by them; but is no incentive either to his courage or his ambition.

(. . .)

The towering ambition of Richard, and the weakness of that passion in Macbeth, are further instances wherein Shakespere has accommodated their characters to the fabulous parts of their stories. The necessity for the most extraordinary incitements to stimulate the latter, thereby becomes apparent; and the meaning of the omens, which attended the birth of the former, is explained. Upon the same principle, a distinction still stronger is made in the article of courage, though both are possessed of it even to an eminent degree; but in Richard it is intrepidity, and in Macbeth no more than resolution: in him it proceeds from exertion, not from nature; in enterprise he betrays a degree of fear, though he is able, when occasion requires, to stifle and subdue it. When he and his wife are concerting the murder, his doubt,

—If we should fail,[8]

is a difficulty raised by apprehension; and as soon as that is removed by the contrivance of Lady Macbeth, to make the officers drunk, and lay the crime upon them, he runs with violence into the other extreme of confidence, and cries out, with a rapture unusual to him,

—Bring forth men-children only!
For thy undaunted metal should compose
Nothing but males. Will it not be receiv'd,
When we have mark'd with blood these sleepy two
Of his own chamber, and us'd their very daggers,
That they have done it?[9]—

Which question he puts to her, who but the moment before had suggested the thought of

His spongy officers, who shall bear the guilt
Of our great quell.[10]—

And his asking it again proceeds from that extravagance, with which a delivery from apprehension and doubt is always accompanied.

Then summoning all his fortitude, he says,

—I am settled, and bend up
Each corporal agent to this terrible feat;[11]

and proceeds to the bloody business without any further recoils. But a certain degree of restlessness and anxiety still continues, such as is constantly felt by a man not naturally very bold, worked up to a momentous achievement. His imagination dwells entirely on the circumstances of horror which surround him; the vision of the dagger; the darkness and the stillness of the night; and the terrors and the prayers of the chamberlains. Lady Macbeth, who is cool and undismayed, attends to the business only; considers of the place where she had laid the daggers ready; the impossibility of his missing them; and is afraid of nothing but a disappointment. She is earnest and eager; he is uneasy and impatient, and therefore wishes it over:

I go, and it is done; the bell invites me.
Hear it not, Duncan, for it is a knell
Which summons thee to heaven or to hell.[12]

But a resolution, thus forced, cannot hold longer than the immediate occasion for it: the moment after that is accomplished for which it was necessary, his thoughts take the contrary turn, and he cries out in agony and despair,

Wake, Duncan, with this knocking; would thou could'st![13]

That courage, which had supported him while he was *settled and bent up*, forsakes him so immediately after he has performed the *terrible feat* for which it had been exerted, that he forgets the favourite circumstance of laying it on the officers of the bed-chamber; and when reminded of it, he refuses to return and complete his work, acknowledging that

I am afraid to think what I have done;
Look on't again I dare not.[14]—

His disordered senses deceive him, and his debilitated spirits fail him; he owns that

—every noise appals him.[15]

He listens when nothing stirs; he mistakes the sounds he does hear; he is so confused, as not to distinguish whence the knocking proceeds. She, who is more calm, knows that it is at the south entry; she gives clear and direct answers to all the incoherent questions he asks her: but he returns none to that which she puts to him; and though after some time, and when necessity again urges him to recollect himself, he recovers so far as to conceal his distress, yet he still is not able to divert his thoughts from it: all his answers to the trivial questions of Lenox and Macduff are evidently given by a man thinking of something else; and by taking a tincture from the subject of his attention, they become equivocal:

Macd. Is the king stirring, worthy Thane?
Macb. Not yet.
Len. Goes the king hence to-day?
Macb. He did appoint so.
Len. The night has been unruly; where we lay,
Our chimneys were blown down; and, as they say,
Lamentings heard i' the air, strange screams of death,
And prophesying, with accents terrible,

Of dire combustions, and confus'd events,
blew hatch'd to th' woful time. The obscure bird
Clamour'd the live-long night. Some say the earth
Was fev'rous, and did shake.
Macb. 'Twas a rough night.
Len. My young remembrance cannot parallel
A fellow to it.[16]

Not yet, implies that he will by and by, and is a kind of guard against any suspicion of his knowing that the king would never stir more: *He did appoint so*, is the very counterpart of that which he had said to Lady Macbeth, when, on his first meeting her, she asked him,

Lady. When goes he hence?
Macb. To-morrow, as he purposes.[17]

In both which answers he alludes to his disappointing the king's intention. And when forced to make some reply to the long description given by Lenox, he puts off the subject which the other was so much inclined to dwell upon, by a slight acquiescence in what had been said of the roughness of the night; but not like a man who had been attentive to the account, or was willing to keep up the conversation.

NOTES

1. Macbeth, Act I. sc. 7.
2. Macbeth, Act I, sc. 10.
3. Ibid. Act I. sc. 9.
4. Ibid. Act I. sc. 10.
5. Macbeth, Act III. sc. 2.
6. Macbeth, Act III. sc. 2.
7. Macbeth, Act I. sc. 10.
8. Macbeth, Act I. sc. 10.
9. Macbeth, Act I. sc. 10.
10. Ibid.
11. Macbeth, Act I. sc. 10.
12. Macbeth, Act II. sc. 2.
13. Ibid. sc. 3.
14. Macbeth, Act II. sc. 3.
15. Ibid.
16. Macbeth, Act II. sc. 4.
17. Macbeth, Act I. sc. 7.

MACBETH
IN THE NINETEENTH CENTURY
 ❧

Nineteenth-century critics continued to admire *Macbeth* both for its unparalleled insight into human nature and its aesthetic achievement. In his 1809 *Lectures on Dramatic Art and Literature*, August Wilhelm von Schlegel proclaimed Shakespeare's imagination to be nonpareil, having reached a height that no other poet, save Dante, had achieved.

> In general we find in *The Midsummer Night's Dream*, in *The Tempest*, in the magical part of *Macbeth*, and wherever Shakespeare avails himself of the popular belief in the invisible presence of spirits, and the possibility of coming in contact with them, a profound view of the inward life of Nature and her mysterious springs, which, it is true, ought never to be altogether unknown to the genuine poet, as poetry is altogether incompatible with mechanical physics, but which few have possessed in an equal degree with Dante and himself.

Schlegel's praise for *Macbeth* continues, as he compares it to one of the ancient Greek tragedians, stating that Shakespeare has illuminated that which is most fundamental and profound in human nature and admonishing any attempt to improve upon his work as a foolhardy endeavor: "Since *The Eumenides* of Aeschylus, nothing so grand and terrible has ever been written."

Shakespeare's unparalleled imagination was emphasized by three of the greatest Romantic critics: William Hazlitt, Samuel Taylor Coleridge, and Thomas De Quincey. For Hazlitt, Shakespeare's genius was without comparison, as he "alone appeared to possess the resources of nature," creating lasting images of the preternatural with a force and a passion that seemed real. In his "Notes on *Macbeth*," Coleridge finds the "Weird Sisters" to be on an imaginative level with Ariel and Caliban. He also praises the eloquence of the speeches within *Macbeth* as comparable to those of Milton's Messiah and Satan. However, in contrast to Coleridge's disgust with the porter scene, which Coleridge was convinced was a mere interpolation, De Quincey questions why the famous "knocking at the gate" would have any effect and finally answers his question after seeing an 1812 performance at Ratcliffe Highway. De Quincey concludes that the porter scene, which immediately follows the murder of Duncan, creates the necessary interval so that the audience's attention would be directed away from the victim, with whom they would sympathize, and refocused toward Macbeth and the "hell within him."

In her essay on Lady Macbeth, Anna Jameson discusses the way in which Shakespeare's time was well-suited for the "vigorous delineation of natural character," whereby the individual can be judged by his actions. Jameson further attests to Shakespeare's fashioning of a story so engrossing that the characters cannot be separated from it. For example, Lady Macbeth's sublime rhetoric is ultimately outweighed by the commonplace notion of a brutal woman who encourages her husband's savage acts. On the other hand, Sarah Siddons's commentary on playing the part of Lady Macbeth, recorded in Thomas Campbell's *The Life of Mrs. Siddons*, defends Lady Macbeth as an "astonishing creature . . . in whose composition are associated . . . all the charms and graces of personal beauty" and admires her ability to captivate and seduce Macbeth. For Siddons, Lady Macbeth is an exemplary wife, supportive of her husband's appalling agenda, so much so that Macbeth's captivity to her elicits our sympathy:

> In one point of view, at least, this guilty pair extort from us, in spite of
> ourselves, a certain respect and approbation. Their grandeur of character
> sustains them both above recrimination (the despicable accustomed
> resort of vulgar minds) in adversity; for the wretched husband, though
> almost impelled into this gulf of destruction by the instigations of
> his wife, feels no abatement of his love for her, while she, on her part,
> appears to have known no tenderness for him, till, with a heart bleeding
> at every pore, she beholds in him the miserable victim of their mutual
> ambition. Unlike the first frail pair in Paradise, they spent not the
> fruitless hours in mutual accusation.

For his own part, Campbell responds to Jameson and Siddons's mutual adulation for Lady Macbeth, stating that though he agrees with them that Lady Macbeth has received unfair treatment from those critics who have portrayed her as an unmitigated villain, she is instead a formidable personality, lacking any personal feelings of revenge or petty vices and driven by only one motive—a "determined feeling of ambition." Campbell finds sublimity in Lady Macbeth, a character whose brilliance and determination rescue her from being totally contemptible.

The great French writer Victor Hugo assigns Macbeth's fatal flaw to something more powerful than ambition, namely, a deficiency of character in the face of temptation. For Hugo, that weakness is an uncontrollable appetite in the soul.

Comparing Macbeth and his wife to Adam and Eve, Hugo charts Macbeth's downfall as progressing from covetousness to violence and, finally, to madness, all of which place the drama within an important historical context: "This drama has epic proportions. Macbeth represents that frightful hungry creature who prowls throughout history. . . . The ancestor of Macbeth is Nimrod."

Beginning with the premise that Shakespeare must be understood and appreciated for his ability to project himself imaginatively into his characters, P. W. Clayden challenges the popular notion that Macbeth is essentially a good person persuaded by opportunity and a bad wife to commit criminal acts. Clayden maintains that Macbeth's temptation to usurp the throne is not the source of his tragic downfall but, rather, merely the catalyst, for he has already decided on his course of action long before he writes a letter to his wife. "It is impossible that an honest man should fall at such a temptation, or should be so familiar with the thought of a fearful crime as to be able to talk it over with his wife at once. The murder must have been in his thought long before, and all that the temptation did was to transfer it suddenly from thought to purpose." Additionally, Clayden dismisses those instances where Macbeth's conscience can possibly be inferred, stating that any hesitancy he displays is the result of having to act suddenly on a plan which he conceived well before the opportunity presented itself.

The famous actor Henry Irving makes a persuasive argument that the Third Murderer in *Macbeth*, who remains nameless and receives scant attention or stage direction, is in fact a trusted servant, entirely under his master's power and aware to some degree of Macbeth's diabolical plans. By focusing on such details as the chamber doors, which afford an opportunity for the attendant to exit one side and the murderers by another door, Irving contends that Macbeth is thus able to gain complete control. "[Macbeth] secures to himself a check upon the two murderers in the person of this attendant, who is made an accomplice, and whose lips are sealed. A very slight and legitimate change in the accepted stage-business would make all this stratagem clear to the audience, and it fits in with my theory that the attendant was a trusty, and not a common servant."

H. N. Hudson's essay on *Macbeth* reflects the Victorian concern for historical accuracy and continues in the critical tradition of praising Shakespeare's psychological insight. In his discussion of the Weird Sisters, he returns to the Anglo-Saxon origins of the word "weird," meaning "fate," and affirms that they are not the witches of superstition, because their malice stems not from personal animosity but, rather, "is of a higher strain, and savours as little of any such human ranklings as the thunder-storms and elemental perturbations amidst which they come and go." Indeed, Hudson sees the witches as vehicles of truth in that they are projections of Macbeth's guilt.

Frances Kemble's "Notes on Macbeth's Character" focuses on another Victorian concern, namely the didactic message of *Macbeth*. Describing the play as a "Drama of Conscience," Kemble praises Shakespeare's supreme artistry in depicting the insidious consequences of temptation within a sublimely beautiful story.

Richard G. Moulton's essay on *Macbeth* is a complex structural analysis of the play. Moulton identifies a subtlety of plot in *Macbeth* whereby the events in the play are a combination of the modern concept of Nemesis, which concerns the changing fortunes of an individual, where "the rise is a crime of which the fall is the retribution" or justice, and the ancient notion of Destiny or fate. In his chapter on Macbeth's character, Moulton makes a distinction between the outer life of action, a social sphere where things are accomplished through interaction with others, and the interior or intellectual life. As these two sides must act in concert with each other, Moulton maintains that this balance does not work for Macbeth.

> There are two flaws in Macbeth's completeness. For one, his lack
> of training in thought has left him without protection against the
> superstition of his age. He is a passive prey to supernatural imaginings.
> . . . And we see throughout the play how he never for an instant
> doubts the reality of the supernatural appearances: a feature the more
> striking from its contrast with the scepticism of Lady Macbeth, and
> the hesitating doubt of Banquo. Again: no active career can be without
> its periods when action is impossible, and it is in such periods that
> the training given by the intellectual life makes itself felt, with its self-
> control and passive courage. All this Macbeth lacks.

Finally, the Danish critic Georg Brandes points out connections between *Macbeth* and *Hamlet*. For example, he calls Macbeth's personality a "counterpart" to Hamlet's. He also points out the elements of the supernatural in both plays, which are absent in *King Lear* and *Othello*.

—⁓⁓⁓—   —⁓⁓⁓—   —⁓⁓⁓—

1809—August Wilhelm von Schlegel.
From *Lectures on Dramatic Art and Literature*

An important figure in German Romanticism, August Wilhelm von Schlegel (1767–1845) was a poet, translator, and critic. In 1796 he went to the university of Jena and in 1798 was appointed extraordinary professor. It is here that he began his translation of Shakespeare, one of the finest in German.

Of *Macbeth* I have already spoken once in passing, and who could exhaust the praises of this sublime work? Since *The Eumenides* of Aeschylus, nothing so grand and terrible has ever been written. The witches are not, it is true, divine Eumenides, and are not intended to be: they are ignoble and vulgar instruments of hell. A German poet, therefore, very ill understood their meaning, when he transformed them into mongrel beings, a mixture of fates, furies, and enchantresses, and clothed them with tragic dignity. Let no man venture to lay hand on Shakspeare's works thinking to improve anything essential: he will be sure to punish himself. The bad is radically odious, and to endeavour in any manner to ennoble it, is to violate the laws of propriety. Hence, in my opinion, Dante, and even Tasso, have been much more successful in their portraiture of demons than Milton. Whether the age of Shakspeare still believed in ghosts and witches, is a matter of perfect indifference for the justification of the use which in *Hamlet* and *Macbeth* he has made of pre-existing traditions. No superstition can be widely diffused without having a foundation in human nature: on this the poet builds; he calls up from their hidden abysses that dread of the unknown, that presage of a dark side of nature, and a world of spirits, which philosophy now imagines it has altogether exploded. In this manner he is in some degree both the portrayer and the philosopher of superstition; that is, not the philosopher who denies and turns it into ridicule, but, what is still more difficult, who distinctly exhibits its origin in apparently irrational and yet natural opinions. But when he ventures to make arbitrary changes in these popular traditions, he altogether forfeits his right to them, and merely holds up his own idle fancies to our ridicule. Shakspeare's picture of the witches is truly magical in the short scenes where they enter, he has created for them a peculiar language, which, although composed of the usual elements, still seems to be a collection of formulae of incantation. The sound of the words, the accumulation of rhymes, and the rhythmus of the verse, form, as it were, the hollow music of a dreary witch-dance. He has been abused for using the names of disgusting objects; but he who fancies the kettle of the witches can be made effective with agreeable aromatics, is as wise as those who desire that hell should sincerely and honestly give good advice. These repulsive things, from which the imagination shrinks, are here emblems of the hostile powers which operate in nature; and the repugnance of our senses is outweighed by the mental horror. With one another the witches discourse like women of the very lowest class; for this was the class to which witches were ordinarily supposed to belong: when, however, they address Macbeth they assume a loftier tone: their predictions, which they either themselves pronounce, or allow their apparitions to deliver, have all the obscure brevity, the majestic solemnity of oracles.

We here see that the witches are merely instruments; they are governed by an invisible spirit, or the operation of such great and dreadful events would be above their sphere. With what intent did Shakspeare assign the same place to them in his play, which they occupy in the history of Macbeth as related in the old chronicles? A monstrous crime is committed; Duncan, a venerable old man, and the best of kings, is, in defenceless sleep, under the hospitable roof, murdered by his subject, whom he has loaded with honours and rewards. Natural motives alone seem inadequate, or the perpetrator must have been portrayed as a hardened villain. Shakspeare wished to exhibit a more sublime picture: an ambitious but noble hero, yielding to a deep-laid hellish temptation; and in whom all the crimes to which, in order to secure the fruits of his first crime, he is impelled by necessity, cannot altogether eradicate the stamp of native heroism. He has, therefore, given a threefold division to the guilt of that crime. The first idea comes from that being whose whole activity is guided by a lust of wickedness. The Weird Sisters surprise Macbeth in the moment of intoxication of victory, when his love of glory has been gratified; they cheat his eyes by exhibiting to him as the work of fate what in reality can only be accomplished by his own deed, and gain credence for all their words by the immediate fulfilment of the first prediction. The opportunity of murdering the King immediately offers; the wife of Macbeth conjures him not to let it slip; she urges him on with a fiery eloquence, which has at command all those sophisms that serve to throw a false splendour over crime. Little more than the mere execution falls to the share of Macbeth; he is driven into it, as it were, in a tumult of fascination. Repentance immediately follows, nay, even precedes the deed, and the stings of conscience leave him rest neither night nor day. But he is now fairly entangled in the snares of hell; truly frightful is it to behold that same Macbeth, who once as a warrior could spurn at death, now that he dreads the prospect of the life to come, clinging with growing anxiety to his earthly existence the more miserable it becomes, and pitilessly removing out of the way whatever to his dark and suspicious mind seems to threaten danger. However much we may abhor his actions, we cannot altogether refuse to compassionate the state of his mind; we lament the ruin of so many noble qualities, and even in his last defence we are compelled to admire the struggle of a brave will with a cowardly conscience. We might believe that we witness in this tragedy the over-ruling destiny of the ancients represented in perfect accordance with their ideas: the whole originates in a supernatural influence, to which the subsequent events seem inevitably linked. Moreover, we even find here the same ambiguous oracles which, by their literal fulfilment, deceive those who confide in them. Yet it may be easily shown that the poet has, in his work, displayed more enlightened views. He wishes to show that the conflict of good and evil in this world can only take place by the permission of Providence, which converts the curse that individual mortals draw down on their heads into a blessing to others. An accurate scale is followed in the retaliation. Lady Macbeth, who of all the human participators in the king's murder is the most guilty, is thrown by the terrors of her conscience into a state of incurable bodily and mental disease; she dies, unlamented by her husband, with all the symptoms of reprobation. Macbeth is still found worthy to die the death of a hero on the field of battle. The noble Macduff is allowed the satisfaction of saving his country by punishing with his own hand the tyrant who had murdered his wife and children. Banquo, by an early death, atones for the ambitious curiosity which prompted the wish to know his glorious descendants, as he thereby has roused Macbeth's jealousy; but he preserved his mind pure from the evil suggestions of the witches: his name is blessed in his race, destined to enjoy for a long succession of ages that royal dignity which Macbeth could only hold for his own life. In the progress of the action, this piece is altogether the reverse of *Hamlet:* it strides forward with amazing rapidity, from the first catastrophe (for Duncan's murder may be called a catastrophe) to the last. "Thought, and done!" is the general motto; for as Macbeth says,

> The flighty purpose never is o'ertook,
> Unless the deed go with it.

In every feature we see an energetic heroic age, in the hardy North which steels every nerve. The precise duration of the action cannot be ascertained,—years perhaps, according to the story; but we know that to the imagination the most crowded time appears always the shortest. Here we can hardly conceive how so very much could ever have been compressed into so narrow a space; not merely external events,—the very inmost recesses in the minds of the dramatic personages are laid open to us. It is as if the drags were taken from the wheels of time, and they rolled along without interruption in their descent. Nothing can equal this picture in its power to excite terror. We need only allude to the circumstances attending the murder of Duncan, the dagger that hovers before the eyes of Macbeth, the vision of Banquo at the feast, the madness of Lady Macbeth; what can possibly be said on the subject that will not rather weaken the impression they naturally leave? Such scenes stand alone, and are to be found only in this poet; otherwise the tragic muse might exchange her mask for the *head of Medusa.* I wish merely to point out as a secondary circumstance the prudent dexterity of Shakspeare, who could still contrive to flatter a king by a work in every part of whose plan nevertheless the poetical views are evident. James the First drew his lineage from Banquo; he was the first who united the threefold sceptre of England, Scotland, and Ireland: this is foreshown in the magical vision, when a long series of glorious successors is promised to Banquo. Even the gift of the English kings to heal certain maladies by the touch, which James pretended to have inherited from Edward the Confessor, and on which he set a great value, is brought in very naturally.—With such occasional matters we may well allow ourselves to be pleased without fearing from them any danger to poetry: by similar allusions Aeschylus endeavoured to recommend the Areopagus to his fellow-citizens, and Sophocles to celebrate the glory of Athens.

1817—William Hazlitt.
"Macbeth," from *Characters of Shakespear's Plays*

William Hazlitt (1778–1830) was a great English essayist and literary critic. He is the author of *Characters of Shakespear's Plays* (1817), *Lectures on the English Poets* (1818), and *The Spirit of the Age* (1825).

The poet's eye in a fine frenzy rolling
Doth glance from heaven to earth, from earth to heaven;
And as imagination bodies forth
The forms of things unknown, the poet's pen
Turns them to shape, and gives to airy nothing
A local habitation and a name.

Macbeth and *Lear, Othello* and *Hamlet*, are usually reckoned Shakespear's four principal tragedies. *Lear* stands first for the profound intensity of the passion; *Macbeth* for the wildness of the imagination and the rapidity of the action; *Othello* for the progressive interest and powerful alternations of feeling; *Hamlet* for the refined development of thought and sentiment. If the force of genius shewn in each of these works is astonishing, their variety is not less so. They are like different creations of the same mind, not one of which has the slightest reference to the rest. This distinctness and originality is indeed the necessary consequence of truth and nature. Shakespear's genius alone appeared to possess the resources of nature. He is 'your only *tragedy-maker.*' His plays have the force of things upon the mind. What he represents is brought home to the bosom as a part of our experience, implanted in the memory as if we had known the places, persons, and things of which he treats. *Macbeth* is like a record of a preternatural and tragical event. It has the rugged severity of an old chronicle with all that the imagination of the poet can engraft upon traditional belief. The castle of Macbeth, round which 'the air smells wooingly,' and where 'the temple-haunting martlet builds,' has a real subsistence in the mind; the Weird Sisters meet us in person on 'the blasted heath'; the 'air-drawn dagger' moves slowly before our eyes; the 'gracious Duncan,' the 'blood-boultered Banquo' stand before us; all that passed through the mind of Macbeth passes, without the loss of a title, through ours. All that could actually take place, and all that is only possible to be conceived, what was said and what was done, the workings of passion, the spells of magic, are brought before us with the same absolute truth and vividness.—Shakespear excelled in the openings of his plays: that of *Macbeth* is the most striking of any. The wildness of the scenery, the sudden shifting of the situations and characters, the bustle, the expectations excited, are equally extraordinary. From the first entrance of the Witches and the description of them when they meet Macbeth,

> What are these
> So wither'd and so wild in their attire,
> That look not like the inhabitants of th' earth
> And yet are on 't?

the mind is prepared for all that follows.

This tragedy is alike distinguished for the lofty imagination it displays, and for the tumultuous vehemence of the action; and the one is made the moving principle of the other. The overwhelming pressure of preternatural agency urges on the tide of human passion with redoubled force. Macbeth himself appears driven along by the violence of his fate like a vessel drifting before a storm: he reels to and fro like a drunken man; he staggers under the weight of his own purposes and the suggestions of others; he stands at bay with his situation; and from the superstitious awe and breathless suspense into which the communications of the Weird Sisters throw him, is hurried on with daring impatience to verify their predictions, and with impious and bloody hand to tear aside the veil which hides the uncertainty of the future. He is not equal to the struggle with fate and conscience. He now 'bends up each corporal instrument to the terrible feat'; at other times his heart misgives him, and he is cowed and abashed by his success. 'The deed, no less than the attempt, confounds him.' His mind is assailed by the stings of remorse, and full of 'preternatural solicitings.' His speeches and soliloquies are dark riddles on human life, baffling solution, and entangling him in their labyrinths. In thought he is absent and perplexed, sudden and desperate in act, from a distrust of his own resolution. His energy springs from the anxiety and agitation of his mind. His blindly rushing forward on the objects of his ambition and revenge, or his recoiling from them, equally betrays the harassed state of his feelings.—This part of his character is admirably set off by being brought in connection with that of Lady Macbeth, whose obdurate strength of will and masculine firmness give her the ascendancy over her husband's faultering virtue. She at once seizes on the opportunity that offers for the accomplishment of all their wished-for greatness, and never flinches from her object till all is over. The magnitude of her resolution almost covers the magnitude of her guilt. She is a great bad woman, whom we hate, but whom we fear more than we hate. She does not excite our loathing and abhorrence like Regan and Gonerill. She is only wicked to gain a great end; and is perhaps more distinguished by her commanding presence of mind and inexorable self-will, which do not suffer her to be diverted from a bad purpose, when once formed, by weak and womanly regrets, than by the hardness of her heart or want of natural affections. The impression which her lofty determination of character makes on the mind of Macbeth is well described where he exclaims,

> Bring forth men children only;
> For thy undaunted mettle should compose
> Nothing but males!

Nor do the pains she is at to 'screw his courage to the sticking-place,' the reproach to him, not to be 'lost so poorly in himself,' the assurance that 'a little water clears them of this deed,' show anything but her greater consistency in depravity. Her strong-nerved ambition furnishes ribs of steel to 'the sides of his intent'; and she is herself wound up to the execution of her baneful project with the same unshrinking fortitude in crime, that in other cricumstances she would probably have shown patience in suffering. The deliberate sacrifice of all other considerations to the gaining 'for their future days and nights sole sovereign sway and masterdom,' by the murder of Duncan, is gorgeously expressed in her invocation on hearing of 'his fatal entrance under her battlements':—

> Come all you spirits
> That tend on mortal thoughts, unsex me here:
> And fill me, from the crown to th' toe, top-full
> Of direst cruelty; make thick my blood,
> Stop up the access and passage to remorse,
> That no compunctious visitings of nature
> Shake my fell purpose, nor keep peace between
> The effect and it. Come to my woman's breasts,
> And take my milk for gall, you murthering ministers,
> Wherever in your sightless substances
> You wait on nature's mischief. Come, thick night!
> And pall thee in the dunnest smoke of hell,
> That my keen knife see not the wound it makes,
> Nor heav'n peep through the blanket of the dark,
> To cry, hold, hold!

When she first hears that 'Duncan comes here to sleep' she is so overcome by the news, which is beyond her utmost expectations, that she answers the messenger, 'Thou 'rt mad to say it': and on receiving her husband's account of the predictions of the Witches, conscious of his instability of purpose, and that her presence is necessary to goad him on to the consummation of his promised greatness, she exclaims—

> Hie thee hither,
> That I may pour my spirits in thine ear,
> And chastise with the valour of my tongue
> All that impedes thee from the golden round,
> Which fate and metaphysical aid doth seem
> To have thee crowned withal.

This swelling exultation and keen spirit of triumph, this uncontroulable eagerness of anticipation, which seems to dilate her form and take possession of all her faculties, this solid, substantial flesh and blood display of passion, exhibit a striking contrast to the cold, abstracted, gratuitous, servile malignity of the Witches, who are equally instrumental in urging Macbeth to his fate for the mere love of mischief, and from a disinterested delight in deformity and cruelty. They are hags of mischief, obscene panders to iniquity, malicious from their impotence of enjoyment, enamoured of destruction, because they are themselves unreal, abortive, half-existences—who become sublime from their exemption from all human sympathies and contempt for all human affairs, as Lady Macbeth does by the force of passion! Her fault seems to have been an excess of that strong principle of self-interest and family aggrandisement, not amenable to the common feelings of compassion and justice, which is so marked a feature in barbarous nations and times. A passing reflection of this kind, on the resemblance of the sleeping king to her father, alone prevents her from slaying Duncan with her own hand.

The dramatic beauty of the character of Duncan, which excites the respect and pity even of his murderers, has been often pointed out. It forms a picture of itself. An instance of the author's power of giving a striking effect to a common reflection, by the manner of introducing it, occurs in a speech of Duncan, complaining of his having been deceived in his opinion of the Thane of Cawdor, at the very moment that he is expressing the most unbounded confidence in the loyalty and services of Macbeth.

> There is no art
> To find the mind's construction in the face:
> He was a gentleman, on whom I built
> An absolute trust.
> O worthiest cousin, (*addressing himself to Macbeth.*)
> The sin of my ingratitude e'en now
> Was great upon me, etc.

Another passage to show that Shakespear lost sight of nothing that could in any way give relief or heightening to his subject, is the conversation which takes place between Banquo and Fleance immediately before the murder-scene of Duncan.

Banquo: How goes the night, boy?
Fleance: The moon is down: I have not heard the
clock.
Banquo: And she goes down at twelve.
Fleance: I take 't, 'tis later, Sir.
Banquo: Hold, take my sword. There's husbandry
in heav'n,
Their candles are all out.—
A heavy summons lies like lead upon me, And yet I would not sleep:
Merciful Powers,
Restrain in me the cursed thoughts that nature
Gives way to in repose.

In like manner, a fine idea is given of the gloomy coming on of evening, just as
Banquo is going to be assassinated.

    Light thickens and the crow
Makes wing to the rooky wood.
. . .
Now spurs the lated traveller apace
To gain the timely inn.

Macbeth (generally speaking) is done upon a stronger and more systematic
principle of contrast than any other of Shakespear's plays. It moves upon the
verge of an abyss, and is a constant struggle between life and death. The action is
desperate and the reaction is dreadful. It is a huddling together of fierce extremes,
a war of opposite natures which of them shall destroy the other. There is nothing
but what has a violent end or violent beginnings. The lights and shades are laid
on with a determined hand; the transitions from triumph to despair, from the
height of terror to the repose of death, are sudden and startling; every passion
brings in its fellow-contrary, and the thoughts pitch and jostle against each
other as in the dark. The whole play is an unruly chaos of strange and forbidden
things, where the ground rocks under our feet. Shakespear's genius here took
its full swing, and trod upon the farthest bounds of nature and passion. This
circumstance will account for the abruptness and violent antitheses of the style,
the throes and labour which run through the expression, and from defects
will turn them into beauties. 'So fair and foul a day I have not seen,' etc. 'Such
welcome and unwelcome news together.' 'Men's lives are like the flowers in their
caps, dying or ere they sicken.' 'Look like the innocent flower, but be the serpent
under it.' The scene before the castle-gate follows the appearance of the Witches
on the heath, and is followed by a midnight murder. Duncan is cut off betimes
by treason leagued with witchcraft, and Macduff is ripped untimely from his

mother's womb to avenge his death. Macbeth, after the death of Banquo, wishes for his presence in extravagant terms, 'To him and all we thirst,' and when his ghost appears, cries out, 'Avaunt and quit my sight,' and being gone, he is 'himself again.' Macbeth resolves to get rid of Macduff, that 'he may sleep in spite of thunder'; and cheers his wife on the doubtful intelligence of Banquo's taking-off with the encouragement— 'Then be thou jocund: ere the bat has flown his cloistered flight; ere to black Hecate's summons the shard-born beetle has rung night's yawning peal, there shall be done—a deed of dreadful note.' In Lady Macbeth's speech 'Had he not resembled my father as he slept, I had done 't,' there is murder and filial piety together; and in urging him to fulfil his vengeance against the defenceless king, her thoughts spare the blood neither of infants nor old age. The description of the Witches is full of the same contradictory principle; they 'rejoice when good kings bleed,' they are neither of the earth nor the air, but both; 'they should be women, but their beards forbid it'; they take all the pains possible to lead Macbeth on to the height of his ambition, only to betray him 'in deeper consequence,' and after showing him all the pomp of their art, discover their malignant delight in his disappointed hopes, by that bitter taunt, 'Why stands Macbeth thus amazedly?' We might multiply such instances every where.

The leading features in the character of Macbeth are striking enough, and they form what may be thought at first only a bold, rude, Gothic outline. By comparing it with other characters of the same author we shall perceive the absolute truth and identity which is observed in the midst of the giddy whirl and rapid career of events. Macbeth in Shakespear no more loses his identity of character in the fluctuations of fortune or the storm of passion, than Macbeth in himself would have lost the identity of his person. Thus he is as distinct a being from Richard III as it is possible to imagine, though these two characters in common hands, and indeed in the hands of any other poet, would have been a repetition of the same general idea, more or less exaggerated. For both are tyrants, usurpers, murderers, both aspiring and ambitious, both courageous, cruel, treacherous. But Richard is cruel from nature and constitution. Macbeth becomes so from accidental circumstances. Richard is from his birth deformed in body and mind, and naturally incapable of good. Macbeth is full of 'the milk of human kindness,' is frank, sociable, generous. He is tempted to the commission of guilt by golden opportunities, by the instigations of his wife, and by prophetic warnings. Fate and metaphysical aid conspire against his virtue and his loyalty. Richard on the contrary needs no prompter, but wades through a series of crimes to the height of his ambition from the ungovernable violence of his temper and a reckless love of mischief. He is never gay but in the prospect or in the success of his villainies: Macbeth is full of horror at the thoughts of the murder of Duncan, which he is with difficulty prevailed on to commit, and of remorse after its perpetration. Richard has no mixture of common humanity in his composition, no regard to kindred or posterity, he owns no fellowship with others, he is 'himself alone.' Macbeth is not destitute of feelings of sympathy, is accessible to pity, is even made in some measure the dupe of his uxoriousness, ranks the loss of friends, of the cordial love of his followers, and of his good name, among the causes which have made him weary of life, and regrets that he has ever seized the crown by unjust means, since he cannot transmit it to his posterity—

> For Banquo's issue have I fil'd my mind—
> For them the gracious Duncan have I murther'd,
> To make them kings, the seed of Banquo kings.

In the agitation of his mind, he envies those whom he has sent to peace. 'Duncan is in his grave; after life's fitful fever he sleeps well.'—It is true, he becomes more callous as he plunges deeper in guilt, 'direness is thus rendered familiar to his slaughterous thoughts,' and he in the end anticipates his wife in the boldness and bloodiness of his enterprises, while she for want of the same stimulus of action, 'is troubled with thick-coming fancies that rob her of her rest,' goes mad and dies. Macbeth endeavours to escape from reflection on his crimes by repelling their consequences, and banishes remorse for the past by the meditation of future mischief. This is not the principle of Richard's cruelty, which displays the wanton malice of a fiend as much as the frailty of human passion. Macbeth is goaded on to acts of violence and retaliation by necessity; to Richard, blood is a pastime.—There are other decisive differences inherent in the two characters. Richard may be regarded as a man of the world, a plotting, hardened knave, wholly regardless of every thing but his own ends, and the means to secure them.—Not so Macbeth. The superstitions of the age, the rude state of society, the local scenery and customs, all give a wildness and imaginary grandeur to his character. From the strangeness of the events that surround him, he is full of amazement and fear; and stands in doubt between the world of reality and the world of fancy. He sees sights not shown to mortal eye, and hears unearthly music. All is tumult and disorder within and without his mind; his purposes recoil upon himself, are broken and disjointed; he is the double thrall of his passions and his evil destiny. Richard is not a character either of imagination or pathos, but of pure self-will. There is no conflict of opposite feelings in his breast. The apparitions which he sees only haunt him in his sleep; nor does he live like Macbeth in a waking dream. Macbeth has considerable energy and manliness of character; but then he is 'subject to all the skyey influences.' He is sure of nothing but the present moment. Richard in the busy turbulence of his projects never loses his self-possession, and makes use of every circumstance that happens as an instrument of his long-reaching designs. In his last extremity we can only regard him as a wild beast taken in the toils:

while we never entirely lose our concern for Macbeth; and he calls back all our sympathy by that fine close of thoughtful melancholy—

> My way of life is fallen into the sear,
> The yellow leaf; and that which should accompany old age,
> As honour, troops of friends, I must not look to have;
> But in their stead, curses not loud but deep,
> Mouth-honour, breath, which the poor heart
> Would fain deny, and dare not.

1818—Samuel Taylor Coleridge.
"Notes on *Macbeth*," from *Shakspeare, with Introductory Remarks on Poetry, the Drama, and the Stage*

Samuel Taylor Coleridge (1772-1834) was an English poet, critic, and philosopher. Along with his friend William Wordsworth, he was one of the founders of the Romantic Movement in England and one of the Lake Poets. He is the author of *Biographia Literaria* (1817) and *Lectures and Notes on Shakespere and other English Poets* (1884).

Macbeth stands in contrast throughout with *Hamlet;* in the manner of opening more especially. In the latter, there is a gradual ascent from the simplest forms of conversation to the language of impassioned intellect,—yet the intellect still remaining the seat of passion: in the former, the invocation is at once made to the imagination and the emotions connected therewith. Hence the movement throughout is the most rapid of all Shakspeare's plays; and hence also, with the exception of the disgusting passage of the Porter (Act ii. sc. 3.), which I dare pledge myself to demonstrate to be an interpolation of the actors, there is not, to the best of my remembrance, a single pun or play on words in the whole drama. I have previously given an answer to the thousand times repeated charge against Shakspeare upon the subject of his punning, and I here merely mention the fact of the absence of any puns in *Macbeth*, as justifying a candid doubt at least, whether even in these figures of speech and fanciful modifications of language, Shakspeare may not have followed rules and principles that merit and would stand the test of philosophic examination. And hence, also, there is an entire absence of comedy, nay, even of irony and philosophic contemplation in *Macbeth*,—the play being wholly and purely tragic. For the same cause, there are no reasonings of equivocal morality, which would have required a more leisurely state and a consequently greater activity of mind;—no sophistry of self-delusion,—except only that previously to the dreadful act, Macbeth mistranslates the recoilings and ominous whispers of conscience into prudential and selfish reasonings, and, after the deed done, the terrors of remorse into fear from external dangers,—like delirious men who run away from the phantoms of their own brains, or, raised by terror to rage, stab the real object that is within their reach:—whilst Lady Macbeth merely endeavours to reconcile his and her own sinkings of heart by anticipations of the worst, and an affected bravado in confronting them. In all the rest, Macbeth's language is the grave utterance of the very heart, conscience-sick, even to the last faintings of moral death. It is the same in all the other characters. The variety arises from rage, caused ever and anon by disruption of anxious thought, and the quick transition of fear into it.

In *Hamlet* and *Macbeth* the scene opens with superstition; but, in each it is not merely different, but opposite. In the first it is connected with the best and holiest feelings; in the second with the shadowy, turbulent, and unsanctified cravings of the individual will. Nor is the purpose the same; in the one the object is to excite, whilst in the other it is to mark a mind already excited. Superstition, of one sort or another, is natural to victorious generals; the instances are too notorious to need mentioning. There is so much of chance in warfare, and such vast events are connected with the acts of a single individual,— the representative, in truth, of the efforts of myriads, and yet to the public and, doubtless, to his own feelings, the aggregate of all,—that the proper temperament for generating or receiving superstitious impressions is naturally produced. Hope, the master element of a commanding genius, meeting with an active and combining intellect, and an imagination of just that degree of vividness which disquiets and impels the soul to try to realize its images, greatly increases the creative power of the mind; and hence the images become a satisfying world of themselves, as is the case in every poet and original philosopher:—but hope fully gratified, and yet the elementary basis of the passion remaining, becomes fear; and, indeed, the general, who must often feel, even though he may hide it from his own consciousness, how large a share chance had in his successes, may very naturally be irresolute in a new scene, where he knows that all will depend on his own act and election.

The Wierd Sisters are as true a creation of Shakspeare's, as his Ariel and Caliban,—fates, furies, and materializing witches being the elements. They are wholly different from any representation of witches in the contemporary writers, and yet presented a sufficient external resemblance to the creatures of vulgar prejudice to act immediately on the audience. Their character consists in the imaginative disconnected from the good; they are the shadowy obscure and fearfully anomalous of physical nature, the lawless of human nature,—elemental avengers without sex or kin:

> Fair is foul, and foul is fair;
> Hover thro' the fog and filthy air.

How much it were to be wished in playing Macbeth, that an attempt should be made to introduce the flexile character-mask of the ancient pantomime;—that Flaxman would contribute his genius to the embodying and making sensuously perceptible that of Shakspeare!

The style and rhythm of the Captain's speeches in the second scene should be illustrated by reference to the interlude in *Hamlet,* in which the epic is substituted for the tragic, in order to make the latter be felt as the real-life diction. In *Macbeth,* the poet's object was to raise the mind at once to the high tragic tone, that the audience might be ready for the precipitate consummation of guilt in the early part of the play. The true reason for the first appearance of the Witches is to strike the key-note of the character of the whole drama, as is proved by their re-appearance in the third scene, after such an order of the king's as establishes their supernatural power of information. I say information,—for so it only is as to Glamis and Cawdor; the 'king hereafter' was still contingent,—still in Macbeth's moral will; although, if he should yield to the temptation, and thus forfeit his free agency, the link of cause and effect *more physico* would then commence. I need not say, that the general idea is all that can be required from the poet,—not a scholastic logical consistency in all the parts so as to meet metaphysical objectors. But O! how truly Shakspearian is the opening of Macbeth's character given in the *unpossessedness* of Banquo's mind, wholly present to the present object,—an unsullied, unscarified mirror!—And how strictly true to nature it is, that Banquo, and not Macbeth himself, directs our notice to the effect produced on Macbeth's mind, rendered temptible by previous dalliance of the fancy with ambitious thoughts:

Good Sir, why do you start; and seem to fear
Things that do sound so fair?

And then, again, still unintroitive, addresses the Witches:—

I' the name of truth,
Are ye fantastical, or that indeed
Which outwardly ye show?

Banquo's questions are those of natural curiosity,—such as a girl would put after hearing a gipsy tell her schoolfellow's fortune;—all perfectly general, or rather planless. But Macbeth, lost in thought, raises himself to speech only by the Witches being about to depart:—

Stay, you imperfect speakers, tell me more:—

and all that follows is reasoning on a problem already discussed in his mind,—on a hope which he welcomes, and the doubts concerning the attainment of which he wishes to have cleared up. Compare his eagerness,—the keen eye with which he has pursued the Witches' evanishing—

> Speak, I charge you!

with the easily satisfied mind of the self-uninterested Banquo:—

> The air hath bubbles, as the water has,
> And these are of them:—Whither are they vanish'd?

and then Macbeth's earnest reply,—

> Into the air; and what seem'd corporal, melted
> As breath into the wind.—'*Would they had staid!*

Is it too minute to notice the appropriateness of the simile 'as breath,' &c. in a cold climate?

Still again Banquo goes on wondering like any common spectator:

> Were such things here as we do speak about?

whilst Macbeth persists in recurring to the self-concerning:—

> Your children shall be kings.
> *Ban.:* You shall be king.
> *Macb.:* And thane of Cawdor too: went it not so?

So surely is the guilt in its germ anterior to the supposed cause, and immediate temptation! Before he can cool, the confirmation of the tempting half of the prophecy arrives, and the concatenating tendency of the imagination is fostered by the sudden coincidence:—

> Glamis, and thane of Cawdor:
> The greatest is behind.

Oppose this to Banquo's simple surprise:—

> What, can the devil speak true?

1823—Thomas De Quincey.
From "On the Knocking at the Gate in *Macbeth*"

Thomas De Quincey (1785-1859) was an English memoirist and critic. He is the author of *Confessions of an English Opium-Eater*, the long essay "On Milton," and two essays on Pope, "The Poetry of Pope" and "Lord Carlisle on Pope." He also wrote numerous articles for the *London Magazine* and *Blackwood's*.

Murder, in ordinary cases, where the sympathy is wholly directed to the case of the murdered person, is an incident of coarse and vulgar horror; and for this reason,—that it flings the interest exclusively upon the natural but ignoble instinct by which we cleave to life: an instinct which, as being indispensable to the primal law of self-preservation, is the same in kind (though different in degree) amongst all living creatures. This instinct, therefore, because it annihilates all distinctions, and degrades the greatest of men to the level of "the poor beetle that we tread on," exhibits human nature in its most abject and humiliating attitude. Such an attitude would little suit the purposes ot the poet. What then must he do? He must throw the interest on the murderer. Our sympathy must be with him (of course I mean a sympathy of comprehension, a sympathy by which we enter into his feelings, and are made to understand them,—not a sympathy of pity or approbation). In the murdered person, all strife of thought, all flux and reflux of passion and of purpose, are crushed by one overwhelming panic; the fear of instant death smites him "with its petrific mace." But in the murderer, such a murderer as a poet will condescend to, there must be raging some great storm of passion,—jealousy, ambition, vengeance, hatred—which will create a hell within him; and into this hell we are to look.

In *Macbeth*, for the sake of gratifying his own enormous and teeming faculty of creation, Shakspere has introduced two murderers: and, as usual in his hands, they are remarkably discriminated: but,—though in Macbeth the strife of mind is greater than in his wife, the tiger spirit not so awake, and his feelings caught chiefly by contagion from her,—yet, as both were finally involved in the guilt of murder, the murderous mind of necessity is finally to be presumed in both. This was to be expressed; and, on its own account, as well as to make it a more proportionable antagonist to the unoffending nature of their victim, "the gracious Duncan," and adequately to expound "the deep damnation of his taking off," this was to be expressed with peculiar energy. We were to be made to feel that the human nature,—*i.e.* the divine nature of love and mercy, spread through the hearts of all creatures, and seldom utterly withdrawn from man,—was gone, vanished, extinct, and that the fiendish nature had taken its place. And, as this effect is marvellously accomplished in the *dialogues* and *soliloquies* themselves, so it is finally consummated by the expedient under consideration; and it is to this that I now solicit the reader's attention. If the reader has ever witnessed a wife, daughter, or sister in a fainting fit, he may chance to have observed that the most affecting moment in such a spectacle is *that* in which a sigh and a stirring announce the recommencement of suspended life. Or, if the reader has ever been present in a vast metropolis on the day when some great national idol was carried in funeral pomp to his grave, and, chancing to walk near the course through which it passed, has felt powerfully, in the silence and desertion of the streets, and in the stagnation of ordinary business, the deep interest which at that moment was possessing the heart of man,—if all at once he should hear the death-like stillness broken up by the sound of wheels rattling away from the scene, and making known that the transitory vision was dissolved, he will be aware that at no moment was his sense of the complete suspension and pause in ordinary human concerns so full and affecting as at that moment when the suspension ceases, and the goings-on of human life are suddenly resumed. All action in any direction is best expounded, measured, and made apprehensible, by reaction. Now, apply this to the case in *Macbeth*. Here, as I have said, the retiring of the human heart and the entrance of the fiendish heart was to be expressed and made sensible. Another world has stept in; and the murderers are taken out of the region of human things, human purposes, human desires. They are transfigured: Lady Macbeth is "unsexed"; Macbeth has forgot that he was born of woman; both are conformed to the image of devils; and the world of devils is suddenly revealed. But how shall this be conveyed and made palpable? In order that a new world may step in, this world must for a time disappear. The murderers and the murder must be insulated—cut off by an immeasurable gulf from the ordinary tide and succession of human affairs—locked up and sequestered in some deep recess; we must be made sensible that the world of ordinary life is suddenly arrested, laid asleep, tranced, racked into a dread armistice; time must be annihilated, relation to things without abolished; and all must pass self-withdrawn into a deep syncope and suspension of earthly passion. Hence it is that, when the deed is done, when the work of darkness is perfect, then the world of darkness passes away like a pageantry in the clouds: the knocking at the gate is heard, and it makes known audibly that the reaction is commenced; the human has made its reflux upon the fiendish; the pulses of life are beginning to beat again; and the re-establishment of the goings-on of the world in which we live first makes us profoundly sensible of the awful parenthesis that had suspended them.

O mighty poet! Thy works are not as those of other men, simply and merely great works of art, but are also like the phenomena of nature, like the sun and the sea, the stars and the flowers, like frost and snow, rain and dew, hail-storm and thunder, which are to be studied with entire submission of our own faculties, and in the perfect faith that in them there can be no too much or too little, nothing useless or inert, but that, the farther we press in our discoveries, the more we shall see proofs of design and self-supporting arrangement where the careless eye had seen nothing but accident!

—~/\/\/~—   —~/\/\/~—   —~/\/\/~—

1832—Anna Jameson. "Lady Macbeth," from *Shakespeare's Heroines: Characteristics of Women: Moral, Poetical and Historical*

Anna Jameson (1794–1860) was an English essayist, born in Dublin. In addition to her work on Shakespeare, *Characteristics of Women: Moral, Poetical and Historical* (1832), she kept a diary of her travels on the Continent as governess to a wealthy family, later published as *The Diary of an Ennuyée* (1826); edited the *Memoirs of the Early Italian Painters* (1845) and wrote *Sacred and Legendary Art* (1848–60; edited by E. M. Hurll, 1896).

I doubt whether the epithet *historical* can properly apply to the character of Lady Macbeth; for though the subject of the play be taken from history, we never think of her with any reference to historical associations, as we do with regard to Constance, Volumnia, Katherine of Arragon, and others. I remember reading some critique, in which Lady Macbeth was styled the "*Scottish Queen*"; and methought the title, as applied to *her*, sounded like a vulgarism. It appears that the real wife of Macbeth,—she who lives only in the obscure record of an obscure age,—bore the very unmusical appellation of Graoch, and was instigated to the murder of Duncan, not only by ambition, but by motives of vengeance. She was the granddaughter of Kenneth the Fourth, killed in 1003, fighting against Malcolm the Second, the father of Duncan. Macbeth reigned over Scotland from the year 1039 to 1053;—but what is all this to the purpose? The sternly magnificent creation of the poet stands before us independent of all these aids of fancy; she is Lady Macbeth; as such she lives, she reigns, and is immortal in the world of imagination. What earthly title could add to her grandeur? what human record or attestation strengthen our impression of her reality?

Characters in history trove before us like a procession of figures in *basso relievo*: we see one side only, that which the artist chose to exhibit to us; the rest is sunk in the block: the same characters in Shakespeare are like the statues *cut out* of the block, fashioned, finished, tangible in every part: we may consider them under every aspect, we may examine them on every side. As the classical times, when the garb did not make the man, were peculiarly favorable to the development and delineation of the human form, and have handed down to us the purest models of strength and grace, so the times in which Shakespeare lived were favorable to the vigorous delineation of natural character. Society was not then one vast conventional masquerade of manners. In his revelations, the accidental circumstances are to the individual character what the drapery of the antique statue is to the statue itself; it is evident, that, though adapted to each other, and studied relatively, they were also studied separately. We trace through the folds the fine and true proportions of the figure beneath: they seem and are independent of each other to the practised eye, though carved together from the same enduring substance; at once perfectly distinct and eternally inseparable. In history we can but study character in relation to events, to situation and circumstances, which disguise and encumber it; we are left to imagine, to infer, what certain people must have been, from the manner in which they have acted or suffered. Shakespeare and nature bring us back to the true order of things; and showing us what the human being *is*, enable us to judge of the possible as well as the positive result in acting and suffering. Here, instead of judging the individual by his actions, we are enabled to judge of actions by a reference to the individual. When we can carry this power into the experience of real life, we shall perhaps be more just to one another, and not consider ourselves aggrieved because we cannot gather figs from thistles and grapes from thorns.

In the play or poem of "Macbeth," the interest of the story is so engrossing, the events so rapid and so appalling, the accessories so sublimely conceived and so skilfully combined, that it is difficult to detach Lady Macbeth from the dramatic situations, or consider her apart from the terrible associations of our first and earliest impressions. As the vulgar idea of a Juliet—that all-beautiful and heaven-gifted child of the south—is merely a love-sick girl in white satin, so the commonplace idea of Lady Macbeth, though endowed with the rarest powers, the loftiest energies, and the profoundest affections, is nothing but a fierce, cruel woman, brandishing a couple of daggers, and inciting her husband to butcher a poor old king.

Even those who reflect more deeply are apt to consider rather the mode in which a certain character is manifested, than the combination of abstract qualities making up that individual human being: so what should be last, is first; effects are mistaken for causes, qualities are confounded with their results, and the perversion of what is essentially good with the operation of positive evil. Hence it is, that those who can feel and estimate the magnificent conception and poetical development of the character, have overlooked the grand moral lesson it conveys; they forget that the crime of Lady Macbeth terrifies us in proportion as we sympathize with her; and that this sympathy is in proportion to the degree of pride, passion, and intellect we may ourselves possess. It is good to behold and to tremble at the possible result of the noblest faculties uncontrolled or perverted. True it is, that the ambitious women of these civilized times do not murder sleeping kings: but are there, therefore, no Lady Macbeths in the world? no women who, under the influence of a diseased or excited appetite for power or distinction, would sacrifice the happiness of a daughter, the fortunes of a husband, the principles of a son, and peril their own souls?

*   *   *   *   *

The character of Macbeth is considered as one of the most complex in the whole range of Shakespeare's dramatic creations. He is represented in the course of the action under such a variety of aspects, the good and evil qualities of his mind are so poised and blended, and instead of being gradually and successively developed, evolve themselves so like shifting lights and shadows playing over the "unstable waters," that his character has afforded a continual and interesting subject of analysis and contemplation. None of Shakespeare's personages have been treated of more at large; none have been more minutely criticized and profoundly examined. A single feature in his character—the question, for instance, as to whether his courage be personal or constitutional, or excited by mere desperation—has been canvassed, asserted, and refuted in two masterly essays.

On the other hand, the character of Lady Macbeth resolves itself into few and simple elements. The grand features of her character are so distinctly and prominently marked, that though acknowledged to be one of the poet's most sublime creations, she has been passed over with comparatively few words: generally speaking, the commentators seem to have considered Lady Macbeth rather with reference to her husband, and as influencing the action of the drama, than as an individual conception of amazing power, poetry, and beauty: or if they do individualize her, it is ever with those associations of scenic representation which Mrs. Siddons has identified with the character. Those who have been accustomed to see it arrayed in the form and lineaments of that magnificent woman, and developed with her wonder-working powers, seem satisfied to leave it there, as if nothing more could be said or added.[44]

But the generation which beheld Mrs. Siddons in her glory is passing away, and we are again left to our own unassisted feelings, or to all the satisfaction to be derived from the sagacity of critics and the reflections of commentators. Let us turn to them for a moment.

Dr. Johnson, who seems to have regarded her as nothing better than a kind of ogress, tells us in so many words that "Lady Macbeth is merely detested." Schlegel dismisses her in haste, as a species of female Fury. In the two essays on Macbeth already mentioned, she is passed over with one or two slight allusions. The only justice that has yet been done to her is by Hazlitt, in "The Characters of Shakespeare's Plays." Nothing can be finer than his remarks as far as they go, but his plan did not allow him sufficient space to work out his own conception of the character with the minuteness it requires. All that he says is just in sentiment, and most eloquent in the expression; but in leaving some of the finest points altogether untouched, he has also left us in doubt whether he even felt or perceived them: and his masterly criticism stops short of the *whole* truth—it is a little superficial, and a little too harsh.[45]

In the mind of Lady Macbeth, ambition is represented as the ruling motive, an intense, over-mastering passion, which is gratified at the expense of every just and generous principle, and every feminine feeling. In the pursuit of her object, she is cruel, treacherous, and daring. She is doubly, trebly, dyed in guilt and blood; for the murder she instigates is rendered more frightful by disloyalty and ingratitude, and by the violation of all the most sacred claims of kindred and hospitality. When her husband's more kindly nature shrinks from the perpetration of the deed of horror, she, like an evil genius, whispers him on to his damnation. The full measure of her wickedness is never disguised, the magnitude and atrocity of her crime is never extenuated, forgotten, or forgiven, in the whole course of the play. Our judgment is not bewildered, nor our moral feeling insulted, by the sentimental jumble of great crimes and dazzling virtues, after the fashion of the German school, and of some admirable writers of our own time. Lady Macbeth's amazing power of intellect, her inexorable determination of purpose, her superhuman strength of nerve, render her as fearful in herself as her deeds are hateful; yet she is not a mere monster of depravity, with whom we have nothing in common, nor a meteor whose destroying path we watch in ignorant affright and amaze. She is a terrible impersonation of evil passions and mighty powers, never so far removed from our own nature as to be cast beyond the pale of our sympathies; for the woman herself remains a woman to the last,—still linked with her sex and with humanity.

This impression is produced partly by the essential truth in the conception of the character, and partly by the manner in which it is evolved; by a combination of minute and delicate touches, in some instances by speech, in others by silence at one time by what is revealed, at another by what we are left to infer. As in real life, we perceive distinctions in character we cannot always explain, and receive impressions for which we cannot always account, without going back to the beginning of an acquaintance and recalling many and trifling circumstances— looks, and tones, and words: thus, to explain that hold which Lady Macbeth, in the midst of all her atrocities, still keeps upon our feelings, it is necessary to trace minutely the action of the play, as far as she is concerned in it, from its very commencement to its close.

We must then bear in mind, that the first idea of murdering Duncan is not suggested by Lady Macbeth to her husband: it springs within *his* mind, and is revealed to us before his first interview with his wife,—before she is introduced, or even alluded to.

    Macbeth. This supernatural soliciting
Cannot be ill; cannot be good. If ill,

Why hath it given me earnest of success,
Commencing in a truth? I am thane of Cawdor—
If good, why do I yield to that suggestion
Whose horrid image doth unfix my hair,
And make my seated heart knock at my ribs,
Against the use of nature?

It will be said, that the same "horrid suggestion" presents itself spontaneously to her on the reception of his letter; or rather, that the letter itself acts upon her mind as the prophecy of the Weird Sisters on the mind of her husband, kindling the latent passion for empire into a quenchless flame. We are prepared to see the train of evil, first lighted by hellish agency, extend itself to *her* through the medium of her husband; but we are spared the more revolting idea that it originated with her. The guilt is thus more equally divided than we should suppose when we hear people pitying "the noble nature of Macbeth," bewildered and goaded on to crime, solely or chiefly by the instigation of his wife.

It is true that she afterwards appears the more active agent of the two; but it is less through her pre-eminence in wickedness than through her superiority of intellect. The eloquence—the fierce, fervid eloquence, with which she bears down the relenting and reluctant spirit of her husband, the dexterous sophistry with which she wards off his objections, her artful and affected doubts of his courage, the sarcastic manner in which she lets fall the word coward—a word which no man can endure from another, still less from a woman, and least of all from the woman he loves—and the bold address with which she removes all obstacles, silences all arguments, overpowers all scruples and marshals the way before him, absolutely make us shrink before the commanding intellect of the woman with a terror in which interest and admiration are strangely mingled.

> *Lady Macbeth.* He has almost supp'd: why have you left the chamber?
> *Macbeth.* Hath he asked for me?
> *Lady Macbeth.* Know ye not he has?
> *Macbeth.* We will proceed no further in this business:
> He hath honour'd me of late; and I have bought
> Golden opinions from all sorts of people,
> Which would be worn now in their newest gloss,
> Not cast aside so soon.
> *Lady Macbeth.* Was the hope drunk,
> Wherein you dress'd yourself? hath it slept since?
> And wakes it now, to look so green and pale
> At what it did so freely? From this time,
> Such I account thy love. Art thou afear'd
> To be the same in thine own act and valour.

As thou art in desire? Would'st thou have that
Which thou esteem'st the ornament of life,
And live a coward in thine own esteem;
Letting I dare not wait upon I would,
Like the poor cat i' the adage?
    Macbeth. Pr'ythee, peace:
I dare do all that may become a man;
Who dares do more, is none.
Lady Macbeth. What beast was 't then,
That made you break this enterprize to me?
When you durst do it, then you were a man;
And, to be more than what you were, you would
Be so much more the man. Nor time, nor place,
Did then adhere, and yet you would make both;
They have made themselves, and that their fitness now
Does unmake you. I have given suck; and know
How tender 'tis to love the babe that milks me:
I would, while it was smiling in my face,
Have pluck'd my nipple from his boneless gums,
And dash'd the brains out, had I so sworn, as you
Have done to this.
    Macbeth. If we should fail,
    Lady Macbeth. We fail.[46]
But screw your courage to the sticking-place,
And we'll not fail.

Again, in the murdering scene, the obdurate inflexibility of purpose with which she drives on Macbeth to the execution of their project, and her masculine indifference to blood and death, would inspire unmitigated disgust and horror, but for the involuntary consciousness that it is produced rather by the exertion of a strong power over herself than by absolute depravity of disposition and ferocity of temper. This impression of her character is brought home at once to our very hearts with the most profound knowledge of the springs of nature within us, the most subtle mastery over their various operations, and a feeling of dramatic effect not less wonderful. The very passages in which Lady Macbeth displays the most savage and relentless determination are so worded as to fill the mind with the idea of sex, and place the *woman* before us in all her dearest attributes, at once softening and refining the horror, and rendering it more intense. Thus, when she reproaches her husband for his weakness—

            From this time,
Such I account thy love!

Again,

> Come to my woman's breasts,
> And take my milk for gall, ye murd'ring ministers,
> . . .
> That no compunctious visitings of nature
> Shake my fell purpose, &c.

> . . . . I have given suck, and know
> How tender 'tis to love the babe that milks me, &c.

And lastly, in the moment of extremest horror comes that unexpected touch of feeling, so startling, yet so wonderfully true to nature—

> . . . . . . Had he not resembled
> My father as he slept, I had done it!

Thus in one of Weber's or Beethoven's grand symphonies, some unexpected soft minor chord or passage will steal on the ear, heard amid the magnificent crash of harmony, making the blood pause, and filling the eye with unbidden tears.

It is particularly observable that in Lady Macbeth's concentrated, strong-nerved ambition, the ruling passion of her mind, there is yet a touch of womanhood; she is ambitious less for herself than for her husband. It is fair to think this, because we have no reason to draw any other inference either from her words or actions. In her famous soliloquy, after reading her husband's letter, she does not once refer to herself. It is of him she thinks: she wishes to see her husband on the throne, and to place the sceptre within *his* grasp. The strength of her affections adds strength to her ambition. Although in the old story of Boethius we are told that the wife of Macbeth "burned with unquenchable desire to bear the name of queen," yet, in the aspect under which Shakespeare has represented the character to us, the selfish part of this ambition is kept out of sight. We must remark also, that in Lady Macbeth's reflections on her husband's character, and on that milkiness of nature which she fears "may impede him from the golden round," there is no indication of female scorn: there is exceeding pride, but no egotism in the sentiment or the expression; no want of wifely and womanly respect and love for *him*, but on the contrary, a sort of unconsciousness of her own mental superiority, which she betrays rather than asserts, as interesting in itself as it is most admirably conceived and delineated.

> Glamis thou art, and Cawdor; and shalt be
> What thou art promis'd:—Yet do I fear thy nature;

It is too full o' the milk of human kindness
To catch the nearest way: Thou would'st be great;
Art not without ambition; but without
The illness should attend it. What thou would'st highly,
That would'st thou holily: would'st not play false,
And yet would'st wrongly win: thou'dst have, great Glamis,
That which cries, *Thus thou must do, if thou have it;*
And that which rather thou dost fear to do,
Than wishest should be done. Hie thee hither,
That I may pour my spirits in thine ear;
And chastise with the valour of my tongue
All that impedes thee from the golden round,
Which fate and metaphysical[47] aid doth seem
To have thee crown'd withal.

Nor is there anything vulgar in her ambition as the strength of her affections lend to it something profound and concentrated, so her splendid imagination invests the object of her desire with its own radiance. We cannot trace in her grand and capacious mind that it is the mere baubles and trappings of royalty which dazzle and allure her: hers is the sin of the "star-bright apostate," and she plunges with her husband into the abyss of guilt, to procure for "all their days and nights sole sovereign sway and masterdom." She revels, she luxuriates in her dream of power. She reaches at the golden diadem which is to sear her brain; she perils life and soul for its attainment, with an enthusiasm as perfect, a faith as settled, as that of the martyr, who sees at the stake heaven and its crowns of glory opening upon him.

> Great Glamis! worthy Cawdor!
> Greater than both, by the all-hail *hereafter!*
> Thy letters have transported me beyond
> This ignorant present, and I feel now
> The future in the instant!

This is surely the very rapture of ambition! and those who have heard Mrs. Siddons pronounce the word *hereafter*, cannot forget the look, the tone, which seemed to give her auditors a glimpse of that awful *future*, which she, in her prophetic fury, beholds upon the instant.

But to return to the text before us: Lady Macbeth having proposed the object to herself, and arrayed it with an ideal glory, fixes her eye steadily upon it, soars far above all womanish feelings and scruples to attain it, and swoops upon her victim with the strength and velocity of a vulture; but having committed unflinchingly the crime necessary for the attainment of her purpose, she stops there. After the murder of Duncan, we see Lady Macbeth, during the rest of the play, occupied in supporting the nervous weakness and sustaining the fortitude of her husband; for instance, Macbeth is at one time on the verge of frenzy, between fear and horror, and it is clear that if she loses her self-command, both must perish.

> *Macbeth.* One cried, God bless us! and Amen! the other;
> As they had seen me, with these hangman's hands.
> Listening their fear; I could not say *Amen!*
> When they did cry *God bless us!*
> *Lady Macbeth.* Consider it not so deeply!
> *Macbeth.* But wherefrom could not pronounce Amen?
> I had most need of blessing, and Amen
> Stuck in my throat.
> *Lady Macbeth.* These deeds must not be thought
> After these ways: so, it will make us mad.
> *Macbeth.* Methought I heard a voice cry "Sleep no more!" &c.
> *Lady Macbeth.* What do you mean?
> Who was it that thus cried? Why, worthy Thane,
> You do unbend your noble strength, to think
> So brainsickly of things:—Go, get some water, &c.

Afterwards (in act iii.) she is represented as muttering to herself:

> Nought's had, all's spent,
> When our desire is got without content:

yet immediately addresses her moody and conscience-stricken husband:

> How now, my lord? why do you keep alone,
> Of sorriest fancies your companions making?
> Using those thoughts, which should indeed have died
> With them they think on? Things without all remedy
> Should be without regard; what's done, is done.

But she is nowhere represented as urging him on to new crimes; so far from it, that when Macbeth darkly hints his purposed assassination of Banquo, and she inquires his meaning, he replies:

> Be innocent of the knowledge, dearest chuck,
> Till thou applaud the deed.

The same may be said of the destruction of Macduff's family. Every one must perceive how our detestation of the woman had been increased, if she had been placed before us as suggesting and abetting those additional cruelties into which Macbeth is hurried by his mental cowardice.

If my feeling of Lady Macbeth's character be just to the conception of the poet, then she is one who could steel herself to the commission of a crime from necessity and expediency, and be daringly wicked for a great end, but not likely to perpetuate gratuitous murders from any vague or selfish fears. I do not mean to say that the perfect confidence existing between herself and Macbeth could possibly leave her in ignorance of his actions or designs: that heart-broken and shuddering allusion to the murder of Lady Macduff (in the sleepwalking scene) proves the contrary:

The thane of Fife had a wife: where is she now?

But she is nowhere brought before us in immediate connection with these horrors, and we are spared any flagrant proof of her participation in them. This may not strike us at first, but most undoubtedly has an effect on the general bearing of the character, considered as a whole.

Another more obvious and pervading source of interest arises from that bond of entire affection and confidence which, through the whole of this dreadful tissue of crime and its consequences, unites Macbeth and his wife; claiming from us an involuntary respect and sympathy, and shedding a softening influence over the whole tragedy. Macbeth leans upon her strength, trusts in her fidelity, and throws himself on her tenderness.

O, full of scorpions is my mind, dear wife!

She sustains him, calms him, soothes him—

. . . . . . Come on; gentle my lord,
Sleek o'er your rugged looks; be bright and jovial
Among your guests to-night.

The endearing epithets, the terms of fondness in which he addresses her, and the tone of respect she invariably maintains towards him, even when most exasperated by his vacillation of mind and his brain-sick terrors, have by the very force of contrast a powerful effect on the fancy.

By these tender redeeming touches we are impressed with a feeling that Lady Macbeth's influence over the affections of her husband, as a wife and a woman, is at least equal to her power over him as a superior mind. Another thing has always struck me. During the supper scene, in which Macbeth is haunted by the spectre of the murdered Banquo, and his reason appears unsettled by the extremity of his horror and dismay, her indignant rebuke, her low whispered remonstrance, the sarcastic emphasis with which she combats his sick fancies and endeavors to recall him to himself, have an intenseness, a severity, a bitterness, which makes the blood creep.

> *Lady Macbeth*. Are you a man?
> *Macbeth*. Ay, and a bold one, that dare look on that
> Which might appal the devil.
>   *Lady Macbeth*. O proper stuff!
> This is the very painting of your fear:
> This is the air-drawn dagger, which, you said
> Led you to Duncan. O, these flaws, and starts,
> (Impostors to true fear), would well become
> A woman's story at a winter's fire,
> Authoriz'd by her grandam! Shame itself!
> Why do you make such faces? When all's done,
> You look but on a stool.
> . . . . What! quite unmann'd in folly?

Yet when the guests are dismissed, and they are left alone, she says no more, and not a syllable of reproach or scorn escapes her: a few words in submissive reply to his questions, and an entreaty to seek repose, are all she permits herself to utter. There is a touch of pathos and of tenderness in this silence which has always affected me beyond expression: it is one of the most masterly and most beautiful traits of character in the whole play.

Lastly, it is clear that in a mind constituted like that of Lady Macbeth, and not utterly depraved and hardened by the habit of crime, conscience must wake some time or other, and bring with it remorse closed by despair, and despair by death. This great moral retribution was to be displayed to us—but how? Lady Macbeth is not a woman to start at shadows; she mocks at air-drawn daggers: she sees no imagined spectres rise from the tomb to appal or accuse her.[48] The towering bravery of *her* mind disdains the visionary terrors which haunt her weaker husband. We know, or rather we feel, that she who could give a voice to the most direful intent, and call on the spirits that wait on mortal thoughts to "unsex her" and "stop up all access and passage of remorse"—to that remorse would have given nor tongue nor sound; and that rather than have uttered a complaint, she would have held her breath and died. To have given her a confidant, though in the partner of her guilt, would have been a degrading resource, and have disappointed and enfeebled all our previous impressions of her character; yet justice is to be done, and we are to be made acquainted with that which the woman herself would have suffered a thousand deaths of torture rather than have betrayed. In the sleeping scene we have a glimpse into the depths of that inward hell: the seared brain and broken heart are laid bare before us in the helplessness of slumber. By a judgment the most sublime ever imagined, yet the most unforced, natural, and inevitable, the sleep of her who murdered sleep is no longer repose, but a condensation of resistless horrors which the prostrate intellect and the powerless will can neither baffle nor repel. We shudder and are satisfied; yet our human sympathies are again touched: we rather sigh over the ruin than exult in it; and after watching her through this wonderful scene with a sort of fascination, dismiss the unconscious, helpless, despair-stricken murderess, with a feeling which Lady Macbeth, in her waking strength, with all her awe-commanding powers about her, could never have excited.

It is here especially we perceive that sweetness of nature which in Shakespeare went hand in hand with his astonishing powers. He never confounds that line of demarcation which eternally separates good from evil, yet he never places evil before us without exciting in some way a consciousness of the opposite good which shall balance and relieve it.

I do not deny that he has represented in Lady Macbeth a woman "naturally cruel,"[49] "invariably savage,"[50] or endued with "*pure demoniac firmness.*"[51] If ever there could have existed a woman to whom such phrases could apply—a woman without touch of modesty, pity, or fear,—Shakespeare knew that a thing so monstrous was unfit for all the purposes of poetry. If Lady Macbeth had been naturally cruel, she needed not so solemnly to have abjured all pity, and called on the spirits that wait on mortal thoughts to unsex her; nor would she have been loved to excess by a man of Macbeth's character; for it is the sense of intellectual energy and strength of will overpowering her feminine nature which draws from him that burst of intense admiration—

> Bring forth men-children only!
> For thy undaunted metal should compose
> Nothing but males.

If she had been *invariably* savage, her love would not have comforted and sustained her husband in his despair, nor would her uplifted dagger have been arrested by a dear and venerable image rising between her soul and its fell purpose. If endued with pure *demoniac firmness*, her woman's nature would not, by the reaction, have been so horribly venged,—she would not have died of remorse and despair.

*   *   *   *   *   *   *

We cannot but observe, that through the whole of the dialogue appropriated to Lady Macbeth, there is something very peculiar and characteristic in the turn of expression: her compliments, when she is playing the hostess or the queen, are elaborately elegant and verbose: but, when in earnest, she speaks in short, energetic sentences—sometimes abrupt, but always full of meaning, her thoughts are rapid and clear, her expressions forcible, and the imagery like sudden flashes of lightning: all the foregoing extracts exhibit this, but I will venture one more, as an immediate illustration.

> *Macbeth.* My dearest love,
> Duncan comes here to-night.
>   *Lady Macbeth.* And when goes hence?
>   *Macbeth.* To-morrow,—as he purposes.
>   *Lady Macbeth.* O never
> Shall sun that morrow see!
> Thy face, my Thane, is as a book, where men
> May read strange matters: To beguile the time,—
> Look like the time; bear welcome in your eye,
> Your hand, your tongue; look like the innocent flower,
> But be the serpent under it.

What would not the firmness, the self-command, the enthusiasm, the intellect, the ardent affections of this woman have performed, if properly directed? but the object being unworthy of the effort, the end is disappointment, despair, and death.

The power of religion could alone have controlled such a mind; but it is the misery of a very proud, strong, and gifted spirit, without sense of religion, that instead of looking upward to find a superior, it looks round and sees all things as subject to itself. Lady Macbeth is placed in a dark, ignorant, iron age; her powerful intellect is slightly tinged with its credulity and superstitions, but she has no religious feeling to restrain the force of will. She is a stern fatalist in principal and action—"what is done, is done," and would be done over again under the same circumstances: her remorse is without repentance, or any reference to an offended Deity; it arises from the pang of a wounded conscience, the recoil of the violated feelings of nature: it is the horror of the past, not the terror of the future; the torture of self-condemnation, not the fear of judgment: it is strong as her soul, deep as her guilt, fatal as her resolve, and terrible as her crime.

If it should be objected to this view of Lady Macbeth's character that it engages our sympathies in behalf of a perverted being—and that to leave her so strong a power upon our feelings in the midst of such supreme wickedness involves a moral wrong, I can only reply, in the words of Dr. Channing, that "in this and the like cases our interest fastens on what is *not* evil in the character—

that there is something kindling and ennobling in the consciousness, however awakened, of the energy which resides in mind; and many a virtuous man has borrowed new strength from the force, constancy, and dauntless courage of evil agents."[52]

This is true; and might he not have added that many a powerful and gifted spirit has learnt humility and self-government, from beholding how far the energy which resides in mind may be degraded and perverted?

*   *   *   *   *   *   *

In general, when a woman is introduced into a tragedy to be the presiding genius of evil in herself, or the cause of evil to others, she is either too feebly or too darkly portrayed; either crime is heaped on crime, and horror on horror, till our sympathy is lost in incredulity, or the stimulus is sought in unnatural or impossible situations, or in situations that ought to be impossible (as in the Myrrha or the Cenci), or the character is enfeebled by a mixture of degrading propensities and sexual weakness, as in Vittoria Corombona. But Lady Macbeth, though so supremely wicked, and so consistently feminine, is still kept aloof from all base alloy. When Shakespeare created a female character purely detestable, he made her an accessory, never a principal. Thus Regan and Goneril are two powerful sketches of selfishness, cruelty, and ingratitude; we abhor them whenever we see or think of them, but we think very little about them, except as necessary to the action of the drama. They are to cause the madness of Lear, and call forth the filial devotion of Cordelia, and their depravity is forgotten in its effects. A comparison has been made between Lady Macbeth and the Greek Clytemnestra in the "Agamemnon" of Aeschylus. The Clytemnestra of Sophocles is something more in Shakespeare's spirit, for she is something less impudently atrocious: but, considered as a woman and an individual, would any one compare this shameless adulteress, cruel murderess, and unnatural mother, with Lady Macbeth? Lady Macbeth herself would certainly shrink from the approximation.[53]

The Electra of Sophocles comes nearer to Lady Macbeth as a poetical conception, with this strong distinction, that she commands more respect and esteem, and less sympathy. The murder in which she participates is ordained by the oracle—is an act of justice, and therefore less a murder than a sacrifice. Electra is drawn with magnificent simplicity, an intensity of feeling and purpose, but there is a want of light and shade and relief. Thus the scene in which Orestes stabs his mother within her chamber, and she is heard pleading for mercy, while Electra stands forward listening exultingly to her mother's cries, and urging her brother to strike again, "another blow! another!" etc., is terribly fine, but the horror is too shocking, too *physical*—if I may use such an expression; it will not surely bear a comparison with the murdering scene in Macbeth, where the exhibition of various passions—the irresolution of Macbeth, the bold determination of his wife, the deep suspense, the rage of the elements without, the horrid stillness within, and the secret feeling of that infernal agency which is ever present to the fancy, even when not visible on the scene—throw a rich coloring of poetry over the whole, which does not take from "the present horror of the time," and yet relieves it. Shakespeare's blackest shadows are like those of Rembrandt; so intense, that the gloom which brooded over Egypt in her day of wrath was pale in comparison,—yet so transparent, that we seem to see the light of heaven through their depth.

In the whole compass of dramatic poetry, there is but one female character which can be placed near that of Lady Macbeth;—the "Medea." Not the vulgar, voluble fury of the Latin tragedy,[54] nor the Medea in a hoop petticoat of Corneille, but the genuine Greek Medea—the Medea of Euripides.[55]

There is something in the Medea which seizes irresistibly on the imagination. Her passionate devotion to Jason for whom she had left her parents and country—to whom she had given all, and

> Would have drawn the spirit from her breast
> Had he but asked it, sighing forth her soul
> Into his bosom.[56]

the wrongs and insults which drive her to desperation—the horrid refinement of cruelty with which she plans and executes her revenge upon her faithless husband—the gush of fondness with which she weep over her children, whom in the next moment she devotes to destruction in a paroxysm of insane fury, carry the terror and pathos of tragic situation to their extreme height. But if we may be allowed to judge through the medium of a translation, there is a certain hardness in the manner of treating the character, which in some degree defeats the effect. Medea talks too much: her human feelings and superhuman power are not sufficiently blended. Taking into consideration the different impulses which actuate Medea and Lady Macbeth, as love, jealousy, and revenge, on the one side, and ambition on the other, we expect to find more of female nature in the first than in the last; and yet the contrary is the fact: at least, my own impression, as far as a woman may judge of a woman, is, that although the passions of Medea are more feminine, the character is less so; we seem to require more feeling in her fierceness, more passion in her frenzy; something less of poetical abstraction,—less art,—fewer words; her delirious vengeance we might forgive, but her calmness and subtlety are rather revolting.

These two admirable characters, placed in contrast to each other, afford a fine illustration of Schlegel's distinction between the ancient or Greek drama, which he compares to sculpture, and the modern or romantic drama, which he compares to painting. The gothic grandeur, the rich chiaroscuro, and deep-toned colors of Lady Macbeth, stand thus opposed to the classical elegance and mythological splendor, the delicate yet inflexible outline of the Medea. If I might be permitted to carry this illustration still further, I would add, that there exists the same distinction between the Lady Macbeth and the Medea, as between the Medusa of Leonardo da Vinci and the Medusa of the Greek gems and bas-reliefs. In the painting, the horror of the subject is at once exalted and softened by the most vivid coloring and the most magical contrast of light and shade. We gaze, until from the murky depths of the background the serpent hair seems to stir and glitter as if instinct with life, and the head itself, in all its ghastliness and brightness, appears to rise from the canvas with the glare of reality. In the Medusa of sculpture how different is the effect on the imagination? We have here the snakes convolving round the winged and graceful head: the brows contracted with horror and pain: but every feature is chiselled into the most regular and faultless perfection; and amid the gorgon terrors there rests a marbly, fixed, supernatural grace, which, without reminding us for a moment of common life or nature, stands before us a presence, a power, and an enchantment!

NOTES

44. Mrs. Siddons left among her papers an analysis of the character of Lady Macbeth, which I have never seen, but I have heard her say, that after playing the part for thirty years, she never read it over without discovering in it something new. She had an idea that Lady Macbeth must, from her Celtic origin, have been a small, fair, blue-eyed woman. Bonduca, Fredegonde, Brunehault, and other Amazons of the gothic ages, were of this complexion; yet I cannot help fancying Lady Macbeth was dark, like Black Agnes of Douglas—a sort of Lady Macbeth in her way.

45. The German critic Tieck also leans to this harsher opinion, judging rather from the manner in which the character is usually played in Germany than from its intrinsic and poetical construction.

46. In her impersonation of the part of Lady Macbeth, Mrs. Siddons adopted successively three different intonations in giving the words we fail. At first, as a quick, contemptuous interrogation—"*we fail?*" Afterwards, with the note of admiration—*we fail!* and an accent of indignant astonishment, laying the principal emphasis on the word *we*—*we* fail! Lastly, she fixes on what I am convinced is the true reading—we fail.—with the simple period, modulating her voice to a deep, low, resolute tone, which settled the issue at once—as though, she had said, "If we fail, why then we fail, and all is over." This is consistent with the dark fatalism of the character and the sense of the line following, and the effect was sublime—almost awful.

47. *Metaphysical* is here used in the sense of spiritual or preternatural.

48. Mrs. Siddons, I believe, had an idea that Lady Macbeth beheld the spectre of Banquo in the supper scene, and that her self-control and presence of mind enabled her to surmount her consciousness of the ghastly presence. This would be superhuman, and I do not see that either the character or the text bear out the supposition.

49. Cumberland.

50. Professor Richardson.

51. Foster's "Essays."

52. See Dr. Charming's remarks on Satan, in his essay, "On the Character and Writings of Milton."—*Works*, p. 131.

53. The vision of Clytemnestra the night before she is murdered, in which she dreams that she has given birth to a dragon, and that in laying it to her bosom it draws blood instead of milk, has been greatly admired, but I suppose that those who most admire it would not place it in comparison with Lady Macbeth's sleeping scene. Lady Ashton, in "The Bride of Lammermoor," is a domestic Lady Macbeth; but the development being in the narrative, not the dramatic form, it follows hence that we have a masterly portrait, not a complete individual: and the relief of poetry and sympathy being wanting, the detestation she inspires is so unmixed as to be almost intolerable: consequently the character, considered in relation to the other personages of the story, is perfect; but abstractedly, it is imperfect; a basso relievo—not a statue.

54. Attributed to Seneca.

55. The comparison has already been made in an article in the "Reflector." It will be seen, on a reference to that very masterly Essay, that I differ from the author in his conception of Lady Macbeth's character.

56. Apollonius Rhodius.—Vide Elton's "Specimens of the Classic Poets."

1836—Peter Eckermann.
From *Conversations with Goethe*

Peter Eckermann (1792–1854) was the private secretary of the great German writer Johann Wolfgang von Goethe (1749–1842), the author of *Faust*, among other masterpieces, and the dominant figure of German Romanticism. Eckermann's book was translated in English and helped popularize Goethe's work in the English-speaking world.

"Are there not," said I, "bold strokes of artistic fiction, similar to this double light of Rubens, to be found in literature?"

"We need not go far," said Goethe, after some reflection; "I could show you a dozen of them in Shakespeare. Only take *Macbeth*. When the lady would animate her husband to the deed, she says:

I have given suck, etc.

Whether this be true or not does not appear; but the lady says it, and she must say it, in order to give emphasis to her speech. But in the course of the piece, when Macduff hears of the account of the destruction of his family, he exclaims in wild rage:

He has no children!

These words of Macduff contradict those of Lady Macbeth; but this does not trouble Shakespeare. The grand point with him is the force of each speech; and as the lady, in order to give the highest emphasis to her words, must say 'I have given suck,' so, for the same purpose, Macduff must say 'He has no children.'

"Generally," continued Goethe, "we must not judge too exactly and narrowly of the pencil touches of a painter, or the words of a poet; we should rather contemplate and enjoy a work of art that has been produced in a bold and free spirit, and if possible with the same spirit.

"Thus it would be foolish, if, from the words of Macbeth:

Bring forth men children only! etc.

it were concluded that the lady was a young creature who had not yet borne any children. It would be equally foolish if we were to go still further, and say that the lady must be represented on the stage as a very youthful person.

"Shakespeare does not make Macbeth say these words to show the youth of the lady. Like those of Lady Macbeth and Macduff, which I quoted just now, they are introduced merely for rhetorical purposes, and prove nothing more than that the poet always makes his character say whatever is proper, effective, and good in each *particular place*, without troubling himself to calculate whether these words may perhaps fall into apparent contradiction with some other passage."

1839—Thomas Campbell. "Mrs. Siddons Acts Lady Macbeth—Her Own Remarks on the Character" and "Observations on Mrs. Siddons Estimate," from *The Life of Mrs. Siddons*

Thomas Campbell (1777-1844) was a Scottish poet chiefly remembered for his sentimental poetry dealing specially with human affairs. In 1799, six months after the publication of the *Lyrical Ballads* of Wordsworth and Coleridge, he wrote, "The Pleasures of Hope," a traditional eighteenth-century-style poem in heroic couplets, as well as several patriotic war songs, including "The Battle of Baltic" in 1801. In 1812, Campbell delivered a series of lectures on poetry at the Royal Institution in London, and Sir Walter Scott urged him to become a candidate for the chair of literature at Edinburgh University. Years later, he was elected Lord Rector of Glasgow University (1826–1829) in competition against Sir Walter Scott.

CHAPTER VIII.

Mrs. Siddons acts *Lady Macbeth*—Her own Remarks on the Character.

No performer was destined oftener than Mrs. Siddons to expend superlative genius on the acting of indifferent dramas. It is true that she sometimes turned this misfortune into the means of creating additional astonishment. Where there was little or no poetry, she made it for herself; and might be said to have become at once both the dramatist and the actress. Where but a hint of a fine situation was given, she caught up the vague conception, and produced it in a shape that was at once ample and defined; and, with the sorriest text to justify the outpouring of her own radiant and fervid spirit, she turned into a glowing picture what she had found but a comparative blank.

Much, however, as we may wonder at this high degree of theatrical art, I doubt if its practice would be desirable, as a general advantage, either to the actor's profession or to dramatic poetry. Actors, in parts beneath their powers, are, after all, only like musicians performing on instruments unworthy of their skill. They overcome us, it is true, with wonder and delight. I have heard the inspired Neukomm draw magical sounds from a common parish-church organ, which, under any other touch than his own, was about as musical as the bell overhead that summoned the parishioners. But this did not prevent me from devoutly wishing that I had heard him perform on the Haarlem organ.

The stage-artist's inspiration ought never to depend on shining by its own light: for it never can be perfect, unless it meets and kindles with the correspondent inspiration of poetry. The temporary triumph which this marvellous acting affords to indifferent plays is unjust to the truly poetical drama, and perplexing to popular taste. Mrs. Siddons's *Margaret of Anjou*, for instance, I dare say, persuaded half her spectators that Franklin's "Earl of Warwick" was a noble poem. The reading man, who had seen the piece at night adorned by her acting, would, no doubt, next morning, on perusal, find that her performance alone had given splendour to the meteor: but the unreading spectator would probably for ever consider "The Earl of Warwick" a tragedy as good as any of Shakspeare's.

The most pleasing points, therefore, in Mrs. Siddons's history, are her returns to the plays of Shakspeare. She chose the part of *Lady Macbeth* for her second benefit this season, February 2, 1785.[1]

I regard the tragedy of "Macbeth," upon the whole, as the greatest treasure of our dramatic literature. We may look, as Britons, at Greek sculpture and Italian paintings, with a humble consciousness that our native art has never reached their perfection; but, in the drama, we can confront Aeschylus himself with Shakspeare: and, of all modern theatres, ours alone can compete with the Greek in the unborrowed nativeness and sublimity of its superstition. In the grandeur of tragedy, "Macbeth" has no parallel, till we go back to the "Prometheus and the Furies" of the Attic stage. I could even produce, if it were not digressing too far from my subject, innumerable instances of striking similarity between the metaphorical mintage of Shakspeare's and of Aeschylus's style,—a similarity, both in beauty and in the fault of excess, that, unless the contrary had been proved, would lead me to suspect our great dramatist to have been a studious Greek scholar. But their resemblance arose only from the consanguinity of nature.

In one respect, the tragedy of "Macbeth" always reminds me of Aeschylus's poetry. It has scenes and conceptions absolutely too bold for representation. What stage could do justice to Aeschylus, when the Titan Prometheus makes his appeal to the elements; and when the hammer is heard in the Scythian Desert that rivets his chains? Or when the ghost of Clytemnestra rushes into Apollo's temple, and rouses the sleeping Furies? I wish to imagine these scenes: I should be sorry to see the acting of them attempted.

In like manner, there are parts of "Macbeth" which I delight to read much more than to see in the theatre. When the drum of the Scottish army is heard on the wild heath, and when I fancy it advancing, with its bowmen in front, and its spears and banners in the distance, I am always disappointed with *Macbeth*'s entrance at the head of a few kilted actors. Perhaps more effect might be given to this scene by stage preparation; though with the science of stage-effect I can pretend to little acquaintance. But, be that as it may, I strongly suspect that the appearance of the *Weird Sisters* is too wild and poetical for the possibility of its being ever duly acted in a theatre. Even with the exquisite music of Lock, the orgies of the *Witches* at their boiling caldron is a burlesque and revolting exhibition. Could any stage contrivance make it seem sublime? No! I think it defies theatrical art to render it half so welcome as when we read it by the *mere* light of our own imaginations. Nevertheless, I feel no inconsistency in reverting from these remarks to my first assertion, that, all in all, "Macbeth" is our greatest possession in dramatic poetry. With the exception of the *Weird Sisters*, it is not only admirably suited for stage representation, but it has given the widest scope to the greatest powers of British acting. It was restored to our theatre by Garrick, with much fewer alterations than have generally mutilated the plays of Shakspeare. For two-thirds of a century before Garrick's time, "Macbeth" had been worse than banished from the stage: for it had been acted with D'Avenant's alterations, produced in 1672, in which every original beauty was either awkwardly disguised or arbitrarily omitted. Yet, so ignorant were Englishmen, that "The Tatler" quotes Shakspeare's "Macbeth" from D'Avenant's alteration of it; and when Quin heard of Garrick's intention to restore the original, he asked, with astonishment, "Have I not all this time been acting Shakspeare's play?"

Lady Macbeth, though not so intensely impassioned as *Constance*, is a more important character in the tragedy to which she belongs. She is a larger occupant of our interest on the stage, and a more full and finished poetical creation. The part accordingly proved, as might have been expected, Mrs. Siddons's masterpiece. It was an era in one's life to have seen her in it. She was Tragedy personified.

Mrs. Siddons has left, in her Memoranda, the following

"*Remarks on the Character of Lady Macbeth.*

"In this astonishing creature one sees a woman in whose bosom the passion of ambition has almost obliterated all the characteristics of human nature; in whose composition are associated all the subjugating powers of intellect, and all the charms and graces of personal beauty. You will probably not agree with me as to the character of that beauty; yet, perhaps, this difference of opinion will be entirely attributable to the difficulty of your imagination disengaging itself from that idea of the person of her representative which you have been so long accustomed to contemplate. According to my notion, it is of that character which I believe is generally allowed to be most captivating to the other sex,—fair, feminine, nay, perhaps even fragile—

'Fair as the forms that, wove in Fancy's loom,
Float in light visions round the poet's head.'

Such a combination only, respectable in energy and strength of mind, and captivating in feminine loveliness, could have composed a charm of such potency as to fascinate the mind of a hero so dauntless, a character so amiable, so honourable as *Macbeth*,—to seduce him to brave all the dangers of the present and all the terrors of a future world; and we are constrained, even while we abhor his crimes, to pity the infatuated victim of such a thraldom. His letters, which have informed her of the predictions of those preternatural beings who accosted him on the heath, have lighted up into daring and desperate determinations all those pernicious slumbering fires which the enemy of man is ever watchful to awaken in the bosoms of his unwary victims. To his direful suggestions she is so far from offering the least opposition, as not only to yield up her soul to them, but moreover to invoke the sightless ministers of remorseless cruelty to extinguish in her breast all those compunctious visitings of nature which otherwise might have been mercifully interposed to counteract, and perhaps eventually to overcome, their unholy instigations. But having impiously delivered herself up to the excitements of hell, the pitifulness of heaven itself is withdrawn from her, and she is abandoned to the guidance of the demons whom she has invoked.

"Here I cannot resist a little digression, to observe how sweetly contrasted with the conduct of this splendid fiend is that of the noble, single-minded Banquo. He, when under the same species of temptation, having been alarmed, as it appears, by some wicked suggestions of the *Weird Sisters* in his last night's dream, puts up an earnest prayer to heaven to have these cursed thoughts restrained in him, '*which nature gives way to in repose.*' Yes, even as to that time when he is not accountable either for their access or continuance, he remembers the precept, 'Keep thy heart with all diligence; for out of it are the issues of life.'

"To return to the subject. *Lady Macbeth*, thus adorned with every fascination of mind and person, enters for the first time, reading a part of one of those portentous letters from her husband. 'They met me in the day of success; and I have learned by the perfectest report they have more in them than mortal knowledge. When I burned with desire to question them further, they made themselves into thin air, into which they vanished. While I stood wrapped in the wonder of it, came missives from the king, who all hailed me 'Thane of Cawdor,' by which title, before these Sisters had saluted me, and referred me to the coming on of time with '*Hail, king that shall be!*' This I have thought good to deliver thee, my dearest partner of greatness, that thou mightst not lose the dues of rejoicing, by being ignorant of what greatness is promised. Lay it to thy heart, and farewell.' Now vaulting ambition and intrepid daring rekindle in a moment all the splendours of her dark blue eyes. She fatally resolves that *Glamis* and *Cawdor* shall be also that which the mysterious agents of the Evil One have promised. She then proceeds to the investigation of her husband's character:

> 'Yet I do fear thy nature,
> It is too full of the milk of human kindness
> To catch the nearest way. Thou wouldst be great,
> Art not without ambition, but without
> The illness should attend it. What thou wouldst highly,
> That thou wouldst holily. Wouldst not play false,
> And yet wouldst wrongly win. Thou'dst have, great Glamis,
> That which cries, *Thus thou must do if thou have it!*
> *And that which rather thou dost fear to do*
> *Than wishest should be undone.*'

"In this development, we find that, though ambitious, he is yet amiable, conscientious, nay, pious; and yet of a temper so irresolute and fluctuating as to require all the efforts, all the excitement which her uncontrollable spirit and her unbounded influence over him can perform. She continues—

> 'Hie thee hither,
> That I may pour my spirits in thine ear,
> And chastise with the valour of my tongue
> All that impedes thee from the golden round,
> Which fate and metaphysical aid doth seem
> To have thee crown'd withal.'

"Shortly *Macbeth* appears. He announces the king's approach; and she, insensible it should seem to all the perils which he has encountered in battle, and to all the happiness of his safe return to her,—for not one kind word of greeting or congratulation does she offer,—is so entirely swallowed up by the horrible design, which has probably been suggested to her by his letters, as to have entirely forgotten both the one and the other. It is very remarkable that *Macbeth* is frequent in expressions of tenderness to his wife, while she never betrays one symptom of affection towards him, till, in the fiery furnace of affection, her iron heart is melted down to softness. For the present, she flies to welcome the venerable gracious *Duncan*, with such a show of eagerness as if allegiance in her bosom sat crowned with devotion and gratitude.

"*The Second Act.*
"There can be no doubt that *Macbeth*, in the first instance, suggested his design of assassinating the king, and it is probable that he has invited his gracious sovereign to his castle, in order the more speedily and expeditiously to realize those thoughts, '*whose murder, though but yet fantastical, so shook his single state of man.*' Yet, on the arrival of the amiable monarch who had so honoured him of late, his naturally benevolent and good feelings resume their wonted power. He then solemnly communes with his heart, and after much powerful reasoning upon the danger of the undertaking, calling to mind that *Duncan* his king, of the mildest virtues, and his kinsman, lay as his guest;—all those accumulated determents, with the violated rights of sacred hospitality bringing up the rear, rising all at once in terrible array to his awakened conscience, he relinquishes the atrocious purpose, and wisely determines to proceed no further in the business. But, now, behold his evil genius, his grave-charm, appears, and by the force of her revilings, her contemptuous taunts, and, above all, by her opprobrious aspersion of cowardice, chases the gathering drops of humanity from his eyes, and drives before her impetuous and destructive career all those kindly charities, those impressions of loyalty, and pity, and gratitude, which, but the moment before, had taken full possession of his mind. She says,

'I have given suck, and know
How tender 'tis to love the babe that milks me.
I would, while it was smiling in my face,
Have pluck'd my nipple from its boneless gums,
And dash'd the brains out,—had I but so sworn
As you have done to this.'

"Even here, horrific as she is, she shows herself made by ambition, but not by nature, a perfectly savage creature. The very use of such a tender allusion in the midst of her dreadful language, persuades one unequivocally that she has really felt the maternal yearnings of a mother towards her babe, and that she considered this action the most enormous that ever required the strength of human nerves for its perpetration. Her language to *Macbeth* is the most potently eloquent that guilt could use. It is only in soliloquy that she invokes the powers of hell to unsex her. To her husband she avows, and the naturalness of her language makes us believe her, that she had felt the instinct of filial as well as maternal love. But she makes her very virtues the means of a taunt to her lord;—'You have the milk of human kindness in your heart,' she says (in substance) to him, 'but ambition, which is my ruling passion, would be also yours if you had courage. With a hankering desire to suppress, if you could, all your weaknesses of sympathy, you are too cowardly to will the deed, and can only dare to wish it. You speak of sympathies and feelings. I too have felt with a tenderness which your sex cannot know; but I am resolute in my ambition to trample on all that obstructs my way to a crown. Look to me, and be ashamed of your weakness.' Abashed, perhaps, to find his own courage humbled before this unimaginable instance of female fortitude, he at last screws up his courage to the sticking-place, and binds up each corporal agent to this terrible feat. It is the dead of night. The gracious *Duncan*, now shut up in measureless content, reposes sweetly, while the restless spirit of wickedness resolves that he shall wake no more. The daring fiend, whose pernicious potions have stupefied his attendants, and who even laid their daggers ready,—her own spirit, as it seems, exalted by the power of wine,—proceeds, 'That which hath made them drunk hath made me bold,' now enters the gallery, in eager expectation of the results of her diabolical diligence. In the tremendous suspense of these moments, while she recollects her habitual humanity, one trait of tender feeling is expressed, 'Had he not resembled my father as he slept, I had done it.' Her humanity vanishes, however, in the same instant; for when she observes that *Macbeth*, in the terror and confusion of his faculties, has brought the daggers from the place where they had agreed they should remain for the crimination of the grooms, she exhorts him to return with them to that place, and to smear those attendants of the sovereign with blood. He, shuddering, exclaims, 'I'll go no more! I am affear'd to think of what I have done. Look on't again I dare not.'

"Then instantaneously the solitary particle of her human feeling is swallowed up in her remorseless ambition; and wrenching the daggers from the feeble grasp of her husband, she finishes the act which the infirm of purpose had not courage to complete, and calmly and steadily returns to her accomplice with the fiend-like boast,

> 'My hands are of your colour;
> But I would scorn to wear a heart so white.'

"How beautifully contrasted is this exclamation with the bolder image of *Macbeth*, in expressing the same feeling!

'Will all great Neptune's ocean wash the blood
Clean from this hand?'

And how appropriately either sex illustrates the same idea!

"During this appalling scene, which, to my sense, is the most so of them all, the wretched creature, in imagination, acts over again the accumulated horrors of her whole conduct. These dreadful images, accompanied with the agitations they have induced, have obviously accelerated her untimely end; for in a few moments the tidings of her death are brought to her unhappy husband. It is conjectured that she died by her own hand. Too certain it is, that she dies, and makes no sign. I have now to account to you for the weakness which I have, a few lines back, ascribed to *Macbeth*; and I am not quite without hope that the following observations will bear me out in my opinion. Please to observe, that he (I must think pusillanimously, when I compare his conduct to her forbearance,) has been continually pouring out his miseries to his wife. His heart has therefore been eased, from time to time, by unloading its weight of woe; while she, on the contrary, has perseveringly endured in silence the uttermost anguish of a wounded spirit.

'The grief that does not speak
Whispers the o'erfraught heart, and bids it break.'

"Her feminine nature, her delicate structure, it is too evident, are soon overwhelmed by the enormous pressure of her crimes. Yet it will be granted, that she gives proofs of naturally higher toned mind than that of *Macbeth*. The different physical powers of the two sexes are finely delineated, in the different effects which their mutual crimes produce. Her frailer frame, and keener feelings, have now sunk under the struggle—his robust and less sensitive constitution has not only resisted it, but bears him on to deeper wickedness, and to, experience the fatal fecundity of crime.

'For mine own good—All causes shall give way.
I am in blood so far stepp'd in, that should I wade no more,
Returning were as tedious as go o'er.'

Henceforth, accordingly, he perpetrates horrors to the day of his doom.

"In one point of view, at least, this guilty pair extort from us, in spite of ourselves, a certain respect and approbation. Their grandeur of character sustains them both above recrimination (the despicable accustomed resort of vulgar minds) in adversity; for the wretched husband, though almost impelled into this gulf of destruction by the instigations of his wife, feels no abatement of his love for her, while she, on her part, appears to have known no tenderness for him, till, with a heart bleeding at every pore, she beholds in him the miserable victim of their mutual ambition. Unlike the first frail pair in Paradise, they spent not the fruitless hours in mutual accusation."

Mrs. Siddons had played *Lady Macbeth* in the provincial theatres many years before she attempted the character in London. Adverting to the first time this part was allotted to her, she says, "It was my custom to study my characters at night, when all the domestic cares and business of the day were over. On the night preceding that in which I was to appear in this part for the first time, I shut myself up, as usual, when all the family were retired, and commenced my study of *Lady Macbeth*. As the character is very short, I thought I should soon accomplish it. Being then only twenty years of age, I believed, as many others do believe, that little more was necessary than to get the words into my head; for the necessity of discrimination, and the development of character, at that time of my life, had scarcely entered into my imagination. But, to proceed. I went on with tolerable composure, in the silence of the night, (a night I never can forget,) till I came to the assassination scene, when the horrors of the scene rose to a degree that made it impossible for me to get farther. I snatched up my candle, and hurried out of the room, in a paroxysm of terror. My dress was of silk, and the rustling of it, as I ascended the stairs to go to bed, seemed to my panic-struck fancy like the movement of a spectre pursuing me. At last I reached my chamber, where I found my husband fast asleep. I clapt my candlestick down upon the table, without the power of putting the candle out; and I threw myself on my bed, without daring to stay even to take off my clothes. At peep of day I rose to resume my task; but so little did I know of my part when I appeared in it, at night, that my shame and confusion cured me of procrastinating my business for the remainder of my life.

"About six years afterwards I was called upon to act the same character in London. By this time I had perceived the difficulty of assuming a personage with whom no one feeling of common general nature was congenial or assistant. One's own heart could prompt one to express, with some degree of truth, the sentiments of a mother, a daughter, a wife, a lover, a sister, &c., but to adopt this character must be an effort of the judgment alone.

"Therefore it was with the utmost diffidence, nay, terror, that I undertook it, and with the additional fear of Mrs. Pritchard's reputation in it before my eyes. The dreaded first night at length arrived, when, just as I had finished my toilette, and was pondering with fearfulness my first appearance in the grand fiendish part, comes Mr. Sheridan, knocking at my door, and insisting, in spite of all my entreaties not to be interrupted at this to me tremendous moment, to be admitted. He would not be denied admittance; for he protested he must speak to me on a circumstance which so deeply concerned my own interest, that it was of the most serious nature. Well, after much squabbling, I was compelled to admit him, that I might dismiss him the sooner, and compose myself before the play began. But, what was my distress and astonishment, when I found that he wanted me, even at this moment of anxiety and terror, to adopt another mode of acting the sleeping scene. He told me he had heard with the greatest surprise and concern that I meant to act it without holding the candle in my hand; and, when I urged the impracticability of washing out that '*damned spot*,' with the vehemence that was certainly implied by both her own words and by those of her gentlewoman, he insisted, that if I did put the candle out of my hand, it would be thought a presumptuous innovation, as Mrs. Pritchard had always retained it in hers. My mind, however, was made up, and it was then too late to make me alter it; for I was too agitated to adopt another method. My deference for Mr. Sheridan's taste and judgment was, however, so great, that, had he proposed the alteration while it was possible for me to change my own plan, I should have yielded to his suggestion; though, even then, it would have been against my own opinion, and my observation of the accuracy with which somnambulists perform all the acts of waking persons. The scene, of course, was acted as I had myself conceived it; and the innovation, as Mr. Sheridan called it, was received with approbation. Mr. Sheridan himself came to me, after the play, and most ingenuously congratulated me on my obstinacy. When he was gone out of the room I began to undress; and, while standing up before my glass, and taking off my mantle, a diverting circumstance occurred, to chase away the feelings of this anxious night; for, while I was repeating, and endeavouring to call to mind the appropriate tone and action to the following words, 'Here's the smell of blood still!' my dresser innocently exclaimed, 'Dear me, ma'am, how very hysterical you are to-night; I protest and vow, ma'am, it was not blood, but rose-pink and water; for I saw the property-man mix it up with my own eyes.'"

CHAPTER IX.

Observations on Mrs. Siddons's Estimate of *Lady Macbeth*'s Character, and on that given by Mrs. Jameson, in her "Characteristics of Women."

Those who have read Mrs. Jameson's admirable "Characteristics of Women," must have remarked the general similarity of her opinions respecting *Lady Macbeth*'s character, to those delivered by Mrs. Siddons in the foregoing critique. If there be any difference, it is that the former goes a shade farther than Mrs. Siddons in her advocacy of Shakspeare's heroine.

Whether Mrs. Jameson heard of Mrs. Siddons's ideas on the subject, which she might by possibility, as the great actress made no secret of them, I have never been in the least anxious to ascertain, because it is plain, from her writings, that

Mrs. Jameson has a mind too original to require or to borrow suggestions from any one. But, in deprecating all suspicion of obligation on the one side, I have an equal right to exclude the possibility of its being suspected on the other. Mrs. Siddons showed me these Remarks on the Character of *Lady Macbeth* some nineteen years ago, so that there can be little doubt of their having been earlier written than those of the authoress of "The Characteristics."

In a general view, I agree with both of the fair advocates of *Lady Macbeth*, that the language of preceding critics was rather unmeasured, when they described her as "*thoroughly hateful, invariably savage, and purely demoniac.*" It is true, that the ungentlemanly epithet, fiend-like, is applied to her by Shakspeare himself, but then he puts it into the mouth of *King Malcolm*, who might naturally be incensed.

Lady Macbeth is not thoroughly hateful, for she is not a virago, not an adultress, not impelled by revenge. On the contrary, she expresses no feeling of personal malignity towards any human being in the whole course of her part. Shakspeare could have easily displayed her crimes in a more commonplace and accountable light, by assigning some feudal grudge as a mixed motive of her cruelty to *Duncan*; but he makes her a murderess in cold blood, and from the sole motive of ambition, well knowing, that if he had broken up the inhuman serenity of her remorselessness by the ruffling of anger, he would have vulgarised the features of the splendid Titaness.

By this entire absence of petty vice and personal virulence, and by concentrating all the springs of her conduct into the one determined feeling of ambition, the mighty poet has given her character a statue-like simplicity, which, though cold, is spirit-stirring, from the wonder it excites, and which is imposing, although its respectability consists, as far as the heart is concerned, in merely negative decencies. How many villains walk the world in credit to their graves, from the mere fulfilment of those negative decencies! Had *Lady Macbeth* been able to smother her husband's babblings, she might have been one of them.

Shakspeare makes her a great character, by calming down all the pettiness of vice, and by giving her only one ruling passion, which, though criminal, has at least a lofty object, corresponding with the firmness of her will and the force of her intellect. The object of her ambition was a crown, which, in the days in which we suppose her to have lived, was a miniature symbol of divinity. Under the full impression of her intellectual powers, and with a certain allowance which we make for the illusion of sorcery, the imagination suggests to us something like a half-apology for her ambition. Though I can vaguely imagine the supernatural agency of the spiritual world, yet I know so little precisely about fiends or demons, that I cannot pretend to estimate the relation of their natures to that of Shakspeare's heroine. But, as a human being, *Lady Macbeth* is too intellectual to be thoroughly hateful. Moreover, I hold it no paradox to say, that the strong idea which Shakspeare conveys to us of her intelligence, is heightened by its contrast with that partial shade which is thrown over it by her sinful will giving way to superstitious influences. At times she is deceived, we should say, prosaically speaking, by the infatuation of her own wickedness, or, poetically speaking, by the agency of infernal tempters; otherwise she could not have imagined for a moment that she could palm upon the world the chamberlains of *Duncan* for his real murderers. Yet her mind, under the approach of this portentous and unnatural eclipse, in spite of its black illusions, has light enough remaining to show us a reading of *Macbeth*'s character such as Lord Bacon could not have given to us more philosophically, or in fewer words.

All this, however, only proves *Lady Macbeth* to be a character of brilliant understanding, lofty determination, and negative decency. That the poet meant us to conceive her more than a piece of august atrocity, or to leave a tacit understanding of her being naturally amiable, I make bold to doubt. Mrs. Siddons, disposed by her own nature to take the most softened views of her heroine, discovers, in her conduct towards *Macbeth*, a dutiful and unselfish tenderness, which, I own, is far from striking me. "*Lady Macbeth*," she says, "seeks out *Macbeth*, that she may, at least, participate in his wretchedness." But is *that* her real motive? No; *Lady Macbeth*, in that scene, seems to me to have no other object than their common preservation. She finds that he is shunning society, and is giving himself up to "*his sorry fancies.*" Her trying to snatch him from these is a matter of policy;—a proof of her sagacity, and not of her social sensibility. At least, insensitive as we have seen her to the slightest joy at the return of her husband, it seems unnecessary to ascribe to her any new-sprung tenderness, when self-interest sufficiently accounts for her conduct.

Both of her fair advocates lay much stress on her abstaining from vituperation towards *Macbeth*, when she exhorts him to retire to rest, after the banquet. But, here I must own, that I can see no proof of her positive tenderness. Repose was necessary to *Macbeth*'s recovery. Their joint fate was hanging by a hair; and she knew that a breath of her reproach, by inflaming him to madness, would break that hair, and plunge them both into exposure and ruin. Common sense is always respectable; and here it is joined with command of temper and matrimonial faith. But still her object includes her own preservation; and we have no proof of her alleged tenderness and sensibility.

If *Lady Macbeth*'s male critics have dismissed her with ungallant haste and harshness, I think the eloquent authoress of the "Characteristics of Women" has tried rather too elaborately to prove her positive virtues, by speculations which, to say the least of them, if they be true, are not certain. She goes beyond Mrs. Siddons's toleration of the heroine; and, getting absolutely in love with her, exclaims, "What would not the firmness, the self-command, the ardent affections of this woman have performed, if properly directed!" Why, her firmness and self-command are very evident; but, as to her ardent affections, I would ask, on what other object on earth she bestows them except the crown of Scotland?

We are told, however, that her husband loves her, and that, therefore, she could not be naturally bad. But, in the first place, though we are not directly told so, we may be fairly allowed to imagine her a very beautiful woman; and, with beauty and superior intellect, it is easy to conceive her managing and making herself necessary to *Macbeth*, a man comparatively weak, and, as we see, facile to wickedness. There are instances of atrocious women having swayed the hearts of more amiable men. What debars me from imagining that *Lady Macbeth* had obtained this conjugal ascendancy by anything amiable in her nature, is, that she elicits *Macbeth's* warmest admiration in the utterance of atrocious feelings; at least, such I consider those expressions to be which precede his saying to her, "Bring forth men-children only."

But here I am again at issue with the ingenious authoress of the "Characteristics," who reads in those very expressions that strike me as proofs of atrocity, distinct evidence of *Lady Macbeth's amiable character*: since, she declares that she had known what it was to have loved the offspring she suckled. The majority of she-wolves, I conceive, would make the same declaration if they could speak, though they would probably omit the addition about dashing out the suckling's brains. Again; she is amiably unable to murder the sleeping king, because, to use Mrs. Jameson's words, "he brings to her the dear and venerable image of her father." Yes: but she can send in her husband to do it for her. Did Shakspeare intend us to believe this murderess naturally compassionate?

It seems to me, also, to be far from self-evident that *Lady Macbeth* is not naturally cruel, because she calls on all the demons of human thought to unsex her; or because she dies of what her apologist calls remorse. If by that word we mean true contrition, Shakspeare gives no proof of her having shown such a feeling. Her death is mysterious; and we generally attribute it to despair and suicide. Even her terrible and thrice-repeated sob of agony, in the sleep-walking scene, shows a conscience haunted indeed by terrors, but not penitent; for she still adheres to her godless old ground of comfort, that "*Banquo is in his grave.*"

She dies,—she is swept away darkly from before us to her great account. I say that we have a tragic satisfaction in her death: and though I grant that we do not exult over her fate, yet I find no argument in this circumstance against her natural enormity. To see a fellow-creature, a beautiful woman, with a bright, bold intellect, thus summoned to her destiny, creates a religious feeling too profound for exultation.

In this terrible swift succession of her punishment to her crimes, lies one of the master-traits of skill by which Shakspeare contrives to make us blend an awful feeling, somewhat akin to pity, with our satisfaction at her death.

Still I am persuaded that Shakspeare never meant her for anything better than a character of superb depravity, and a being, with all her decorum and force of mind, naturally cold and remorseless. When Mrs. Jameson asks us, what might not religion have made of such a character? she puts a question that will equally apply to every other enormous criminal; for, the worst heart that ever beat in a human breast would be at once rectified, if you could impress it with a genuine religious faith. But if Shakspeare intended us to believe *Lady Macbeth's* nature a soil peculiarly adapted for the growth of religion, he has chosen a way very unlike his own wisdom in portraying her, for he exhibits her as a practical infidel in a simple age: and he makes her words sum up all the essence of that unnatural irreligion, which cannot spring up to the head without having its root in a callous heart. She holds that

> "The sleeping and the dead
> Are but as pictures."

And that

> "Things without remedy,
> Should be without regard."

There is something hideous in the very strength of her mind, that can dive down, like a wounded monster, to such depths of consolation.

She is a splendid picture of evil, nevertheless,—a sort of sister of Milton's *Lucifer*; and, like him, we surely imagine her externally majestic and beautiful. Mrs. Siddons's idea of her having been a delicate and blonde beauty, seems to me to be a pure caprice. The public would have ill exchanged such a representative of *Lady Macbeth*, for the dark locks and the eagle eyes of Mrs. Siddons.

In some other characters which Mrs. Siddons performed, the memory of the old, or the imagination of the young, might possibly conceive her to have had a substitute; but not in *Lady Macbeth*. The moment she seized the part, she identified her image with it in the minds of the living generation.

NOTE

1. Cast of the other parts in the performance of "Macbeth," Feb. 2, 1785. *Macbeth*, Smith; *Macduff*, Brereton; *Banquo*, Bensley; *Witches*, Parsons, Moody, and Baddely.

1864—Victor Hugo. From *William Shakespeare*

Victor Hugo (1802–1885) was a leader of the Romantic movement in France. The author of *Les Misérables* (1862) and *The Hunchback of Notre Dame* (1830) and many other works, Hugo also wrote a study of Shakespeare in 1864.

To say "Macbeth is ambition," is to say nothing. Macbeth is hunger. What hunger? The hunger of the monster, always possible in man. Certain souls have teeth. Do not arouse their hunger.

To bite at the apple is a fearful thing. The apple is named "Omnia," says Filesac, that doctor of the Sorbonne who confessed Ravaillac. Macbeth has a wife whom the chronicle calls Gruoch. This Eve tempts this Adam. Once Macbeth has taken the first bite, he is lost. The first thing that Adam produces with Eve is Cain; the first thing that Macbeth accomplishes with Gruoch is murder.

Covetousness easily becoming violence, violence easily becoming crime, crime easily becoming madness: this progression is in Macbeth. Covetousness, Crime, Madness—these three night-hags have spoken to him in the solitude, and have invited him to the throne. The cat Gray-malkin has called him: Macbeth will be cunning; the toad Paddock has called him: Macbeth will be horror. The unsexed being, Gruoch, completes him. It is done; Macbeth is no longer a man. He is no longer anything but an unconscious energy rushing wildly toward evil. Henceforth, no notion of right; appetite is everything. The transitory right of royalty, the eternal right of hospitality—Macbeth murders both. He does more than slay them: he ignores them. Before they fell bleeding under his hand, they already lay dead within his soul. Macbeth begins by this parricide,—the murder of Duncan, his guest; a crime so terrible that, as a consequence, in the night when their master is stabbed, the horses of Duncan become wild again. The first step taken, the ground begins to crumble; it is the avalanche. Macbeth rolls headlong; he is precipitated; he falls and rebounds from one crime to another, ever deeper and deeper. He undergoes the mournful gravitation of matter invading the soul. He is a thing that destroys. He is a stone of ruin, a flame of war, a beast of prey, a scourge. He marches over all Scotland, king as he is, his barelegged kernes and his heavily armed gallow-glasses slaughtering, pillaging, massacring. He decimates the thanes, he murders Banquo, he murders all the Macduffs except the one that shall slay him, he murders the nobility, he murders the people, he murders his country, he murders "sleep." At length the catastrophe arrives,—the forest of Birnam moves against him. Macbeth has infringed all, overstepped all, destroyed all, violated all; and this desperation ends in arousing even Nature. Nature loses patience, Nature enters into action against Macbeth, Nature becomes soul against the man who has become brute force.

This drama has epic proportions. Macbeth represents that frightful hungry creature who prowls throughout history—in the forest called brigand, and on the throne, conqueror. The ancestor of Macbeth is Nimrod. These men of force, are they forever furious? Let us be just; no. They have a goal, which being attained, they stop. Give to Alexander, to Cyrus, to Sesostris, to Caesar—what?—the world; they are appeased. Geoffrey St. Hilaire said to me one day: "When the lion has eaten, he is at peace with Nature." For Cambyses, Sennacherib, Genghis Khan, and the like, to have eaten is to possess the whole earth. They would calm themselves down in the process of digesting the human race.

1867—P. W. Clayden. From "Macbeth and Lady Macbeth," in *The Fortnightly Review*

Peter William Clayden (1827-1902) was a British historian, biographer, and lifelong journalist. One of his nonpolitical topics of interest was poetry, and in the 1880s he wrote a biography of the poet Samuel Rogers.

He (Shakespeare) puts on the character he conceives, transfers himself in this character to the scenes he imagines, kindles within himself the emotions those scenes excite, and then utters what he feels. The force of his imagination is such that he can put off his own personality and put on another. He has in him the hero he describes. He realises in imagination heroic situations and does heroic deeds. He does not describe emotions—he expresses them. He does not write about Hamlet or Macbeth—he embodies them. Shakespeare was Hamlet when he was developing Hamlet's tragic history; he was Macbeth when he was writing Macbeth's speeches. His many-sided, comprehensive, magnificent nature has written itself upon his pages, has given in every creation an aspect of what was possible to itself, so that all his characters stand before us full of life, full of reality, and full of nature. How could it be otherwise? They live; they are real; they are Nature.

A canon of criticism, or principle of interpretation, is therefore not far to find. It is simply this,—interpret the works of genius as you would interpret Nature, a character of Shakespeare's as you would a character of history. All talk about central ideas of the character, or about the object Shakespeare had in view in making Macbeth do this or Hamlet say that, is beside the mark. Nor is it of any use to talk of what Shakespeare may have meant to teach. We can dismiss all such questions, and all that we have to ask is, What has he accomplished? He may have accomplished more than he intended, for it is sometimes the prerogative of genius to utter words the full meaning of which is hidden from the mind that utters them. A man of genius may create a man or a woman whom he does not fully understand. He feels that his delineation is true to Nature, but he cannot tell us why. He knows instinctively what the person he imagines would say and do in given circumstances, but he leaves to others—to critics and expositors who feel their painful way along a path over which he has been lightly borne upon the wings of fancy—to find reasons why he should have said and done those particular things and no other.

Macbeth and Lady Macbeth are remarkable examples in proof of all that I have said. Everybody knows that Shakespeare did not create them out of nothing, did not build up the characters around some central idea, as Goethe did those of Faust and Wilhelm Meister, but that he found them in a dead tradition and breathed into them life. We are, therefore, in an attempt to estimate them, liberated from the necessity of seeking for Shakespeare's didactic purpose. But we must equally free ourselves from prepossession by the popular view of them, which is founded on the assumption of such a purpose. Macbeth is usually regarded as his wife regards him in the opening of the play, while she herself is judged entirely by her words. He is usually represented as a tolerably good man up to the time when evil opportunity and a bad wife conspired to transform him into a villain. His murders are supposed to be done at her instigation. Her ambition, for which she had "unsexed" herself, led him away. She is said to have tempted him to crime, to have pushed him over the boundary line which divides criminality from innocence, though when once he had crossed it he became indeed a villain. But she is considered to be far worse than he. She was a born demon; he was only a man who had been sorely tempted and had awfully fallen.

Now when we come to regard Macbeth and his wife as two real characters of whom all that we know is recorded in this play, we arrive at a conclusion the very opposite of the popular one. Macbeth himself is probably an elderly man when he is introduced to us. He and his wife have had a past, and in that past the future which becomes present in the play has been prepared. Our first glance of him is indirect. The soldier describes him, Act i. Scene 2:—

> Brave Macbeth (well he deserves that name),
> Disdaining fortune, with his brandished steel,
> Which smoked with bloody execution,
> Like valour's minion,
> Carved out his passage, till he faced the slave,
> And ne'er shook hands, nor bade farewell to him,
> Till he unseamed him from the nave to the chaps,
> And fixed his head upon our battlements.

Were that our only glimpse of him, we should say that he was a brave but cruel warrior of a barbarous time.

When we first actually see him he is on the heath with Banquo meeting the witches. He is returning from the fight, just described, full of honours. It is the moment of his temptation. A diabolical suggestion comes to him—for the witches evidently do but give voice to his own unspoken thoughts. They call him "Thane of Glamis," which he already was; "Thane of Cawdor," which he was about to be; and "King," which he had dreamed of being. For this is clearly not the first time these thoughts have come to him. When he receives the suggestion that he should be king, he is at once perfectly familiar with the obstacles in his way. The witches make no suggestion to him as to the way in which the obstacles are to be removed, yet we find him saying directly after the king's messenger has told him of the rewards his sovereign had heaped upon him—

> Glamis and Thane of Cawdor:
> The greatest is behind.

And when Banquo utters a warning against ambition, Macbeth meditates thus:—

> Two truths are told
> As happy prologue to the swelling act
> Of the imperial theme. I thank you, gentlemen.
> This supernatural soliciting
> Cannot be ill, cannot be good. If ill,
> Why hath it given me earnest of success
> Commencing in a truth? I am Thane of Cawdor.
> If good, why do I yield to that suggestion
> Whose horrid image doth unfix my hair,
> And make my seated heart knock at my ribs
> Against the use of Nature? Present fears
> Are less than horrible imaginings.
> My thought, whose murder yet is but fantastical,
> Shakes so my single state of man, that function
> Is smothered in surmise, and nothing is,
> But what is not.

The plain meaning of that is, that on the very first day of his temptation, amid the very honours the king is heaping on him, he has conceived the idea of murdering him, and is frightened at it. But the fear is not moral. Conscience has nothing to do with it. He does not repel the suggestion. He does not scorn himself for being capable of receiving it. He is frightened at it, but he accepts it and bides his time.

In the fourth scene they have got to the king, who receives them nobly, and to whom Macbeth makes a fine speech. But during the interview the king names his eldest son as his heir, making him Prince of Cumberland. On this Macbeth meditates thus:—

The Prince of Cumberland! That is a step
On which I must fall down, or else o'erleap,
For in my way it lies. Stars, hide your fires!
Let not light see my black and deep desires:
The eye wink at the hand! yet let that be
Which the eye fears, when it is done, to see.

His mind is already made up. But conscience has no whisper against his resolution. The eye fears to see what the hand must nevertheless do; and, horrible as the thing is, he says, "Let it be." Meanwhile, he has written a letter to his wife, and she instantly conceives the same murderous purpose, and divines that her husband has done so too, although his letter does not even hint it. While their thoughts are thus full of murder the opportunity suddenly comes. The king resolves to rest under their roof, and Lady Macbeth hears of his determination to do so while she is meditating on her husband's letter. She immediately resolves that once under their roof, the king shall never leave it alive; and while she is reflecting on this, her husband arrives, and the very first sentences of their conversation reveal to each the purpose that animates both. But does not that pre-suppose some previous conversations on the subject? Could a wife and husband, while apart from each other, arrive at the same design of murder, and mention it to each other as soon as they met, had they not talked about it before, and allowed themselves to dally with the guilty thoughts and cherish the guilty ambitions their position suggested long before the moment of opportunity and temptation? Macbeth had been thought an honest man up to this time; but beneath the surface there was the villain. It is impossible that an honest man should fall at such a temptation, or should be so familiar with the thought of a fearful crime as to be able to talk it over with his wife at once. The murder must have been in his thought long before, and all that the temptation did was to transfer it suddenly from thought to purpose. He had indulged in guilty imaginings, had fed his fancy upon guilty hopes, and conscience had not rebuked them, and now they sprang to active life in guilty purposes and plans. The king came to their house on the very day on which he had greatly honoured Macbeth, and he and his wife both knew at once that he came as their victim.

The seventh scene brings Macbeth to the very verge of the accomplishment of his guilty purpose. He pauses for a moment and hesitates. In his soliloquy there is almost an echo of conscience. Still his hesitancy is rather intellectual than moral. He has no great horror of the deed. What he fears is that it should get abroad. He sees reasons against the murder; reasons which would rouse conscience, if it were possible so to do; but he sees them intellectually, and does not appreciate their moral bearing. What he says of "even-handed justice," which

Commends the ingredients of our poisoned chalice
To our own lips,

does not refer to the moral results of crime, but merely to the danger of rousing popular resentment against the murderer of one whose virtues plead so loud against "the deep damnation of his taking off," and to the other danger of setting an example, which may be followed when he is king:—

We teach
Bloody instructions, which, being taught, return
To plague the inventor.

After the soliloquy follows the remarkable interview with his wife. In this interview he seems to come nearest to conscientiousness, but if we analyse his expressions there is no conscience in them:—

We will proceed no further in this business.
He hath honoured me of late, and I have bought
Golden opinions from all sorts of people,
Which would be worn now in their newest gloss,
Not cast aside so soon.

This is his only objection to proceed. There is neither conscience nor pity in it, nothing but the fear of losing the good opinion he had won. Farther on he pleads:—

I dare do all that may become a man;
Who dares do more, is none;

and she makes him a very remarkable reply:—

What beast was it, then,
That made you break this enterprise to me?
When you durst do it, then you were a man,
And to be more than what you were you would
Be so much more the man. Nor time, nor place,
Did then adhere, and yet you would make both:
They have made themselves, and that their fitness now
Does unmake you.

This is the most important passage in the play in the elucidation of Macbeth's character. The meaning is plain. It proves that they had actually talked this matter over together long before the time at which the action of the play begins. We concluded before that murder could not ripen in an honest mind so suddenly as we see it do in Macbeth's, that he must have dallied with the guilty thought and hope so long that it was quite ready to develop into purpose; and here is the proof, not only that it was so, but that the suggestion came first from him, that he had been planning and purposing some opportunity of doing this base and bloody deed, and that it was only now, when the opportunity he had sought had suddenly and unexpectedly come, that he was staggered and frightened. All experience shows this to be just what we might expect to happen. It is sometimes only by a shock and an effort that thought passes over into action—purpose into accomplishment. An opportunity for which we have worked seldom takes us by surprise, but one for which we have only watched and waited, when it suddenly comes, finds us unprepared. Many a man has had an exceedingly happy speech to make at a public meeting. He watches for his opportunity while one after another rises to speak, but no chance seems to offer itself for him. But all at once there is silence. His opportunity has come, but with it the hesitancy sudden opportunity so often brings. He fidgets on his seat—

> Letting I dare not wait upon I would,
> Like the poor cat i' the adage;

and if he has no wife at hand to urge him to be equal to the occasion, he will most likely let the opportunity pass, and "live a coward in his own esteem." Had Macbeth gone on plotting and planning for an opportunity to murder Duncan, there would have been none of the hesitancy we see in him now. It is the sudden necessity to decide and act which makes him hesitate. He would have gone into it gradually without any hesitation. A scheme to mature to-day, a plot to lay to-morrow, a false part to play next day, would have familiarised him gradually with his position, and he would have passed easily and smoothly into crime. But here was the opportunity before him. It was now or never. A turn in his road, and there was the Rubicon. On this side "honour, love, obedience, troops of friends," but not the crown. On that side the crown, but with it possibly exposure and calamity, certainly suspicion and

> Curses not loud but deep, mouth honour, breath
> Which the poor heart would fain deny, but dare not.

No wonder at his hesitancy. Caesar paused, and then struck across the stream. Macbeth paused. The awful grandeur of his situation came clearly before him. All its possibilities of danger and disgrace were present to his mind. It wanted but one word from conscience, one glance back to the innocence of earlier days, and the crime would never have been committed. But these did not come; and in place of them there was the evil prompting of his wife, whom he had familiarised with the thought of murder, who found it easy to urge him on, and whose taunting words so dissipate his intellectual fears that he is able to say—

> I am settled, and bend up
> Each corporal agent to this terrible feat.

But while he is afterwards waiting for the signal from his wife to commit the murder, he makes another soliloquy, addressing the dagger:—

> Is this a dagger which I see before me,
> The handle toward my hand? Come, let me clutch thee.
> I have thee not, and yet I see thee still.
> Art thou not, fatal vision, sensible
> To feeling as to sight? Or art thou but
> A dagger of the mind, a false creation,
> Proceeding from the heat-oppressed brain?
> I see thee yet, in form as palpable
> As this which now I draw.
> Thou marshal'st me the way that I was going,
> And such an instrument I was to use.

Here is still further proof of his previous familiarity with the thought of crime. These thoughts are drawn from him by the fact that a situation he had long contemplated was now realised; that a position with which he had been long familiar in imagination had now become actual. The dagger he had grasped in foul and wayward fancy was now really in his hand, marshalling him the way he was to go. The situation waked his intellect, and kindled all the powers of his imagination; but did not wake his conscience, for he had none to wake.

After the murder there seem to be some gleams of remorse. But we have only to put side by side with Macbeth's exclamations the bitter reflections of Milton's Satan, and we see at once how widely different were Macbeth's fears from real remorse. Milton says of Satan—

> Now conscience wakes despair
> That slumbered; wakes the bitter memory
> Of what he was, what is, and what must be.

And Satan himself reflects—

> Ah, wherefore, he deserved no such return
> From me, whom he created what I was

In that bright eminence, and with his good
Upbraided none.

And again—

Me miserable, which way shall I fly
Infinite wrath and infinite despair?
Which way I fly is hell; myself am hell;
And in the lowest deep a lower deep,
Still threatening to devour me, opens wide,
To which the hell I suffer seems a heaven.
Oh, then, at last relent. Is there no place
Left for repentance, none for pardon left?

That is remorse. But how different the ring of those words from any that are uttered by Macbeth. He felt Amen stick in his throat. He heard a voice crying "Macbeth doth murder sleep." He was afraid to look on what he had done. He had become irritable and dreamy. Noises frightened him, and he saw ghosts. But there were no regrets, there was no bitter self-reproach, no longing after the peace he had slain, no looking back to the state of innocence from which he had fallen, no sense of the hell he had lighted within. It is imagination, and not conscience, which makes Macbeth afraid; and even the things invisible that alarm him are only the airy evanescent products of a morbid fancy. All his after actions strictly accord with this view of his nature. He plots the murder of Banquo, fearing his "royalty of nature," and tells the murderer—

We wear our health but sickly in his life,
Which in his death were perfect;

and when he hears that Fleance has escaped, he says—

Then comes my fit again; I had else been perfect,
Whole as the marble, founded as the rock,
As broad and general as the casing air;
But now I am cabined, cribbed, confined, bound in
To saucy doubts and fears.

—but is encouraged by the assurance that "Banquo's safe." From that time an awful necessity impels him forward in his career of crime. He yields to that necessity without even a show of resistance, and earns the evil reputation which was the only thing he feared. Again he takes counsel with the witches, and his imagination permits itself to be soothed by their false words, and it is not till the last moment of his fate that he finds in what fancied security his evil arts have lulled him. He then falls back, as his last resource, on the brute courage he possessed, and though his imagination is a source of weakness even in his last fight, he dies "with the harness on his back."

The character of Macbeth is, I venture to suggest, nearly related to that of Hamlet, though so wonderfully different in its development. Hamlet is a man under the power of a tyrannous imagination, but with a sensitive conscience. Macbeth is also subject to the sway of his imagination, but he has no conscience. Hence Hamlet's imagination is a source of strength to him, but Macbeth's imagination is to him a source of weakness. Of a large intellectual nature, with vast power to do and dare, his imagination is his master. In the honest part of his life that imagination was allowed to dwell on scenes of sin, to picture to itself the means by which he might in a few sudden leaps reach the throne; and this dalliance with guilty thoughts, this playing with a criminal design, so familiarised him with it that it grew at length to be his master, and he became a criminal at its bidding. In such a nature there must at first have been a conscience; but his imagination had smothered it, and all that remained within him now was the dim echo of a diviner voice than that of his ambition or his pride. Satisfied with a phrase, contented by a well-turned expression, silenced by a metaphor, conscience was now a merely intellectual thing, its moral function was abnegated, and its rightful authority lost. But the echo of its voice remained, and dwelling in his fancy were vague words and phrases, meaningless now, but haunting his thoughts and wandering amid his images of terror, like the ghost of that better nature he had slain. He therefore presents himself to us during the short acquaintance we have with him in the action of the play as a brave man who is a coward, a man of large poetic mind who is a murderer and a tyrant, a great soul lost, one who might have been a hero and is nothing but a villain.

The popular misunderstanding of the character of Macbeth is due, probably, to the description his wife gives of him in the first interview we have with her:—

> Thou shalt be
> What thou art promised:—Yet do I fear thy nature.
> It is too full of the milk of human kindness
> To catch the nearest way. Thou would'st be great;
> Art not without ambition, but without
> The illness should attend it. What thou would'st highly
> That would'st thou holily; would'st not play false,
> And yet would'st wrongly win.

But it is obvious that so far as we see Macbeth in the play, nothing could be wider of the mark than this estimate of him. That it was the estimate his wife had formed of him, before temptation had come and turned his criminal imaginings into schemes of crime, gives us no real insight into his character, but throws much light on hers. For nothing can be farther from the truth than the popular view of Lady Macbeth. That wonderful characteristic of genius which enables it to put on the character it conceives, reaches its highest manifestation in this marvellous portrait, in which Shakespeare has realised the feelings of a woman who, with all a woman's nature, has one unwomanly passion—a great ambition in place of a great love. But all the truth and force of the delineation are lost when Lady Macbeth is regarded as a mere tempter and fiend. She is, in reality, nothing of the kind. Her part is simply that of a woman and a wife who shares her husband's ambition, and supports him in it. So far from suggesting his crimes, she distinctly declares that he broke the enterprise to her. Of Macbeth's murders, it was only that of Duncan in which she had a share, or of which she even definitely knew beforehand, and we have seen that, before he saw his wife, Macbeth had made up his mind to this first step in his career of crime. All that she does is to back him in the execution of his own design; and she does this at immense cost and by enormous effort. That first soliloquy does not describe her husband's character, but it reveals her own. Her concluding words are a self-revelation—unconscious but complete:—

> Hie thee hither,
> That I may pour my spirits in thine ear,
> And chastise with the valour of my tongue
> All that impedes thee from the gold round
> Which fate and metaphysical aid doth seem
> To have thee crowned withal.

In those words, "chastise with the valour of my tongue," we have an exact description of Lady Macbeth's attitude, not merely towards her husband, but towards herself. In her continuation of the soliloquy after its interruption by the messenger who announced the approach of the king, we find her thus "chastising" all that impedes her in her own nature:—

> Come, come, you spirits
> That tend on mortal thoughts, unsex me here,
> And fill me from the crown to the toe top full
> Of direst cruelty! Make thick my blood,
> Stop up the access and passage to remorse,
> That no compunctious visitings of nature
> Shake my fell purpose, nor keep pace between
> The effect and it. Come to my woman's breasts
> And take my milk for gall, you murd'ring ministers,
> Wherever in your sightless substances

You wait on Nature's mischief. Come, thick night,
And pall thee in the dunnest smoke of hell,
That my keen knife see not the wound it makes,
Nor heaven peep through the blanket of the dark
To cry, Hold, hold!

These words are more frightful in their sound than any that Macbeth uses, but their whole tone and meaning are entirely different from his. He strives with external fears,—this is a fight with internal weakness. He calls to the "sure and firm set earth"—

Hear not my steps which way they walk, for fear
Thy very stones prate of my whereabout.

She calls to supernatural powers to help her to subdue the rising protests of her conscience, and school her better nature to submission. For that soliloquy clearly shows that hers was not a nature that was utterly without good, but that she had resolved to slay the good that was still in it. A man who feels no fear never whistles to keep up his courage. A man without compunctious visitings never talks about remorse. The utterly depraved never strive with themselves to put down their virtuous impulses; they have no such impulses to put down, no "compunctious visitings" to dread, no better part to scold into subjection. But Lady Macbeth was not utterly depraved. Her whole soul was on fire with ambition, and with a woman's energy and wholeness of devotion she gave herself up to it. She shows all a woman's wonderful self-control; but she must keep it up by using valiant words, living in public, and chastising her husband and herself "with the valour of her tongue." She had a woman's will, unswerving so long as it could keep on, but which once broken was broken for ever. It was now like a bow full-strung; but it was an immense and constant effort to keep it bent. She was afraid of her own nature. Had she been utterly unsexed, she would not have called on spirits to unsex her. Had she not feared remorse—which, indeed, did come at last and kill her—she would not have cried out to have the "access and passage" to it stopped by supernatural means. Had she not had eyes which could see the light, and some sense of Heaven's watching eye still left, she would not have called to thick night to hide her, and to "the dunnest smoke of hell" to shut out Heaven. This terrible imprecation is the expression of her will—not the ebullition of her feelings. It was indicative of a struggle. Her human, womanly nature was down beneath the fiery onset of her baser passions—throttled but not dead—held forcibly down, not slain and done with; and this language is the voice of her worse and baser part, scolding the better into silence and submission. The same thing is seen all through her character. She is not long before us, but she keeps up wonderfully. But it is emphatically what ladies call "keeping up." It is far more "the valour of her tongue" than the valour of her heart which gets expression in her speeches. Her language is everywhere that of a woman who, in screwing her husband's courage to the sticking place, as she says, is also screwing her own. That she is so entirely successful in screwing up herself and keeping up, is not at all wonderful. In this art women excel. They "keep up" through labour, and anxiety, and trouble, through pain and loss, and keep up till the need is over, and then break down. So long as the stress remains, and there is need to wear a brave front to the public, they show no sign of failure; full-bred, they keep on like blood-horses, who will drop upon the course. Lady Macbeth is a wonderful example of a woman of this kind; keeping herself up in hideous crime, showing herself always equal to the occasion while it lasts, but when the stress is over, breaking utterly down. Through the first act she is in her heroic mood, putting down her better self, and rebuking her husband's weakness. But in the first scene of the second act she falters a little, and her words show that she has had recourse to a stimulant to keep up her courage, and that even then she can only do so by being perpetually busy.

> That which hath made them drunk hath made me bold;
> What hath quenched them hath given me fire. Hark! Peace!
> It was the owl that shrieked, the fatal bellman
> That gives the stern'st good night. He is about it.

There was, too, a little "compunctious visiting of nature" while she was alone, for she reflected, as only a woman would—

> Had he not resembled
> My father as he slept, I had done it.

But the presence of her husband helps her, and she is entirely herself as soon as he appears. She can completely school herself in rousing him; the friction rekindles her fire, and so long as there is anything to busy herself about, whether it is urging him or doing something herself, all her energy is at command and the valour of her tongue is perfect. She knows nothing of those outward fears which are all that Macbeth himself seems to appreciate. Chastising his fancies and chastising her own nature as well, she exclaims:—

> Infirm of purpose!
> Give me the daggers. The sleeping and the dead
> Are but as pictures; 'tis the eye of childhood
> That fears a painted devil;

and in a sudden access of fiery energy she reddens her own hands in Duncan's blood, and prints a vision of terror on her fancy from which she never after rids herself. But at the moment she feels nothing. Her husband loses his presence of mind and stands weakly lost in his thoughts. Her presence of mind never leaves her for a moment; she comprehends all the necessities of their situation in one rapid glance of intuition, and urges her husband—

> Get on your nightgown, lest occasion call us,
> And show us to be watchers. Be not lost
> So poorly in your thoughts.

But when the necessity for action is over, all her ready wit forsakes her; she faints and must be carried away when the murder is out, and she can only hear others talk about it but has nothing to say or do that will keep up her courage, and from that time she is no longer what she was. Her husband only hints Banquo's murder to her, and though she pretty well understands the hint, it is clearly a loss to her that her husband no longer needs the valour of her tongue. Her meditation just before Banquo's murder is hinted to her is very painful.

> 'Tis safer to be that which we destroy,
> Than by destruction dwell in doubtful joy;

though no sooner does her husband come in with gloom on his face than she turns upon herself in rousing him, and says:—

> Things without remedy
> Should be without regard. What's done is done.

Her last successful effort is at the banquet. Here she is in public, and her husband needs her, and she is quite equal to the occasion. The presence of his weakness always enables her to overcome her own. At this banquet she is truly Macbeth's helpmate, saving him by her readiness and self-possession from the consequences of his fears. But after that she breaks down, and for a time we see nothing of her. Other murders follow that of Banquo, but she knows little of them, and when we next see her it is in that awful scene where she is no longer the strong-minded woman she was; when she has felt the force of that reaction which always follows woman's wilder moods; when she can keep up no longer, but even in her broken sleep cannot avoid the awful whispers of the avenger Remorse. Even in this sad scene her words are still valiant—yet her character, as I have described it, shows itself more clearly than ever. There is the echo of her resolute language, but it is only an echo. The excitement has passed and the reaction has come. Conscience is awake. Her woman's nature has asserted itself. She could not be unsexed. The access and passage to remorse could not be stopped, and it has poured in upon her conscience and overwhelmed her reason. She had strung herself up to full tension, but had overstretched the string. Her doctor soon saw that her condition was one

> More needing the divine than the physician,

and her husband described her case with far more accuracy than that with which she in her first soliloquy had described him:—

> Canst thou not minister to a mind diseased,
> Pluck from the memory a rooted sorrow,
> Raze out the written troubles of the mind,
> And with some sweet oblivious antidote
> Cleanse the stuffed bosom of that perilous stuff
> Which weighs upon the heart?

It weighed lightly enough on the heart of Macbeth, but it pressed the life out of his wife. It was the resurrection of her better self which really slew her. The fiend in her did not triumph, but succumbed at length, and she died of that remorse which is only possible to those who are still alive to their degradation, whose evil triumphs are the rooted sorrows of a memory which looks back to better times and better things, and on whose hearts, not yet hardened to stone, the perilous stuff of an ambition which has been gratified by crime weighs with a fatal pressure.

Macbeth and his wife were well mated. She had in her the making of a heroine, and he had the making of a hero. Ambition destroyed them both. She sustained her husband, but it was in a course he had himself chosen and in motives he had inspired. At one great crisis in his fate and hers, she not only went with him, but played the woman's part in keeping him to his chosen course, and played it only too well for his welfare and for her own. Her husband's meditation on her death is no fit epitaph for her, but is only the culminating revelation of his own less noble nature and far inferior character.

> Life's but a walking shadow, a poor player
> That struts and frets his hour upon the stage,
> And then is heard no more. It is a tale
> Told by an idiot, full of sound and fury,
> Signifying nothing.

The fit reflection of such a man, put into his mouth by the instinct of genius, and telling us how life may look to those who view it from the stand-point of a career of crime. "Full of sound and fury," that is Macbeth's own character. But so far from "signifying nothing," his life signified the danger of all dalliance with thoughts of crime and the fatal necessity by which such criminal imaginings, beneath the stimulus of opportunity, become criminal deeds. It signified, too, that the fight with conscience may be fought upon the field of fancy; that when the victory has been won by evil dreams there will be no resistance to the most evil deeds; and that to a man thus made a villain only one consolation remains, the consolation of a wild hope that the world is but a vain show, and life an idiot's tale "signifying nothing."

1877—Henry Irving. "The Third Murderer in *Macbeth*," from *The Nineteenth Century*

Henry Irving (1838–1905) was a famous actor and theater manager. According to the Royal Shakespeare Company, his 1888 production "restored Macbeth as a serious and dark play."

There have been various theories and much discussion among students of Shakspeare as to the Third Murderer in *Macbeth*. It has even been maintained that Macbeth himself was the man, and that only upon this assumption can the difficulties attending the character be solved. Anyone curious to follow out that suggestion will find it discussed in *Notes and Queries* for September 11 and November 13, 1869.

A theory on this subject has struck me, which has not, so far as I am aware, been hitherto advanced.

The stage directions in *Macbeth* concerning one particular character (who, curiously enough, is not mentioned in the *dramatis personae* of any edition which I bear in mind) are minute, and I believe that, where such directions are so particularly given by Shakspeare, they are for a purpose, because he is generally careless about those matters, and leaves them, as it were, for the actors to carry out.

This character is described simply as 'an Attendant,' and what I wish to contend is that this 'Attendant' is the Third Murderer.

My reasons are as follows:—Macbeth utters what little he does say to this attendant in a tone of marked contempt—strangely suggestive, to my mind, of his being some wretched creature who was entirely in Macbeth's power—not an ordinary servant, but one whom he might use as a tool, and who had no courage to disobey or withstand him.

Supposing this to have been the case, such a servant (from whatever causes), in such a state of moral bondage to his master, would be just the man employed upon the work of watching without 'the palace gate' for the two murderers whose services he had, by Macbeth's orders, secured.

He need not have known the precise object of their interview with Macbeth, and I think it was probable, from the action of the scene, that he was not told of it until after Macbeth's conversation (act iii. sc. 1) with the two murderers, at the conclusion of which, I infer, he was commanded to watch them.

Now the stage direction in act iii. sc. 1 is: 'Exeunt all but Macbeth and an Attendant.' With a confidential servant, this is just what might happen without exciting notice.

The words are:

Macb.: Sirrah, a word with you. Attend those men
Our pleasure?
Attend.: They are, my lord, without the palace gate.
Macb.: Bring them before us.

The tone of contempt is obvious, and also the fact that this attendant had been taken, to a certain extent, into his master's confidence, with a sort of careless assurance of his secrecy. We learn that he has been just now on the watch for the two men, and presume that he had conducted them to Macbeth the day before.

The next direction is: 'Re-enter Attendant with Two Murderers;' when Macbeth says to him, in the same tone and manner,

Now go to the door and stay there till we call.

The attendant then retires, and is not recalled by Macbeth; but the action which I am about to suggest, and which the text fully warrants, would, if carried out, afford the opportunity for Macbeth to communicate to him the undertaking of the two murderers, and give him instructions to follow and observe them. If the attendant left the chamber by one door ('Now go to the door and stay there till we call') and the murderers by another, and if Macbeth used the former egress, the suggestion would be that at this moment, while he kept the murderers waiting, and in expectation of seeing him again (I'll call upon you straight—abide within'), he went after the attendant and gave him his instructions.

By this device Macbeth gains the object which he has been seeking. He secures to himself a check upon the two murderers in the person of this attendant, who is made an accomplice, and whose lips are sealed. A very slight and legitimate change in the accepted stage-business would make all this stratagem clear to the audience, and it fits in with my theory that the attendant was a trusty, and not a common, servant. Had he been otherwise, the most momentous and secret transaction of the play would never have been committed to him.

Coming now to the murder of Banquo (act iii. sc. 3), we find that the words prove that one man is a stranger to the other two, at any rate so far as his privity to the enterprise is concerned. But the manner in which the Second Murderer satisfies the First that the newcomer need not be mistrusted strengthens my theory. For either the Second Murderer did not recognise the stranger at all, owing to the darkness of the night, and so distrusted him until he had delivered his credentials in shape of his intimate acquaintance with the whole place and scheme, or else perhaps they did recognise him as the attendant whom they had seen before; in which case also they would have been chary of confiding in him, as they had received from Macbeth no instructions to trust him in this matter. Indeed the instant reply of the Second Murderer, in order to allay the fears and misgivings expressed by the First, would favour the assumption that the stranger was a man they already knew, and who, up to a certain point at all events, was aware of their project. His further knowledge of the matter would be less surprising to them than if shown by anybody else, and he would thus be more easily taken into comradeship. Except upon the theory that they had seen or known something of him previously, they would hardly be likely so soon to accept his mere word.

> *Enter* Three Murderers.
> 1st *Mur.:* But who bid thee join us?
> 3rd Mur.:   Macbeth.
> 2nd *Mur.:* He needs not our mistrust; since he delivers
> Our offices, and what we have to do,
> To the direction just.
> *1st Mur.:*   Then stand with us.
> 3rd Mur: Hark! I hear horses.
> *Ban.:* (*within.*) Give us a light there, hoa!
> 2nd *Mur.:*   Then 'tis he; the rest
> That are within the note of expectation,
> Already are i' the court.
> *1st Mur.:*   His horses go about.
> 3rd *Mur.:* Almost a mile; *but he does usually,*
> *So all men do, from hence to the palace gate*
> *Make it their walk.*
> *2nd Mur.:*   A light! A light!
> 3rd *Mur.:*   *'Tis* he!

The exact familiarity which the Third Murderer shows with the surroundings of the palace and the readiness with which his information is accepted by the others, suggest that he must have been somebody quite conversant with the palace usages and approaches. This familiar knowledge may very well have been another reason in Macbeth's mind for connecting his attendant with the deed, if only by an after-thought, lest it might fail through the ignorance of the strangers as to the spot where they should post themselves, and other necessary precautions.

My theory would account for this familiar acquaintance with the locality on the part of the Third Murderer without recourse to any such violent improbability as that the Third Murderer was Macbeth himself.

It may now be considered what a difference in the usual arrangement of the banquet scene this supposition would make. We have no knowledge that it may not have been originally acted upon in the manner which I will briefly describe.

Think of the effect of the First Murderer being brought to the banquet-room by the attendant, and the latter standing by during the ghastly recital of the murder. If this expedient were adopted, there would be no intrinsic absurdity in the appearance of the strange man at the feast. He might come there with a secrecy the more effectual because of its apparent openness, for he would be in the company of one of Macbeth's chief retainers, with whom many of the guests were familiar, and with whom he might naturally, even at such a time, be obliged to speak aside a few words on some urgent and private matter. The conversation so conducted, even under the eyes, and only just out of earshot, of the whole company, might and would be no violation of probability, and need attract no special notice from the guests, even though the deadliest secret were clothed under the audacious but complete and natural disguise. But the effect upon the audience would be widely different from that of the present almost unmanageable tradition, which necessitates an improbability so absurd as almost, if not quite, to render ridiculous what might be one of the most thrilling horrors of the tragedy.

1880—H. N. Hudson. "Macbeth,"
from *Shakespeare: His Life, Art, and Characters*

Henry Norman Hudson (1814-1886) was an American essayist and noted Shakespearean scholar. He served as chaplain with General B. F. Butler during the Civil War and later arraigned Butler in *A Chaplain's Campaign with General Butler* (1865).

. . .Thomas Middleton has a play called *The Witch*, wherein are delineated with considerable skill the vulgar hags of old superstition, whose delight it was to "raise jars, jealousies, strifes, and heart-burning disagreements, like a thick scurf o'er life." Much question has been had whether this play or *Macbeth* was written first; with the view on one side, as would seem, to make out for Middleton the honour of contributing somewhat towards the Poet's Weird Sisters. Malone has perhaps done all that the case admits of, to show that *The Witch* was not written before 1613; but, in truth, there is hardly enough to ground an opinion upon, one way or the other. And the question may be justly dismissed as vain;

for the two plays have nothing in common but what may well enough have been derived: from Scot's *Discovery of Witchcraft*, or from the floating witchcraft lore of the time; some relics of which have drifted down in the popular belief to our own day.

Weird is from an Anglo-Saxon word meaning the same as the Latin *fatum*; so that weird sisters is *fatal sisters*, or *sisters of fate*. And there is an old translation of Virgil by Gawin Douglas, wherein *Parcoe* is rendered by *weird sisters*. So, again, in Holinshed's account of Macbeth: "The common opinion was, that these women were either the weird sisters, that is, the *goddesses of destiny*, or else some nymphs or fairies endued with prophecy by their necromantical science; because every thing came to pass as they had spoken." And Dr. Forman in his note of this play says, "there stood before them three women, *fairies* or *nymphs*, and saluted Macbeth, saying unto him three times, Hail, Macbeth." Which looks as if this dealer in occult science knew better than to call them witches, yet hardly knew what else to call them.

Shakespeare takes the old Hecate of classical mythology as the queen or chief of his Weird Sisters. This has been censured by some as a confounding of ancient and modern superstitions. Now, in the first place, the common notions of witchcraft in the Poet's time took classical names for the chiefs or leaders of the witches. Thus, in Ben Jonson's *Sad Shepherd*, the witches speak of Hecate as their mistress, "our *dame* Hecate." And the same course is taken by Middleton in the play just referred to. But, in the second place, the censure itself in this case is at fault, since it proceeds by confounding the Weird Sisters with the witches of popular belief. It was reserved for the best critics of our own time to set this matter right. "The Weird Sisters," says Coleridge, "are as true a creation of Shakespeare's as his Ariel and Caliban; fates, furies, and materializing witches being the elements. They are wholly different from any representation of witches in the contemporary writers, and yet presented a sufficient external resemblance to the creatures of vulgar prejudice, to act immediately on the audience." Charles Lamb, also, speaks to the same purpose, having the witches of Rowley and Dekker in his eye. "They are," says he, "the plain, traditional, old-woman witches of our ancestors,—poor, deformed, and ignorant, the terror of villages,—themselves amenable to a justice. That should be a hardy sheriff, with the power of the county at his heels, that should lay hands on the Weird Sisters. They are of another jurisdiction." All which, I believe, sufficiently clears the way for what seems to me a right statement of the matter in hand.

The old witches of superstition were foul, ugly, mischievous beings, generally actuated by vulgar envy or hate; not so much wicked as mean, and more apt to excite disgust, than to inspire terror or awe; who could inflict injury, but not guilt; and could work men's temporal ruin, but not win them to work their own spiritual ruin. The Weird Sisters are cast in quite another mould, and are beholden to those old witches for little if any thing more than the drapery of the representation. Resembling old women, save that they have long beards, they bubble up in human shape, but own no human relations; are without age, or sex, or kin; without birth or death; passionless and motiveless. A combination of the terrible and the grotesque, unlike the Furies of the Greek drama they are petrific, not to the senses, but to the thoughts. At first, indeed, on merely looking at them, we can scarce help laughing, so uncouth and grotesque is their appearance; but afterwards, on looking into them, we find them terrible beyond description; and the more we look, the more terrible do they become; the blood almost curdling in our veins, as, dancing, and singing their infernal glees over embryo murders, they unfold to our thoughts the cold, passionless, inexhaustible malignity and deformity of their nature. Towards Macbeth they have nothing of personal hatred or revenge; their malice is of a higher strain, and savours as little of any such human ranklings as the thunder-storms and elemental perturbations amidst which they come and go. Coleridge describes their character as "consisting in the imaginative disconnected from the good"; than which I can scarce frame an idea of any thing more dreadful to contemplate. But, with all their essential wickedness, the Weird Sisters have nothing gross or vulgar or sensual about them. "Fair is foul, and foul is fair," to them, by constitution of nature; darkness is their light, storms their sunshine, tumults, terrors, hideous rites, and Satanic liturgies their religion. They are indeed the very purity of sin incarnate; the vestal virgins, so to speak, of Hell; in whom every thing is reversed; whose ascent is downwards; whose proper eucharist is a sacrament of evil; and the law of whose being is violation of law!

In sorting the materials out of which the Weird Sisters weave their incantations, and compound their "hell-broth," so as to "make the gruel thick and slab," the Poet gathered and condensed the popular belief of his time. Ben Jonson, whose mind dwelt more in the circumstantial, and who spun his poetry much more out of the local and particular, made a grand showing from the same source in his *Masque of Queens*. But his powers did not permit, nor did his purpose require, him to select and dispose his materials so as to cause any thing like the mixed impression of the terrible and the grotesque, which is here conveyed. Shakespeare so spins his incantations as to cast a spell upon the mind, and engage its acquiescence in what he represents.

But is there any thing of permanent truth in the matter of the Weird Sisters? and, if so, what? These are questions that may fairly claim to be considered in any attempt to interpret the drama.

Probably no form of superstition ever prevailed to much extent, but that it had a ground and principle of truth. The old system of witchcraft, I take it, was an embodiment of some natural law, a local and temporary outgrowth from something as general and permanent as human nature. Our moral being must breathe; and therefore, in default of other provision, it puts forth some such arrangement of breathing-organs spontaneously, just as a tree puts forth leaves.

The point of art, then, in the case before us, was to raise and transfigure the literal into the symbolical; to take the body, so brittle and perishable in itself and endow it with immortality; which could be done only by filling and animating it with the efficacy of imperishable truth. Accordingly the Poet took enough of current and traditionary matter to enlist old credulity in behalf of agents suited to his peculiar purpose; representing to the age its own thoughts, and at the same time informing that representation with a moral significance suited to all ages alike. In *The Witch* of Middleton we have the literal form of a transient superstition; in *Macbeth* that form is made the transparent vehicle of a truth coeval and coextensive with the workings of human guilt. In their literal character the Weird Sisters answer to something that was, and is not; in their symbolical character they answer to something that was, and is, and will abide; for they represent the mysterious action and reaction between the evil mind and external nature.

For the external world serves in some sort as a looking-glass wherein we behold the image of our inner man. And the evil suggestions, which seem to us, written in the face or speaking from the mouth of outward objects and occasions, are in reality but projections from our own evil hearts. In a moral sense, the world around us only gives us back ourselves; its aspect is but a reflection of what we bring to it. So that, if the things we look on seem inviting us to crime, it is only because our depraved lusts and most frail affections construe their innocent meanings into wicked invitations.

In the spirit and virtue of this principle, the Weird Sisters symbolize the inward moral history of each and every man; and therefore they may be expected to live in the faith of reason so long as the present moral order or disorder of things shall last. So that they may be aptly enough described as poetical or mythical impersonations of evil influences. They body forth in living forms the fearful echo which the natural world gives back to the evil that speaks out from the human heart. And the secret of their power over Macbeth lies mainly in that they present to him his embryo wishes and half-formed thoughts. At one time they harp his fear aright, at another his hope; and this too before his hope and fear have distinctly reported themselves in his consciousness; and, by thus harping them, nurse them into purpose and draw them into act. As men often know they would something, yet know not clearly what they would, till an articulation of it, or what seems such, comes to them from without. For so we are naturally made conscious of what is within us by the shadow it casts in the light of occasion; and therefore it is that trials and opportunities have such an effect in revealing us to ourselves.

All which may serve to suggest the real nature and scope of the Weird influences on the action of the play. The office of the Weird Sisters is not so properly to deprave as to develop the characters whereon they act. They do not create the evil heart, they only untie the evil hands. They put nothing into Macbeth's mind, but merely draw out what was already there; breathing fructification upon his indwelling germs of sin, and thus acting as mediators between the secret upspringing purpose and the final accomplishment of crime. He was already minded to act as he does, only there needed something to "trammel up the consequence"; which, in his apprehension, is just what the Weird Sisters do.

—≈⁄⁄⁄⁄≈— —≈⁄⁄⁄⁄≈— —≈⁄⁄⁄⁄≈—

1882—Frances Anne Kemble. "Some Notes upon the Characters in Shakespeare's Play of *Macbeth,*" from *Notes Upon Some of Shakespeare's Plays*

Frances Anne Kemble (1809–1893) was a Shakespearean actress, a writer, and a prominent figure in the social scene of London. She is the author of *Journal of a Residence on a Georgian Plantation in 1838–1839, Record of a Girlhood* (1878) and *Records of Later Life* (1882).

No. I.

Macbeth is pre-eminently the Drama of Conscience. It is the most wonderful history of temptation, in its various agency upon the human soul, that is to be found in the universal range of imaginative literature. Viewed in this aspect, the solemn march of the tragedy becomes awful, and its development a personal appeal, of the profoundest nature, to every one who considers it with that serious attention that its excellence as a work of art alone entitles it to command. To every human soul it tells the story of its own experience, rendered indeed more impressive by the sublime poetry in which it is uttered; but it is the truth itself, and not the form in which it is presented, which makes the force of its appeal; and the terrible truth with which the insidious approach of temptation—its imperceptible advances, its gradual progress, its clinging pertinacity, its recurring importunity, its prevailing fascination, its bewildering sophistry, its pitiless tenacity, its imperious tyranny, and its final hideous triumph over the moral sense—is delineated, that makes *Macbeth* the grandest of all poetical lessons, the most powerful of all purely fictitious moralities, the most solemn of all lay sermons drawn from the text of human nature.

In a small pamphlet, written many years ago by Mr. John Kemble, upon the subject of the character of Macbeth, and which now survives as a mere curiosity of literature, he defends with considerable warmth the hero of the play from a charge of cowardice, brought against him either by Malone or Steevens in some of their strictures on the tragedy.

This charge appeared to me singular, as it would never have occurred to me that there could be two opinions upon the subject of the personal prowess of the soldier; who comes before us heralded by the martial title of Bellona's bridegroom, and wearing the garland of a double victory. But, in treating his view of the question, Mr. Kemble dwells, with extreme and just admiration, upon the skill with which Shakespeare has thrown all the other characters into a shadowy background, in order to bring out with redoubled brilliancy the form of Macbeth when it is first presented to us. Banquo, his fellow in fight and coadjutor in conquest, shares both the dangers and rewards of his expedition; and yet it is the figure of Macbeth which stands out prominently in the van of the battle so finely described by Rosse—it is he whom the king selects as heir to the dignities of the treacherous Thane of Cawdor—it is to meet him that the withered ambassadresses of the powers of darkness float through the lurid twilight of the battle day; and when the throb of the distant drum is heard across the blasted heath, among the host whose tread it times over the gloomy expanse, the approach of one man alone is greeted by the infernal ministers. Their appointed prey draws near, and, with the presentiment of their dire victory over the victor, they exclaim, "A drum! a drum! Macbeth doth come!"

Marshalled with triumphant strains of warlike melody; paged at the heels by his victorious soldiers; surrounded by their brave and noble leaders, himself the leader of them all; flushed with success and crowned with triumph—Macbeth stands before us; and the shaggy brown heath seems illuminated around him with the keen glitter of arms, the waving of bright banners, and broad tartan folds, and the light that emanates from, and surrounds as with a dazzling halo, the face and form of a heroic man in the hour of his success.

Wonderful indeed, in execution as in conception, is this brilliant image of warlike glory! But how much more wonderful, in conception as in execution, is that representation of moral power which Shakespeare has placed beside it in the character of Banquo! Masterly as is the splendour shed around, and by, the prominent figure on the canvas, the solemn grace and dignity of the one standing in the shadow behind it is more remarkable still. How with almost the first words that he speaks the majesty of right asserts itself over that of might, and the serene power of a steadfast soul sheds forth a radiance which eclipses the glare of mere martial glory, as the clear moonlight spreads itself above and beyond the flaring of ten thousand torches.

When the unearthly forms and greeting of the witches have arrested the attention of the warriors, and to the amazement excited in both of them is added, in the breast of one, the first shuddering thrill of a guilty thought which betrays itself in the start with which he receives prophecies which to the ear of Banquo seem only as "things that do sound so fair;" Macbeth has already accepted the first inspiration of guilt—the evil within his heart has quickened and stirred at the greeting of the visible agents of evil, and he is already sin-struck and terror-struck at their first utterance; but like a radiant shield, such as we read of in old magic stories, of virtue to protect its bearer from the devil's assault, the clear integrity of Banquo's soul remains unsullied by the serpent's breath, and, while accepting all the wonder of the encounter, he feels none of the dismay which shakes the spirit of Macbeth—

> "Good sir, why do you start, and seem to fear
> Things that do sound so fair?"

The fair sound has conveyed no foul sense to his perception, but, incited rather by the fear and bewilderment of his usually dauntless companion than by any misgiving of his own (which indeed his calm and measured adjuration shows him to be free from), he turns to these mysterious oracles, and, with that authority before which the devils of old trembled and dispossessed themselves of their prey, he questions, and they reply. Mark the power—higher than any, save that of God, from which it directly emanates—of the intrepid utterance of an upright human soul—

> "In the name of *Truth*, are ye fantastical?"

At that solemn appeal, does one not see hell's agents start and cower like the foul toad touched by the celestial spear? How pales the glitter of the hero of the battle-field before the steadfast shining of this honest man, when to his sacred summons the subject ministers of hell reply true oracles, though uttered by lying lips—sincere homage, such as was rendered on the fields of Palestine by the defeated powers of darkness, to the divine virtue that overthrew them—such as for ever unwilling evil pays to the good which predominates over it, the everlasting subjection of hell to heaven.

> "Hail, hail, hail!—lesser than Macbeth, but greater," etc.

And now the confused and troubled workings of Macbeth's mind pour themselves forth in rapid questions, urging one upon another the evident obstacles which crowd, faster than his eager thought can beat them aside, between him and the bait held forth to his ambitious desires; but to *his* challenge, made, not in the name or spirit of truth, but at the suggestion of the grasping devil which is fast growing into entire possession of his heart, no answer is vouchsafed; the witches vanish, leaving the words of impotent and passionate command to fall upon the empty air. The reply to his vehement questioning has already been made; he has *seen*, at one glimpse, in the very darkest depths of his imagination, *how* the things foretold *may* be, and to that fatal answer alone is he left by the silence of those whose mission to him is thenceforth fully accomplished. Twice does he endeavour to draw from Banquo some comment other than that of mere astonishment upon the fortunes thus foretold them:—

> "Your children shall be kings?
> You shall be king?
> And Thane of Cawdor too—went it not so?
> To the self-same tune and words?"

But the careless answers of Banquo unconsciously evade the snare; and it is not until the arrival of Rosse, and his ceremonious greeting of Macbeth by his new dignity of Thane of Cawdor, that Banquo's exclamation of—

> "What! can the devil speak true?"

proves at once that he had hitherto attached no importance to the prophecy of the witches, and that, now that its partial fulfilment compelled him to do so, he unhesitatingly pronounces the agency through which their foreknowledge had reached them to be evil. Most significant indeed is the direct, rapid, unhesitating intuition by which the one mind instantly repels the approach of evil, pronouncing it at once to be so, compared with the troubled, perplexed, imperfect process, half mental, half moral, by which the other labours to strangle within himself the pleadings of his better angel:—

> "This supernatural soliciting cannot be ill—
> Cannot be good! If ill,
> Why hath it given me earnest of success
> Beginning in a truth? I *am* Thane of Cawdor."

The devil's own logic: the inference of right drawn from the successful issue, the seal whose stamp, whether false or genuine, still satisfies the world of the validity of every deed to which it is appended. Wiser than all the wisdom that ever was elaborated by human intellect, brighter than any light that ever yet was obtained by process of human thought, juster and more unerringly infallible than any scientific deduction ever produced by the acutest human logic, is the simple instinct of good and evil in the soul that loves the one and hates the other. Like those fine perceptions by which certain delicate and powerful organisations detect with amazing accuracy the hidden proximity of certain sympathetic or antipathetic existences, so the moral sensibility of the true soul recoils at once from the antagonistic principles which it detects with electric rapidity and certainty, leaving the intellect to toil after and discover, discriminate and describe, the cause of the unutterable instantaneous revulsion.

Having now not only determined the nature of the visitation they have received, but become observant of the absorbed and distracted demeanour and countenance of Macbeth, for which he at first accounted guilelessly according to his wont, by the mere fact of natural astonishment at the witches' prophecy and its fulfilment, together with the uneasy novelty of his lately acquired dignities—

"Look how our partner's rapt,
New honours come upon him like our new garments," etc.

Banquo is called upon by Macbeth directly for some expression of his own opinion of these mysterious events, and the impression they have made on his mind.

"Do you not hope your children *shall* be kings," etc.

He answers with that solemn warning, almost approaching to a rebuke of the evil suggestion that he now for the first time perceives invading his companion's mind:—

"That trusted home
Might yet enkindle you unto the crown," etc.

It is not a little remarkable that, having in the first instance expressed so strongly his surprise at finding a truth among the progeny of the father of lies, and uttered that fine instinctive exclamation, "What! can the devil speak true?" Banquo, in the final deliberate expression of his opinion to Macbeth upon the subject of the witches' prophecy, warns him against the semblance of truth, that combined with his own treacherous infirmity, is strengthening the temptation by which his whole soul is being searched:—

"But it is strange,
And oftentimes to win us to our harm
The instruments of darkness tell us truths," etc.

Although these two passages may appear at first to involve a contradiction almost, it seems to me that both the sentiments—the brave, sudden denial of any kindred between the devil and truth, and the subsequent admission of the awful mystery by which truth sometimes is permitted to be a two-edged weapon in the armoury of hell—are eminently characteristic of the same mind. Obliged to confess that the devil does speak true sometimes, Banquo, nevertheless, can only admit that he does so for an evil purpose, and this passage is one of innumerable proofs of the general coherence, in spite of apparent discrepancy, in Shakespeare's delineations of character. The same soul of the one man may, with no inconsistency but what is perfectly compatible with spiritual harmony, utter both the sentiments: the one on impulse, the other on reflection.

Here, for the first time, Macbeth encounters the barrier of that uncompromising spirit, that sovereignty of nature, which as he afterwards himself acknowledges "would be feared," and which he does fear and hate accordingly, more and more savagely and bitterly, till detestation of him as his natural superior, terror of him as the possible avenger of blood, and envy of him as the future father of a line of kings, fill up the measure of his murderous ill-will, and thrust him upon the determination of Banquo's assassination; and when, in the midst of his royal banquet-hall, filled with hollow-hearted feasting and ominous revelry and splendour, his conscience conjures up the hideous image of the missing guest, whose health he invokes with lips white with terror, while he knows that his gashed and mangled corpse is lying stark under the midnight rain; surely it is again with this solemn warning, uttered in vain to stay his soul from the perdition yawning for it in the first hour of their joint temptation,—

> "That trusted home
> Might yet enkindle you unto the crown," etc.

that the dead lips appear to move, and the dead eyes are sadly fixed on him, and the heavy locks, dripping with gore, are shaken in silent intolerable rebuke.

In the meeting with the kind-hearted old king, the loyal professions of the two generals are, as might be expected, precisely in inverse ratio to their sincere devotion to Duncan. Banquo answers in a few simple words the affectionate demonstration of his sovereign, while Macbeth, with his whole mind churning round and round like some black whirlpool the murderous but yet unformed designs which have taken possession of it, utters his hollow professions of attachment in terms of infinitely greater warmth and devotion. On the nomination of the king's eldest son to the dignity of Prince of Cumberland, the bloody task which he had already proposed to himself is in an instant doubled on his hands; and instantly, without any of his late misgivings, he deals in imagination with the second human life that intercepts his direct attainment of the crown. This short soliloquy of his ends with some lines which are not more remarkable for the power with which they exhibit the confused and dark heavings of his stormy thoughts than for being the first of three similar adjurations, of various expression, but almost equal poetic beauty:—

> "Stars, hide your fires!
> Let not light see my black and deep desires!

The eye wink at the hand, yet let that be
Which the eye fears, when it is done, to see!"

In the very next scene, we have the invocation to darkness with which Lady
Macbeth closes her terrible dedication of herself to its ruling powers:—

"Come, thick night,
And pall thee in the dunnest smoke of hell," etc.

What can be finer than this peculiar use of the word *pall*; suggestive not only of
blackness, but of that funereal blackness in which death is folded up; an image
conveying at once absence of light and of life?—

"That my keen knife see not the wound it makes,
Nor heaven peep through the blanket of the dark,
To cry, Hold! hold!" etc.

The third of these murderous adjurations to the powers of nature for their
complicity is uttered by Macbeth in the scene preceding the banquet, when,
having contrived the mode of Banquo's death, he apostrophises the approaching
night thus:—

"Come, sealing night!
Scarf up the tender eye of pitiful day," etc.

(what an exquisite grace and beauty there is in this wonderful line!)

"And with thy bloody and invisible hand
Cancel, and tear to pieces, that great bond,
Which keeps me pale!"

Who but Shakespeare would thus have multiplied expressions of the very
same idea with such wonderful variety of power and beauty in each of them?—
images at once so similar in their general character, and so exquisitely different in
their particular form. This last quoted passage precedes lines which appear to me
incomparable in harmony of sound and in the perfect beauty of their imagery:
lines on which the tongue dwells, which linger on the ear with a charm enhanced
by the dark horror of the speaker's purpose in uttering them, and which remind
one of the fatal fascination of the Gorgon's beauty, as it lies in its frame of
writhing reptiles, terrible and lovely at once to the beholder:—

"Light thickens, and the crow
Makes wing to the rooky wood."

We see the violet-coloured sky, we feel the soft intermitting wind of evening, we hear the solemn lullaby of the dark fir-forest; the homeward flight of the bird suggests the sweetest images of rest and peace; and, coupled and contrasting with the gradual falling of the dim veil of twilight over the placid face of nature, the remote horror "of the deed of fearful note" about to desecrate the solemn repose of the approaching night, gives to these harmonious and lovely lines a wonderful effect of mingled beauty and terror. The combination of vowels in this line will not escape the ear of a nice observer of the melody of our language: the "rooky wood" is a specimen of a happiness of a sound not so frequent perhaps in Shakespeare as in Milton, who was a greater master of the melody of words.

To return to Banquo: in the scene where he and Macbeth are received with such overflowing demonstrations of gratitude by Duncan, we have already observed he speaks but little; only once indeed, when in answer to the king's exclamation,

"Let me unfold thee, and hold thee to my heart,"

he simply replies—

"There if I grow, the harvest is your own."

But while Macbeth is rapidly revolving in his mind the new difficulties thrown in the way of his ambition, and devising new crimes to overleap lest he fall down upon them, we are left to imagine Banquo as dilating upon his achievements to the king, and finding in his praise the eloquence that had failed him in the professions of his own honest loyalty; for no sooner had Macbeth departed to announce the king's approach to his wife, than Duncan answers to the words spoken aside to him by Banquo:—

"True, worthy Banquo, he *is* full so valiant,
And in his praises I am fed."

This slight indication of the generous disposition that usually lives in holy alliance with integrity and truth is a specimen of that infinite virtue which pervades all Shakespeare's works, the effect of which is felt in the moral harmony of the whole, even by those who overlook the wonderful details by which the general result is produced. Most fitting is it, too, that Banquo should speak the delicious lines by which the pleasant seat of Macbeth's castle is brought so vividly to our senses. The man of temperate passions and calm mind is the devout observer of nature; and thus it is that, in the grave soldier's mouth, the notice of the habits of the guest of summer, "the temple-haunting martlet," is an appropriate beauty of profound significance. Here again are lines whose intrinsic exquisiteness is keenly enhanced by the impending doom which hovers over the kind old king. With a heart overflowing with joy for the success of his arms, and gratitude towards his victorious generals, Duncan stands inhaling the serene summer air, receiving none but sensations of the most pleasurable exhilaration on the threshold of his slaughter-house. The sunny breezy eminence before the hospitable castle gate of his devoted kinsman and subject betrays no glimpse to his delighted spirits of the glimmering midnight chamber, where, between his drunken grooms and his devil-driven assassin, with none to hear his stifled cries for help but the female fiend who listens by the darkened door, his life-blood is to ooze away before the daylight again strikes at the portal by which he now stands rejoicing in the ruddy glow of its departure. Banquo next meets us, as the dark climax is just at hand; the heavens, obedient to the invocation of guilt, have shut their eyes, unwilling to behold the perpetration of the crime about to be committed. The good old king has retired to rest in unusual satisfaction, his host and hostess have made their last lying demonstrations, and are gone to the secret councils of the chamber—where they lie in wait. Banquo, unwilling to yield himself to the sleep which treacherously presents to his mind, through the disturbed agency of dreams, the temptation so sternly repelled by his waking thoughts, is about to withdraw, supposing himself the last of all who wake in the castle; for on meeting Macbeth he expresses astonishment that he is not yet abed. How beautiful is the prayer with which he fortifies himself against the nightly visitation of his soul's enemy!—

> "Merciful powers,
> Restrain in me the accursed thoughts that nature
> Gives way to in repose."

Further on the explanation of these lines is found in the brief conversation that follows between himself and Macbeth when he says: "I dreamed last night of the three weird sisters;" and it is against a similar visitation of the powers of darkness during his helpless hours of slumber that he prays to be defended before surrendering himself to the heavy summons that "lies like lead upon him." It is remarkable that Banquo, though his temptation assails him from without in dreams of the infernal prophetesses, prays to be delivered not from them, but from the "accursed thoughts that *nature* gives way to in repose;" referring, and justly, his danger to the complicity with evil in his own nature—that noble nature of which Macbeth speaks as sovereignly virtuous, but of which the mortal infirmity is thus confessed by him who best knows its treacherous weakness.

Banquo next appears in the midst of the hideous uproar consequent upon Duncan's murder, when the vaulted chambers of the castle ring with Macduff's cries to the dead man's sleeping sons—when every door bursts open as with the sweeping of a whirlwind, and half-naked forms, and faces white with sudden terror, lean from every gallery overlooking the great hall, into which pour, like the in-rushing ridges of the tide, the scared and staring denizens of the upper chambers; while along remote corridors echoes the sound of hurrying feet, and inarticulate cries of terror are prolonged through dismal distant passages, and the flare of sudden torches flashes above and below, making the intermediate darkness blacker; and the great stone fortress seems to reel from base to battlement with the horror that has seized like a frenzy on all its inmates. From the midst of this appalling tumult rises the calm voice of the man who remembers that he "stands in the great hand of God," and thence confronts the furious elements of human passion surging and swaying before him.

Banquo stands in the hall of Macbeth's castle, in that sudden surprise of dreadful circumstances alone master of his soul, alone able to appeal to the All-seeing Judge of human events, alone able to advise the actions and guide the counsels of the passion-shaken men around him—a wonderful image of steadfastness in that tremendous chaos of universal dismay and doubt and terror.

This is the last individual and characteristic manifestation of the man. The inevitable conviction of Macbeth's crime, and equally inevitable conviction of the probable truth of the promised royalty of his own children, are the only two important utterances of his that succeed, and these are followed so immediately by his own death that the regretful condemnation of the guilty man, once the object of his affectionate admiration, cannot assume the bitterer character of personal detestation, or the reluctant admission of the truth of the infernal prophecy beguile him into dangerous speculations as to the manner of its fulfilment. The noble integrity of the character is unimpaired to the last.

—◊◊◊◊— —◊◊◊◊— —◊◊◊◊—

1893—Richard G. Moulton. From Chapter VII, "Macbeth, Lord and Lady: A Study in Character-Contrast," in *Shakespeare as a Dramatic Artist*

Richard G. Moulton (1849–1924) was an English author and critic who also served as professor of literary theory and interpretation at the University of Chicago (1891–1919). He is the author of *Shakespeare as a Dramatic Artist: A Popular Illustration of the Principles of Scientific Criticism* (1893), *The Moral System of Shakespeare: A Popular Illustration of Fiction as the Experimental Side of Philosophy* (1903), and *The Literary Study of The Bible: An Account of the Leading Forms of Literature Represented in the Sacred Writings: Intended for English Readers* (1899).

. . .[Macbeth's] is pre-eminently the practical nature, moulded in a world of action, but uninfluenced by the cultivation of the inner life. Yet he is not perfect as a man of action: for the practical cannot reach its perfection without the assistance of the inner life. There are two flaws in Macbeth's completeness. For one, his lack of training in thought has left him without protection against the superstition of his age. He is a passive prey to supernatural imaginings. He himself tells us he is a man whose senses would cool to hear a night-shriek, and his fell of hair rouse at a dismal treatise. And we see throughout the play how he never for an instant doubts the reality of the supernatural appearances: a feature the more striking from its contrast with the scepticism of Lady Macbeth, and the hesitating doubt of Banquo. Again: no active career can be without its periods when action is impossible, and it is in such periods that the training given by the intellectual life makes itself felt, with its self-control and passive courage. All this Macbeth lacks: in suspense he has no power of self-restraint. . . .[O]ne of these two flaws springing out of Macbeth's lack of the inner life, his superstition and his helplessness in suspense, is at every turn the source of his betrayal.

In the case of Lady Macbeth, the old-fashioned view of her as a second Clytaemnestra has long been steadily giving way before a conception higher at least on the intellectual side. The exact key to her character is given by regarding her as the antithesis of her husband, and an embodiment of the inner life and its intellectual culture so markedly wanting in him. She has had the feminine lot of being shut out from active life, and her genius and energy have been turned inwards; her soul—like her 'little hand'—is not hardened for the working-day world, but is quick, delicate, sensitive. She has the keenest insight into the characters of those around her. She is accustomed to moral loneliness and at home in mental struggles. She has even solved for herself some of their problems. In the very crisis of Duncan's murder she gives utterance to the sentiment:

> the sleeping and the dead
> Are but as pictures.

When we remember that she must have started with the superstitions of her age such an expression, simple enough in modern lips, opens up to us a whole drama of personal history: we can picture the trembling curiosity, the struggle between will and quivering nerves, the triumph chequered with awe, the resurrection of doubts, the swayings between natural repulsion and intellectual thirst, the growing courage and the reiterated victories settling down into calm principle. Accordingly, Lady Macbeth has won the grand prize of the inner life: in the kingdom of her personal experience her WILL is unquestioned king. It may seem strange to some readers that Lady Macbeth should be held up as the type of the inner life, so associated is that phrase to modern ears with the life fostered by religion. But the two things must not be confused—religion and the sphere in which religion is exercised. 'The kingdom of God is within you,' was the proclamation of Christ, but the world within *may* be subjugated to other kings than God. Mental discipline and perfect self-control, like that of Lady Macbeth, would hold their sway over evil passions, but they would also be true to her when she chose to contend against goodness, and even against the deepest instincts of her feminine nature. This was ignored in the old conception of the character, and a struggle *against* the softer side of her nature was mistaken for its total absence. But her intellectual culture must have quickened her finer sensibilities at the same time that it built up a will strong enough to hold them down; nor is the subjugation so perfect but that a sympathetic insight can throughout trace a keen delicacy of nature striving to assert itself. In particular, when she calls upon the spirits that tend on mortal thoughts to unsex and fill her from crown to toe with direst cruelty she is thrilling all over with feminine repugnance to the bloody enterprise, which nevertheless her royal will insists upon her undertaking. Lady Macbeth's career in the play is one long mental civil war; and the strain ends, as such a strain could only end, in madness.

Such is the general conception of Lord and Lady Macbeth from the point of view of the antithesis between the outer and inner life. . . .

⸺⁓⸺ ⸺⁓⸺ ⸺⁓⸺

1898—Georg Brandes. "*Macbeth* in Comparison to *Hamlet*," from *William Shakespeare: A Critical Study*

Georg Brandes (1842–1927) was an important Danish literary critic and opponent of Romanticism. He wrote extensively on Shakespeare's plays.

There is much to indicate that an unbroken train of thought led Shakespeare from *Hamlet* to *Macbeth*. The personality of Macbeth is a sort of counterpart to that of Hamlet. The Danish prince's nature is passionate, but refined and thoughtful. Before the deed of vengeance which is imposed upon him he is restless, self-reproachful, and self-tormenting; but he never betrays the slightest remorse for a murder once committed, though he kills four persons before he stabs the King. The Scottish thane is the rough, blunt soldier, the man of action. He takes little time for deliberation before he strikes; but immediately after the murder he is attacked by hallucinations both of sight and hearing, and is hounded on, wild and vacillating and frenzied, from crime to crime. He stifles his self-reproaches and falls at last, after defending himself with the hopeless fury of the "bear tied to the stake."

Hamlet says:—

And thus the native hue of resolution
Is sicklied o'er with the pale cast of thought.

Macbeth, on the contrary, declares (iv. 1)—

> From this moment
> The very firstlings of my heart shall be
> The firstlings of my hand.

They stand at opposite poles—Hamlet, the dreamer; Macbeth, the captain, "Bellona's bridegroom." Hamlet has a superabundance of culture and of intellectual power. His strength is of the kind that wears a mask; he is a master in the art of dissimulation. Macbeth is unsophisticated to the point of clumsiness, betraying himself when he tries to deceive. His wife has to beg him not to show a troubled countenance, but to "sleek o'er his rugged looks."

Hamlet is the born aristocrat: very proud, keenly alive to his worth, very self-critical—too self-critical to be ambitious in the common acceptation of the word. To Macbeth, on the contrary, a sounding title is honour, and a wreath on the head, a crown on the brow, greatness. When the Witches on the heath, and another witch, his wife in the castle, have held up before his eyes the glory of the crown and the power of the sceptre, he has found his great goal—a tangible prize in this life, for which he is willing to risk his welfare in "the life to come." Whilst Hamlet, with his hereditary right, hardly gives a thought to the throne of which he has been robbed, Macbeth murders his king, his benefactor, his guest, that he may plunder him and his sons of a chair with a purple canopy.

And yet there is a certain resemblance between Macbeth and Hamlet. One feels that the two tragedies must have been written close upon each other. In his first monologue (i. 7) Macbeth stands hesitating with Hamlet-like misgivings:—

> If it were done, when 't is done, then 't were well
> It were done quickly: if the assassination
> Could trammel up the consequence, and catch
> With his surcease success; that but this blow
> Might be the be-all and the end-all here,
> But here, upon this bank and shoal of time,—
> We'd jump the life to come.—But in these cases
> We still have judgment here.

Hamlet says: Were we sure that there is no future life, we should seek death. Macbeth thinks: Did we not know that judgment would come upon us here, we should care little about the life to come. There is a kinship in these contradictory reflections. But Macbeth is not hindered by his cogitations. He pricks the sides of his intent, as he says, with the spur of ambition, well knowing that it will o'erleap itself and fall. He cannot resist when he is goaded onward by a being superior to himself, a woman.

Like Hamlet, he has imagination, but of a more timorous and visionary cast. It is through no peculiar faculty in Hamlet that he sees his father's ghost; others had seen it before him and see it with him. Macbeth constantly sees apparitions that no one else sees, and hears voices that are inaudible to others.

When he has resolved on the king's death he sees a dagger in the air:—

Is this a dagger which I see before me,
The handle toward my hand? Come, let me clutch thee:—
I have thee not, and yet I see thee still.
Art thou not, fatal vision, sensible
To feeling, as to sight? or art thou but
A dagger of the mind, a false creation,
Proceeding from the heat-oppressed brain?

Directly after the murder he has an illusion of hearing:—

Methought I heard a voice cry, "Sleep no more!
Macbeth does murder sleep."

And, very significantly, Macbeth hears this same voice give him the different titles which are his pride:—

Still it cried, "Sleep no more!" to all the house:
"Glamis hath murder'd sleep, and therefore Cawdor
Shall sleep no more, Macbeth shall sleep no more!"

Yet another parallel shows the kinship between the Danish and the Scottish tragedy. It is in these dramas alone that the dead leave their graves and reappear on the scene of life; in them alone a breath from the spirit-world reaches the atmosphere of the living. There is no trace of the supernatural either in *Othello* or in *King Lear*.

MACBETH
IN THE TWENTIETH CENTURY

☙

Twentieth-century criticism of *Macbeth* ranged from in-depth psychoanalytical character studies to detailed examinations of the ways in which history, philosophy, politics and gender relate to the play. Discussed below are but a few of the most important critical works.

Criticism of *Macbeth* during the first three decades was defined by two important writers, A. C. Bradley and Sigmund Freud. In 1904, A. C. Bradley published a definitive and very influential work, titled *Shakespearean Tragedy*, in which he studies all dimensions of *Macbeth,* including imagery, timing of action, and supernatural agencies, and thoroughly examines the ways in which the play's characters evolve. After setting forth the similarities between Macbeth and Lady Macbeth, Bradley identifies the defining moment to be the encounter in which they display different attitudes toward the anticipated murder of Duncan; according to Bradley, from that point forward, Macbeth becomes the more complex character while Lady Macbeth recedes into the background.

In Freud's seminal work, *Some Character-types Met With in Psycho-analytic Work*, published in 1916, the legendary psychoanalyst discusses the complex ways in which conscience works in the human psyche vis-à-vis an understanding of literature. For Freud, Lady Macbeth's character provides a perfect opportunity to analyze the ways in which a guilty conscience manifests itself. He writes:

> We may take as an example of a person who collapses on reaching success, after striving for it with single-minded energy, the figure of Shakespeare's Lady Macbeth. Beforehand there is no hesitation, no sign of any internal conflict in her, no endeavour but that of overcoming the scruples of her ambitious and yet tender-minded husband. She is ready to sacrifice even her womanliness to her murderous intention, without reflecting on the decisive part which this womanliness must play when the question afterwards arises of preserving the aim of her ambition, which has been attained through a crime.

For the critic Arthur Quiller-Couch, *Macbeth* is a consummate work of art, "single or complete in itself, strongly imagined, simply constructed, and in its way excellent beyond any challenging." Quiller-Couch begins his examination by imagining the audience for whom Shakespeare wrote and the physical conditions of the stage at the Globe Theatre in Southwark, proceeds through the historical sources that the playwright read and re-imagined for Macbeth, and ends with praise for Shakespeare's presentation of absolute evil. "Instead of extenuating Macbeth's criminality, Shakespeare doubles and redoubles it. Deliberately this magnificent artist locks every door on condonation, plunges the guilt deep as hell, and then—tucks up his sleeves."

G. Wilson Knight's essay focuses on a clarification of Macbeth's malevolence and argues that his speech in Act I ("My thought whose murder yet is but fantastical / Shakes so my single state of man that function / Is smother'd in surmise, and nothing is / But what is not") is the most critical, for it both encapsulates and sets forth the dynamics of evil that will permeate the entire play and also marks the moment that Macbeth contemplates the actualization of his frightening imagination. Ultimately, as Knight points out, any understanding of Macbeth's motivation for blood lust can only be reached through our imagination: "[I]t expresses its vision, not to a critical intellect, but to the responsive imagination; and, working in terms not of 'character' or any ethical code, but of the abysmal deeps of a spirit-world untuned to human reality."

The middle of the century produced many important works. Cleanth Brooks, one of the most prominent of the New Critics, wrote an essay titled "The Naked Babe and the Cloak of Manliness," in which he applies the techniques of explicating a lyric poem to such longer works as *Macbeth*. Brooks considers, among other things, the significance of the unclothed baby in light of the phrase, "Pity, like a naked new-born babe," finding two ambiguous readings in that the baby is either a heavenly being, able to "stride the blast," or simply a helpless human infant. Henry Paul's book, *The Royal Play of Macbeth: When, Why and How It Was Written by Shakespeare* (1950), though some of its inferences have been contested, provides a carefully documented examination of the Jacobean era, discussing King James I's writings and ideology, as well as a discussion of the ramifications of the Gunpowder Plot. In his chapter, "Macbeth's Imagination," Paul maintains that Macbeth's extraordinary and hallucinatory imagination serves a dual purpose, on both a dramatic and political/moral level. In the first instance there is Macbeth's self-incrimination, in which he exposes, through his hallucinations, the crime he has committed; secondly, there is Shakespeare's intention to enlighten King James as to the consequences of a belief in witchcraft and the terrible wrongs already committed in punishing those accused. Harold Goddard, whom Harold Bloom has called his favorite American critic of Shakespeare, discusses the unrelenting nightmare world depicted in *Macbeth*. He identifies two opening scenes—the inaugural scene of the witches' colloquy and the following scene, with its bloody description of Macbeth's military victory over the rebels. For Goddard, these two scenes, one concerned with the supernatural and the other dominated by violence, work together as the fundamental structure and theme of *Macbeth*, namely a study of human passion. Francis Fergusson's essay sees Macbeth as a protagonist who assumes a dual role as both an ambitious soldier and a suffering poet and seer, one whose imagination makes him so vulnerable to temptation. Interestingly, unlike Coleridge, who found the porter in very bad taste, Fergusson finds an important contrast in this scene, whereby the drunken porter underscores the far more terrifying inebriation of the Macbeths. Fergusson writes: "Shakespeare knew that a deep motive affects the whole being, including the body and its functions. Having shown the insane drive of evil in the high moral imagination of Macbeth, he now reveals it in the most homely, lewd, and farcical analogies."

L. C. Knights, probably best known for his essay "How Many Children Had Lady Macbeth," also wrote on Macbeth's "Lust for Power." In this essay, Knights maintains that Macbeth's malevolence emanates from this lust and, further, that our understanding of his penchant for evil can only come about through an emotional response to the play. Knights argues that our ability to come to terms with the overwhelming darkness of Macbeth rests on the poetry, which has a haunting, almost tactile presence, and on our ability to feel the events as they unfold. "The logic is not formal but experiential, and demands from us, if we are to test its validity and feel its force, a fullness of imaginative response and a closeness of realization, in which both sensation and feeling becomes modes of understanding."

In his essay contrasting Macbeth with Lady Macbeth, the American poet John Berryman maintains that Lady Macbeth is marginalized by the third act because of a fundamental flaw in her character—a shallowness and inability to follow through with her plans. Though she shares Macbeth's ambitious motives, Berryman finds that she lacks the complexity of Macbeth, a soldier who has proven his bravery and valor: "Macbeth [also] believes in 'justice,' . . . and he believes in eternal life, punishment, and would like to skip it ('jump the life to come')."

Another fine critic, William Empson, used his disagreement with the critic Dover Wilson as the springboard for his own meditations on *Macbeth*.

Thomas McAlindon argues that Macbeth's primary motivation and ensuing downfall are the result of his pursuit of greatness, a distinction which he maintains is different from a desire for power and wealth. "It proceeds from a restless striving which he himself [Macbeth] scarcely understands and which compels him to 'o'erleap' all obstacles of person, time and place so as to win, as tokens of his transcendent worth, golden opinions and the golden round."

A good deal of the Shakespearean criticism in the latter decades of the twentieth-century followed various trends in academic teaching, including such critical approaches as New Historicism, feminist criticism, and cultural studies, to name just a few. Critics identified with the new historicist movement took up several new issues. One new historicist critic stated that the driving force in *Macbeth* is the establishment of a civil society. Others identified a new source of equivocation in Macbeth through an analysis of conflicting Renaissance perspectives on witchcraft. Feminist critics also examined the issue of witchcraft, focusing, for example, on the status of witches as "heroines" in the Renaissance, from their first stage appearance at Shakespeare's Globe to their comic nature in Davenant's Restoration version. Other feminist critics maintained that Macbeth and his wife are the most domestic of couples.

Critics of the deconstructionist movement characteristically seized upon the many examples of ambiguity in the play. Some argued for issues of indeterminacy in the text, citing Macbeth's unrelenting dilemma as to the deciphering of messages. Marxist critics focused on aspects of a prevailing ideology in Macbeth, such as cultural symbols of class distinctions and underlying power structures.

Despite this, there were critics who remained focused on the aesthetic. One of the best known of these is Harold Bloom, who distinguishes this play as Shakespeare's most imaginative in its unmitigated terror. In his 1998 essay, Bloom classifies *Macbeth* as a visionary drama and takes up the enigmatic question of why we feel sympathetic toward its evil protagonist. Describing Macbeth as "a great killing-machine," Bloom argues that for all of his bloody acts, it is his imagination that captures our fascination and compels us to participate in his indignation toward false assurances. "Indeed, as Macbeth increasingly becomes outraged by the equivocal nature of the occult promises that have been made to him, his sense of being outraged contaminates us, so that we come to share in his outrage. He becomes our paradigm of confounded expectations." Bloom further argues that Macbeth ultimately presents us with a negative transcendence in that his fantasy of the future, with its supernatural attendants, affords him a sense of "a realm free of time."

1904—A. C. Bradley. "Lecture IX: Macbeth" and "Lecture X: Macbeth," from *Shakespearean Tragedy*

A. C. Bradley (1851–1935) was a key Shakespearean scholar of the late nineteenth and early twentieth centuries. He held professorships of modern literature at the University of Liverpool, of English language and literature at the University of Glasgow, and of poetry at Oxford University. Bradley is best known for his book *Shakespearean Tragedy* (1904). But he also published *Oxford Lectures on Poetry* (1909), which includes an essay on Shakespeare's *Antony and Cleopatra*, and *A Miscellany*

(1929), in which appears a well-known commentary on Tennyson's *In Memoriam*.

[Lecture IX]

Macbeth, it is probable, was the last-written of the four great tragedies, and immediately preceded *Antony and Cleopatra*. In that play Shakespeare's final style appears for the first time completely formed, and the transition to this style is much more decidedly visible in *Macbeth* than in *King Lear*. Yet in certain respects *Macbeth* recalls *Hamlet* rather than *Othello* or *King Lear*. In the heroes of both plays the passage from thought to a critical resolution and action is difficult, and excites the keenest interest. In neither play, as in *Othello* and *King Lear*, is painful pathos one of the main effects. Evil, again, though it shows in Macbeth a prodigious energy, is not the icy or stony inhumanity of Iago or Goneril; and, as in *Hamlet*, it is pursued by remorse. Finally, Shakespeare no longer restricts the action to purely human agencies, as in the two preceding tragedies; portents once more fill the heavens, ghosts rise from their graves, an unearthly light flickers about the head of the doomed man. The special popularity of *Hamlet* and *Macbeth* is due in part to some of these common characteristics, notably to the fascination of the supernatural, the absence of the spectacle of extreme undeserved suffering, the absence of characters which horrify and repel and yet are destitute of grandeur. The reader who looks unwillingly at Iago gazes at Lady Macbeth in awe, because though she is dreadful she is also sublime. The whole tragedy is sublime.

In this, however, and in other respects, *Macbeth* makes an impression quite different from that of *Hamlet*. The dimensions of the principal characters, the rate of movement in the action, the supernatural effect, the style, the versification, are all changed; and they are all changed in much the same manner. In many parts of *Macbeth* there is in the language a peculiar compression, pregnancy, energy, even violence; the harmonious grace and even flow, often conspicuous in *Hamlet*, have almost disappeared. The chief characters, built on a scale at least as large as that of *Othello*, seem to attain at times an almost superhuman stature. The diction has in places a huge and rugged grandeur, which degenerates here and there into tumidity. The solemn majesty of the royal Ghost in *Hamlet*, appearing in armour and standing silent in the moonlight, is exchanged for shapes of horror, dimly seen in the murky air or revealed by the glare of the caldron fire in a dark cavern, or for the ghastly face of Banquo badged with blood and staring with blank eyes. The other three tragedies all open with conversations which lead into the action: here the action bursts into wild life amidst the sounds of a thunderstorm and the echoes of a distant battle. It hurries through seven very brief scenes of mounting suspense to a terrible crisis, which is reached, in the murder of Duncan, at the beginning of the Second Act. Pausing a moment and changing its shape, it hastes

again with scarcely diminished speed to fresh horrors. And even when the speed
of the outward action is slackened, the same effect is continued in another form:
we are shown a soul tortured by an agony which admits not a moment's repose,
and rushing in frenzy towards its doom. *Macbeth* is very much shorter than
the other three tragedies, but our experience in traversing it is so crowded and
intense that it leaves an impression not of brevity but of speed. It is the most
vehement, the most concentrated, perhaps we may say the most tremendous, of
the tragedies.

1

A Shakespearean tragedy, as a rule, has a special tone or atmosphere of its
own, quite perceptible, however difficult to describe. The effect of this atmosphere
is marked with unusual strength in *Macbeth*. It is due to a variety of influences
which combine with those just noticed, so that, acting and reacting, they form
a whole; and the desolation of the blasted heath, the design of the Witches, the
guilt in the hero's soul, the darkness of the night, seem to emanate from one
and the same source. This effect is strengthened by a multitude of small touches,
which at the moment may be little noticed but still leave their mark on the
imagination. We may approach the consideration of the characters and the action
by distinguishing some of the ingredients of this general effect.

Darkness, we may even say blackness, broods over this tragedy. It is remarkable
that almost all the scenes which at once recur to memory take place either at
night or in some dark spot. The vision of the dagger, the murder of Duncan, the
murder of Banquo, the sleep-walking of Lady Macbeth, all come in night-scenes.
The Witches dance in the thick air of a storm, or, 'black and midnight hags,'
receive Macbeth in a cavern. The blackness of night is to the hero a thing of fear,
even of horror; and that which he feels becomes the spirit of the play. The faint
glimmerings of the western sky at twilight are here menacing: it is the hour when
the traveller hastens to reach safety in his inn, and when Banquo rides homeward
to meet his assassins; the hour when 'light thickens,' when 'night's black agents
to their prey do rouse,' when the wolf begins to howl, and the owl to scream,
and withered murder steals forth to his work. Macbeth bids the stars hide their
fires that his 'black' desires may be concealed; Lady Macbeth calls on thick night
to come, palled in the dunnest smoke of hell. The moon is down and no stars
shine when Banquo, dreading the dreams of the coming night, goes unwillingly
to bed, and leaves Macbeth to wait for the summons of the little bell. When
the next day should dawn, its light is 'strangled,' and 'darkness does the face of
earth entomb.' In the whole drama the sun seems to shine only twice: first, in
the beautiful but ironical passage where Duncan sees the swallows flitting round
the castle of death; and, afterwards, when at the close the avenging army gathers
to rid the earth of its shame. Of the many slighter touches which deepen this
effect I notice only one. The failure of nature in Lady Macbeth is marked by her

fear of darkness; 'she has light by her continually.' And in the one phrase of fear that escapes her lips even in sleep, it is of the darkness of the place of torment that she speaks.[2]

The atmosphere of *Macbeth*, however, is not that of unrelieved blackness. On the contrary, as compared with *King Lear* and its cold dim gloom, *Macbeth* leaves a decided impression of colour; it is really the impression of a black night broken by flashes of light and colour, sometimes vivid and even glaring. They are the lights and colours of the thunder-storm in the first scene; of the dagger hanging before Macbeth's eyes and glittering alone in the midnight air; of the torch borne by the servant when he and his lord come upon Banquo crossing the castle-court to his room; of the torch, again, which Fleance carried to light his father to death, and which was dashed out by one of the murderers; of the torches that flared in the hall on the face of the Ghost and the blanched cheeks of Macbeth; of the flames beneath the boiling caldron from which the apparitions in the cavern rose; of the taper which showed to the Doctor and Gentlewoman the wasted face and blank eyes of Lady Macbeth. And, above all, the colour is the colour of blood. It cannot be an accident that the image of blood is forced upon us continually, not merely by the events themselves, but by full descriptions, and even by reiteration of the word in unlikely parts of the dialogue. The Witches, after their first wild appearance, have hardly quitted the stage when there staggers onto it a 'bloody man,' gashed with wounds. His tale is of a hero whose 'brandished steel smoked with bloody execution,' 'carved out a passage to his enemy,' and 'unseam'd him from the nave to the chaps.' And then he tells of a second battle so bloody that the combatants seemed as if they 'meant to bathe in reeking wounds.' What metaphors! What a dreadful image is that with which Lady Macbeth greets us almost as she enters, when she prays the spirits of cruelty so to thicken her blood that pity cannot flow along her veins! What pictures are those of the murderer appearing at the door of the banquet-room with Banquo's 'blood upon his face'; of Banquo himself 'with twenty trenched gashes on his head,' or 'blood-bolter'd' and smiling in derision at his murderer; of Macbeth, gazing at his hand, and watching it dye the whole green ocean red; of Lady Macbeth, gazing at hers, and stretching it away from her face to escape the smell of blood that all the perfumes of Arabia will not subdue! The most horrible lines in the whole tragedy are those of her shuddering cry, 'Yet who would have thought the old man to have had so much blood in him?' And it is not only at such moments that these images occur. Even in the quiet conversation of Malcolm and Macduff, Macbeth is imagined as holding a bloody sceptre, and Scotland as a country bleeding and receiving every day a new gash added to her wounds. It is as if the poet saw the whole story through an ensanguined mist, and as if it stained the very blackness of the night. When Macbeth, before Banquo's murder, invokes night to scarf up the tender eye of pitiful day, and to tear in pieces the great bond that keeps him pale, even the invisible hand that is to tear the bond is imagined as covered with blood.

Let us observe another point. The vividness, magnitude, and violence of the imagery in some of these passages are characteristic of Macbeth almost throughout; and their influence contributes to form its atmosphere. Images like those of the babe torn smiling from the breast and dashed to death; of pouring the sweet milk of concord into hell; of the earth shaking in fever; of the frame of things disjointed; of sorrows striking heaven on the face, so that it resounds and yells out like syllables of dolour; of the mind lying in restless ecstasy on a rack; of the mind full of scorpions; of the tale told by an idiot, full of sound and fury;—all keep the imagination moving on a 'wild and violent sea,' while it is scarcely for a moment permitted to dwell on thoughts of peace and beauty. In its language, as in its action, the drama is full of tumult and storm. Whenever the Witches are present we see and hear a thunder-storm: when they are absent we hear of ship-wrecking storms and direful thunders; of tempests that blow down trees and churches, castles, palaces and pyramids; of the frightful hurricane of the night when Duncan was murdered; of the blast on which pity rides like a new-born babe, or on which Heaven's cherubim are horsed. There is thus something magnificently appropriate in the cry 'Blow, wind! Come, wrack!' with which Macbeth, turning from the sight of the moving wood of Birnam, bursts from his castle. He was borne to his throne on a whirlwind, and the fate he goes to meet comes on the wings of storm.

Now all these agencies—darkness, the lights and colours that illuminate it, the storm that rushes through it, the violent and gigantic images—conspire with the appearances of the Witches and the Ghost to awaken horror, and in some degree also a supernatural dread. And to this effect other influences contribute. The pictures called up by the mere words of the Witches stir the same feelings,—those, for example, of the spell-bound sailor driven tempest-tost for nine times nine weary weeks, and never visited by sleep night or day; of the drop of poisonous foam that forms on the moon, and, falling to earth, is collected for pernicious ends; of the sweltering venom of the toad, the finger of the babe killed at its birth by its own mother, the tricklings from the murderer's gibbet. In Nature, again, something is felt to be at work, sympathetic with human guilt and supernatural malice. She labours with portents.

> Lamentings heard in the air, strange screams of death,
> And prophesying with accents terrible,

burst from her. The owl clamours all through the night; Duncan's horses devour each other in frenzy; the dawn comes, but no light with it. Common sights and sounds, the crying of crickets, the croak of the raven, the light thickening after sunset, the home-coming of the rooks, are all ominous. Then, as if to deepen these impressions, Shakespeare has concentrated attention on the obscurer regions of man's being, on phenomena which make it seem that he is in the power of secret forces lurking below, and independent of his consciousness and will: such as the relapse of Macbeth from conversation into a reverie, during which he gazes fascinated at the image of murder drawing closer and closer; the writing on his face of strange things he never meant to show; the pressure of imagination heightening into illusion, like the vision of a dagger in the air, at first bright, then suddenly splashed with blood, or the sound of a voice that cried 'Sleep no more' and would not be silenced.[3] To these are added other, and constant, allusions to sleep, man's strange half-conscious life; to the misery of its withholding; to the terrible dreams of remorse; to the cursed thoughts from which Banquo is free by day, but which tempt him in his sleep: and again to abnormal disturbances of sleep; in the two men, of whom one during the murder of Duncan laughed in his sleep, and the other raised a cry of murder; and in Lady Macbeth, who rises to re-enact in somnambulism those scenes the memory of which is pushing her on to madness or suicide. All this has one effect, to excite supernatural alarm and, even more, a dread of the presence of evil not only in its recognised seat but all through and around our mysterious nature. Perhaps there is no other work equal to *Macbeth* in the production of this effect.[4]

It is enhanced—to take a last point—by the use of a literary expedient. Not even in *Richard III.*, which in this, as in other respects, has resemblances to *Macbeth*, is there so much of Irony. I do not refer to irony in the ordinary sense; to speeches, for example, where the speaker is intentionally ironical, like that of Lennox in III. vi. I refer to irony on the part of the author himself, to ironical juxtapositions of persons and events, and especially to the 'Sophoclean irony' by which a speaker is made to use words bearing to the audience, in addition to his own meaning, a further and ominous sense, hidden from himself and, usually, from the other persons on the stage. The very first words uttered by Macbeth,

So foul and fair a day I have not seen,

are an example to which attention has often been drawn; for they startle the reader by recalling the words of the Witches in the first scene,

Fair is foul, and foul is fair.

When Macbeth, emerging from his murderous reverie, turns to the nobles saying, 'Let us toward the King,' his words are innocent, but to the reader have a double meaning. Duncan's comment on the treachery of Cawdor,

There's no art
To find the mind's construction in the face:
He was a gentleman on whom I built
An absolute trust,

is interrupted[5] by the entrance of the traitor Macbeth, who is greeted with effusive gratitude and a like 'absolute trust.' I have already referred to the ironical effect of the beautiful lines in which Duncan and Banquo describe the castle they are about to enter. To the reader Lady Macbeth's light words,

> A little water clears us of this deed:
> How easy is it then,

summon up the picture of the sleep-walking scene. The idea of the Porter's speech, in which he imagines himself the keeper of hell-gate, shows the same irony. So does the contrast between the obvious and the hidden meanings of the apparitions of the armed head, the bloody child, and the child with the tree in his hand. It would be easy to add further examples. Perhaps the most striking is the answer which Banquo, as he rides away, never to return alive, gives to Macbeth's reminder, 'Fail not our feast.' 'My lord, I will not,' he replies, and he keeps his promise. It cannot be by accident that Shakespeare so frequently in this play uses a device which contributes to excite the vague fear of hidden forces operating on minds unconscious of their influence.[6]

2

But of course he had for this purpose an agency more potent than any yet considered. It would be almost an impertinence to attempt to describe anew the influence of the Witch-scenes on the imagination of the reader.[7] Nor do I believe that among different readers this influence differs greatly except in degree. But when critics begin to analyse the imaginative effect, and still more when, going behind it, they try to determine the truth which lay for Shakespeare or lies for us in these creations, they too often offer us results which, either through perversion or through inadequacy, fail to correspond with that effect. This happens in opposite ways. On the one hand the Witches, whose contribution to the 'atmosphere' of *Macbeth* can hardly be exaggerated, are credited with far too great an influence upon the action; sometimes they are described as goddesses, or even as fates, whom Macbeth is powerless to resist. And this is perversion. On the other hand, we are told that, great as is their influence on the action, it is so because they are merely symbolic representations of the unconscious or half-conscious guilt in Macbeth himself. And this is inadequate. The few remarks I have to make may take the form of a criticism on these views.

(1) As to the former, Shakespeare took, as material for his purposes, the ideas about witch-craft that he found existing in people around him and in books like Reginald Scot's *Discovery* (1584). And he used these ideas without changing their substance at all. He selected and improved, avoiding the merely ridiculous, dismissing (unlike Middleton) the sexually loathsome or stimulating, rehandling and heightening whatever could touch the imagination with fear, horror, and

mysterious attraction. The Witches, that is to say, are not goddesses, or fates, or, in any way whatever, supernatural beings. They are old women, poor and ragged, skinny and hideous, full of vulgar spite, occupied in killing their neighbours' swine or revenging themselves on sailors' wives who have refused them chestnuts. If Banquo considers their beards a proof that they are not women, that only shows his ignorance: Sir Hugh Evans would have known better.[8] There is not a syllable in *Macbeth* to imply that they are anything but women. But, again in accordance with the popular ideas, they have received from evil spirits certain supernatural powers. They can 'raise haile, tempests, and hurtfull weather; as lightening, thunder, etc.' They can 'passe from place to place in the aire invisible.' They can 'keepe divels and spirits in the likenesse of todes and cats,' Paddock or Graymalkin. They can 'transferre corne in the blade from one place to another.' They can 'manifest unto others things hidden and lost, and foreshew things to come, and see them as though they were present.' The reader will apply these phrases and sentences at once to passages in *Macbeth*. They are all taken from Scot's first chapter, where he is retailing the popular superstitions of his time; and, in regard to the Witches, Shakespeare mentions scarcely anything, if anything, that was not to be found, of course in a more prosaic shape, either in Scot or in some other easily accessible authority.[9] He read, to be sure, in Holinshed, his main source for the story of Macbeth, that, according to the common opinion, the 'women' who met Macbeth 'were eyther the weird sisters, that is (as ye would say) ye Goddesses of destinee, or els some Nimphes or Feiries.' But what does that matter? What he read in his authority was absolutely nothing to his audience, and remains nothing to us, unless he *used* what he read. And he did not use this idea. He used nothing but the phrase 'weird sisters,'[10] which certainly no more suggested to a London audience the Parcae of one mythology or the Norns of another than it does to-day. His Witches owe all their power to the spirits; they are '*instruments* of darkness'; the spirits are their 'masters' (IV. i. 63). Fancy the fates having masters! Even if the passages where Hecate appears are Shakespeare's,[11] that will not help the Witches; for they are subject to Hecate, who is herself a goddess, not a fate.[12]

Next, while the influence of the Witches' prophecies on Macbeth is very great, it is quite clearly shown to be an influence and nothing more. There is no sign whatever in the play that Shakespeare meant the actions of Macbeth to be forced on him by an external power, whether that of the Witches, or of their 'masters,' or of Hecate. It is needless therefore to insist that such a conception would be in contradiction with his whole tragic practice. The prophecies of the Witches are presented simply as dangerous circumstances with which Macbeth has to deal: they are dramatically on the same level as the story of the Ghost in *Hamlet*, or the falsehoods told by Iago to Othello. Macbeth is, in the ordinary sense, perfectly free in regard to them: and if we speak of decrees of freedom, he is even more free than Hamlet, who was crippled by melancholy when the

Ghost appeared to him. That the influence of the first prophecies upon him came as much from himself as from them, is made abundantly clear by the obviously intentional contrast between him and Banquo. Banquo, ambitious but perfectly honest, is scarcely even startled by them, and he remains throughout the scene indifferent to them. But when Macbeth heard them he was not an innocent man. Precisely how far his mind was guilty may be a question; but no innocent man would have started, as he did, with a start of *fear* at the mere prophecy of a crown, or have conceived thereupon *immediately* the thought of murder. Either this thought was not new to him,[13] or he had cherished at least some vaguer dishonourable dream, the instantaneous recurrence of which, at the moment of his hearing the prophecy, revealed to him an inward and terrifying guilt. In either case not only was he free to accept or resist the temptation, but the temptation was already within him. We are admitting too much, therefore, when we compare him with Othello, for Othello's mind was perfectly free from suspicion when his temptation came to him. And we are admitting, again, too much when we use the word 'temptation' in reference to the first prophecies of the Witches. Speaking strictly we must affirm that he was tempted only by himself. *He* speaks indeed of their 'supernatural soliciting'; but in fact they did not solicit. They merely announced events: they hailed him as Thane of Glamis, Thane of Cawdor, and King hereafter. No connection of these announcements with any action of his was even hinted by them. For all that appears, the natural death of an old man might have fulfilled the prophecy any day.[14] In any case, the idea of fulfilling it by murder was entirely his own.[15]

When Macbeth sees the Witches again, after the murders of Duncan and Banquo, we observe, however, a striking change. They no longer need to go and meet him; he seeks them out. He has committed himself to his course of evil. Now accordingly they do 'solicit.' They prophesy, but they also give advice: they bid him be bloody, bold, and secure. We have no hope that he will reject their advice; but so far are they from having, even now, any power to compel him to accept it, that they make careful preparations to deceive him into doing so. And, almost as though to intimate how entirely the responsibility for his deeds still lies with Macbeth, Shakespeare makes his first act after this interview one for which his tempters gave him not a hint—the slaughter of Macduff's wife and children.

To all this we must add that Macbeth himself nowhere betrays a suspicion that his action is, or has been, thrust on him by an external power. He curses the Witches for deceiving him, but he never attempts to shift to them the burden of his guilt. Neither has Shakespeare placed in the mouth of any other character in this play such fatalistic expressions as may be found in *King Lear* and occasionally elsewhere. He appears actually to have taken pains to make the natural psychological genesis of Macbeth's crimes perfectly clear, and it was a most unfortunate notion of Schlegel's that the Witches were required because natural agencies would have seemed too weak to drive such a man as Macbeth to his first murder.

'Still,' it may be said, 'the Witches did foreknow Macbeth's future; and what is foreknown is fixed; and how can a man be responsible when his future is fixed?' With this question, as a speculative one, we have no concern here; but, in so far as it relates to the play, I answer, first, that not one of the things foreknown is an action. This is just as true of the later prophecies as of the first. That Macbeth will be harmed by none of woman born, and will never be vanquished till Birnam Wood shall come against him, involves (so far as we are informed) no action of his. It may be doubted, indeed, whether Shakespeare would have introduced prophecies of Macbeth's deeds, even if it had been convenient to do so; he would probably have felt that to do so would interfere with the interest of the inward struggle and suffering. And, in the second place, *Macbeth* was not written for students of metaphysics or theology, but for people at large; and, however it may be with prophecies of actions, prophecies of mere events do not suggest to people at large any sort of difficulty about responsibility. Many people, perhaps most, habitually think of their 'future' as something fixed, and of themselves as 'free.' The Witches nowadays take a room in Bond Street and charge a guinea; and when the victim enters they hail him the possessor of £1000 a year, or prophesy to him of journeys, wives, and children. But though he is struck dumb by their prescience, it does not even cross his mind that he is going to lose his glorious 'freedom'—not though journeys and marriages imply much more agency on his part than anything foretold to Macbeth. This whole difficulty is undramatic; and I may add that Shakespeare nowhere shows, like Chaucer, any interest in speculative problems concerning foreknowledge, predestination and freedom.

(2) We may deal more briefly with the opposite interpretation. According to it the Witches and their prophecies are to be taken merely as symbolical representations of thoughts and desires which have slumbered in Macbeth's breast and now rise into consciousness and confront him. With this idea, which springs from the wish to get rid of a mere external supernaturalism, and to find a psychological and spiritual meaning in that which the groundlings probably received as hard facts, one may feel sympathy. But it is evident that it is rather a 'philosophy' of the Witches than an immediate dramatic apprehension of them; and even so it will be found both incomplete and, in other respects, inadequate.

It is incomplete because it cannot possibly be applied to all the facts. Let us grant that it will apply to the most important prophecy, that of the crown; and that the later warning which Macbeth receives, to beware of Macduff, also answers to something in his own breast and 'harps his fear aright.' But there we have to stop. Macbeth had evidently no suspicion of that treachery in Cawdor through which he himself became Thane; and who will suggest that he had any idea, however subconscious, about Birnam Wood or the man not born of woman? It may be held—and rightly, I think—that the prophecies which answer to nothing inward, the prophecies which are merely supernatural, produce, now at any rate, much less imaginative effect than the others,—even that they are in *Macbeth* an element which was of an age and not for all time; but still they are there, and they are essential to the plot.[16] And as the theory under consideration will not apply to them at all, it is not likely that it gives an adequate account even of those prophecies to which it can in some measure be applied.

It is inadequate here chiefly because it is much too narrow. The Witches and their prophecies, if they are to be rationalised or taken symbolically, must represent not only the evil slumbering in the hero's soul, but all those obscurer influences of the evil around him in the world which aid his own ambition and the incitements of his wife. Such influences, even if we put aside all belief in evil 'spirits,' are as certain, momentous, and terrifying facts as the presence of inchoate evil in the soul itself; and if we exclude all reference to these facts from our idea of the Witches, it will be greatly impoverished and will certainly fail to correspond with the imaginative effect. The union of the outward and inward here may be compared with something of the same kind in Greek poetry.[17] In the first book of the *Iliad* we are told that, when Agamemnon threatened to take Briseis from Achilles, 'grief came upon Peleus' son, and his heart within his shaggy breast was divided in counsel, whether to draw his keen blade from his thigh and set the company aside and so slay Atreides, or to assuage his anger and curb his soul. While yet he doubted thereof in heart and soul, and was drawing his great sword from his sheath, Athene came to him from heaven, sent forth of the white-armed goddess Hera, whose heart loved both alike and had care for them. She stood behind Peleus' son and caught him by his golden hair, to him only visible, and of the rest no man beheld her.' And at her bidding he mastered his wrath, 'and stayed his heavy hand on the silver hilt, and thrust the great sword back into the sheath, and was not disobedient to the saying of Athene.'[18] The succour of the goddess here only strengthens an inward movement in the mind of Achilles, but we should lose something besides a poetic effect if for that reason we struck her out of the account. We should lose the idea that the inward powers of the soul answer in their essence to vaster powers without, which support them and assure the effect of their exertion. So it is in *Macbeth*.[19] The words of the Witches are fatal to the hero only because there is in him something which leaps into light at the sound of them; but they are at the same time the witness of forces which never cease to work in the world around him, and, on the instant of his surrender to them, entangle him inextricably in the web of Fate. If the inward connection is once realised (and Shakespeare has left us no excuse for missing it), we need not fear, and indeed shall scarcely be able, to exaggerate the effect of the Witch-scenes in heightening and deepening the sense of fear, horror, and mystery which pervades the atmosphere of the tragedy.

3

From this murky background stand out the two great terrible figures, who dwarf all the remaining characters of the drama. Both are sublime, and both inspire, far more than the other tragic heroes, the feeling of awe. They are never detached in imagination from the atmosphere which surrounds them and adds to their grandeur and terror. It is, as it were, continued into their souls. For within them is all that we felt without—the darkness of night, lit with the flame of tempest and the hues of blood, and haunted by wild and direful shapes, 'murdering ministers,' spirits of remorse and maddening visions of peace lost and judgment to come. The way to be untrue to Shakespeare here, as always, is to relax the tension of imagination, to conventionalise, to conceive Macbeth, for example, as a half-hearted cowardly criminal, and Lady Macbeth as a whole-hearted fiend.

These two characters are fired by one and the same passion of ambition; and to a considerable extent they are alike. The disposition of each is high, proud, and commanding. They are born to rule, if not to reign. They are peremptory or contemptuous to their inferiors. They are not children of light, like Brutus and Hamlet; they are of the world. We observe in them no love of country, and no interest in the welfare of anyone outside their family. Their habitual thoughts and aims are, and, we imagine, long have been, all of station and power. And though in both there is something, and in one much, of what is higher—honour, conscience, humanity—they do not live consciously in the light of these things or speak their language. Not that they are egoists, like Iago; or, if they are egoists, theirs is an *egoïsme à deux*. They have no separate ambitions.[20] They support and love one another. They suffer together. And if, as time goes on, they drift a little apart, they are not vulgar souls, to be alienated and recriminate when they experience the fruitlessness of their ambition. They remain to the end tragic, even grand.

So far there is much likeness between them. Otherwise they are contrasted, and the action is built upon this contrast. Their attitudes towards the projected murder of Duncan are quite different; and it produces in them equally different effects. In consequence, they appear in the earlier part of the play as of equal importance, if indeed Lady Macbeth does not overshadow her husband; but afterwards she retires more and more into the background, and he becomes unmistakably the leading figure. His is indeed far the more complex character: and I will speak of it first.

Macbeth, the cousin of a King mild, just, and beloved, but now too old to lead his army, is introduced to us as a general of extraordinary prowess, who has covered himself with glory in putting down a rebellion and repelling the invasion of a foreign army. In these conflicts he showed great personal courage, a quality which he continues to display throughout the drama in regard to all plain dangers. It is difficult to be sure of his customary demeanour, for in the play we see him either in what appears to be an exceptional relation to his wife, or else in the throes of remorse and desperation; but from his behaviour during his journey home after the war, from his *later* conversations with Lady Macbeth, and from his language to the murderers of Banquo and to others, we imagine him as a great warrior, somewhat masterful, rough, and abrupt, a man to inspire some fear and much admiration. He was thought 'honest,' or honourable; he was trusted, apparently, by everyone; Macduff, a man of the highest integrity, 'loved him well.' And there was, in fact, much good in him. We have no warrant, I think, for describing, him, with many writers, as of a 'noble' nature, like Hamlet or Othello;[21] but he had a keen sense both of honour and of the worth of a good name. The phrase, again, 'too much of the milk of human kindness,' is applied to him in impatience by his wife, who did not fully understand him; but certainly he was far from devoid of humanity and pity.

At the same time he was exceedingly ambitious. He must have been so by temper. The tendency must have been greatly strengthened by his marriage. When we see him, it has been further stimulated by his remarkable success and by the consciousness of exceptional powers and merit. It becomes a passion. The course of action suggested by it is extremely perilous: it sets his good name, his position, and even his life on the hazard. It is also abhorrent to his better feelings. Their defeat in the struggle with ambition leaves him utterly wretched, and would have kept him so, however complete had been his outward success and security. On the other hand, his passion for power and his instinct of self-assertion are so vehement that no inward misery could persuade him to relinquish the fruits of crime, or to advance from remorse to repentance.

In the character as so far sketched there is nothing very peculiar, though the strength of the forces contending in it is unusual. But there is in Macbeth one marked peculiarity, the true apprehension of which is the key to Shakespeare's conception.[22] This bold ambitious man of action has, within certain limits, the imagination of a poet,—an imagination on the one hand extremely sensitive to impressions of a certain kind, and, on the other, productive of violent disturbance both of mind and body. Through it he is kept in contact with supernatural impressions and is liable to supernatural fears. And through it, especially, come to him the intimations of conscience and honour. Macbeth's better nature—to put the matter for clearness' sake too broadly—instead of speaking to him in the overt language of moral ideas, commands, and prohibitions, incorporates itself in images which alarm and horrify. His imagination is thus the best of him, something usually deeper and higher than his conscious thoughts; and if he had obeyed it he would have been safe. But his wife quite misunderstands it, and he himself understands it only in part. The terrifying images which deter him from crime and follow its commission, and which are really the protest of his deepest self, seem to his wife the creations of mere nervous fear, and are sometimes referred by himself to the dread of vengeance or the restlessness of insecurity.[23] His conscious or reflective mind, that is, moves chiefly among considerations of outward success and failure, while his inner being is convulsed by conscience. And his inability to understand himself is repeated and exaggerated in the interpretations of actors and critics, who represent him as a coward, cold-blooded, calculating, and pitiless, who shrinks from crime simply because it is dangerous, and suffers afterwards simply because he is not safe. In reality his courage is frightful. He strides from crime to crime, though his soul never ceases to bar his advance with shapes of terror, or to clamour in his ears that he is murdering his peace and casting away his 'eternal jewel.'

It is of the first importance to realise the strength, and also (what has not been so clearly recognised) the limits, of Macbeth's imagination. It is not the universal meditative imagination of Hamlet. He came to see in man, as Hamlet sometimes did, the 'quintessence of dust'; but he must always have been incapable of Hamlet's reflections on man's noble reason and infinite faculty, or of seeing with Hamlet's eyes 'this brave o'erhanging firmament, this majestical roof fretted with golden fire.' Nor could he feel, like Othello, the romance of war or the infinity of love. He shows no sign of any unusual sensitiveness to the glory or beauty in the world or the soul; and it is partly for this reason that we have no inclination to love him, and that we regard him with more of awe than of pity. His imagination is excitable and intense, but narrow. That which stimulates it is, almost solely, that which thrills with sudden, startling, and often supernatural fear.[24] There is a famous passage late in the play (V. v. 10) which is here very significant, because it refers to a time before his conscience was burdened, and so shows his native disposition:

> The time has been, my senses would have cool'd
> To hear a night-shriek; and my fell of hair
> Would at a dismal treatise rise and stir
> As life were in't.

This 'time' must have been in his youth, or at least before we see him. And, in the drama, everything which terrifies him is of this character, only it has now a deeper and a moral significance. Palpable dangers leave him unmoved or fill him with fire. He does himself mere justice when he asserts he 'dare do all that may become a man,' or when he exclaims to Banquo's ghost,

> What man dare, I dare:
> Approach thou like the rugged Russian bear,
> The arm'd rhinoceros, or the Hyrcan tiger;
> Take any shape but that, and my firm nerves
> Shall never tremble.

What appals him is always the image of his own guilty heart or bloody deed, or some image which derives from them its terror or gloom. These, when they arise, hold him spell-bound and possess him wholly, like a hypnotic trance which is at the same time the ecstasy of a poet. As the first 'horrid image' of Duncan's murder—of himself murdering Duncan—rises from unconsciousness and confronts him, his hair stands on end and the outward scene vanishes from his eyes. Why? For fear of 'consequences'? The idea is ridiculous. Or because the deed is bloody? The man who with his 'smoking' steel 'carved out his passage' to the rebel leader, and 'unseam'd him from the nave to the chaps,' would hardly be frightened by blood. How could fear of consequences make the dagger he is to use hang suddenly glittering before him in the air, and then as suddenly dash it with gouts of blood? Even when he *talks* of consequences, and declares that if he were safe against them he would 'jump the life to come,' his imagination bears witness against him, and shows us that what really holds him back is the hideous vileness of the deed:

> He's here in double trust;
> First, as I am his kinsman and his subject,
> Strong both against the deed; then, as his host,
> Who should against his murderer shut the door,
> Not bear the knife myself. Besides, this Duncan
> Hath borne his faculties so meek, hath been
> So clear in his great office, that his virtues
> Will plead like angels, trumpet-tongued, against
> The deep damnation of his taking-off;
> And pity, like a naked new-born babe,
> Striding the blast, or heaven's cherubim, horsed
> Upon the sightless couriers of the air,
> Shall blow the horrid deed in every eye,
> That tears shall drown the wind.

It may be said that he is here thinking of the horror that others will feel at the deed—thinking therefore of consequences. Yes, but could he realise thus how horrible the deed would look to others if it were not equally horrible to himself?

It is the same when the murder is done. He is well-nigh mad with horror, but it is not the horror of detection. It is not he who thinks of washing his hands or getting his nightgown on. He has brought away the daggers he should have left on the pillows of the grooms, but what does he care for that? What *he* thinks of is that, when he heard one of the men awaked from sleep say 'God bless us,' he could not say 'Amen'; for his imagination presents to him the parching of his throat as an immediate judgment from heaven. His wife heard the owl scream and the crickets cry; but what *he* heard was the voice that first cried 'Macbeth doth murder sleep,' and then, a minute later, with a change of tense, denounced on him, as if his three names gave him three personalities to suffer in, the doom of sleeplessness:

Glamis hath murdered sleep, and therefore Cawdor
Shall sleep no more, Macbeth shall sleep no more.

There comes a sound of knocking. It should be perfectly familiar to him; but he knows not whence, or from what world, it comes. He looks down at his hands, and starts violently: 'What hands are here?' For they seem alive, they move, they mean to pluck out his eyes. He looks at one of them again; it does not move; but the blood upon it is enough to dye the whole ocean red. What has all this to do with fear of 'consequences'? It is his soul speaking in the only shape in which it can speak freely, that of imagination.

So long as Macbeth's imagination is active, we watch him fascinated; we feel suspense, horror, awe; in which are latent, also, admiration and sympathy. But so soon as it is quiescent these feelings vanish. He is no longer 'infirm of purpose': he becomes domineering, even brutal, or he becomes a cool pitiless hypocrite. He is generally said to be a very bad actor, but this is not wholly true. Whenever his imagination stirs, he acts badly. It so possesses him, and is so much stronger than his reason, that his face betrays him, and his voice utters the most improbable untruths[25] or the most artificial rhetoric.[26] But when it is asleep he is firm, self-controlled and practical, as in the conversation where he skilfully elicits from Banquo that information about his movements which is required for the successful arrangement of his murder.[27] Here he is hateful; and so he is in the conversation with the murderers, who are not professional cut-throats but old soldiers, and whom, without a vestige of remorse, he beguiles with calumnies against Banquo and with such appeals as his wife had used to him.[28] On the other hand, we feel much pity as well as anxiety in the scene (I. vii.) where she overcomes his opposition to the murder; and we feel it (though his imagination is not specially active) because this scene shows us how little he understands himself. This is his great misfortune here. Not that he fails to realise in reflection the baseness of the deed (the soliloquy with which the scene opens shows that he does not). But he has never, to put it pedantically, accepted as the principle of his conduct the morality which takes shape in his imaginative fears. Had he done so, and said plainly to his wife, 'The thing is vile, and, however much I have sworn to do it, I will not,' she would have been helpless; for all her arguments proceed on the assumption that there is for them no such point of view. Macbeth does approach this position once, when, resenting the accusation of cowardice, he answers,

> I dare do all that may become a man;
> Who dares do more is none.

She feels in an instant that everything is at stake, and, ignoring the point, overwhelms him with indignant and contemptuous personal reproach. But he yields to it because he is himself half-ashamed of that answer of his, and because, for want of habit, the simple idea which it expresses has no hold on him comparable to the force it acquires when it becomes incarnate in visionary fears and warnings.

Yet these were so insistent, and they offered to his ambition a resistance so strong, that it is impossible to regard him as falling through the blindness or delusion of passion. On the contrary, he himself feels with such intensity the enormity of his purpose that, it seems clear, neither his ambition nor yet the prophecy of the Witches would ever without the aid of Lady Macbeth have overcome this feeling. As it is, the deed is done in horror and without the faintest desire or sense of glory,—done, one may almost say, as if it were an appalling duty; and, the instant it is finished, its futility is revealed to Macbeth as clearly as its vileness had been revealed beforehand. As he staggers from the scene he mutters in despair,

> Wake Duncan with thy knocking! I would thou could'st.

When, half an hour later, he returns with Lennox from the room of the murder, he breaks out:

> Had I but died an hour before this chance,
> I had lived a blessed time; for from this instant
> There's nothing serious in mortality:
> All is but toys: renown and grace is dead;
> The wine of life is drawn, and the mere lees
> Is left this vault to brag of.

This is no mere acting. The language here has none of the false rhetoric of his merely hypocritical speeches. It is meant to deceive, but it utters at the same time his profoundest feeling. And this he can henceforth never hide from himself for long. However he may try to drown it in further enormities, he hears it murmuring,

> Duncan is in his grave:
> After life's fitful fever he sleeps well:

or,

better be with the dead:

or,

I have lived long enough:

and it speaks its last words on the last day of his life:

> Out, out, brief candle!
> Life's but a walking shadow, a poor player
> That struts and frets his hour upon the stage
> And then is heard no more: it is a tale
> Told by an idiot, full of sound and fury,
> Signifying nothing.

How strange that this judgment on life, the despair of a man who had knowingly made mortal war on his own soul, should be frequently quoted as Shakespeare's own judgment, and should even be adduced, in serious criticism, as a proof of his pessimism!

It remains to look a little more fully at the history of Macbeth after the murder of Duncan. Unlike his first struggle this history excites little suspense or anxiety on his account: we have now no hope for him. But it is an engrossing spectacle, and psychologically it is perhaps the most remarkable exhibition of the *development* of a character to be found in Shakespeare's tragedies.

That heart-sickness which comes from Macbeth's perception of the futility of his crime, and which never leaves him for long, is not, however, his habitual state. It could not be so, for two reasons. In the first place the consciousness of guilt is stronger in him than the consciousness of failure; and it keeps him in a perpetual agony of restlessness, and forbids him simply to droop and pine. His mind is 'full of scorpions.' He cannot sleep. He 'keeps alone,' moody and savage. 'All that is within him does condemn itself for being there.' There is a fever in his blood which urges him to ceaseless action in the search for oblivion. And, in the second place, ambition, the love of power, the instinct of self-assertion, are much too potent in Macbeth to permit him to resign, even in spirit, the prize for which he has put rancours in the vessel of his peace. The 'will to live' is mighty in him. The forces which impelled him to aim at the crown re-assert themselves. He faces the world, and his own conscience, desperate, but never dreaming of acknowledging defeat. He will see 'the frame of things disjoint' first. He challenges fate into the lists.

The result is frightful. He speaks no more, as before Duncan's murder, of honour or pity. That sleepless torture, he tells himself, is nothing but the sense of insecurity and the fear of retaliation. If only he were safe, it would vanish. And he looks about for the cause of his fear; and his eye falls on Banquo. Banquo, who cannot fail to suspect him, has not fled or turned against him: Banquo has become his chief, counsellor. Why? Because, he answers, the kingdom was promised to Banquo's children. Banquo, then, is waiting to attack him, to make a way for them. The 'bloody instructions' he himself taught when he murdered Duncan, are about to return, as he said they would, to plague the inventor. *This* then, he tells himself, is the fear that will not let him sleep; and it will die with Banquo. There is no hesitation now, and no remorse: he has nearly learned his lesson. He hastens feverishly, not to murder Banquo, but to procure his murder: some strange idea is in his mind that the thought of the dead man will not haunt him, like the memory of Duncan, if the deed is done by other hands.[29] The deed is done: but, instead of peace descending on him, from the depths of his nature his half-murdered conscience rises; his deed confronts him in the apparition of Banquo's Ghost, and the horror of the night of his first murder returns. But, alas, *it* has less power, and *he* has more will. Agonised and trembling, he still faces this rebel image, and it yields:

> Why, so: being gone,
> I am a man again.

Yes, but his secret is in the hands of the assembled lords. And, worse, this deed is as futile as the first. For, though Banquo is dead and even his Ghost is conquered, that inner torture is unassuaged. But he will not bear it. His guests have hardly left him when he turns roughly to his wife:

> How say'st thou, that Macduff denies his person
> At our great bidding?

Macduff it is that spoils his sleep. He shall perish,—he and aught else that bars the road to peace.

> For mine own good
> All causes shall give way: I am in blood
> Stepp'd in so far that, should I wade no more,
> Returning were as tedious as go o'er:
> Strange things I have in head that will to hand,
> Which must be acted ere they may be scann'd.

She answers, sick at heart,

> You lack the season of all natures, sleep.

No doubt: but he has found the way to it now:

> Come, we'll to sleep. My strange and self-abuse
> Is the initiate fear that wants hard use:
> We are yet but young in deed.

What a change from the man who thought of Duncan's virtues, and of pity like a naked new-born babe! What a frightful clearness of self-consciousness in this descent to hell, and yet what a furious force in the instinct of life and self-assertion that drives him on!

He goes to seek the Witches. He will know, by the worst means, the worst. He has no longer any awe of them.

> How now, you secret, black and midnight hags!

—so he greets them, and at once he demands and threatens. They tell him he is right to fear Macduff. They tell him to fear nothing, for none of woman born can harm him. He feels that the two statements are at variance; infatuated, suspects no double meaning; but, that he may 'sleep in spite of thunder,' determines not to spare Macduff. But his heart throbs to know one thing, and he forces from the Witches the vision of Banquo's children crowned. The old intolerable thought returns, 'for Banquo's issue have I filed my mind'; and with it, for all the absolute security apparently promised him, there returns that inward fever. Will nothing quiet it? Nothing but destruction. Macduff, one comes to tell him, has escaped him; but that does not matter: he can still destroy:[30]

> And even now,
> To crown my thoughts with acts, be it thought and done:
> The castle of Macduff I will surprise;
> Seize upon Fife; give to the edge o' the sword
> His wife, his babes, and all unfortunate souls
> That trace him in's line. No boasting like a fool;
> This deed I'll do before this purpose cool.
> But no more sights!

No, he need fear no more 'sights.' The Witches have done their work, and after this purposeless butchery his own imagination will trouble him no more.[31] He has dealt his last blow at the conscience and pity which spoke through it.

The whole flood of evil in his nature is now let loose. He becomes an open tyrant, dreaded by everyone about him, and a terror to his country. She 'sinks beneath the yoke.'

> Each new morn
> New widows howl, new orphans cry, new sorrows
> Strike heaven on the face.

She weeps, she bleeds, 'and each new day a gash is added to her wounds.' She is not the mother of her children, but their grave;

> where nothing,
> But who knows nothing, is once seen to smile:
> Where sighs and groans and shrieks that rend the air
> Are made, not mark'd.

For this wild rage and furious cruelty we are prepared; but vices of another kind start up as he plunges on his downward way.

> I grant him bloody,
> Luxurious, avaricious, false, deceitful,
> Sudden, malicious,

says Malcolm; and two of these epithets surprise us. Who would have expected avarice or lechery[32] in Macbeth? His ruin seems complete.

Yet it is never complete. To the end he never totally loses our sympathy; we never feel towards him as we do to those who appear the born children of darkness. There remains something sublime in the defiance with which, even when cheated of his last hope, he faces earth and hell and heaven. Nor would any soul to whom evil was congenial be capable of that heart-sickness which overcomes him when he thinks of the 'honour, love, obedience, troops of friends' which 'he must not look to have' (and which Iago would never have cared to have), and contrasts with them

> Curses, not loud but deep, mouth-honour, breath,
> Which the poor heart would fain deny, and dare not,

(and which Iago would have accepted with indifference). Neither can I agree with those who find in his reception of the news of his wife's death proof of alienation or utter carelessness. There is no proof of these in such words as

> She should have died hereafter;
> There would have been a time for such a word,

spoken as they are from a man already in some measure prepared for such news, and now transported by the frenzy of his last fight for life. He has no time now to feel.[33] Only, as he thinks of the morrow when time to feel will come—if anything comes, the vanity of all hopes and forward-lookings sinks deep into his soul with an infinite weariness, and he murmurs,

> To-morrow, and to-morrow, and to-morrow,
> Creeps in this petty pace from day to day
> To the last syllable of recorded time,
> And all our yesterdays have lighted fools
> The way to dusty death.

In the very depths a gleam of his native love of goodness, and with it a touch of tragic grandeur, rests upon him. The evil he has desperately embraced continues to madden or to wither his inmost heart. No experience in the world could bring him to glory in it or make his peace with it, or to forget what he once was and Iago and Goneril never were.

NOTES

2. 'Hell is murky' (V. i. 35). This, surely, is not meant for a scornful repetition of something said long ago by Macbeth. He would hardly in those days have used an argument or expressed a fear that could provoke nothing but contempt.

3. Whether Banquo's ghost is a mere illusion, like the dagger, is discussed in Note FF.

4. In parts of this paragraph I am indebted to Hunter's *Illustrations of Shakespeare*.

5. The line is a foot short.

6. It should be observed that in some cases the irony would escape an audience ignorant of the story and watching the play for the first time,—another indication that Shakespeare did not write solely for immediate stage purposes.

7. Their influence on spectators is, I believe, very inferior. These scenes, like the Storm-scenes in *King Lear*, belong properly to the world of imagination.

8. 'By yea and no, I think the 'oman is a witch indeed: I like not when a 'oman has a great peard' (*Merry Wives*, IV. ii. 202).

9. Even the metaphor in the lines (II. iii. 127),

> What should be spoken here, where our fate,
> Hid in an auger-hole, may rush and seize us?

was probably suggested by the words in Scot's first chapter, 'They can go in and out at awger-holes.'

10. Once, 'weird women.' Whether Shakespeare knew that 'weird' meant 'fateful' we cannot tell, but it is probable that he did. The word occurs six times in *Macbeth* (it does not occur elsewhere in Shakespeare). The first three times it is spelt in the Folio *weyward*, the last three *weyard*. This may suggest a miswriting or misprinting of *wayward*; but, as that word is always spelt in the Folio either rightly or *weiward*, it is more likely that the *weyward* and *weyard* of *Macbeth* are the copyist's or printer's misreading of Shakespeare's *weird* or *weyrd*.

11. The doubt as to these passages (see Note Z) does not arise from the mere appearance of this figure. The idea of Hecate's connection with witches appears also at II. i. 52, and she is mentioned again at III. ii. 41 (cf *Mid. Night's Dream*, V. i. 391, for her connection with fairies). It is part of the common traditional notion of the heathen gods being now devils. Scot refers to it several times. See the notes in the Clarendon Press edition on III. v. 1, or those in Furness's Variorum.

Of course in the popular notion the witch's spirits are devils or servants of Satan. If Shakespeare openly introduces this idea only in Banquo's phrases 'the instruments of darkness' and 'what! can the devil speak true?' the reason is probably his unwillingness to give too much prominence to distinctively religious ideas.

12. If this paragraph is true, some of the statements even of Lamb and of Coleridge about the Witches are, taken literally, incorrect. What these critics, and notably the former, describe so well is the poetic aspect abstracted from the remainder; and in describing this they attribute to the Witches themselves what belongs really to the complex of Witches, Spirits, and Hecate. For the purposes of imagination, no doubt, this inaccuracy is of small consequence; and it is these purposes that matter. [I have not attempted to fulfil them.]

13. See Note CC.

14. The proclamation of Malcolm as Duncan's successor (I. iv.) changes the position, but the design of murder is prior to this.

15. Schlegel's assertion that the first thought of the murder comes from the Witches is thus in flat contradiction with the text. (The sentence in which he asserts this is, I may observe, badly mistranslated in the English version, which, wherever I have consulted the original, shows itself untrustworthy. It ought to be revised, for Schlegel is well worth reading.)

16. It is noticeable that Dr. Forman, who saw the play in 1610 and wrote a sketch of it in his journal, says nothing about the later prophecies. Perhaps he despised them as mere stuff for the groundlings. The reader will find, I think, that the great poetic effect of Act IV. Sc. i. depends much more on the 'charm' which precedes Macbeth's entrance, and on Macbeth himself, than on the predictions.

17. This comparison was suggested by a passage in Hegel's *Aesthetik*, i. 291 ff.

18. *Il.* i. 188 ff. (Leaf's translation).

19. The supernaturalism of the modern poet, indeed, is more 'external' than that of the ancient. We have already had evidence of this, and shall find more when we come to the character of Banquo.

20. The assertion that Lady Macbeth sought a crown for herself, or sought anything for herself, apart from her husband, is absolutely unjustified by anything in the play. It is based on a sentence of Holinshed's which Shakespeare did *not* use.

21. The word is used of him (I. ii. 67), but not in a way that decides this question or even bears on it.

22. This view, thus generally stated, is not original, but I cannot say who first stated it.

23. The latter, and more important, point was put quite clearly by Coleridge.

24. It is the consequent insistence on the idea of fear, and the frequent repetition of the word, that have principally led to misinterpretation.

25. *E.g.* I. iii. 149, where he excuses his abstraction by saying that his 'dull brain was wrought with things forgotten,' when nothing could be more natural than that he should be thinking of his new honour.

26. *E.g.* in I. iv. This is so also in II. iii. 114 ff., though here there is some real imaginative excitement mingled with the rhetorical antitheses and balanced clauses and forced bombast.

27. III. i. Lady Macbeth herself could not more naturally have introduced at intervals the questions 'Ride you this afternoon?' (l. 19), 'Is't far you ride?' (l. 24), 'Goes Fleance with you?' (l. 36).

28. We feel here, however, an underlying subdued frenzy which awakes some sympathy. There is an almost unendurable impatience expressed even in the rhythm of many of the lines; *e.g.*:

> Well then, now
> Have you consider'd of my speeches? Know
> That it was he in the times past which held you
> So under fortune, which you thought had been
> Our innocent self: this I made good to you
> In our last conference, pass'd in probation with you,
> How you were borne in hand, how cross'd, the instruments,
> Who wrought with them, and all things else that might
> To half a soul and to a notion crazed
> Say, 'Thus did Banquo.'

This effect is heard to the end of the play in Macbeth's less poetic speeches, and leaves the same impression of burning energy, though not of imaginative exaltation, as his great speeches. In these we find either violent, huge, sublime imagery, or a torrent of figurative expressions (as in the famous lines about 'the innocent sleep'). Our impressions as to the diction of the play are largely derived from these speeches of the hero, but not wholly so. The writing almost throughout leaves an impression of intense, almost feverish, activity.

29. See his first words to the Ghost: 'Thou canst not say I did it.'

30.   For only in destroying I find ease
> To my relentless thoughts.—*Paradise Lost*, ix. 129.

Milton's portrait of Satan's misery here, and at the beginning of Book IV., might well have been suggested by *Macbeth*. Coleridge, after quoting Duncan's speech, I. iv. 35 ff., says: 'It is a fancy; but I can never read this, and the following speeches of Macbeth, without involuntarily thinking of the Miltonic Messiah and Satan.' I doubt if it was a mere fancy. (It will be remembered that Milton thought at one time of writing a tragedy on Macbeth.)

31. The immediate reference in 'But no more sights' is doubtless to the visions called up by the Witches; but one of these, the 'blood-bolter'd Banquo,' recalls to him the vision of the preceding night, of which he had said,

> You make me strange
> Even to the disposition that I owe,
> When now I think you can behold such *sights*,
> And keep the natural ruby of your cheeks,
> When mine is blanch'd with fear.

32. 'Luxurious' and 'luxury' are used by Shakespeare only in this older sense. It must be remembered that these lines are spoken by Malcolm, but it seems likely that they are meant to be taken as true throughout.

33. I do not at all suggest that his love for his wife remains what it was when he greeted her with the words 'My dearest love, Duncan comes here to-night.' He has greatly changed; she has ceased to help him, sunk in her own despair; and there is no intensity of anxiety in the questions he puts to the doctor about her. But his love for her was probably never unselfish, never the love of Brutus, who, in somewhat similar circumstances, uses, on the death of Cassius, words which remind us of Macbeth's:

> I shall find time, Cassius, I shall find time.

For the opposite strain of feeling cf. Sonnet 90:

> Then hate me if thou wilt; if ever, now,
> Now while the world is bent my deeds to cross.

[Lecture X]

1

To regard Macbeth as a play, like the love-tragedies *Romeo and Juliet* and *Antony and Cleopatra*, in which there are two central characters of equal importance, is certainly a mistake. But Shakespeare himself is in a measure responsible for it, because the first half of *Macbeth* is greater than the second, and in the first half Lady Macbeth not only appears more than in the second but exerts the ultimate deciding influence on the action. And, in the opening Act at least, Lady Macbeth is the most commanding and perhaps the most awe-inspiring figure that Shakespeare drew. Sharing, as we have seen, certain traits with her husband, she is at once clearly distinguished from him by an inflexibility of will, which appears to hold imagination, feeling, and conscience completely in check. To her the prophecy of things that will be becomes instantaneously the determination that they shall be:

> Glamis thou art, and Cawdor, and shalt be
> That thou art promised.

She knows her husband's weakness, how he scruples 'to catch the nearest way' to the object he desires; and she sets herself without a trace of doubt or conflict to counteract this weakness. To her there is no separation between will and deed; and, as the deed falls in part to her, she is sure it will be done:

> The raven himself is hoarse
> That croaks the fatal entrance of Duncan
> Under my battlements.

On the moment of Macbeth's rejoining her, after braving infinite dangers and winning infinite praise, without a syllable on these subjects or a word of affection, she goes straight to her purpose and permits him to speak of nothing else. She takes the superior position and assumes the direction of affairs,—appears to assume it even more than she really can, that she may spur him on. She animates him by picturing the deed as heroic, 'this night's *great* business,' or 'our *great* quell,' while she ignores its cruelty and faithlessness. She bears down his faint resistance by presenting him with a prepared scheme which may remove from him the terror and danger of deliberation. She rouses him with a taunt no man can bear, and least of all a soldier,—the word 'coward.' When he still hesitates, she appeals even to his love for her:

> from this time
> Such I account thy love;

—such, that is, as the protestations of a drunkard. Her reasonings are mere sophisms; they could persuade no man. It is not by them, it is by personal appeals, through the admiration she extorts from him, and through sheer force of will, that she impels him to the deed. Her eyes are fixed upon the crown and the means to it; she does not attend to the consequences. Her plan of laying the guilt upon the chamberlains is invented on the spur of the moment, and simply to satisfy her husband. Her true mind is heard in the ringing cry with which she answers his question, 'Will it not be received . . . that they have done it?'

> Who *dares* receive it other?

And this is repeated in the sleep-walking scene: 'What need we fear who knows it, when none can call our power to account?' Her passionate courage sweeps him off his feet. His decision is taken in a moment of enthusiasm:

> Bring forth men-children only;
> For thy undaunted mettle should compose
> Nothing but males.

And even when passion has quite died away her will remains supreme. In presence of overwhelming horror and danger, in the murder scene and the banquet scene, her self-control is perfect. When the truth of what she has done dawns on her, no word of complaint, scarcely a word of her own suffering, not a single word of her own as apart from his, escapes her when others are by. She helps him, but never asks his help. She leans on nothing but herself. And from the beginning to the end though she makes once or twice a slip in acting her part—her will never fails her. Its grasp upon her nature may destroy her, but it is never relaxed. We are sure that she never betrayed her husband or herself by a word or even a look, save in sleep. However appalling she may be, she is sublime.

In the earlier scenes of the play this aspect of Lady Macbeth's character is far the most prominent. And if she seems invincible she seems also inhuman. We find no trace of pity for the kind old king; no consciousness of the treachery and baseness of the murder; no sense of the value of the lives of the wretched men on whom the guilt is to be laid; no shrinking even from the condemnation or hatred of the world. Yet if the Lady Macbeth of these scenes were really utterly inhuman, or a 'fiend-like queen,' as Malcolm calls her, the Lady Macbeth of the sleep-walking scene would be an impossibility. The one woman could never become the other. And in fact, if we look below the surface, there is evidence enough in the earlier scenes of preparation for the later. I do not mean that Lady Macbeth was naturally humane. There is nothing in the play to show this, and several passages subsequent to the murder-scene supply proof to the contrary. One is that where she exclaims, on being informed of Duncan's murder,

> Woe, alas!
> What, in our house?

This mistake in acting shows that she does not even know what the natural feeling in such circumstances would be; and Banquo's curt answer, 'Too cruel anywhere,' is almost a reproof of her insensibility. But, admitting this, we have in the first place to remember, in imagining the opening scenes, that she is deliberately bent on counteracting the 'human kindness' of her husband, and also that she is evidently not merely inflexibly determined but in a condition of abnormal excitability. That exaltation in the project which is so entirely lacking in Macbeth is strongly marked in her. When she tries to help him by representing their enterprise as heroic, she is deceiving herself as much as him. Their attainment of the crown presents itself to her, perhaps has long presented itself, as something so glorious, and she has fixed her will upon it so completely, that for the time she sees the enterprise in no other light than that of its greatness. When she soliloquises,

> Yet do I fear thy nature:
> It is too full o' the milk of human kindness
> To catch the nearest way: thou wouldst be great;
> Art not without ambition, but without
> The illness should attend it; what thou wouldst highly,
> That wouldst thou holily,

one sees that 'ambition' and 'great' and 'highly' and even 'illness' are to her simply terms of praise, and 'holily' and 'human kindness' simply terms of blame. Moral distinctions do not in this exaltation exist for her; or rather they are inverted: 'good' means to her the crown and whatever is required to obtain it, 'evil' whatever stands in the way of its attainment. This attitude of mind is evident even when she is alone, though it becomes still more pronounced when she has to work upon her husband. And it persists until her end is attained. But, without being exactly forced, it betrays a strain which could not long endure.

Besides this, in these earlier scenes the traces of feminine weakness and human feeling, which account for her later failure, are not absent. Her will, it is clear, was exerted to overpower not only her husband's resistance but some resistance in herself. Imagine Goneril uttering the famous words,

> Had he not resembled
> My father as he slept, I had done 't.

They are spoken, I think, without any sentiment—impatiently, as though she regretted her weakness: but it was there. And in reality, quite apart from this recollection of her father, she could never have done the murder if her husband had failed. She had to nerve herself with wine to give her 'boldness' enough to go through her minor part. That appalling invocation to the spirits of evil, to unsex her and fill her from the crown to the toe topfull of direst cruelty, tells the same tale of determination to crush the inward protest. Goneril had no need of such a prayer. In the utterance of the frightful lines,

> I have given suck, and know
> How tender 'tis to love the babe that milks me:
> I would, while it was smiling in my face,
> Have pluck'd my nipple from his boneless gums,
> And dash'd the brains out, had I so sworn as you
> Have done to this,

her voice should doubtless rise until it reaches, in 'dash'd the brains out,' an almost hysterical scream.[1] These lines show unmistakably that strained exaltation which, as soon as the end is reached, vanishes, never to return.

The greatness of Lady Macbeth lies almost wholly in courage and force of will. It is an error to regard her as remarkable on the intellectual side. In acting a part she shows immense self-control, but not much skill. Whatever may be thought of the plan of attributing the murder of Duncan to the chamberlains, to lay their bloody daggers on their pillows, as if they were determined to advertise their guilt, was a mistake which can be accounted for only by the excitement of the moment. But the limitations of her mind appear most in the point where she is most strongly contrasted with Macbeth,—in her comparative dullness of imagination. I say 'comparative,' for she sometimes uses highly poetic language, as indeed does everyone in Shakespeare who has any greatness of soul. Nor is she perhaps less imaginative than the majority of his heroines. But as compared with her husband she has little imagination. It is not *simply* that she suppresses what she has. To her, things remain at the most terrible moment precisely what they were at the calmest, plain facts which stand in a given relation to a certain deed, not visions which tremble and flicker in the light of other worlds. The probability that the old king will sleep soundly after his long journey to Inverness is to her simply a fortunate circumstance; but one can fancy the shoot of horror across Macbeth's face as she mentions it. She uses familiar and prosaic illustrations, like

> Letting 'I dare not' wait upon 'I would,'
> Like the poor cat i' the adage,

(the cat who wanted fish but did not like to wet her feet); or,

> We fail?
> But screw your courage to the sticking-place,
> And we'll not fail;[2]

or,

> Was the hope drunk
> Wherein you dress'd yourself? hath it slept since?
> And wakes it now, to look so green and pale
> At what it did so freely?

The Witches are practically nothing to her. She feels no sympathy in Nature with her guilty purpose, and would never bid the earth not hear her steps, which way they walk. The noises before the murder, and during it, are heard by her as simple facts, and are referred to their true sources. The knocking has no mystery for her: it comes from 'the south entry.' She calculates on the drunkenness of the grooms, compares the different effects of wine on herself and on them, and listens to their snoring. To her the blood upon her husband's hands suggests only the taunt,

> My hands are of your colour, but I shame
> To wear a heart so white;

and the blood to her is merely 'this filthy witness,'—words impossible to her husband, to whom it suggested something quite other than sensuous disgust or practical danger. The literalism of her mind appears fully in two contemptuous speeches where she dismisses his imaginings; in the murder scene:

> Infirm of purpose!
> Give me the daggers! The sleeping and the dead
> Are but as pictures: 'tis the eye of childhood
> That fears a painted devil;

and in the banquet scene:

> O these flaws and starts,
> Impostors to true fear, would well become
> A woman's story at a winter's fire,
> Authorised by her grandam. Shame itself!
> Why do you make such faces? When all's done,
> You look but on a stool.

Even in the awful scene where her imagination breaks loose in sleep she uses no such images as Macbeth's. It is the direct appeal of the facts to sense that has fastened on her memory. The ghastly realism of 'Yet who would have thought the old man to have had so much blood in him?' or 'Here's the smell of the blood still,' is wholly unlike him. Her most poetical words, 'All the perfumes of Arabia will not sweeten this little hand,' are equally unlike his words about great Neptune's ocean. Hers, like some of her other speeches, are the more moving, from their greater simplicity and because they seem to tell of that self-restraint in suffering which is so totally lacking in him; but there is in them comparatively little of imagination. If we consider most of the passages to which I have referred, we shall find that the quality which moves our admiration is courage or force of will.

This want of imagination, though it helps to make Lady Macbeth strong for immediate action, is fatal to her. If she does not feel beforehand the cruelty of Duncan's murder, this is mainly because she hardly imagines the act, or at most imagines its outward show, 'the motion of a muscle this way or that.' Nor does she in the least foresee those inward consequences which reveal themselves immediately in her husband, and less quickly in herself. It is often said that she understands him well. Had she done so, she never would have urged him on. She knows that he is given to strange fancies; but, not realising what they spring from, she has no idea either that they may gain such power as to ruin the scheme, or that, while they mean present weakness, they mean also perception of the future. At one point in the murder scene the force of his imagination impresses her, and for a moment she is startled; a light threatens to break on her:

> These deeds must not be thought
> After these ways: so, it will make us mad,

she says, with a sudden and great seriousness. And when he goes panting on, 'Methought I heard a voice cry, "Sleep no more,"' . . . she breaks in, 'What do you mean?' half-doubting whether this was not a real voice that he heard. Then, almost directly, she recovers herself, convinced of the vanity of his fancy. Nor does she understand herself any better than him. She never suspects that these deeds *must* be thought after these ways; that her facile realism,

> A little water clears us of this deed,

will one day be answered by herself, 'Will these hands ne'er be clean?' or that the fatal commonplace, 'What's done is done,' will make way for her last despairing sentence, 'What's done cannot be undone.'

Hence the development of her character—perhaps it would be more strictly accurate to say, the change in her state of mind—is both inevitable, and the opposite of the development we traced in Macbeth. When the murder has been done, the discovery of its hideousness, first reflected in the faces of her guests, comes to Lady Macbeth with the shock of a sudden disclosure, and at once her nature begins to sink. The first intimation of the change is given when, in the scene of the discovery, she faints.[3] When next we see her, Queen of Scotland, the glory of her dream has faded. She enters, disillusioned, and weary with want of sleep: she has thrown away everything and gained nothing:

> Nought's had, all's spent,
> Where our desire is got without content:
> 'Tis safer to be that which we destroy
> Than by destruction dwell in doubtful joy.

Henceforth she has no initiative: the stem of her being seems to be cut through. Her husband, physically the stronger, maddened by pangs he had foreseen, but still flaming with life, comes into the foreground, and she retires. Her will remains, and she does her best to help him; but he rarely needs her help. Her chief anxiety appears to be that he should not betray his misery. He plans the murder of Banquo without her knowledge (not in order to spare her, I think, for he never shows love of this quality, but merely because he does not need her now); and even when she is told vaguely of his intention she appears but little interested. In the sudden emergency of the banquet scene she makes a prodigious and magnificent effort; her strength, and with it her ascendancy, returns, and she saves her husband at least from an open disclosure. But after this she takes no part whatever in the action. We only know from her shuddering words in the sleep-walking scene, 'The Thane of Fife had a wife: where is she now?' that she has even learned of her husband's worst crime; and in all the horrors of his tyranny over Scotland she has, so far as we hear, no part. Disillusionment and despair prey upon her more and more. That she should seek any relief in speech, or should ask for sympathy, would seem to her mere weakness, and would be to Macbeth's defiant fury an irritation. Thinking of the change in him, we imagine the bond between them slackened, and Lady Macbeth left much alone. She sinks slowly downward. She cannot bear darkness, and has light by her continually: 'tis her command. At last her nature, not her will, gives way. The secrets of the past find vent in a disorder of sleep, the beginning perhaps of madness. What the doctor fears is clear. He reports to her husband no great physical mischief, but bids her attendant to remove from her all means by which she could harm herself, and to keep eyes on her constantly. It is in vain. Her death is announced by a cry from her women so sudden and direful that it would thrill her husband with horror if he were any longer capable of fear. In the last words of the play Malcolm tells us it is believed in the hostile army that she died by her own hand. And (not to speak of the indications just referred to) it is in accordance with her character that even in her weakest hour she should cut short by one determined stroke the agony of her life.

The sinking of Lady Macbeth's nature, and the marked change in her demeanour to her husband, are most strikingly shown in the conclusion of the banquet scene; and from this point pathos is mingled with awe. The guests are gone. She is completely exhausted, and answers Macbeth in listless, submissive words which seem to come with difficulty. How strange sounds the reply 'Did you send to him, sir?' to his imperious question about Macduff! And when he goes on, 'waxing desperate in imagination,' to speak of new deeds of blood, she seems to sicken at the thought, and there is a deep pathos in that answer which tells at once of her care for him and of the misery she herself has silently endured,

You lack the season of all natures, sleep.

We begin to think of her now less as the awful instigator of murder than as a woman with much that is grand in her, and much that is piteous. Strange and almost ludicrous as the statement may sound,[4] she is, up to her light, a perfect wife. She gives her husband the best she has; and the fact that she never uses to him the terms of affection which, up to this point in the play, he employs to her, is certainly no indication of want of love. She urges, appeals, reproaches, for a practical end, but she never recriminates. The harshness of her taunts is free from mere personal feeling, and also from any deep or more than momentary contempt. She despises what she thinks the weakness which stands in the way of her husband's ambition; but she does not despise *him*. She evidently admires him and thinks him a great man, for whom the throne is the proper place. Her commanding attitude in the moments of his hesitation or fear is probably confined to them. If we consider the peculiar circumstances of the earlier scenes and the banquet scene, and if we examine the language of the wife and husband at other times, we shall come, I think, to the conclusion that their habitual relations are better represented by the later scenes than by the earlier, though naturally they are not truly represented by either. Her ambition for her husband and herself (there was no distinction to her mind) proved fatal to him, far more so than the prophecies of the Witches; but even when she pushed him into murder she believed she was helping him to do what he merely lacked the nerve to attempt; and her part in the crime was so much less open-eyed than his, that, if the impossible and undramatic task of estimating degrees of culpability were forced on us, we should surely have to assign the larger share to Macbeth.

'Lady Macbeth,' says Dr. Johnson, 'is merely detested'; and for a long time critics generally spoke of her as though she were Malcolm's 'fiend-like queen.' In natural reaction we tend to insist, as I have been doing, on the other and less obvious side; and in the criticism of the last century there is even a tendency to sentimentalise the character. But it can hardly be doubted that Shakespeare meant the predominant impression to be one of awe, grandeur, and horror, and that he never meant this impression to be lost, however it might be modified, as Lady Macbeth's activity diminishes and her misery increases. I cannot believe that, when she said of Banquo and Fleance,

> But in them nature's copy's not eterne,

she meant only that they would some day die; or that she felt any surprise when Macbeth replied,

> There's comfort yet: they are assailable;

though I am sure no light came into her eyes when he added those dreadful words, 'Then be thou jocund.' She was listless. She herself would not have moved a finger against Banquo. But she thought his death, and his son's death, might ease her husband's mind, and she suggested the murders indifferently and without remorse. The sleepwalking scene, again, inspires pity, but its main effect is one of awe. There is great horror in the references to blood, but it cannot be said that there is more than horror; and Campbell was surely right when, in alluding to Mrs. Jameson's analysis, he insisted that in Lady Macbeth's misery there is no trace of contrition.[5] Doubtless she would have given the world to undo what she had done; and the thought of it killed her; but, regarding her from the tragic point of view, we may truly say she was too great to repent.[6]

2

The main interest of the character of Banquo arises from the changes that take place in him, and from the influence of the Witches upon him. And it is curious that Shakespeare's intention here is so frequently missed. Banquo being at first strongly contrasted with Macbeth, as an innocent man with a guilty, it seems to be supposed that this contrast must be continued to his death; while, in reality, though it is never removed, it is gradually diminished. Banquo in fact may be described much more truly than Macbeth as the victim of the Witches. If we follow his story this will be evident.

He bore a part only less distinguished than Macbeth's in the battles against Sweno and Macdonwald. He and Macbeth are called 'our captains,' and when they meet the Witches they are traversing, the 'blasted heath'⁷ alone together. Banquo accosts the strange shapes without the slightest fear. They lay their fingers on their lips, as if to signify that they will not, or must not, speak to *him*. To Macbeth's brief appeal, 'Speak, if you can: what are you?' they at once reply, not by saying what they are, but by hailing him Thane of Glamis, Thane of Cawdor, and King hereafter. Banquo is greatly surprised that his partner should start as if in fear, and observes that he is at once 'rapt'; and he bids the Witches, if they know the future, to prophesy to *him*, who neither begs their favour nor fears their hate. Macbeth, looking back at a later time, remembers Banquo's daring, and how

> he chid the sisters,
> When first they put the name of king upon me,
> And bade them speak to him.

'Chid' is an exaggeration; but Banquo is evidently a bold man, probably an ambitious one, and certainly has no lurking guilt in his ambition. On hearing the predictions concerning himself and his descendants he makes no answer, and when the Witches are about to vanish he shows none of Macbeth's feverish anxiety to know more. On their vanishing, he is simply amazed, wonders if they were anything but hallucinations, makes no reference to the predictions till Macbeth mentions them, and then answers lightly.

When Ross and Angus, entering, announce to Macbeth that he has been made Thane of Cawdor, Banquo exclaims, aside, to himself or Macbeth, 'What! can the devil speak true?' He now believes that the Witches were real beings and the 'instruments of darkness.' When Macbeth, turning to him, whispers,

> Do you not hope your children shall be kings,
> When those that gave the Thane of Cawdor to me
> Promised no less to them?

he draws with the boldness of innocence the inference which is really occupying Macbeth, and answers,

> That, trusted home,
> Might yet enkindle you unto the crown
> Beside the thane of Cawdor.

Here he still speaks, I think, in a free, off-hand, even jesting,[8] manner ('enkindle' meaning merely 'excite you to *hope* for'). But then, possibly from noticing something in Macbeth's face, he becomes graver, and goes on, with a significant 'but,'

> But 'tis strange:
> And oftentimes, to win us to our harm,
> The instruments of darkness tell us truths,
> Win us with honest trifles, to betray's
> In deepest consequence.

He afterwards observes for the second time that his partner is 'rapt'; but he explains his abstraction naturally and sincerely by referring to the surprise of his new honours; and at the close of the scene, when Macbeth proposes that they shall discuss the predictions together at some later time, he answers in the cheerful, rather bluff manner, which he has used almost throughout, 'Very gladly.' Nor was there any reason why Macbeth's rejoinder, 'Till then, enough,' should excite misgivings in him, though it implied a request for silence, and though the whole behaviour of his partner during the scene must have looked very suspicious to him when the prediction of the crown was made good through the murder of Duncan.

In the next scene Macbeth and Banquo join the King, who welcomes them both with the kindest expressions of gratitude and with promises of favours to come. Macbeth has indeed already received a noble reward. Banquo, who is said by the King to have 'no less deserved,' receives as yet mere thanks. His brief and frank acknowledgment is contrasted with Macbeth's laboured rhetoric; and, as Macbeth goes out, Banquo turns with hearty praises of him to the King.

And when next we see him, approaching Macbeth's castle in company with Duncan, there is still no sign of change. Indeed he gains on us. It is he who speaks the beautiful lines,

> This guest of summer,
> The temple-haunting martlet, does approve,
> By his loved mansionry, that the heaven's breath

Smells wooingly here: no jutty, frieze,
Buttress, nor coign of vantage, but this bird
Hath made his pendent bed and procreant cradle:
Where they most breed and haunt, I have observed,
The air is delicate;

—lines which tell of that freedom of heart, and that sympathetic sense of peace and beauty, which the Macbeth of the tragedy could never feel.

But now Banquo's sky begins to darken. At the opening of the Second Act we see him with Fleance crossing the court of the castle on his way to bed. The blackness of the moonless, starless night seems to oppress him. And he is oppressed by something else.

A heavy summons lies like lead upon me,
And yet I would not sleep: merciful powers,
Restrain in me the cursed thoughts that nature
Gives way to in repose!

On Macbeth's entrance we know what Banquo means: he says to Macbeth—and it is the first time he refers to the subject unprovoked,

I dreamt last night of the three weird sisters.

His will is still untouched: he would repel the 'cursed thoughts'; and they are mere thoughts, not intentions. But still they are 'thoughts,' something more, probably, than mere recollections; and they bring with them an undefined sense of guilt. The poison has begun to work.

The passage that follows Banquo's words to Macbeth is difficult to interpret:

I dreamt last night of the three weird sisters:
To you they have show'd some truth.
    Macb. I think not of them:
Yet, when we can entreat an hour to serve,
We would spend it in some words upon that business,
If you would grant the time.
    Ban. At your kind'st leisure.
    Macb. If you shall cleave to my consent, when 'tis,
It shall make honour for you.
    Ban. So I lose none
In seeking to augment it, but still keep
My bosom franchised and allegiance clear,
I shall be counselled.

Macb. Good repose the while!
Ban. Thanks, sir: the like to you!

Macbeth's first idea is, apparently, simply to free himself from any suspicion which the discovery of the murder might suggest, by showing himself, just before it, quite indifferent to the predictions, and merely looking forward to a conversation about them at some future time. But why does he go on, 'If you shall cleave,' etc.? Perhaps he foresees that, on the discovery, Banquo cannot fail to suspect him, and thinks it safest to prepare the way at once for an understanding with him (in the original story he makes Banquo his accomplice *before* the murder). Banquo's answer shows three things,— that he fears a treasonable proposal, that he has no idea of accepting it, and that he has no fear of Macbeth to restrain him from showing what is in his mind.

Duncan is murdered. In the scene of discovery Banquo of course appears, and his behaviour is significant. When he enters, and Macduff cries out to him,

> O Banquo, Banquo,
> Our royal master's murdered,

and Lady Macbeth, who has entered a moment before, exclaims,

> Woe, alas!
> What, in our house?

his answer,

> Too cruel anywhere,

shows, as I have pointed out, repulsion, and we may be pretty sure that he suspects the truth at once. After a few words to Macduff he remains absolutely silent while the scene is continued for nearly forty lines. He is watching Macbeth and listening as he tells how he put the chamberlains to death in a frenzy of loyal rage. At last Banquo appears to have made up his mind. On Lady Macbeth's fainting he proposes that they shall all retire, and that they shall afterwards meet,

> And question this most bloody piece of work
> To know it further. Fears and scruples[9] shake us:
> In the great hand of God I stand, and thence
> Against the undivulged pretence[10] I fight
> Of treasonous malice.

His solemn language here reminds us of his grave words about 'the instruments of darkness,' and of his later prayer to the 'merciful powers.' He is profoundly shocked, full of indignation, and determined to play the part of a brave and honest man.

But he plays no such part. When next we see him, on the last day of his life, we find that he has yielded to evil. The Witches and his own ambition have conquered him. He alone of the lords knew of the prophecies, but he has said nothing of them. He has acquiesced in Macbeth's accession, and in the official theory that Duncan's sons had suborned the chamberlains to murder him. Doubtless, unlike Macduff, he was present at Scone to see the new king invested. He has, not formally but in effect, 'cloven to' Macbeth's 'consent'; he is knit to him by 'a most indissoluble tie'; his advice in council has been 'most grave and prosperous'; he is to be the 'chief guest' at that night's supper. And his soliloquy tells us why:

> Thou hast it now: king, Cawdor, Glamis, all,
> As the weird women promised, and, I fear,
> Thou play'dst most foully for't: yet it was said
> It should not stand in thy posterity,
> But that myself should be the root and father
> Of many kings. If there come truth from them—
> As upon thee, Macbeth, their speeches shine—
> Why, by the verities on thee made good,
> May they not be my oracles as well,
> And set me up in hope? But hush! no more.

This 'hush! no more' is not the dismissal of 'cursed thoughts': it only means that he hears the trumpets announcing the entrance of the King and Queen.

His punishment comes swiftly, much more swiftly than Macbeth's, and saves him from any further fall. He is a very fearless man, and still so far honourable that he has no thought of *acting* to bring about the fulfilment of the prophecy which has beguiled him. And therefore he has no fear of Macbeth. But he little understands him. To Macbeth's tormented mind Banquo's conduct appears highly suspicious. *Why* has this bold and circumspect[11] man kept his secret and become his chief adviser? In order to make good *his* part of the predictions after Macbeth's own precedent. Banquo, he is sure, will suddenly and secretly attack him. It is not the far-off accession of Banquo's descendants that he fears; it is (so he tells himself) swift murder; not that the 'barren sceptre' will some day droop from his dying hand, but that it will be 'wrenched' away now (III. i. 62).[12] So he kills Banquo. But the Banquo he kills is not the innocent soldier who met the Witches and daffed their prophecies aside, nor the man who prayed to be delivered from the temptation of his dreams.

Macbeth leaves on most readers a profound impression of the misery of a guilty conscience and the retribution of crime. And the strength of this impression is one of the reasons why the tragedy is admired by readers who shrink from Othello and are made unhappy by *Lear*. But what Shakespeare perhaps felt even more deeply, when he wrote this play, was the *incalculability* of evil,—that in meddling with it human beings do they know not what. The soul, he seems to feel, is a thing of such inconceivable depth, complexity, and delicacy, that when you introduce into it, or suffer to develop in it, any change, and particularly the change called evil, you can form only the vaguest idea of the reaction you will provoke. All you can be sure of is that it will not be what you expected, and that you cannot possibly escape it. Banquo's story, if truly apprehended, produces this impression quite as strongly as the more terrific stories of the chief characters, and perhaps even more clearly, inasmuch as he is nearer to average human nature, has obviously at first a quiet conscience, and uses with evident sincerity the language of religion.

3

Apart from his story Banquo's character is not very interesting, nor is it, I think, perfectly individual. And this holds good of the rest of the minor characters. They are sketched lightly, and are seldom developed further than the strict purposes of the action required. From this point of view they are inferior to several of the less important figures in each of the other three tragedies. The scene in which Lady Macduff and her child appear, and the passage where their slaughter is reported to Macduff, have much dramatic value, but in neither case is the effect due to any great extent to the special characters of the persons concerned. Neither they, nor Duncan, nor Malcolm, nor even Banquo himself, have been imagined intensely, and therefore they do not produce that sense of unique personality which Shakespeare could convey in a much smaller number of lines than he gives to most of them.[13] And this is of course even more the case with persons like Ross, Angus, and Lennox, though each of these has distinguishable features. I doubt if any other great play of Shakespeare's contains so many speeches which a student of the play, if they were quoted to him, would be puzzled to assign to the speakers. Let the reader turn, for instance, to the second scene of the Fifth Act, and ask himself why the names of the persons should not be interchanged in all the ways mathematically possible. Can he find, again, any signs of character by which to distinguish the speeches of Ross and Angus in Act I. scenes ii and iii, or to determine that Malcolm must have spoken I. iv. 2–11? Most of this writing, we may almost say, is simply Shakespeare's writing, not that of Shakespeare become another person. And can anything like the same proportion of such writing be found in *Hamlet*, *Othello*, or *King Lear*?

Is it possible to guess the reason of this characteristic of Macbeth? I cannot believe it is due to the presence of a second hand. The writing mangled by the printer and perhaps by 'the players,' seems to be sometimes obviously Shakespeare's, sometimes sufficiently Shakespearean to repel any attack not based on external evidence. It may be, as the shortness of the play has suggested to some, that Shakespeare was hurried, and, throwing all his weight on the principal characters, did not exert himself in dealing with the rest. But there is another possibility which may be worth considering. *Macbeth* is distinguished by its simplicity,—by grandeur in simplicity, no doubt, but still by simplicity. The two great figures indeed can hardly be called simple, except in comparison with such characters as Hamlet and Iago; but in almost every other respect the tragedy has this quality. Its plot is quite plain. It has very little intermixture of humour. It has little pathos except of the sternest kind. The style, for Shakespeare, has not much variety, being generally kept at a higher pitch than in the other three tragedies; and there is much less than usual of the interchange of verse and prose.[14] All this makes for simplicity of effect. And, this being so, is it not possible that Shakespeare instinctively felt, or consciously feared, that to give much individuality or attraction to the subordinate figures would diminish this effect, and so, like a good artist, sacrificed a part to the whole? And was he wrong? He has certainly avoided the overloading which distresses us in *King Lear*, and has produced a tragedy utterly unlike it, not much less great as a dramatic poem, and as a drama superior.

I would add, though without much confidence, another suggestion. The simplicity of Macbeth is one of the reasons why many readers feel that, in spite of its being intensely 'romantic,' it is less unlike a classical tragedy than *Hamlet* or *Othello* or *King Lear*. And it is possible that this effect is, in a sense, the result of design. I do not mean that Shakespeare intended to imitate a classical tragedy; I mean only that he may have seen in the bloody story of Macbeth a subject suitable for treatment in a manner somewhat nearer to that of Seneca, or of the English Senecan plays familiar to him in his youth, than was the manner of his own mature tragedies. The Witches doubtless are 'romantic,' but so is the witch-craft in Seneca's *Medea and Hercules Oetaeus*; indeed it is difficult to read the account of Medea's preparations (670–739) without being reminded of the incantations in Macbeth. Banquo's Ghost again is 'romantic,' but so are Seneca's ghosts. For the swelling of the style in some of the great passages—however immeasurably superior these may be to anything in Seneca—and certainly for the turgid bombast which occasionally appears in Macbeth, and which seems to have horrified Jonson, Shakespeare might easily have found a model in Seneca. Did he not think that this was the high Roman manner? Does not the Sergeant's speech, as Coleridge observed, recall the style of the 'passionate speech' of the Player in *Hamlet*,—a speech, be it observed,

on a Roman subject?[15] And is it entirely an accident that parallels between
Seneca and Shakespeare seem to be more frequent in *Macbeth* than in any
other of his undoubtedly genuine works except perhaps *Richard III.*, a tragedy
unquestionably influenced either by Seneca or by English Senecan plays?[16]
If there is anything in these suggestions, and if we suppose that Shakespeare
meant to give to his play a certain classical tinge, he might naturally carry
out this idea in respect to the characters, as well as in other respects, by
concentrating almost the whole interest on the important figures and leaving
the others comparatively shadowy.

4

Macbeth being more simple than the other tragedies, and broader and more
massive in effect, three passages in it are of great importance as securing variety
in tone, and also as affording relief from the feelings excited by the Witch-scenes
and the principal characters. They are the passage where the Porter appears, the
conversation between Lady Macduff and her little boy, and the passage where
Macduff receives the news of the slaughter of his wife and babes. Yet the first of
these, we are told even by Coleridge, is unworthy of Shakespeare and is not his;
and the second, with the rest of the scene which contains it, appears to be usually
omitted in stage representations of *Macbeth*.

I question if either this scene or the exhibition of Macduff's grief is required
to heighten our abhorrence of Macbeth's cruelty. They have a technical value
in helping to give the last stage of the action the form of a conflict between
Macbeth and Macduff. But their chief function is of another kind. It is to touch
the heart with a sense of beauty and pathos, to open the springs of love and
of tears. Shakespeare is loved for the sweetness of his humanity, and because
he makes this kind of appeal with such irresistible persuasion; and the reason
why *Macbeth*, though admired as much as any work of his, is scarcely loved, is
that the characters who predominate cannot make this kind of appeal, and at
no point are able to inspire unmingled sympathy. The two passages in question
supply this want in such measure as Shakespeare thought advisable in *Macbeth*,
and the play would suffer greatly from their excision. The second, on the
stage, is extremely moving, and Macbeth's reception of the news of his wife's
death may be intended to recall it by way of contrast. The first brings a relief
even greater, because here the element of beauty is more marked, and because
humour is mingled with pathos. In both we escape from the oppression of
huge sins and sufferings into the presence of the wholesome affections of
unambitious hearts; and, though both scenes are painful and one dreadful, our
sympathies can flow unchecked.[17]

Lady Macduff is a simple wife and mother, who has no thought for anything
beyond her home. Her love for her children shows her at once that her husband's
flight exposes them to terrible danger. She is in an agony of fear for them, and

full of indignation against him. It does not even occur to her that he has acted from public spirit, or that there is such a thing.

What had he done to make him fly the land?

He must have been mad to do it. He fled for fear. He does not love his wife and children. He is a traitor. The poor soul is almost beside herself—and with too good reason. But when the murderer bursts in with the question 'Where is your husband?' she becomes in a moment the wife, and the great noble's wife:

> I hope, in no place so unsanctified
> Where such as thou may'st find him.

What did Shakespeare mean us to think of Macduff's flight, for which Macduff has been much blamed by others beside his wife? Certainly not that fear for himself, or want of love for his family, had anything to do with it. His love for his country, so strongly marked in the scene with Malcolm, is evidently his one motive.

> He is noble, wise, judicious, and best knows
> The fits o' the season,

says Ross. That his flight was 'noble' is beyond doubt. That it was not wise or judicious in the interest of his family is no less clear. But that does not show that it was wrong; and, even if it were, to represent its consequences as a judgment on him for his want of due consideration is equally monstrous and ludicrous.[18] The further question whether he did fail in due consideration, or whether for his country's sake he deliberately risked a danger which he fully realised, would in Shakespeare's theatre have been answered at once by Macduff's expression and demeanour on hearing Malcolm's words,

> Why in that rawness left you wife and child,
> Those precious motives, those strong knots of love,
> Without leave-taking?

It cannot be decided with certainty from the mere text; but, without going into the considerations on each side, I may express the opinion that Macduff knew well what he was doing, and that he fled without leave-taking for fear his purpose should give way. Perhaps he said to himself, with Coriolanus,

> Not of a woman's tenderness to be,
> Requires nor child nor woman's face to see.

Little Macduff suggests a few words on Shakespeare's boys (there are scarcely any little girls). It is somewhat curious that nearly all of them appear in tragic or semi-tragic dramas. I remember but two exceptions: little William Page, who said his *Hic, haec, hoc* to Sir Hugh Evans; and the page before whom Falstaff walked like a sow that hath overwhelmed all her litter but one; and it is to be feared that even this page, if he is the Boy of *Henry V*, came to an ill end, being killed with the luggage.

So wise so young, they say, do ne'er live long,

as Richard observed of the little Prince of Wales. Of too many of these children (some of the 'boys,' *e.g.* those in *Cymbeline*, are lads, not children) the saying comes true. They are pathetic figures, the more so because they so often appear in company with their unhappy mothers, and can never be thought of apart from them. Perhaps Arthur is even the first creation in which Shakespeare's power of pathos showed itself mature;[19] and the last of his children, Mamillius, assuredly proves that it never decayed. They are almost all of them noble figures, too,—affectionate, frank, brave, high-spirited, 'of an open and free nature' like Shakespeare's best men. And almost all of them, again, are amusing and charming as well as pathetic; comical in their mingled acuteness and *naïveté*, charming in their confidence in themselves and the world, and in the seriousness with which they receive the jocosity of their elders, who commonly address them as strong men, great warriors, or profound politicians.

Little Macduff exemplifies most of these remarks. There is nothing in the scene of a transcendent kind, like the passage about Mamillius' never-finished 'Winter's Tale' of the man who dwelt by a churchyard, or the passage about his death, or that about little Marcius and the butterfly, or the audacity which introduces him, at the supreme moment of the tragedy, outdoing the appeals of Volumnia and Virgilia by the statement,

'A shall not tread on me:
I'll run away till I'm bigger, but then I'll fight.

Still one does not easily forget little Macduff's delightful and well-justified confidence in his ability to defeat his mother in argument; or the deep impression she made on him when she spoke of his father as a 'traitor'; or his immediate response when he heard the murderer call his father by the same name,—

Thou liest, thou shag-haired villain.

Nor am I sure that, if the son of Coriolanus had been murdered, his last words to his mother would have been, 'Run away, I pray you.'

I may add two remarks. The presence of this child is one of the things in which *Macbeth* reminds us of *Richard III*. And he is perhaps the only person in the tragedy who provokes a smile. I say 'perhaps,' for though the anxiety of the Doctor to escape from the company of his patient's husband makes one smile, I am not sure that it was meant to.

5

The Porter does not make me smile: the moment is too terrific. He is grotesque; no doubt the contrast he affords is humorous as well as ghastly; I dare say the groundlings roared with laughter at his coarsest remarks. But they are not comic enough to allow one to forget for a moment what has preceded and what must follow. And I am far from complaining of this. I believe that it is what Shakespeare intended, and that he despised the groundlings if they laughed. Of course he could have written without the least difficulty speeches five times as humorous; but he knew better. The Grave-diggers make us laugh: the old Countryman who brings the asps to Cleopatra makes us smile at least. But the Grave-digger scene does not come at a moment of extreme tension; and it is long. Our distress for Ophelia is not so absorbing that we refuse to be interested in the man who digs her grave, or even continue throughout the long conversation to remember always with pain that the grave is hers. It is fitting, therefore, that he should be made decidedly humorous. The passage in *Antony and Cleopatra* is much nearer to the passage in *Macbeth*, and seems to have been forgotten by those who say that there is nothing in Shakespeare resembling that passage.[20] The old Countryman comes at a moment of tragic exaltation, and the dialogue is appropriately brief. But the moment, though tragic, is emphatically one of exaltation. We have not been feeling horror, nor are we feeling a dreadful suspense. We are going to see Cleopatra die, but she is to die gloriously and to triumph over Octavius. And therefore our amusement at the old Countryman and the contrast he affords to these high passions, is untroubled, and it was right to make him really comic. But the Porter's case is quite different. We cannot forget how the knocking that makes him grumble sounded to Macbeth, or that within a few minutes of his opening the gate Duncan will be discovered in his blood; nor can we help feeling that in pretending to be porter of hell-gate he is terribly near the truth. To give him language so humorous that it would ask us almost to lose the sense of these things would have been a fatal mistake,—the kind of mistake that means want of dramatic imagination. And that was not the sort of error into which Shakespeare fell.

To doubt the genuineness of the passage, then, on the ground that it is not humorous enough for Shakespeare, seems to me to show this want. It is to judge the passage as though it were a separate composition, instead of conceiving it in the fulness of its relations to its surroundings in a stage-play. Taken by itself, I admit, it would bear no indubitable mark of Shakespeare's authorship, not even in the phrase 'the primrose way to the everlasting bonfire,' which Coleridge thought Shakespeare might have added to an interpolation of 'the players.' And if there were reason (as in my judgment there is not) to suppose that Shakespeare thus permitted an interpolation, or that he collaborated with another author, I could believe that he left 'the players' or his collaborator to write the *words* of the passage. But that anyone except the author of the scene of Duncan's murder *conceived* the passage, is incredible.[21]

The speeches of the Porter, a low comic character, are in prose. So is the letter of Macbeth to his wife. In both these cases Shakespeare follows his general rule or custom. The only other prose-speeches occur in the sleep-walking scene, and here the use of prose may seem strange. For in great tragic scenes we expect the more poetic medium of expression, and this is one of the most famous of such scenes. Besides, unless I mistake, Lady Macbeth is the only one of Shakespeare's great tragic characters who on a last appearance is denied the dignity of verse.

Yet in this scene also he adheres to his custom. Somnambulism is an abnormal condition, and it is his general rule to assign prose to persons whose state of mind is abnormal. Thus, to illustrate from these four plays, Hamlet when playing the madman speaks prose, but in soliloquy, in talking with Horatio, and in pleading with his mother, he speaks verse.[22] Ophelia in her madness either sings snatches of songs or speaks prose. Almost all Lear's speeches, after he has become definitely insane, are in prose: where he wakes from sleep recovered, the verse returns. The prose enters with that speech which closes with his trying to tear off his clothes; but he speaks in verse—some of it very irregular—in the Timon-like speeches where his intellect suddenly in his madness seems to regain the force of his best days (IV. vi.). Othello, in IV. i., speaks in verse till the moment when Iago tells him that Cassio has confessed. There follow ten lines of prose—exclamations and mutterings of bewildered horror—and he falls to the ground unconscious.

The idea underlying this custom of Shakespeare's evidently is that the regular rhythm of verse would be inappropriate where the mind is supposed to have lost its balance and to be at the mercy of chance impressions coming from without (as sometimes with Lear), or of ideas emerging from its unconscious depths and pursuing one another across its passive surface. The somnambulism of Lady Macbeth is such a condition. There is no rational connection in the sequence of images and ideas. The sight of blood on her hand, the sound of the clock striking the hour for Duncan's murder, the hesitation of her husband before that hour came, the vision of the old man in his blood, the idea of the murdered wife of Macduff, the sight of the hand again, Macbeth's 'flaws and starts' at the sight of Banquo's ghost, the smell on her hand, the washing of hands after Duncan's murder again, her husband's fear of the buried Banquo, the sound of the knocking at the gate—these possess her, one after another, in this chance order. It is not much less accidental than the order of Ophelia's ideas; the great difference is that with Ophelia total insanity has effaced or greatly weakened the emotional force of the ideas, whereas to Lady Macbeth each new image or perception comes laden with anguish. There is, again, scarcely a sign of the exaltation of disordered imagination; we are conscious rather of an intense suffering which forces its way into light against resistance, and speaks a language for the most part strikingly bare in its diction and simple in its construction. This language stands in strong contrast with that of Macbeth in the surrounding scenes, full of a feverish and almost furious excitement, and seems to express a far more desolating misery.

The effect is extraordinarily impressive. The soaring pride and power of Lady Macbeth's first speeches return on our memory, and the change is felt with a breathless awe. Any attempt, even by Shakespeare, to draw out the moral enfolded in this awe, would but weaken it. For the moment, too, all the language of poetry—even of Macbeth's poetry—seems to be touched with unreality, and these brief toneless sentences seem the only voice of truth.[23]

NOTES

1. So Mrs. Siddons is said to have given the passage.

2. Surely the usual interpretation of 'We fail?' as a question of contemptuous astonishment, is right. 'We fail!' gives practically the same sense, but alters the punctuation of the first two Folios. In either case, 'But,' I think, means 'Only.' On the other hand the proposal to read 'We fail.' with a full stop, as expressive of sublime acceptance of the possibility, seems to me, however attractive at first sight, quite out of harmony with Lady Macbeth's mood throughout these scenes.

3. See Note DD.

4. It is not new.

5. The words about Lady Macduff are of course significant of natural human feeling, and may have been introduced expressly to mark it, but they do not, I think, show any fundamental change in Lady Macbeth, for at no time would she have suggested or approved a purposeless atrocity. It is perhaps characteristic that this human feeling should show itself most clearly in reference to an act for which she was not directly responsible, and in regard to which therefore she does not feel the instinct of self-assertion.

6. The tendency to sentimentalise Lady Macbeth is partly due to Mrs. Siddons's fancy that she was a small, fair, blue-eyed woman, 'perhaps even fragile.' Dr. Bucknill, who was unacquainted with this fancy, independently determined that she was 'beautiful and delicate,' 'unoppressed by weight of flesh,' 'probably small,' but 'a tawny or brown blonde,' with grey eyes: and Brandes affirms that she was lean, slight, and hard. They know much more than Shakespeare, who tells us absolutely nothing on these subjects. That Lady Macbeth, after taking part in a murder, was so exhausted as to faint, will hardly demonstrate her fragility. That she must have been blue-eyed, fair, or red-haired, because she was a Celt, is a bold inference, and it is an idle dream that Shakespeare had any idea of making her or her husband characteristically Celtic. The only evidence ever offered to prove that she was small is the sentence, 'All the perfumes of Arabia will not sweeten this

little hand'; and Goliath might have called his hand 'little' in contrast with all the perfumes of Arabia. One might as well propose to prove that Othello was a small man by quoting,

> I have seen the day,
> That, with this little arm and this good sword,
> I have made my way through more impediments
> Than twenty times your stop.

The reader is at liberty to imagine Lady Macbeth's person in the way that pleases him best, or to leave it, as Shakespeare very likely did, unimagined.

Perhaps it may be well to add that there is not the faintest trace in the play of the idea occasionally met with, and to some extent embodied in Madame Bernhardt's impersonation of Lady Macbeth, that her hold upon her husband lay in seductive attractions deliberately exercised. Shakespeare was not unskilled or squeamish in indicating such ideas.

7. That it is Macbeth who feels the harmony between the desolation of the heath and the figures who appear on it is a characteristic touch.

8. So, in Holinshed, 'Banquho jested with him and sayde, now Makbeth thou haste obtayned those things which the twoo former sisters prophesied, there remayneth onely for thee to purchase that which the third sayd should come to passe.'

9. = doubts.

10. = design.

11.   'tis much he dares,
> And, to that dauntless temper of his mind,
> He hath a wisdom that doth guide his valour
> To act in safety.

12. So when he hears that Fleance has escaped he is not much troubled (III. iv. 29):

> the worm that's fled
> Hath nature that in time will venom breed,
> No teeth for the present.

I have repeated above what I have said before, because the meaning of Macbeth's soliloquy is frequently misconceived.

13. Virgilia in *Coriolanus* is a famous example. She speaks about thirty-five lines.

14. The percentage of prose is, roughly, in *Hamlet* 30⅔, in *Othello* 16⅓, in *King Lear* 27⅓, in *Macbeth* 8½.

15. Cf. Note F. There are also in *Macbeth* several shorter passages which recall the Player's speech. Cf. 'Fortune . . . showed like a rebel's whore' (I. ii. 14) 'Out! out! thou strumpet Fortune!' The form 'eterne' occurs in Shakespeare only in *Macbeth*, III. ii. 38, and in the 'proof eterne' of the Player's speech. Cf. 'So, as a painted tyrant, Pyrrhus stood,' with *Macbeth*, V. viii. 26; 'the rugged Pyrrhus, like the Hyrcanian beast,' with 'the rugged Russian bear . . . or the Hyrcan tiger' (*Macbeth*, III. iv. 100); 'like a neutral to his will and matter' with *Macbeth*, I. v. 47. The words 'Till he unseam'd him from the nave to the chaps,' in the Serjeant's speech, recall the words 'Then from the navel to the throat at once He ript old Priam,' in

Dido Queen of Carthage, where these words follow those others, about Priam falling with the mere wind of Pyrrhus' sword, which seem to have suggested 'the whiff and wind of his fell sword' in the Player's speech.

16. See Cunliffe, *The Influence of Seneca on Elizabethan Tragedy*. The most famous of these parallels is that between 'Will all great Neptune's Ocean,' etc., and the following passages:

> Quis eluet me Tanais? aut quae barbaris
> Maeotis undis Pontico incumbens mari?
> Non ipse toto magnus Oceano pater
> Tantum expiarit sceleris. (*Hipp.* 715.)

> Quis Tanais, aut quis Nilus, aut quis Persica
> Violentus unda Tigris, aut Rhenus ferox,
> Tagusve Ibera turbidus gaza fluens,
> Abluere dextram poterit? Arctoum licet
> Maeotis in me gelida transfundat mare,
> Et tota Tethys per meas currat manus,
> Haerebit altum facinus. (*Herc. Furens*, 1323.)

(The reader will remember Othello's 'Pontic sea' with its 'violent pace.') Medea's incantation in Ovid's *Metamorphoses*, vii. 197 ff., which certainly suggested Prospero's speech, *Tempest*, V. i. 33 ff., should be compared with Seneca, *Herc. Oet.*, 452 ff., 'Artibus magicis,' etc. It is of course highly probable that Shakespeare read some Seneca at school. I may add that in the *Hippolytus*, beside the passage quoted above, there are others which might have furnished him with suggestions. Cf. for instance *Hipp.*, 30 ff., with the lines about the Spartan hounds in *Mids. Night's Dream*, IV. i. 117 ff., and Hippolytus' speech, beginning 483, with the Duke's speech in *As You Like It*, II. i.

17. Cf Coleridge's note on the Lady Macduff scene.

18. It is nothing to the purpose that Macduff himself says,

> Sinful Macduff,
> They were all struck for thee! naught that I am,
> Not for their own demerits, but for mine,
> Fell slaughter on their souls.

There is no reason to suppose that the sin and demerit he speaks of is that of leaving his home. And even if it were, it is Macduff that speaks, not Shakespeare, any more than Shakespeare speaks in the preceding sentence,

> Did heaven look on,
> And would not take their part?

And yet Brandes (ii. 104) hears in these words 'the voice of revolt . . . that sounds later through the despairing philosophy of *King Lear*.' It sounds a good deal earlier too; *e.g.* in *Tit. And.*, IV. i. 81, and *2 Henry VI.*, II. i. 154. The idea is a commonplace of Elizabethan tragedy.

19. And the idea that it was the death of his son Hamnet, aged eleven, that brought this power to maturity is one of the more plausible attempts to find in his dramas a reflection of his private history. It implies however as late a date as 1596 for *King John*.

20. Even if this were true, the retort is obvious that neither is there anything resembling the murder-scene in *Macbeth*.

21. I have confined myself to the single aspect of this question on which I had what seemed something new to say. Professor Hales's defence of the passage on fuller grounds, in the admirable paper reprinted in his *Notes and Essays on Shakespeare*, seems to me quite conclusive. I may add two notes. (1) The references in the Porter's speeches to 'equivocation,' which have naturally, and probably rightly, been taken as allusions to the Jesuit Garnet's appeal to the doctrine of equivocation in defence of his perjury when on trial for participation in the Gunpowder Plot, do not stand alone in *Macbeth*. The later prophecies of the Witches Macbeth calls 'the equivocation of the fiend That lies like truth' (V. v. 43); and the Porter's remarks about the equivocator who 'could swear in both the scales against either scale, who committed treason enough for God's sake, yet could not equivocate to heaven,' may be compared with the following dialogue (IV. ii. 45):

> *Son.* What is a traitor?
> *Lady Macduff.* Why, one that swears and lies.
> *Son.* And be all traitors that do so?
> *Lady Macduff.* Everyone that does so is a traitor, and must be hanged.

Garnet, as a matter of fact, *was* hanged in May, 1606; and it is to be feared that the audience applauded this passage.

(2) The Porter's soliloquy on the different applicants for admittance has, in idea and manner, a marked resemblance to Pompey's soliloquy on the inhabitants of the prison, in *Measure for Measure*, IV. iii. 1 ff.; and the dialogue between him and Abhorson on the 'mystery' of hanging (IV. ii. 22 ff.) is of just the same kind as the Porter's dialogue with Macduff about drink.

22. In the last Act, however, he speaks in verse even in the quarrel with Laertes at Ophelia's grave. It would be plausible to explain this either from his imitating what he thinks the rant of Laertes, or by supposing that his 'towering passion' made him forget to act the madman. But in the final scene also he speaks in verse in the presence of all. This again might be accounted for by saying that he is supposed to be in a lucid interval, as indeed his own language at 239 ff. implies. But the probability is that Shakespeare's real reason for breaking his rule here was simply that he did not choose to deprive Hamlet of verse on his last appearance. I wonder the disuse of prose in these two scenes has not been observed, and used as an argument, by those who think that Hamlet, with the commission in his pocket, is now resolute.

23. The verse-speech of the Doctor, which closes this scene, lowers the tension towards that of the next scene. His introductory conversation with the Gentlewoman is written in prose (sometimes very near verse), partly, perhaps, from its familiar character, but chiefly because Lady Macbeth is to speak in prose.

1916—Sigmund Freud. "Remarks on *Macbeth*," from *Some Character-types Met With in Psychoanalytic Work*

Sigmund Freud (1856-1939) was a neurologist and psychiatrist who cofounded the psychoanalytic school of psychology. Best known for his theories of the unconscious mind, Freud is the author of *The Interpretation of Dreams* (1899), *On Narcissism* (1914), and *Beyond the Pleasure Principle* (1920).

Shakespeare's *Macbeth* is a *pièce d'occasion*, written for the accession of James, who had hitherto been King of Scotland. The plot was ready-made, and had been handled by other contemporary writers, whose work Shakespeare probably made use of in his customary manner. It offered remarkable analogies to the actual situation. The 'virginal' Elizabeth, of whom it was rumoured that she had never been capable of childbearing and who had once described herself as 'a barren stock', in an anguished outcry at the news of James's birth, was obliged by this very childlessness of hers to let the Scottish king become her successor. And he was the son of that Mary Stuart whose execution she, though reluctantly, had decreed, and who, despite the clouding of their relations by political concerns, was yet of her blood and might be called her guest.

The accession of James I. was like a demonstration of the curse of unfruitfulness and the blessings reserved for those who carry on the race. And Shakespeare's *Macbeth* develops on the theme of this same contrast. The three Fates, the 'weird sisters,' have assured him that he shall indeed be king, but to Banquo they promise that *his* children shall obtain possession of the crown. Macbeth is incensed by this decree of destiny; he is not content with the satisfaction of his own ambition, he desires to found a dynasty and not to have murdered for the benefit of strangers. This point is overlooked when Shakespeare's play is regarded only as a tragedy of ambition. It is clear that Macbeth cannot live for ever, and thus there is but one way for him to disprove that part of the prophecy which opposes his wishes—namely, to have children himself, children who can succeed him. And he seems to expect them from his vigorous wife:

Bring forth men-children only!
For thy undaunted mettle should compose
Nothing but males. . . . (Act l. Sc. 7.)

And equally it is clear that if he is deceived in this expectation he must submit to destiny; otherwise his actions lose all purpose and are transformed into the blind fury of one doomed to destruction, who is resolved to destroy beforehand all that he can reach. We watch Macbeth undergo this development, and at the height of the tragedy we hear that shattering cry from Macduff, which has often ere now been recognized to have many meanings and possibly to contain the key to the change in Macbeth:

He has no children! (Act IV. Sc. 3.)

Undoubtedly that signifies 'Only because he is himself childless could he murder my children'; but more may be implied in it, and above all it might be said to lay bare the essential motive which not only forces Macbeth to go far beyond his own true nature, but also assails the hard character of his wife at its only weak place. If one looks back upon *Macbeth* from the culmination reached in these words of Macduff's, one sees that the whole play is sown with references to the father-and-children relation. The murder of the kindly Duncan is little else than parricide; in Banquo's case, Macbeth kills the father while the son escapes him; and he kills Macduff's children because the father has fled from him. A bloody child, and then a crowned one, are shown him by the witches in the conjuration-scene; the armed head seen previously is doubtless Macbeth's own. But in the background arises the sinister form of the avenger, Macduff, who is himself an exception to the laws of generation, since he was not born of his mother but ripp'd from her womb.

It would be a perfect example of poetic justice in the manner of the talion if the childlessness of Macbeth and the barrenness of his Lady were the punishment for their crimes against the sanctity of geniture—if Macbeth could not become a father because he had robbed children of their father and a father of his children, and if Lady Macbeth had suffered the unsexing she had demanded of the spirits of murder. I believe one could without more ado explain the illness of Lady Macbeth, the transformation of her callousness into penitence, as a reaction to her childlessness, by which she is convinced of her impotence against the decrees of nature, and at the same time admonished that she has only herself to blame if her crime has been barren of the better part of its desired results.

In the *Chronicle* of Holinshed (1577), whence Shakespeare took the plot of *Macbeth*, Lady Macbeth is only once mentioned as the ambitious wife who instigates her husband to murder that she may herself be queen. Of her subsequent fate and of the development of her character there is no word at all. On the other hand, it would seem that there the change in Macbeth to a sanguinary tyrant is motivated just in the way we have suggested. For in Holinshed ten years pass between the murder of Duncan, whereby Macbeth becomes king, and his further misdeeds; and in these ten years he is shown as a stern but righteous ruler. It is not until after this period that the change begins in him, under the influence of the tormenting apprehension that the prophecy to Banquo will be fulfilled as was that of his own destiny. Then only does he contrive the murder of Banquo, and, as in Shakespeare, is driven from one crime to another. Holinshed does not expressly say that it was his childlessness which urged him to these courses, but there is warrant enough—both time and occasion—for this probable motivation. Not so in Shakespeare. Events crowd breathlessly on one another in the tragedy, so that to judge by the statements made by the persons in the play about one week represents the duration of time assigned to it. This acceleration takes the ground from under our attempts at reconstructing the motives for the change in the characters of Macbeth and his wife. There is no time for a long-drawn disappointment of their hopes of offspring to enervate the woman and drive the man to an insane defiance; and it remains impossible to resolve the contradiction that so many subtle interrelations in the plot, and between it and its occasion, point to a common origin of them in the motive of childlessness, and that yet the period of time in the tragedy expressly precludes a development of character from any but a motive contained in the play.

What, however, these motives can have been which in so short a space of time could turn the hesitating, ambitious man into an unbridled tyrant, and his steely-hearted instigator into a sick woman gnawed by remorse, it is, in my view, impossible to divine. I think we must renounce the hope of penetrating the triple obscurity of the bad preservation of the text, the unknown intention of the dramatist, and the hidden purport of the legend. But I should not admit that such investigations are idle in view of the powerful effect which the tragedy has upon the spectator. The dramatist can indeed, during the representation, overwhelm us by his art and paralyse our powers of reflection; but he cannot prevent us from subsequently attempting to grasp the psychological mechanism of that effect. And the contention that the dramatist is at liberty to shorten at will the natural time and duration of the events he brings before us, if by the sacrifice of common probability he can enhance the dramatic effect, seems to me irrelevant in this instance. For such a sacrifice is justified only when it merely affronts probability, and not when it breaks the causal connection; besides, the dramatic effect would hardly have suffered if the time-duration had been left in uncertainty, instead of being expressly limited to some few days.

One is so unwilling to dismiss a problem like that of *Macbeth* as insoluble that I will still make another attempt, by introducing another comment which points towards a new issue. Ludwig Jekels, in a recent Shakespearean study, thinks he has divined a technical trick of the poet, which might have to be reckoned with in *Macbeth*, too. He is of opinion that Shakespeare frequently splits up a character into two personages, each of whom then appears not altogether comprehensible until once more conjoined with the other. I might be thus with Macbeth and the Lady: and then it would of course be futile to regard her as an independent personage and seek to discover her motivation without considering the Macbeth who completes her. I shall not follow this hint any further, but I would add, nevertheless, a remark which strikingly confirms the idea—namely, that the stirrings of fear which arise in Macbeth on the night of the murder, do not develop further in him, but in the Lady. It is he who has the hallucination of the dagger before the deed, but it is she who later succumbs to mental disorder; he, after the murder, hears the cry from the house: 'Sleep no more! Macbeth does murder sleep . . .', and so 'Macbeth shall sleep no more,' but we never hear that King Macbeth could not sleep, while we see that the Queen rises from her bed and betrays her guilt in somnambulistic wanderings. He stands helpless with bloody hands, lamenting that not great Neptune's ocean can wash them clean again, while she comforts him: 'A little water clears us of this deed'; but later it is she who washes her hands for a quarter of an hour and cannot get rid of the blood-stains. 'All the perfumes of Arabia will not sweeten this little hand.' Thus is fulfilled in her what his pangs of conscience had apprehended; she is incarnate remorse after the deed, he incarnate defiance—together they exhaust the possibilities of reaction to the crime, like two disunited parts of the mind of a single individuality, and perhaps they are the divided images of a single prototype.

1917—Arthur Quiller-Couch.
"Macbeth," from *Notes on Shakespeare's Workmanship*

Sir Arthur Quiller-Couch (1863–1944) was a Fellow of Jesus College, Cambridge, and King Edward VII Professor of English Literature. He is the author of *On the Art of Reading* (1920), *Charles Dickens and other Victorians* (1925), and *Paternity in Shakespeare* (1932).

---

(1)

I propose to take a single work of art, of admitted excellence, and consider its workmanship. I choose Shakespeare's tragedy of *Macbeth* as being eminently such a work: single or complete in itself, strongly imagined, simply constructed, and in its way excellent beyond any challenging.

There are, of course, many other aspects from which so unchallengeable a masterpiece deserves to be studied. We may seek, for example, and seek usefully, to fix its date and define its place in order of time among Shakespeare's writings; but this has been done for us, nearly enough. Or we may search it for light on Shakespeare, the man himself, and on his history—so obscure in the main, though here and there lit up by flashes of evidence, contemporary and convincing so far as they go. For my part, while admitting such curiosity to be human, and

suffering myself now and again to be intrigued by it, I could never believe in it as
a pursuit that really mattered. All literature must be personal: yet the artist—the
great artist—dies into his work, and in that survives. What dread hand designed
the Sphinx? What dread brain conceived its site, there, overlooking the desert?
What sort of man was he who contrived Memnon, with a voice to answer the
sunrise? What were the domestic or extra-domestic habits of Pheidias? Whom
did Villon rob or Cellini cheat or Molière mock? Why did Shakespeare bequeath
to his wife his second-best bed? These are questions which, as Sir Thomas
Browne would say, admit a wide solution, and I allow some of them to be
fascinating. "Men are we," and must needs wonder, a little wistfully, concerning
the forerunners, our kinsmen who, having achieved certain things we despair to
improve or even to rival, have gone their way, leaving so much to be guessed.
"How splendid," we say, "to have known them! Let us delve back and discover
all we can about them!"

> Brave lads in olden musical centuries
> Sang, night by night, adorable choruses,
>   Sat late by alehouse doors in April,
> Chaunting in joy as the moon was rising.
>
> Moon-seen and merry, under the trellises,
> Flush-faced they played with old polysyllables;
>   Spring scents inspired, old wine diluted,
> Love and Apollo were there to chorus.
>
> Now these, the songs, remain to eternity,
> Those, only those, the bountiful choristers
>   Gone—those are gone, those unremembered
> Sleep and are silent in earth for ever.

No: it is no ignoble quarrel we hold with Time over these men. But, after all,
the moral of it is summed up in a set of verses ascribed to Homer, in which he
addresses the Delian Women. "Farewell to you all," he says, "and remember me
in time to come: and when any one of men on earth, a stranger from far, shall
enquire of you, 'O maidens, who is the sweetest of minstrels here about? and in
whom do you most delight?' then make answer modestly, 'Sir, it is a blind man,
and he lives in steep Chios.'"

But the shutters are up at *The Mermaid*: and, after all, it is the masterpiece
that matters—the Sphinx herself, the *Iliad*, the Parthenon, the Perseus, the song
of the Old Héaulmières, *Tartufe*, *Macbeth*.

Lastly, I shall not attempt a *general* criticism of *Macbeth*, because that work has been done, exquisitely and (I think) perdurably, by Dr. Bradley, in his published *Lectures on Shakespearian Tragedy*, a book which I can hardly start to praise without using the language of extravagance: a book which I hold to belong to the first order of criticism, to be a true ornament of our times. Here and there, to be sure, I cannot accept Dr. Bradley's judgment: but it would profit my readers little to be taken point by point through these smaller questions at issue, and (what is more) I have not the necessary self-confidence.

If, however, we spend a little while in considering *Macbeth* as a *piece of workmanship* (or artistry, if you prefer it), we shall be following a new road which seems worth a trial—perhaps better worth a trial just because it lies off the trodden way; and whether it happen or not to lead us out upon some fresh and lively view of this particular drama, it will at least help us by the way to clear our thoughts upon dramatic writing and its method: while I shall not be false to my belief in the virtue of starting upon any chosen work of literature *absolutely*, with minds intent on discovering just that upon which the author's mind was intent.

I shall assume that *Macbeth* is an eminently effective play; that, by consent, it produces a great, and intended, impression on the mind. It is the shortest of Shakespeare's plays, save only *The Comedy of Errors*. It is told in just under 2,000 lines—scarcely more than half the length of *Hamlet*. We may attribute this brevity in part—and we shall attribute it rightly—to its simplicity of plot, but that does not matter; or, rather, it goes all to *Macbeth*'s credit. The half of artistry consists in learning to make one stroke better than two. The more simply, economically, you produce the impression aimed at, the better workman you may call yourself.

Now what had Shakespeare to *do*? He—a tried and competent dramatist—had to write a play: and if it be answered that everybody knew this without my telling it, I reply that it is the first thing some commentators forget. This play had to be an 'acting play': by which of course I mean a play to succeed on the boards and entertain, for three hours or so,[1] an audience which had paid to be entertained. This differentiates it at once from a literary composition meant to be read by the fireside, where the kettle does all the hissing. Therefore, to understand what Shakespeare as a workman was driving at, we must in imagination seat ourselves amid the audience he had in mind as he worked.

Moreover we must imagine ourselves in the Globe Theatre, Southwark, different in so many respects from the playhouses we know: because at every point of difference we meet with some condition of which Shakespeare had to take account. The stage, raised pretty much as it is nowadays, was bare and ran out for some way into the auditorium, the central area of which was unroofed. Thus—the fashionable time for the theatre being the afternoon—the action, or a part of it, took place in daylight. When daylight waned, lanterns were called in and some may agree with me, after studying Shakespeare's sense of darkness and its artistic value, that it were worth while, with this in mind, to tabulate the times of year, so far as we can ascertain them, at which his several plays were first performed. For my part, I am pretty sure that, among other conditions, he worked with an eye on the almanac.

To return to the stage of the Globe Theatre.—Not only did it run out into the auditorium: the audience returned the compliment by overflowing *it*. Stools, ranged along either side of it, were much in demand by young gentlemen who wished to show off their fine clothes. These young gentlemen smoked—or, as they put it, "drank"—tobacco in clay pipes. So the atmosphere was free and easy; in its way (I suspect) not much unlike that of the old music-halls I frequented in graceless days, where a corpulent chairman called for drinks for which, if privileged to know him and sit beside him, you subsequently paid; where all joined companionably in a chorus; where a wink from the singer would travel—I know not how—around four-fifths of a complete circle.

The Elizabethan theatre had no painted scenery;[2] or little, and that of the rudest. At the back of the stage, at some little height above the heads of the players, projected a narrow gallery, or platform, with (as I suppose) a small doorway behind it, and a 'practicable' ladder to give access to it or be removed, as occasion demanded. Fix the ladder, and it became the stairway leading to Duncan's sleeping-chamber: take it away, and the gallery became the battlements of Dunsinane, or Juliet's balcony, or Brabantio's window, or Shylock's from which Jessica drops the coffer, or Cleopatra's up to which she hales dying Antony. From the door of this gallery to the floor of the stage depended draperies which, as they were drawn close or opened, gave you the arras behind which Falstaff was discovered in slumber, or Polonius stabbed, the tomb of Juliet, Desdemona's bed, the stage for the play-scenes in *Hamlet* and the *Midsummer-Night's Dream*, the cave of Prospero or of Hecate.

To right and left of this draped alcove, beyond the pillars supporting the gallery, were two doors giving on the back and the green-room—*mimorum aedes*—for the entrances and exits of the players.

Such was the Elizabethan theatre, with an audience so disposed that, as Sir Walter Raleigh puts it, "the groups of players were seen from many points of view, and had to aim at statuesque rather than pictorial effect." When we take this into account with the daylight and the lack of scenic background, we at once realise that it *must* have been so, and that these were the conditions under which Shakespeare wrought for success.

I must add another, though without asking it to be taken into account just here. I must add it because, the more we consider it, the more we are likely to count it the heaviest handicap of all. All female parts were taken by boys. Reflect upon this, and listen to Lady Macbeth:

> I have given suck, and know
> How tender 'tis to love the babe that milks me:
> I would, while it was smiling in my face,
> Have pluck'd my nipple from his boneless gums,
> And dash'd the brains out, had I so sworn as you
> Have done to this.

That in the mouth of a boy! Shakespeare's triumph over this condition will remain a wonder, however closely it be studied. Nevertheless, there it was: a condition which, having to lay account with it, he magnificently over-rode.

It were pedantic, of course, to lay upon a modern man the strain of constantly visualising that old theatre on the Bankside when reading Shakespeare, or, when seeing him acted, perpetually reminding himself, "He did not write it for *this*." He did not, to be sure. But so potent was his genius that it has carried his work past the conditions of his own age to reincarnate, to revive, it in unabated vigour in later ages and under new conditions, even as the *Iliad* has survived the harp and the warriors' feast. This adaptable vitality is the test of first-rate genius; and, save Shakespeare's, few dramas of the great Elizabethan age have passed it. But as for Shakespeare, I verily believe that, could his large masculine spirit revisit London, it would—whatever the *dilettante* and the superior person may say—rejoice in what has been done to amplify that cage against which we have his own word that he fretted, and would be proud of the care his countrymen, after three centuries, take to interpret him worthily: and this although I seem to catch, together with a faint smell of brimstone, his comments on the 'star' performer of these days, with the limelight following him about the stage and analysing the rainbow upon his glittering eye. These things, however, Shakespeare could not foresee: and we must seek back to the limitations of *his* theatre for our present purpose, to understand what a workman he was.

(2)

We pass, then, from the *conditions* under which he built his plays to the *material* out of which he had to build this particular one. The material of *Macbeth*, as we know, he found in Raphael Holinshed's *Chronicles of Scotland*, first published in 1578 (but he appears to have read the second edition, of 1587). It lies scattered about in various passages in the separate chronicles of King Duncan, King Duff, King Kenneth, King Macbeth; but we get the gist of it in two passages from the *Chronicle of King Duncan*. There is no need to quote them in full: but the purport of the first may be gathered from its opening:—

> Shortly after happened a strange and uncouth wonder. . . . It fortuned
> as Macbeth and Banquho journeyed towards Fores, where the king as

then lay, they went sporting by the way together without other companie save only themselves, passing through the woodes and fieldes, when sodenly, in the middes of a launde, there met them 3 women in strange and ferly apparell, resembling creatures of an elder worlde; whom they attentively behelde, wondering much at the sight.

Then follow the prophecies: "All hayle, Makbeth, Thane of Glammis," etc., with the promise to Banquho that "contrarily thou in deede shall not reigne at all, but of thee shall be borne which shall governe the Scottish Kingdome by long order of continuall descent." I pause on that for a moment, merely because it gives a reason, if a secondary one, why the story should attract Shakespeare: for James I, a descendant of Banquho, had come to be King of England. Actors and playwrights have ever an eye for 'topical' opportunity, and value that opportunity none the less if it be one to flatter a reigning house.

I take up the quotation at a later point:—

The same night at supper Banquho jested with him and sayde, Nowe Makbeth thou hast obtayned those things which the two former sisters prophesied, there remayneth only for thee to purchase that which the thyrd sayd should come to passe. Whereupon Makbeth, revolving the thing in his mind even then, began to devise how he mighte attayne to the kingdome.

Next we read that Duncan, by appointing his young son, Malcolm, Prince of Cumberland, "as it were thereby to appoint him his successor in the Kingdome," sorely troubled Macbeth's ambition, insomuch that he now began to think of usurping the kingdom by force. The *Chronicle* goes on:—

The wordes of the three weird sisters also (of whome before ye have heard) greatly encouraged him hereunto, but specially his wife lay sore upon him to attempt the thing, as she that was very ambitious, burning in unquenchable desire to beare the name of a Queene. At length, therefore, communicating his proposed intent with his trustie friendes, amongst whom Banquho was the chiefest, upon confidence of their promised ayde, he slewe the king at Envernes (or as some say at Botgosuane) in the VI year of his reygne.

The *Chronicle* proceeds to tell how Macbeth had himself crowned at Scone; how he reigned (actually for a considerable time); how he got rid of Banquho; how Banquho's son escaped; how Birnam Wood came to Dunsinane, with much more that is handled in the tragedy; and ends (so far as we are concerned) as the play ends:—

But Makduffe . . . answered (with his naked sworde in his hande) saying: it is true, Makbeth, and now shall thine insatiable crueltie have an ende, for I am even he that thy wysards have tolde thee of, who was never borne of my mother, but ripped out of her wombe: therewithall he stept unto him, and slue him in the place. Then cutting his heade from the shoulders, he set it upon a poll, and brought it into Malcolme. This was the end of Makbeth, after he had reigned XVII years over the Scottishmen. In the beginning of his raigne he accomplished many worthie actes, right profitable to the common wealth (as ye have heard), but afterwards, by illusion of the Divell, he defamed the same with most horrible crueltie.

There, in brief, we have Shakespeare's material: and patently it holds one element on which an artist's mind (if I understand the artistic mind) would by attraction at once inevitably seize. I mean the element of the supernatural. It is the element which almost every commentator, almost every critic, has done his best to belittle. I shall recur to it, and recur with stress upon it; because, writing as diffidently as a man may who has spent thirty years of his life in learning to understand how stories are begotten, and being old enough to desire to communicate what of knowledge, though too late for me, may yet profit others, I can make affidavit that what first arrested Shakespeare's mind as he read the *Chronicles* was that passage concerning the "three weird sisters"—"All hail, Macbeth, Thane of Glamis!" and the rest.

Let us consider the *Chronicle* with this supernatural element left out, and what have we?—An ordinary sordid story of a disloyal general murdering his king, usurping the throne, reigning with cruelty for seventeen years, and being overcome at length amid every one's approval. There is no material for tragedy in that. "Had Zimri peace, who slew his master?"—Well (if we exclude the supernatural in the *Chronicle*), yes, he had; and for seventeen years: which, for a bloody tyrant, is no short run.

Still, let us exclude the supernatural for a moment. Having excluded it, we shall straightway perceive that the story of the *Chronicle* has one fatal defect as a theme of tragedy. For tragedy demands some sympathy with the fortunes of its hero: but where is there room for sympathy in the fortunes of a disloyal, self-seeking murderer?

Just there lay Shakespeare's capital difficulty.

(3)

Before we follow his genius in coming to grips with it, let us realise the importance as well as the magnitude of that difficulty. "Tragedy [says Aristotle] is the imitation of an action: and an action implies personal agents, who necessarily possess certain qualities both of character and thought. It is these that determine the qualities of actions themselves: these—thought and character—are the two natural causes from which actions spring: on these causes, again, all success or failure depends."[3]

But it comes to this—The success or failure of a tragedy depends on what sort of person we represent, and principally, of course, on what sort of person we make our chief tragic figure, our protagonist. Everything depends really on our protagonist: and it was his true critical insight that directed Dr. Bradley, examining the substance of Shakespearian tragedy, to lead off with these words:

> Such a tragedy brings before us a considerable number of persons (many more than the persons in a Greek play, unless the members of the Chorus are reckoned among them); but it is preeminently the story of one person, the 'hero,' or at most of two, the 'hero' and 'heroine.' Moreover, it is only in the love-tragedies, *Romeo and Juliet, Antony and Cleopatra*, that the heroine is as much the centre of the action as the hero. The rest, including *Macbeth*, are single stars. So that, having noticed the peculiarity of these two dramas, we may henceforth, for the sake of brevity, ignore it, and may speak of the tragic story as being concerned primarily with one person.

So, it makes no difference to this essential of tragedy whether we write our play for an audience of Athenians or of Londoners gathered in the Globe Theatre, Southwark: whether we crowd our *dramatis personae* or are content with a cast of three or four. There must be one central figure (or at most two), and on this figure, as the story unfolds itself, we must concentrate the spectators' emotions of pity or terror, or both. Now, I must, for handiness, quote Aristotle again, because he lays down very succinctly some rules concerning this 'hero' or protagonist, or central figure (call him what we will—I shall use the word 'hero' merely because it is the shortest). But let us understand that though these so-called 'rules' of Aristotle are marvellously enforced—though their wisdom is marvellously confirmed—by Dr. Bradley's examination of the 'rules' which Shakespeare, consciously or unconsciously, obeyed, they do no more than turn into precept, with reasons given, certain inductions drawn by Aristotle from the approved masterpieces of his time. There is no reason to suppose that Shakespeare had ever heard of them; rather, there is good reason to suppose that he had not. But Aristotle says this concerning the hero, or protagonist, of tragic drama, and Shakespeare's practice at every point supports him:—

> (1) A Tragedy must not be the spectacle of a perfectly good man brought from prosperity to adversity. For this merely shocks us.

(2) Nor, of course, must it be that of a bad man passing from adversity to prosperity: for that is not tragedy at all, but the perversion of tragedy, and revolts the moral sense.

(3) Nor, again, should it exhibit the downfall of an utter villain: since pity is aroused by undeserved misfortunes, terror by misfortunes befalling a man like ourselves.

(4) There remains, then, as the only proper subject for Tragedy, the spectacle of a man not absolutely or eminently good or wise who is brought to disaster not by sheer depravity but by some error or frailty.

(5) Lastly, this man must be highly renowned and prosperous—an Oedipus, a Thyestes, or some other illustrious person.

Before dealing with the others, let us get this last rule out of the way; for, to begin with, it presents no difficulty in *Macbeth*, since in the original—in Holinshed's *Chronicles*—Macbeth is an illustrious warrior who makes himself a king; and moreover the rule is patently a secondary one, of artistic expediency rather than of artistic right or wrong. It amounts but to this, that the more eminent we make our persons in Tragedy, the more evident we make the disaster—the dizzier the height, the longer way to fall, and the greater shock on our audience's mind. Dr. Bradley goes further, and remarks, "The pangs of despised love and the anguish of remorse, we say, are the same in a peasant and a prince: but (not to insist that they cannot be so when the prince is really a prince) the story of the prince, the triumvir, or the general, has a greatness and dignity of its own. His fate affects the welfare of a whole; and when he falls suddenly from the height of earthly greatness to the dust, his fall produces a sense of contrast, of the powerlessness of man, and of the omnipotence— perhaps the caprice—of Fortune or Fate, which no tale of private life can possibly rival." In this wider view Dr. Bradley may be right, though some modern dramatists would disagree with him. But we are dealing more humbly with Shakespeare as a *workman*; and for our purpose it is more economical, as well as sufficient, to say that downfall from a high eminence is more spectacular than downfall from a low one; that Shakespeare, who knew most of the tricks of his art, knew this as well as ever did Aristotle, and that those who adduce to us Shakespeare's constant selection of kings and princes for his *dramatis personae* as evidence of his having been a 'snob,' might as triumphantly prove it snobbish in a Greek tragedian to write of Agamemnon and Clytemnestra, or of Cadmus and Harmonia, because

The gods had to their marriage come,
And at the banquet all the Muses sang:

But, touching the other and more essential rules laid down by Aristotle, let me,—very fearfully, knowing how temerarious it is, how impudent, to offer to condense so great and close a thinker,—suggest that, after all, they work down into one:—that a hero of Tragic Drama must, whatever else he miss, engage our sympathy; that, however gross his error or grievous his frailty, it must not exclude our feeling that he is a man like ourselves; that, sitting in the audience, we must know in our hearts that what is befalling him might conceivably in the circumstances have befallen us, and say in our hearts, "There, but for the grace of God, go I."

I think, anticipating a little, I can drive this point home by a single illustration. When the ghost of Banquo seats itself at that dreadful supper, who sees it? Not the company. Not even Lady Macbeth. Whom does it accuse? Not the company, and, again, not even Lady Macbeth. Those who see it are Macbeth and you and I. Those into whom it strikes terror are Macbeth and you and I. Those whom it accuses are Macbeth and you and I. And what it accuses is what, of Macbeth, you and I are hiding in our own breasts. So, if this be granted, I come back upon the capital difficulty that faced Shakespeare as an artist.

(1) It was not to make Macbeth a grandiose or a conspicuous figure. He was already that in the *Chronicle*.

(2) It was not to clothe him in something to illude us with the appearance of real greatness. Shakespeare, with his command of majestic poetical speech, had that in his work-bag surely enough, and knew it. When a writer can make an imaginary person talk like this:—

She should have died hereafter;
There would have been a time for such a word.
To-morrow, and to-morrow, and to-morrow
Creeps in this petty pace from day to day
To the last syllable of recorded time;
And all our yesterdays have lighted fools
The way to dusty death—

I say, when a man knows he can make his Macbeth talk like that, he needs not distrust his power to drape his Macbeth in an illusion of greatness. Moreover, Shakespeare—artist that he was—had other tricks up his sleeve to convince us of Macbeth's greatness. One of these I hope to discuss in a subsequent chapter.

But (here lies the crux) how could he make us *sympathise* with him—make us, sitting or standing in the Globe Theatre some time (say) in the year 1610, feel that Macbeth was even such a man as you or I? He was a murderer, and a murderer for his private profit—a combination which does not appeal to most of us, to unlock the flood-gates of sympathy, or indeed (I hope) as striking home upon any private and pardonable frailty. The *Chronicle* does, indeed, allow just one loop-hole for pardon. It hints that Duncan, nominating his boy to succeed him, thereby cut off Macbeth from a reasonable hope of the crown, which he thereupon (and not until then) by process of murder usurped, "having," says Holinshed, "a juste quarrell so to do (as he took the mater)."

Did Shakespeare use that one hint, enlarge that loophole? He did not.

The more I study Shakespeare as an artist, the more I worship the splendid audacity of what he did, just here, in this play.

Instead of using a paltry chance to condone Macbeth's guilt, he seized on it and plunged it threefold deeper, so that it might verily

the multitudinous seas incarnadine.

Think of it:—

He made this man, a sworn soldier, murder Duncan, his liege-lord.

He made this man, a host, murder Duncan, a guest within his gates.

He made this man, strong and hale, murder Duncan, old, weak, asleep and defenceless.

He made this man commit murder for nothing but his own advancement.

He made this man murder Duncan, who had steadily advanced him hitherto, who had never been aught but trustful, and who (that no detail of reproach might be wanting) had that very night, as he retired, sent, in most kindly thought, the gift of a diamond to his hostess.

To sum up: instead of extenuating Macbeth's criminality, Shakespeare doubles and redoubles it. Deliberately this magnificent artist locks every door on condonation, plunges the guilt deep as hell, and then—tucks up his sleeves.

There was once another man, called John Milton, a Cambridge man of Christ's College; and, as most of us know, he once thought of rewriting this very story of Macbeth. The evidence that he thought of it—the entry in Milton's handwriting—may be examined in the library of Trinity College, Cambridge.

Milton did not eventually write a play on the story of Macbeth. Eventually he preferred to write an epic upon the Fall of Man, and of that poem critics have been found to say that Satan, "enemy of mankind," is in fact the hero and the personage that most claims our sympathy.

Now (still bearing in mind how the subject of Macbeth attracted Milton) let us open *Paradise Lost* at Book IV upon the soliloquy of Satan, which between lines 32–113 admittedly holds the *clou* of the poem:

O! thou that, with surpassing glory crown'd—

Still thinking of Shakespeare and of Milton—of Satan and of Macbeth—let us ponder every line: but especially these:—

Lifted up so high,
I 'sdain'd subjection, and thought one step higher
Would set me highest, and in a moment quit
The debt immense of endless gratitude,
So burdensome, still paying, still to owe:
Forgetful what from him I still receiv'd;
And understood not that a grateful mind
By owing owes not, but still pays, at once
Indebted and discharg'd. . . .

And yet more especially this:—

Farewell, remorse! All good to me is lost:
Evil, be thou my good.

NOTES

1. In the Prologue to *Romeo and Juliet* Shakespeare talks of "the two hours' traffic of our stage." But the actual performance must have taken longer than two hours.

2. "The Elizabethan Stage," "the Elizabethan Drama," are terms which actually cover a considerable period of time. It is certain that—say between 1550 and 1620—the theatre enormously improved its apparatus: upon the masques, as we know, very large sums of money were spent: and I make no doubt that before the close of Shakespeare's theatrical career, painted scenes and tapestries were the fashion.

3. I quote from Butcher's rendering, which gives the sense clearly enough; though, actually, Aristotle's language is simpler, and for "thought" I should substitute "understanding" as a translation of dianoia.

1930—G. Wilson Knight. From *"Macbeth* and the Metaphysic of Evil," from *The Wheel of Fire*

G. Wilson Knight (1875–1965) was professor of English at Leeds University and also taught at the University of Toronto. At both universities he produced and acted in Shakespeare plays. In addition, Knight wrote plays for the British stage and television. His critical books include *The Wheel of Fire, Shakespearean Production* and *Lord Byron: Christian Virtues.*

The central human theme—the temptation and crime of Macbeth—is, however, more easy of analysis. The crucial speech runs as follows:

Why do I yield to that suggestion,
Whose horrid image doth unfix my hair,
And make my seated heart knock at my ribs
Against the use of nature? Present fears
Are less than horrible imaginings.
My thought whose murder yet is but fantastical
Shakes so my single state of man that function
Is smother'd in surmise, and nothing is
But what is not. (I. iii. 134)

These lines, spoken when Macbeth first feels the impending evil, expresses again all those elements I have noticed in the mass-effect of the play: questioning doubt, horror, fear of some unknown power; horrible imaginings of the supernatural and 'fantastical'; an abysm of unreality; disorder on the plane of physical life. This speech is a microcosm of the *Macbeth* vision: it contains the germ of the whole. Like a stone in a pond, this original immediate experience of Macbeth sends ripples of itself expanding over the whole play. This is the moment of the birth of evil in *Macbeth*—he may have had ambitious thoughts before, may even have intended the murder, but now for the first time he feels its oncoming reality. This is the mental experience which he projects into action, thereby plunging his land, too, in fear, horror, darkness, and disorder. In this speech we have a swift interpenetration of idea with idea, from fear and disorder, through sickly imaginings, to abysmal darkness, nothingness. 'Nothing is but what is not': that is the text of the play. Reality and unreality change places. We must see that Macbeth, like the whole universe of this play, is paralysed, mesmerized, as though in a dream. This is not merely 'ambition'—it is fear, a nameless fear which yet fixes itself to a horrid image. He is helpless as a man in a nightmare: and this helplessness is integral to the conception—the will-concept is absent. Macbeth may struggle, but he cannot fight: he can no more resist than a rabbit resists a weasel's teeth fastened in its neck, or a bird the serpent's transfixing eye. Now this evil in Macbeth propels him to an act absolutely evil. For, though no ethical system is ultimate, Macbeth's crime is as near absolute as may be. It is therefore conceived as absolute. Its dastardly nature is emphasized clearly (I. vii. 12–25): Duncan is old, good; he is at once Macbeth's kinsman, king, and guest; he is to be murdered in sleep. No worse act of evil could well be found. So the evil of which Macbeth is at first aware rapidly entraps him in a mesh of events: it makes a tool of Duncan's visit, it dominates Lady Macbeth. It is significant that she, like her husband, is influenced by the Weird Sisters and their prophecy. Eventually Macbeth undertakes the murder, as a grim and hideous duty. He cuts a sorry figure at first, but, once embarked on his allegiant enterprise of evil, his grandeur grows. Throughout he is driven by fear—the fear that paralyses everyone else urges him to an amazing and mysterious action of blood. This action he repeats, again and again.

By his original murder he isolates himself from humanity. He is lonely, endures the uttermost torture of isolation. Yet still a bond unites him to men: that bond he would 'cancel and tear to pieces'—the natural bond of human fellowship and love. He further symbolizes his guilty, pariah soul by murdering Banquo. He fears everyone outside himself but his wife, suspects them. Every act of blood is driven by fear of the horrible disharmony existent between himself and his world. He tries to harmonize the relation by murder. He would let 'the frame of things disjoint, both the worlds suffer' (III. ii. 16) to win back peace. He is living in an unreal world, a fantastic mockery, a ghoulish dream: he strives to make this single nightmare to rule the outward things of his nation. He would make all Scotland a nightmare thing of dripping blood. He knows he cannot return, so determines to go o'er. He seeks out the Weird Sisters a second time. Now he welcomes disorder and confusion, would let them range wide over the earth, since they range unfettered in his own soul:

> . . . though the treasure
> Of nature's germens tumble all together,
> Even till destruction sicken; answer me
> To what I ask you. (IV. i. 58)

So he addresses the Weird Sisters. Castles, palaces, and pyramids—let all fall in general confusion, if only Macbeth be satisfied. He is plunging deeper and deeper into unreality, the severance from mankind and all normal forms of life is now abysmal, deep. Now he is shown Apparitions glassing the future. They promise him success in terms of natural law; no man 'of woman born' shall hurt him, he shall not be vanquished till Birnam Wood come against him. He, based firmly in the unreal, yet thinks to build his future on the laws of reality. He forgets that he is trafficking with things of nightmare fantasy, whose truth is falsehood, falsehood truth. That success they promise is unreal as they themselves. So, once having cancelled the bond of reality he has no home: the unreal he understands not, the real condemns him. In neither can he exist. He asks if Banquo's issue shall reign in Scotland: most horrible thought to him, since, if that be so, it proves that the future takes its natural course irrespective of human acts—that prophecy need not have been interpreted into crime: that he would in truth have been King of Scotland without his own 'stir' (I. iii. 144). Also the very thought of other succeeding and prosperous kings, some of them with 'twofold balls and treble sceptres' (IV. i. 121), is a maddening thing to him who is no real king but only monarch of a nightmare realm. The Weird Sisters who were formerly as the three Parcae, or Fates, foretelling Macbeth's future, now, at this later stage of his story, become the Erinyes, avengers of murder, symbols of the tormented soul. They delude and madden him with their apparitions and ghosts. Yet he does not give way, and raises our admiration at his undaunted severance from good. He contends for his own individual soul against the universal reality. Nor is his contest unavailing. He is fighting himself free from the nightmare fear of his life. He goes on 'till destruction sicken' (IV. i. 60): he actually does 'go o'er', is not lost in the stream of blood he elects to cross. It is true. He wins his battle. He adds crime to crime and emerges at last victorious and fearless:

> I have almost forgot the taste of fears:
> The time has been, my senses would have cool'd
> To hear a night-shriek; and my fell of hair
> Would at a dismal treatise rouse and stir
> As life were in't; I have supp'd full with horrors;
> Direness, familiar to my slaughterous thoughts,
> Cannot once start me. (V. v. 9)

Again, 'Hang those that talk of fear!' (V. iii. 36) he cries, in an ecstasy of courage. He is, at last, 'broad and general as the casing air' (III. iv. 23).

This will appear a strange reversal of the usual commentary; it is, however, true and necessary. Whilst Macbeth lives in conflict with himself there is misery, evil, fear: when, at the end, he and others have openly identified himself with evil, he faces the world fearless nor does he appear evil any longer. The worst element of his suffering has been that secrecy and hypocrisy so often referred to throughout the play (I. iv. 12; I. v. 64; III. ii. 34; V. iii. 27). Dark secrecy and night are in Shakespeare ever the badges of crime. But at the end Macbeth has no need of secrecy. He is no longer 'cabin'd, cribb'd, confined, bound in to saucy doubts and fears' (III. iv. 24). He has won through by excessive crime to an harmonious and honest relation with his surroundings. He has successfully symbolized the disorder of his lonely guilt-stricken soul by creating disorder in the world, and thus restores balance and harmonious contact. The mighty principle of good planted in the nature of things then asserts itself, condemns him openly, brings him peace. Daylight is brought to Macbeth, as to Scotland, by the accusing armies of Malcolm. He now knows himself to be a tyrant confessed, and wins back that integrity of soul which gives us:

> I have lived long enough: my way of life
> Is fallen into the sere, the yellow leaf . . . (V. iii. 22)

Here he touches a recognition deeper than fear, more potent than nightmare. The delirious dream is over. A clear daylight now disperses the imaginative dark that has eclipsed Scotland. The change is remarkable. There is now movement, surety and purpose, colour: horses 'skirr the country round' (V. iii. 35), banners are hung out on the castle walls (V. v. 1), soldiers hew down the bright leaves of Birnam (V. iv. 5). There is, as it were, a paean of triumph as the *Macbeth* universe, having struggled darkly upward, now climbs into radiance. Though they oppose each other in fight, Macbeth and Malcolm share equally in this relief, this awakening from horror. Of a piece with this change is the fulfilment of the Weird Sisters' prophecies. In bright daylight the nightmare reality to which Macbeth has been subdued is insubstantial and transient as sleep-horrors at dawn. Their unreality is emphasized by the very fact that they are nevertheless related to natural phenomena: they are thus parasitic on reality. To these he has trusted, and they fail. But he himself is, at the last, self-reliant and courageous. The words of the Weird Sisters ring true:

> Though his bark cannot be lost
> Yet it shall be tempest-toss'd. (I. iii. 24)

Each shattering report he receives with redoubled life-zest; and meets the fate marked out by the daylight consciousness of normal man for the nightmare reality of crime. Malcolm may talk of 'this dead butcher and his fiend-like queen' (V. vii. 98). We, who have felt the sickly poise over the abysmal deeps of evil, the hideous reality of the unreal, must couch our judgement in a different phrase.

1947—Cleanth Brooks. "The Naked Babe and the Cloak of Manliness," from *The Well Wrought Urn*

Cleanth Brooks (1906-1994), who concluded his teaching career as professor emeritus of rhetoric at Yale, was perhaps the best-known proponent of New Criticism. A prolific scholar, he is the author of numerous critical works, including *Community, Religion, and Literature: Essays* (1995); *Historical Evidence and the Reading of Seventeenth-Century Poetry* (1991); *On the Prejudices, Predilections, and Firm Beliefs of William Faulkner: Essays* (1987); and *William Faulkner: Toward Yoknapatawpha and Beyond* (1978).

I began by suggesting that our reading of Donne might contribute something to our reading of Shakespeare, though I tried to make plain the fact that I had no design of trying to turn Shakespeare into Donne, or—what I regard as nonsense—of trying to exalt Donne above Shakespeare. I have in mind specifically some such matter as this: that since the *Songs and Sonets* of Donne, no less than *Venus and Adonis*, requires a "perpetual activity of attention . . . on the part of the reader from the rapid flow, the quick change, and the playful nature of the thoughts and images," the discipline gained from reading Donne may allow us to see more clearly the survival of such qualities in the later style of Shakespeare. And, again, I have in mind some such matter as this: that if a reading of Donne has taught us that the "rapid flow, the quick change, and the playful nature of the thoughts and images"—qualities which we are all too prone to associate merely with the fancy—can, on occasion, take on imaginative power, we may, thus taught, better appreciate details in Shakespeare which we shall otherwise dismiss as merely fanciful, or, what is more likely, which we shall simply ignore altogether.

With Donne, of course, the chains of imagery, "always vivid" and "often minute," are perfectly evident. For many readers they are all too evident. The difficulty is not to prove that they exist, but that, on occasion, they may subserve a more imaginative unity. With Shakespeare, the difficulty may well be to prove that the chains exist at all. In general, we may say, Shakespeare has made it relatively easy for his admirers to choose what they like and neglect what they like. What he gives on one or another level is usually so magnificent that the reader finds it easy to ignore other levels.

Yet there are passages not easy to ignore and on which even critics with the conventional interests have been forced to comment. One of these passages occurs in *Macbeth*, Act I, scene vii, where Macbeth compares the pity for his victim-to-be, Duncan, to

> a naked new-born babe,
> Striding the blast, or heaven's cherubim, hors'd
> Upon the sightless couriers of the air.

The comparison is odd, to say the least. Is the babe natural or supernatural—an ordinary, helpless baby, who, as newborn, could not, of course, even toddle, much less stride the blast? Or is it some infant Hercules, quite capable of striding the blast, but, since it is powerful and not helpless, hardly the typical pitiable object?

Shakespeare seems bent upon having it both ways—and, if we read on through the passage—bent upon having the best of both worlds; for he proceeds to give us the option: pity is like the babe "or heaven's cherubim" who quite appropriately, of course, do ride the blast. Yet, even if we waive the question of the legitimacy of the alternative (of which Shakespeare so promptly avails himself), is the cherubim comparison really any more successful than is the babe comparison? Would not one of the great warrior archangels be more appropriate to the scene than the cherub? Does Shakespeare mean for pity or for fear of retribution to be dominant in Macbeth's mind?

Or is it possible that Shakespeare could not make up his own mind? Was he merely writing hastily and loosely, letting the word "pity" suggest the typically pitiable object, the babe naked in the blast, and then, stirred by the vague notion that some threat to Macbeth should be hinted, using "heaven's cherubim"—already suggested by "babe"—to convey the hint? Is the passage vague or precise?

Loosely or tightly organized? Comments upon the passage have ranged all the way from one critic's calling it "pure rant, and intended to be so" to another's laudation: "Either like a mortal babe, terrible in helplessness; or like heaven's angel-children, mighty in love and compassion. This magnificent passage . . ."

An even more interesting, and perhaps more disturbing passage in the play is that in which Macbeth describes his discovery of the murder:

> Here lay Duncan,
> His silver skin lac'd with his golden blood;
> And his gash'd stabs look'd like a breach in nature
> For ruin's wasteful entrance: there, the murderers,
> Steep'd in the colours of their trade, their daggers
> Unmannerly breech'd with gore. . . .

It is amusing to watch the textual critics, particularly those of the eighteenth century, fight a stubborn rear-guard action against the acceptance of "breech'd." Warburton emended "breech'd" to "reech'd"; Johnson, to "drench'd"; Seward, to "hatch'd." Other critics argued that the *breeches* implied were really the handles of the daggers, and that, accordingly, "breech'd" actually here meant "sheathed." The Variorum page witnesses the desperate character of the defense, but the position has had to be yielded, after all. *The Shakespeare Glossary* defines "breech'd" as meaning "covered as with breeches," and thus leaves the poet committed to a reading which must still shock the average reader as much as it shocked that nineteenth-century critic who pronounced upon it as follows: "A metaphor must not be far-fetched nor dwell upon the details of a disgusting picture, as in these lines. There is little, and that far-fetched, similarity between *gold lace* and *blood*, or between *bloody daggers* and *breech'd legs*. The slightness of the similarity, recalling the greatness of the dissimilarity, disgusts us with the attempted comparison."

The two passages are not of the utmost importance, I dare say, though the speeches (of which each is a part) are put in Macbeth's mouth and come at moments of great dramatic tension in the play. Yet, in neither case is there any warrant for thinking that Shakespeare was not trying to write as well as he could. Moreover, whether we like it or not, the imagery is fairly typical of Shakespeare's mature style. Either passage ought to raise some qualms among those who retreat to Shakespeare's authority when they seek to urge the claims of "noble simplicity." They are hardly simple. Yet it is possible that such passages as these may illustrate another poetic resource, another type of imagery which, even in spite of its apparent violence and complication, Shakespeare could absorb into the total structure of his work.

Shakespeare, I repeat, is not Donne—is a much greater poet than Donne; yet the example of his typical handling of imagery will scarcely render support to the usual attacks on Donne's imagery—for, with regard to the two passages in question, the second one, at any rate, is about as strained as Donne is at his most extreme pitch.

Yet I think that Shakespeare's daggers attired in their bloody breeches can be defended as poetry, and as characteristically Shakespearean poetry. Furthermore, both this passage and that about the newborn babe, it seems to me, are far more than excrescences, mere extravagances of detail: each, it seems to me, contains a central symbol of the play, and symbols which we must understand if we are to understand either the detailed passage or the play as a whole.

If this be true, then more is at stake than the merit of the quoted lines taken as lines. (The lines as constituting mere details of a larger structure could, of course, be omitted in the acting of the play without seriously damaging the total effect of the tragedy—though this argument obviously cuts two ways. Whole scenes, and admittedly fine scenes, might also be omitted—have in fact *been* omitted—without quite destroying the massive structure of the tragedy.) What is at stake is the whole matter of the relation of Shakespeare's imagery to the total structures of the plays themselves.

I should like to use the passages as convenient points of entry into the larger symbols which dominate the play. They *are* convenient because, even if we judge them to be faulty, they demonstrate how obsessive for Shakespeare the symbols were—they demonstrate how far the conscious (or unconscious) symbolism could take him.

If we see how the passages are related to these symbols, and they to the tragedy as a whole, the main matter is achieved; and having seen this, if we still prefer "to wish the lines away," that, of course, is our privilege. In the meantime, we may have learned something about Shakespeare's methods—not merely of building metaphors—but of encompassing his larger meanings.

One of the most startling things which has come out of Miss Spurgeon's book on Shakespeare's imagery is her discovery of the "old clothes" imagery in *Macbeth*. As she points out: "The idea constantly recurs that Macbeth's new honours sit ill upon him, like a loose and badly fitting garment, belonging to someone else." And she goes on to quote passage after passage in which the idea is expressed. But, though we are all in Miss Spurgeon's debt for having pointed this out, one has to observe that Miss Spurgeon has hardly explored the full implications of her discovery. Perhaps her interest in classifying and cataloguing the imagery of the plays has obscured for her some of the larger and more important relationships. At any rate, for reasons to be given below, she has realized only a part of the potentialities of her discovery.

Her comment on the clothes imagery reaches its climax with the following paragraphs:

And, at the end, when the tyrant is at bay at Dunsinane, and the English troops are advancing, the Scottish lords still have this image in their minds. Caithness sees him as a man vainly trying to fasten a large garment on him with too small a belt:

> He cannot buckle his distemper'd cause
> Within the belt of rule;

while Angus, in a similar image, vividly sums up the essence of what they all have been thinking ever since Macbeth's accession to power:

> now does he feel his title
> Hang loose about him, like a giant's robe
> Upon a dwarfish thief.

This imaginative picture of a small, ignoble man encumbered and degraded by garments unsuited to him, should be put against the view emphasized by some critics (notably Coleridge and Bradley) of the likeness between Macbeth and Milton's Satan in grandeur and sublimity.

Undoubtedly Macbeth . . . is great, magnificently great. . . . But he could never be put beside, say, Hamlet or Othello, in nobility of nature; and there is an aspect in which he is but a poor, vain, cruel, treacherous creature, snatching ruthlessly over the dead bodies of kinsman and friend at place and power he is utterly unfitted to possess. It is worth remembering that it is thus that Shakespeare, with his unshrinking clarity of vision, repeatedly *sees* him.

But this is to make primary what is only one aspect of the old-clothes imagery! And there is no warrant for interpreting the garment imagery as used by Macbeth's enemies, Caithness and Angus, to mean that *Shakespeare* sees Macbeth as a poor and somewhat comic figure.

The crucial point of the comparison, it seems to me, lies not in the smallness of the man and the largeness of the robes, but rather in the fact that—whether the man be large or small—these are not *his* garments; in Macbeth's case they are actually stolen garments. Macbeth is uncomfortable in them because he is continually conscious of the fact that they do not belong to him. There is a further point, and it is one of the utmost importance; the oldest symbol for the hypocrite is that of the man who cloaks his true nature under a disguise. Macbeth loathes playing the part of the hypocrite—and actually does not play it too well. If we keep this in mind as we look back at the instances of the garment images which Miss Spurgeon has collected for us, we shall see that the pattern of imagery becomes very rich indeed. Macbeth says in Act I:

The Thane of Cawdor lives: why do you dress me
In borrow'd robes?

Macbeth at this point wants no honors that are not honestly his. Banquo says
in Act I:

> New honours come upon him,
> Like our strange garments, cleave not to their mould,
> But with the aid of use.

But Banquo's remark, one must observe, is not censorious. It is indeed a
compliment to say of one that he wears new honors with some awkwardness. The
observation becomes ironical only in terms of what is to occur later.
    Macbeth says in Act I:

> He hath honour'd me of late; and I have bought
> Golden opinions from all sorts of people,
> Which would be worn now in their newest gloss,
> Not cast aside so soon.

Macbeth here is proud of his new clothes: he is happy to wear what he has truly
earned. It is the part of simple good husbandry not to throw aside these new
garments and replace them with robes stolen from Duncan.
    But Macbeth has already been wearing Duncan's garments in anticipation, as
his wife implies in the metaphor with which she answers him:

> Was the hope drunk,
> Wherein you dress'd yourself?

(The metaphor may seem hopelessly mixed, and a full and accurate analysis of
such mixed metaphors in terms of the premises of Shakespeare's style waits upon
some critic who will have to consider not only this passage but many more like
it in Shakespeare.) For our purposes here, however, one may observe that the
psychological line, the line of the basic symbolism, runs on unbroken. A man
dressed in a drunken hope is garbed in strange attire indeed—a ridiculous dress
which accords thoroughly with the contemptuous picture that Lady Macbeth
wishes to evoke. Macbeth's earlier dream of glory has been a drunken fantasy
merely, if he flinches from action now.
    But the series of garment metaphors which run through the play is paralleled
by a series of masking or cloaking images which—if we free ourselves of Miss
Spurgeon's rather mechanical scheme of classification—show themselves to be
merely variants of the garments which hide none too well his disgraceful self. He
is consciously hiding that self throughout the play.

"False face must hide what the false heart doth know," he counsels Lady Macbeth before the murder of Duncan; and later, just before the murder of Banquo, he invokes night to "Scarf up the eye of pitiful day."

One of the most powerful of these cloaking images is given to Lady Macbeth in the famous speech in Act I:

> Come, thick night,
> And pall thee in the dunnest smoke of hell,
> That my keen knife see not the wound it makes,
> Nor heaven peep through the blanket of the dark,
> To cry, "Hold, Hold!"

I suppose that it is natural to conceive the "keen knife" here as held in her own hand. Lady Macbeth is capable of wielding it. And in this interpretation, the imagery is thoroughly significant. Night is to be doubly black so that not even her knife may see the wound it makes. But I think that there is good warrant for regarding her "keen knife" as Macbeth himself. She has just, a few lines above, given her analysis of Macbeth's character as one who would "not play false, / And yet [would] wrongly win." To bring him to the point of action, she will have to "chastise [him] with the valour of [her] tongue." There is good reason, then, for her to invoke night to become blacker still—to pall itself in the "dunnest smoke of hell." For night must not only screen the deed from the eye of heaven—conceal it at least until it is too late for heaven to call out to Macbeth "Hold, Hold!" Lady Macbeth would have night blanket the deed from the hesitant doer. The imagery thus repeats and reinforces the substance of Macbeth's anguished aside uttered in the preceding scene:

> Let not light see my black and deep desires;
> The eye wink at the hand; yet let that be
> Which the eye fears, when it is done, to see.

I do not know whether "blanket" and "pall" qualify as garment metaphors in Miss Spurgeon's classification: yet one is the clothing of sleep, and the other, the clothing of death—they are the appropriate garments of night; and they carry on an important aspect of the general clothes imagery. It is not necessary to attempt to give here an exhaustive list of instances of the garment metaphor; but one should say a word about the remarkable passage in II, iii.

Here, after the discovery of Duncan's murder, Banquo says

> And when we have our naked frailties hid,
> That suffer in exposure, let us meet,
> And question this most bloody piece of work—

that is, "When we have clothed ourselves against the chill morning air, let us meet to discuss this bloody piece of work." Macbeth answers, as if his subconscious mind were already taking Banquo's innocent phrase, "naked frailties," in a deeper, ironic sense:

> Let's briefly put on manly readiness.

It is ironic; for the "manly readiness" which he urges the other lords to put on, is, in his own case, a hypocrite's garment: he can only pretend to be the loyal, grief-stricken liege who is almost unstrung by the horror of Duncan's murder.

But the word "manly" carries still a further ironic implication: earlier, Macbeth had told Lady Macbeth that he dared

> do all that may become a man;
> Who dares do more is none.

Under the weight of her reproaches of cowardice, however, he *has* dared do more, and has become less than a man, a beast. He has already laid aside, therefore, one kind of "manly readiness" and has assumed another: he has garbed himself in a sterner composure than that which he counsels to his fellows—the hard and inhuman "manly readiness" of the resolved murderer.

The clothes imagery, used sometimes with emphasis on one aspect of it, sometimes, on another, does pervade the play. And it should be evident that the daggers "breech'd with gore"—though Miss Spurgeon does not include the passage in her examples of clothes imagery—represent one more variant of this general symbol. Consider the passage once more:

> Here lay Duncan,
> His silver skin lac'd with his golden blood;
> And his gash'd stabs look'd like a breach in nature
> For ruin's wasteful entrance: there, the murderers,
> Steep'd in the colours of their trade, their daggers
> Unmannerly breech'd with gore. . . . .

The clothes imagery runs throughout the passage; the body of the king is dressed in the most precious of garments, the blood royal itself; and the daggers too are dressed—in the same garment. The daggers, "naked" except for their lower parts which are reddened with blood, are like men in "unmannerly" dress—men, naked except for their red breeches, lying beside the red-handed grooms. The figure, though vivid, is fantastic; granted. But the basis for the comparison is *not* slight and adventitious. The metaphor fits the real situation on the deepest levels. As Macbeth and Lennox burst into the room, they find the daggers wearing, as Macbeth knows all too well, a horrible masquerade. They have been carefully "clothed" to play a part. They are not honest daggers, honorably naked in readiness to guard the king, or, "mannerly" clothed in their own sheaths. Yet the disguise which they wear will enable Macbeth to assume the robes of Duncan—robes to which he is no more entitled than are the daggers to the royal garments which they now wear, grotesquely.

The reader will, of course, make up his own mind as to the value of the passage. But the metaphor in question, in the light of the other garment imagery, cannot be dismissed as merely a strained ingenuity, irrelevant to the play. And the reader who *does* accept it as poetry will probably be that reader who knows the play best, not the reader who knows it slightly and regards Shakespeare's poetry as a rhetoric more or less loosely draped over the "content" of the play.

And now what can be said of pity, the "naked new-born babe"? Though Miss Spurgeon does not note it (since the governing scheme of her book would have hardly allowed her to see it), there are, by the way, a great many references to babes in this play—references which occur on a number of levels. The babe appears sometimes as a character, such as Macduff's child; sometimes as a symbol, like the crowned babe and the bloody babe which are raised by the witches on the occasion of Macbeth's visit to them; sometimes, in a metaphor, as in the passage under discussion. The number of such references can hardly be accidental; and the babe turns out to be, as a matter of fact, perhaps the most powerful symbol in the tragedy.

But to see this fully, it will be necessary to review the motivation of the play. The stimulus to Duncan's murder, as we know, was the prophecy of the Weird Sisters. But Macbeth's subsequent career of bloodshed stems from the same prophecy. Macbeth was to have the crown, but the crown was to pass to Banquo's children. The second part of the prophecy troubles Macbeth from the start. It does not oppress him, however, until the crown has been won. But from this point on, the effect of the prophecy is to hurry Macbeth into action and more action until he is finally precipitated into ruin.

We need not spend much time in speculating on whether Macbeth, had he been content with Duncan's murder, had he tempted fate no further, had he been willing to court the favor of his nobles, might not have died peaceably in bed. We are dealing, not with history, but with a play. Yet, even in history the usurper sometimes succeeds; and he sometimes succeeds on the stage. Shakespeare himself knew of, and wrote plays about, usurpers who successfully maintained possession of the crown. But, in any case, this much is plain: the train of murders into which Macbeth launches aggravates suspicions of his guilt and alienates the nobles.

Yet, a Macbeth who could act once, and then settle down to enjoy the fruits of this one attempt to meddle with the future would, of course, not be

Macbeth. For it is not merely his great imagination and his warrior courage in defeat which redeem him for tragedy and place him beside the other great tragic protagonists: rather, it is his attempt to conquer the future, an attempt involving him, like Oedipus, in a desperate struggle with fate itself. It is this which holds our imaginative sympathy, even after he has degenerated into a bloody tyrant and has become the slayer of Macduff's wife and children.

To sum up, there can be no question that Macbeth stands at the height of his power after his murder of Duncan, and that the plan—as outlined by Lady Macbeth—has been relatively successful. The road turns toward disaster only when Macbeth decides to murder Banquo. Why does he make this decision? Shakespeare has pointed up the basic motivation very carefully:

> Then prophet-like,
> They hail'd him father to a line of kings.
> Upon my head they plac'd a fruitless crown,
> And put a barren sceptre in my gripe,
> Thence to be wrench'd with an unlineal hand,
> No son of mine succeeding. If't be so,
> For Banquo's issue have I fil'd my mind;
> For them the gracious Duncan have I murder'd;
> Put rancours in the vessel of my peace
> Only for them; and mine eternal jewel
> Given to the common enemy of man,
> To make them kings, the seed of Banquo kings!

Presumably, Macbeth had entered upon his course from sheer personal ambition. Ironically, it is the more human part of Macbeth—his desire to have more than a limited personal satisfaction, his desire to found a line, his wish to pass something on to later generations—which prompts him to dispose of Banquo. There is, of course, a resentment against Banquo, but that resentment is itself closely related to Macbeth's desire to found a dynasty. Banquo, who has risked nothing, who has remained upright, who has not defiled himself, will have kings for children; Macbeth, none. Again, ironically, the Weird Sisters who have given Macbeth, so he has thought, the priceless gift of knowledge of the future, have given the real future to Banquo.

So Banquo's murder is decided upon, and accomplished. But Banquo's son escapes, and once more, the future has eluded Macbeth. The murder of Banquo thus becomes almost meaningless. This general point may be obvious enough, but we shall do well to note some of the further ways in which Shakespeare has pointed up the significance of Macbeth's war with the future.

When Macbeth, at the beginning of scene vii, Act I, contemplates Duncan's murder, it is the future over which he agonizes:

> If it were done, when 'tis done, then 'twere well
> It were done quickly; if the assassination
> Could trammel up the consequence, and catch
> With his surcease success; that but this blow
> Might be the be-all and the end-all here.

But the continuum of time cannot be partitioned off; the future is implicit in the present. There is no net strong enough to trammel up the consequence—not even in this world.

Lady Macbeth, of course, has fewer qualms. When Macbeth hesitates to repudiate the duties which he owes Duncan—duties which, by some accident of imagery perhaps—I hesitate to press the significance—he has earlier actually called "children"—Lady Macbeth cries out that she is willing to crush her own child in order to gain the crown:

> I have given suck, and know
> How tender 'tis to love the babe that milks me;
> I would, while it was smiling in my face,
> Have pluck'd my nipple from his boneless gums
> And dash'd the brains out, had I so sworn as you
> Have done to this.

Robert Penn Warren has made the penetrating observation that all of Shakespeare's villains are rationalists. Lady Macbeth is certainly of their company. She knows what she wants; and she is ruthless in her consideration of means. She will always "catch the nearest way." This is not to say that she ignores the problem of scruples, or that she is ready to oversimplify psychological complexities. But scruples are to be used to entangle one's enemies. One is not to become tangled in the mesh of scruples himself. Even though she loves her husband and though her ambition for herself is a part of her ambition for him, still she seems willing to consider even Macbeth at times as pure instrument, playing upon his hopes and fears and pride.

Her rationalism is quite sincere. She is apparently thoroughly honest in declaring that

> The sleeping and the dead
> Are but as pictures; 'tis the eye of childhood
> That fears a painted devil. If he do bleed,
> I'll gild the faces of the grooms withal,
> For it must seem their guilt.

For her, there is no moral order: *guilt* is something like *gilt*—one can wash it off or paint it on. Her pun is not frivolous and it is deeply expressive.

Lady Macbeth abjures all pity; she is willing to unsex herself; and her continual taunt to Macbeth, when he falters, is that he is acting like a baby—not like a man. This "manhood" Macbeth tries to learn. He is a dogged pupil. For that reason he is almost pathetic when the shallow rationalism which his wife urges upon him fails. His tone is almost one of puzzled bewilderment at nature's unfairness in failing to play the game according to the rules—the rules which have applied to other murders:

> the time has been,
> That, when the brains were out, the man would die,
> And there an end; but now they rise again.

Yet, after the harrowing scene, Macbeth can say, with a sort of dogged weariness:

> Come, we'll to sleep. My strange and self-abuse
> Is the initiate fear that wants hard use:
> We are yet but young in deed.

Ironically, Macbeth is still echoing the dominant metaphor of Lady Macbeth's reproach. He has not yet attained to "manhood"; that *must* be the explanation. He has not yet succeeded in hardening himself into something inhuman.

Tempted by the Weird Sisters and urged on by his wife, Macbeth is thus caught between the irrational and the rational. There is a sense, of course, in which every man is caught between them. Man must try to predict and plan and control his destiny. That is man's fate; and the struggle, if he is to realize himself as a man, cannot be avoided. The question, of course, which has always interested the tragic dramatist involves the terms on which the struggle is accepted and the protagonist's attitude toward fate and toward himself. Macbeth in his general concern for the future is typical—is Every Man. He becomes the typical tragic protagonist when he yields to pride and *hybris*. The occasion for temptation is offered by the prophecy of the Weird Sisters. They offer him knowledge which cannot be arrived at rationally. They offer a key—if only a partial key—to what is otherwise unpredictable. Lady Macbeth, on the other hand, by employing a ruthless clarity of perception, by discounting all emotional claims, offers him the promise of bringing about the course of events which he desires.

Now, in the middle of the play, though he has not lost confidence and though, as he himself says, there can be no turning back, doubts have begun to arise; and he returns to the Weird Sisters to secure unambiguous answers to his fears. But, pathetically and ironically for Macbeth, in returning to the Weird Sisters, he is really trying to impose rationality on what sets itself forth plainly as irrational: that is, Macbeth would force a rigid control on a future which, by definition—by the very fact that the Weird Sisters already know it—stands beyond his manipulation.

It is because of his hopes for his own children and his fears of Banquo's that he has returned to the witches for counsel. It is altogether appropriate, therefore, that two of the apparitions by which their counsel is revealed should be babes, the crowned babe and the bloody babe.

For the babe signifies the future which Macbeth would control and cannot control. It is the unpredictable thing itself—as Yeats has put it magnificently, "The uncontrollable mystery on the bestial floor." It is the one thing that can justify, even in Macbeth's mind, the murders which he has committed. Earlier in the play, Macbeth had declared that if the deed could "trammel up the consequence," he would be willing to "jump the life to come." But he cannot jump the life to come. In his own terms he is betrayed. For it is idle to speak of jumping the life to come if one yearns to found a line of kings. It is the babe that betrays Macbeth—his own babes, most of all.

The logic of Macbeth's distraught mind, thus, forces him to make war on children, a war which in itself reflects his desperation and is a confession of weakness. Macbeth's ruffians, for example, break into Macduff's castle and kill his wife and children. The scene in which the innocent child prattles with his mother about his absent father, and then is murdered, is typical Shakespearean "fourth act" pathos. But the pathos is not adventitious; the scene ties into the inner symbolism of the play. For the child, in its helplessness, defies the murderers. Its defiance testifies to the force which threatens Macbeth and which Macbeth cannot destroy.

But we are not, of course, to placard the child as The Future in a rather stiff and mechanical allegory. *Macbeth* is no such allegory. Shakespeare's symbols are richer and more flexible than that. The babe signifies not only the future; it symbolizes all those enlarging purposes which make life meaningful, and it symbolizes, furthermore, all those emotional and—to Lady Macbeth—irrational ties which make man more than a machine—which render him human. It signifies pre-eminently the pity which Macbeth, under Lady Macbeth's tutelage, would wean himself of as something "unmanly." Lady Macbeth's great speeches early in the play become brilliantly ironical when we realize that Shakespeare is using the same symbol for the unpredictable future that he uses for human compassion. Lady Macbeth is willing to go to any length to grasp the future: she would willingly dash out the brains of her own child if it stood in her way to that future. But this is to repudiate the future, for the child is its symbol.

Shakespeare does not, of course, limit himself to the symbolism of the child: he makes use of other symbols of growth and development, notably that of the plant. And this plant symbolism patterns itself to reflect the development of the play. For example, Banquo says to the Weird Sisters, early in the play:

> If you can look into the seeds of time,
> And say which grain will grow and which will not,
> Speak then to me.

A little later, on welcoming Macbeth, Duncan says to him:

> I have begun to plant thee, and will labour
> To make thee full of growing.

After the murder of Duncan, Macbeth falls into the same metaphor when he comes to resolve on Banquo's death. The Weird Sisters, he reflects, had hailed Banquo as

> father to a line of kings.
> Upon my head they placed a fruitless crown,
> And put a barren sceptre in my gripe.

Late in the play, Macbeth sees himself as the winter-stricken tree:

> I have liv'd long enough: my way of life
> Is fall'n into the sear, the yellow leaf.

The plant symbolism, then, supplements the child symbolism. At points it merges with it, as when Macbeth ponders bitterly that he has damned himself

> To make them kings, the seed of Banquo kings!

And, in at least one brilliant example, the plant symbolism unites with the clothes symbolism. It is a crowning irony that one of the Weird Sisters' prophecies on which Macbeth has staked his hopes is fulfilled when Birnam Wood comes to Dunsinane. For, in a sense, Macbeth is here hoist on his own petard. Macbeth, who has invoked night to "Scarf up the tender eye of pitiful day," and who has, again and again, used the "false face" to "hide what the false heart doth know," here has the trick turned against him. But the garment which cloaks the avengers is the living green of nature itself, and nature seems, to the startled eyes of his sentinels, to be rising up against him.

But it is the babe, the child, that dominates the symbolism. Most fittingly, the last of the prophecies in which Macbeth has placed his confidence, concerns the child: and Macbeth comes to know the final worst when Macduff declares to him that he was not "born of woman" but was from his "mother's womb / Untimely ripp'd." The babe here has defied even the thing which one feels may reasonably be predicted of him—his time of birth. With Macduff's pronouncement, the unpredictable has broken through the last shred of the net of calculation. The future cannot be trammelled up. The naked babe confronts Macbeth to pronounce his doom.

The passage with which we began this essay, then, is an integral part of a larger context, and of a very rich context:

And pity, like a naked new-born babe,
Striding the blast, or heaven's cherubim, hors'd
Upon the sightless couriers of the air,
Shall blow the horrid deed in every eye,
That tears shall drown the wind.

Pity is like the naked babe, the most sensitive and helpless thing; yet, almost as soon as the comparison is announced, the symbol of weakness begins to turn into a symbol of strength; for the babe, though newborn, is pictured as "Striding the blast" like an elemental force—like "heaven's cherubim, hors'd / Upon the sightless couriers of the air." We can give an answer to the question put earlier: is Pity like the human and helpless babe, or powerful as the angel that rides the winds? It is both; and it is strong because of its very weakness. The paradox is inherent in the situation itself; and it is the paradox that will destroy the overbrittle rationalism on which Macbeth founds his career.

For what will it avail Macbeth to cover the deed with the blanket of the dark if the elemental forces that ride the winds will blow the horrid deed in every eye? And what will it avail Macbeth to clothe himself in "manliness"— to become bloody, bold, and resolute—if he is to find himself again and again, viewing his bloody work through the "eye of childhood / That fears a painted devil"? Certainly, the final and climactic appearance of the babe symbol merges all the contradictory elements of the symbol. For, with Macduff's statement about his birth, the naked babe rises before Macbeth as not only the future that eludes calculation but as avenging angel as well.

The clothed daggers and the naked babe—mechanism and life—instrument and end—death and birth—that which should be left bare and clean and that which should be clothed and warmed—these are facets of two of the great symbols which run throughout the play. They are not the only symbols, to be sure; they are not the most obvious symbols: darkness and blood appear more often. But with a flexibility which must amaze the reader, the image of the garment and the image of the babe are so used as to encompass an astonishingly large area of the total situation. And between them—the naked babe, essential humanity, humanity stripped down to the naked thing itself, and yet as various as the future—and the various garbs which humanity assumes, the robes of honor, the hypocrite's disguise, the inhuman "manliness" with which Macbeth endeavors to cover up his essential humanity—between them, they furnish Shakespeare with his most subtle and ironically telling instruments.

—◇◇◇— —◇◇◇— —◇◇◇—

1950—Henry N. Paul. "Macbeth's Imagination," from *The Royal Play of Macbeth: When, Why and How It Was Written by Shakespeare*

Henry Neill Paul (1863-1954) was a Shakespeare scholar and dean of the Shakspere Society of Philadelphia, a club that combined serious Shakespearean scholarship and lively dinners.

In the play of *Macbeth* the dramatist has pictured the "vis phantastica," that is, the force of the imagination, more vividly than in any other play he, or perhaps anyone else, ever wrote. Dr. J. Q. Adams, in his discussion of *Macbeth*, puts it thus:

> Indeed, his abnormal imagination almost completely dominates his mental processes. His thoughts take the form, not of ideas, but of vivid images. For instance, when the purpose to murder Duncan comes into his mind, it promptly shapes itself into a "horrid image." And this is characteristic of his mental activity throughout the play; everywhere we see his thoughts expressing themselves in images so vivid as scarcely to be distinguished from reality [ed. of *Macbeth*, p. 135].

And Dr. Kittredge writes that Macbeth has "an imagination of extraordinary power, which visualizes to the verge of delirium. Every idea that enters his mind takes instant visible shape. He *sees* what another would merely *think*" (ed. of *Macbeth*, p. xiv).

Macbeth's imagination is not only powerful; it is characterized by what has been happily called "the hallucination of self-credulity." The phrase is that of the elder Disraeli.[1] It is finely shown in Shakespeare's disclosure of the mind of Macbeth, who speaks of it as his "strange and self-abuse" (III, iv, 142). In modern parlance, "he fools himself by seeing things." Macbeth thinks about a certain thing. He may wish it true. He may fear it will be true. There follows quickly a state of rapture or ecstasy or hallucination which pictures the thing hoped or feared so vividly that he assumes it to be true, acts as though it were true, and is thus brought to ruin.

This elaborate development by Shakespeare of Macbeth's imagination becomes the more striking when we realize that Holinshed's Macbeth had no imagination at all. He was merely a brave warrior who became a cruel murderer.

This abnormal imagination has great dramatic significance, for the turning point of the plot of *Macbeth* is the exposure of the crime by the hallucination of the criminal. It has an even greater psychological interest, for it is the self-credulity of Macbeth's imagination led by his hopes which tempts him to violate his conscience; and the same powerful imagination led by his fears vastly increases the torments of his violated conscience. Furthermore, the succession of hallucinations created by this imagination is used by the dramatist to lead the king to a better understanding of the delusions of witchcraft, for King James was by now troubled about the reliability of the confessions of the witches whom fifteen years ago he had had tortured with the pilliwinks and burned. He had come to suspect that their stories might be the fictions of an unduly vivid imagination. Shakespeare thought so too, and used his royal play to show the king what extraordinary effects can result from the human imagination.

To do this he shows to us three old hags practicing sorcery and necromancy according to the beliefs of the Scottish people and professing to do strange things. But a running comment put in the mouths of those who see them constantly suggests that their awesome practices are due to hallucination of the beholder, very real subjectively, but objectively nonexistent. When alone, they are only old women of flesh and blood professing sorcery as expounded by King James in his *Daemonologie*; but when Banquo or Macbeth sees them, the audience is kept aware that their doings and sayings are influenced by the imagination of those who see them, suggesting at once to the "judicious" that witchcraft may be but a delusion.

Dr. Johnson failed to see this, and thought it necessary to apologize for the showing of sorcery in *Macbeth*. After describing "the doctrine of witchcraft at once established by law and by the fashion," he said:

> Upon this general infatuation Shakespeare might be easily allowed to found a play, especially since he has followed with great exactness such histories as were then thought true; nor can it be doubted that the scenes of enchantment, however they may now be ridiculed, were both by himself and his audience thought awful and affecting [Johnson's *Shakespeare*, Vol. 6, p. 372].

This literalism is blind to the scope of Shakespeare's enduring art. At the other extreme is such a well phrased statement as the following taken from a short essay on Macbeth by William Preston Johnston:

> The prophetic soul of Shakespeare accepted the popular beliefs as modes of expression, and employed them as symbols for the unseen forces of nature and spirit, in which dwell activities more potent than even

superstition could conjure up. And it was through this high poetic and philosophic power, this eminent gift of imagination and understanding working together, that he produced the terrible and highly idealized conception of supernatural agency embodied in the Weird Sisters. These and Banquo's ghost, the apparitions, the omens, the air-drawn dagger, the mysterious voice, are but the signs and formulas through which he represents the problem of evil, with which Macbeth grapples, and which he solves to his own temporal and eternal ruin.[2]

Neither of these statements is satisfactory. The first is entirely characteristic of the unimaginative eighteenth century criticism which is now out of favor. The latter is a typical nineteenth century romantic generalization which does not take into account the minds of the audience who were to see the play in Shakespeare's day.

The twentieth century has found (as we must hope) the true via media. For an excellent statement of this position I quote the words of Allardyce Nicoll:

> There are thus two distinct points of view from which we may regard the witches. We can see in them evil ministers tempting Macbeth to destruction, or we can look on them merely as embodiments of ambitious thoughts which had already moved Macbeth and his wife to murderous imaginings. The peculiar thing to note is that through Shakespeare's subtle and suggestive art we do not regard these two points of view as mutually antagonistic [*Studies in Shakespeare* (1928), p. 123].

So important is this that I subjoin in a footnote a few other statements to much the same effect, although in differing phraseology.[3]

The way in which the thaumaturgy of the dramatist works this wonder can be seen by the inquiring eye. There truly were on the heath three withered hags of whom Banquo inquired how far they were from Forres. But Macbeth, always prone to substitute the imaginary for the real, transmutes the mumblings of the third witch into greetings corresponding to the hopes which are in his own mind.

Banquo's reaction is different. He, too, is interested in the establishment of a "line of kings" in Scotland (the "imperial theme"), so as to end the lawless succession of fighting kinglets who have ruled and ruined Scotland during the preceding century. Therefore he, too, welcomes words of the witches which seem to promise this to his descendants; but his trouble is that he is not at all sure that they really said it. To his honest mind they seem but "bubbles." He asks them: "Are ye fantastical [imaginary], or that indeed which outwardly you show?"

And he asks Macbeth:

Were such things here as we do speak about?
Or have we eaten on the insane root
That takes the reason prisoner?

This suggestion of the fantastical and imaginary character of the words and doings of the witches runs through the play. Not only does Banquo thus question the reality of the witches but as Macbeth's imaginings take shape, his habit is to seek confirmation from another. When he sees the dagger in the air, he debates with himself whether it really is there. When he sees Banquo's ghost, he debates its reality with his wife. When he sees the procession of the kings, he asks Lennox whether there was really anybody there. The subtle suggestion of this will be lost on the crowd. It still is. To the groundlings what the sisters do or say seems real. To thoughtful men, including the king, the play presses home Banquo's question, whether it is imaginary. Thus the witchery of the play has a different meaning to different people.

It is apt to be overlooked that this difference of opinion as to the powers of the sisters is derived from the ancient sources.

Hector Boece writes (1575 ed., p. 249 v.):

Vana ea Maccabaeo Banquohonique visa. . . . Verum ex eventu postea Parcas, aut nymphas aliquas fatidicas diabolico astu praeditas fuisse interpretatum est vulgo.

Holinshed, freely translating this, states that the strange words and doings of the three sisters were

reputed at the first but some vaine fantastical illusion by Macbeth and Banquo. . . . But afterward the common opinion was, that these women were either the weird sisters, that is (as ye would say) the goddesses of destinie; or else some nymphs or feiries, endued with knowledge of prophecie by their necromantical science, because everything came to pass as they had spoken. p. 171.

The sources thus specify three views: the sisters were (1) imaginary; or (2) the Fates or Norns; or (3) women practicing black art. Shakespeare projected question concerning this throughout his entire play with the result that discussion has continued to this day as to what the dramatist really wished his audience to think.

The first interpretation was the immediate reaction of Banquo and the ultimate acknowledgment of Macbeth, and they were the two who could best judge. It was, as I think, Shakespeare's view, and he hoped that it would be that of the king. The second interpretation has been much insisted upon by a few modern critics, but Dr. Bradley's refutation of it (*Shakespearean Tragedy*, p. 342) seems to me unanswerable.[4] The third is now, as then, the usual view and has always been the "common opinion," as no doubt Shakespeare expected it to be. Everyone is left free to decide whether the deeds of the witches are real or fantastical. For the dramatist did not know how far he might dare to lead his king. He had been told of the general trend of James's thoughts toward a rational position, but just where the king stood at the moment he could not know; and so he left it for him to go as far as he pleased and no farther.

The temptation scene (I, iii, 116–142) is the full showing of how Macbeth's imagination operates. He clings to an evil thought while trying to shift responsibility for it. His hopes created the thought (I, iii, 118). He had already discussed it with his wife, and this had produced an image in his mind of King Duncan murdered that Macbeth may take his throne. The sight of the sisters brings this image again to mind and he yields to what he calls a "supernatural soliciting," although as he yields he knows it to be only a "horrible imagining," a *fantasy*, an unreal thing. His great fault is thus shown to be his habit of taking the unreal to be real, and allowing it to master him because it corresponds precisely with his wishes.[5] It is this reflexive element in the enticements of the witches which teaches the thoughtful auditor that their temptations are imaginary.

The important lines are:

My thought, whose murder yet is but fantastical,
Shakes so my single state of man that function
Is smother'd in surmise, and nothing is
But what is not. [I, iii, 138–142]

In these lines the dramatist took the first opportunity offered in his play to define with the accuracy of a psychologist the devious way in which the imagination of Macbeth does its work. Unfortunately for the modern playgoer, the definition is expressed in words several of which are used in senses now obsolete or unusual. It is therefore necessary in this twentieth century to translate these lines into a more modern, even though less vigorous, mode, thus:

The murder which is part of the design I have in mind, though as yet
existing only in my imagination, so shakes my power to control myself,
that action is overruled by imagination, and nothing exists for me but
that which is not.[6]

Thus we are shown the workings of the mind of the worthy Macbeth as he is transformed into the superstitious Macbeth, a change which marks the first milestone of the play. He well knows that he has put his actions under the control of his imagination. He well knows that he ought not to do this.

Persons with this sort of imagination are at times beside themselves. The mind leaves the body and watches it. "Ecstasy," the Greeks called it. The Latins called it "rapture." Macbeth after first seeing the witches "seems rapt" (I, iii, 57). The fit lasts for some time, until Banquo exclaims, "Look how our partner's rapt." Macbeth, too, knows about these fits. He writes to his wife that he "stood rapt" at the wonder of the witches. But this rapture is not involuntary. He can control the fit if he wants to do so. There is a fine showing of this at the end of the murder scene. Macbeth has been racked by the sight of his bloody hands. To escape his tormenting conscience, he at once flees from reality to unreality. So is he rapt until his wife urges, "Be not lost so poorly in your thoughts" (II, ii, 73). She knows that he can control this matter. So does he. The next words, "To know my deed?," in the folio text make a single line and, as the Clarendon editors prefer (p. 109), should stand as Macbeth's question. For if he obeys his wife, he will know his deed and from that he would escape. His next words, "'Twere best not know myself," are his acknowledgment that he is deceiving himself. But the rapture ends, and as he comes to himself the pangs of remorse begin their torment and he wishes the loud knocking could wake Duncan. Again in the banquet scene we are shown the operation of one of Macbeth's fits, and both he and his wife describe the malady. He says, "I have a strange infirmity which is nothing to those that know me." She tells more. "My lord is often thus, and hath been from his youth. . . . The fit is momentary; upon a thought he will again be well." This process of hallucination and self-deception, begun in boyhood and developed until the mind has become diseased, is the process by which Macbeth's strong imagination brings about his downfall. "Fortis imaginatio generat casum."

The supreme exhibition of the power of Macbeth's imagination is the vision of the bloody dagger which the murderer sees as he goes to Duncan's chamber. The familiar lines (II, i, 33–49) are a debate, "an imaginatio possit producere reales effectus." The mind insists on the reality of that which the bodily sense asserts to be nonexistent. In the end the latter wins ("there's no such thing"), recognizing that the hallucination is due to Macbeth's wish, that is, "the bloody business." It is his responsibility. The handle is "toward his hand" for he wishes it so. It marshals him the way that he was going. The gouts of blood appear on the blade because he wishes them there. In III, iv, 62, Lady Macbeth says that her husband told her that this air-drawn dagger *led him to Duncan*, showing how well he knew that he had let his imagination thus tempt and control him in violation of his conscience.

The actor of this part must make the imaginary dagger so real that not only Macbeth but the audience see it. Burbage could do this. So could Garrick, Macready, Irving, and Booth. For this reason the dagger is not shown to the audience, although some poor actors have called for it. I have seen it lying on a table and revealed by the spotlight. I have also seen it dangled in the air and turned to show the blood on it. Thus will the inferior actor crave help in depicting the imaginary, and thus will the stage strive to give it.

The bloody dagger is only *seen*, not *felt*: "Mine eyes are made the fools of the other senses or else worth all the rest." Other senses are soon brought in. Macbeth *hears* the voice crying, "Sleep no more." In the sleepwalking scene, Lady Macbeth (V, i, 56) *smells* the imagined blood spots on her hands; and Angus tells us (V, iii, 16) that Macbeth *feels* the clotted blood of his victims on his hands. Macbeth's "I have supp'd full with horrors" suggests the *taste* of blood. All of man's senses can thus deceive him.

In the banquet scene the ghost of Banquo is as purely imaginary as the bloody dagger, coming and going according to Macbeth's fitful hallucinations. By De Loier's test, it is a "phantosme" and not a "specter," for it "hath not any will of its own." Heretofore, image had followed the wish of Macbeth, but in this case it twice follows his feigned wish, expressed in a bravado which is really an expression of his fear. Again it occasions a debate as to its reality, this time with Lady Macbeth, terminating in the acknowledgment that it is an "unreal mockery."

We may accept as authoritative Dr. Schelling's estimate of this ghost as expressed in his *Elizabethan Drama* (Vol. I, p. 582):

> Banquo appears among the guests unseen by them and purely as the subjective result of the concentration of Macbeth's mind on his murdered victim; and the apparition disappears as other figures replace the mental image, a phenomenon repeated in this case with cumulative effect most powerful.

There has been much critical pronouncement as to whether Banquo's ghost should appear physically. The stage direction calls for it, for Shakespeare wished to make sure that his audience should know how vividly and horridly Macbeth sees the gory locks. Yet many great actors have been able to attain the desired effect without it, and modernist sentiment generally extols its banishment. But the fact remains that whether or not this ghost should be shown on the stage is really dependent not upon critical literary judgments but upon the intelligence of the audience. My preference is for the manager who follows Shakespeare's stage direction. Playgoers of this age can be relied upon to know that Banquo's ghost, even though appearing visibly, is purely a creation of Macbeth's imagination. Furthermore, the stage direction at IV, i, 112, compels us to treat the procession of the kings as we do this ghost. If the latter is driven from the stage because imaginary, so too must be the kings, and this is most unfortunate. We do best when we follow the expressed judgment of William Shakespeare, dramatist, stage manager, and actor; for there is no good reason to think that anyone but he wrote the stage directions for the play of *Macbeth*.

Taking up next the necromantic scene, it appears that the oracles uttered by the apparitions are essentially subjective. Here it behooves us to advance carefully, for this proposition has been questioned by high authority.

The first apparition warns, "Beware Macduff," which, as Macbeth says, harps his fear. The second tells him, "Be bloody, bold and resolute." This was his own thought when he had recently called for a "bloody and invisible" hand to serve him in his crimes (III, ii, 48). The third says, "Be lion-mettled, proud, and take no care who chafes, who frets or where conspirers are." This, too, is the comfort he longs for. All of these oracles are "sweet bodements" to the frightened king, and spring from his own brain. But to the last two oracles are appended the familiar deceptive pronouncements concerning the man not born of woman and the coming of Birnam Wood, and these prophetical tags admittedly raise the difficulty which is discussed by Dr. A. C. Bradley in his *Shakespearean Tragedy* (p. 346). After expressing sympathy with the view that the play of *Macbeth* is psychological for those who will so take it, although for the groundlings it is "hard fact," he is led to a skeptical intermediate position in regard to the subjectivity of the apparitions, finding the theory which has been outlined "incomplete" and urging that although it applies to the prophecy of the crown and the warning to beware Macduff, yet the prophecies as to Birnam Wood and the man not born of woman "answer to nothing inward"; for which reason he considers that the theory breaks down at this point.

But this judgment needs to be tempered by noting that the two deceptive prophecies are not of Shakespeare's making, but are an essential part of the Macbeth story as known to King James and all the Scotchmen with him. It was necessary to retain them and weave them into the otherwise subjective prophecies which influence Macbeth's conduct; and the dramatist has done this with great skill, for they are only corollaries to words telling Macbeth just what he wants to be told. In this way this scene (otherwise wholly of his own invention) is caused to include the striking utterances which Holinshed records and to pave the way for the dramatic denouement of the play.

But the dramatist wished to make sure that his audience was not deceived by the visible showing of the apparitions and of the kings, and therefore for the third time he resorted to the device of an argument by Macbeth as to the reality of it all. In our current texts this argument is ruined by the unfortunate interpolation of seven lines with their stage directions put into the play later, probably by Thomas Middleton. What Shakespeare wrote (beginning at IV, i, 122) is the following:

> *Macb.* Horrible sight! Now, I see, 'tis true;
> For the blood-bolter'd Banquo smiles upon me,
> And points at them for his. What? Is this so?
> *First Witch.* Ay, sir, all this is so. (*Witches vanish.*)

> *Macb.* Where are they? Gone. Let this pernicious hour
> Stand aye accursed in the calendar!
> Come in, without there! (*Enter Lennox.*)
>   *Len.* What's your grace's will?
>   *Macb.* Saw you the weird sisters?
>   *Len.* No, my lord.
>   *Macb.* Came they not by you?
>   *Len.* No, indeed, my lord.

These lines conclude the debate which began in the first act as to the reality of Macbeth's hallucinations; and they are proportionately important to an understanding of the whole play. No greater misfortune ever happened to a great play than when Thomas Middleton took *Macbeth* in hand and turned it into a spectacle with dancing witches, actually interposing a divertissement of this sort in the midst of Macbeth's argument. [. . .]

Shakespeare's lines, when freed from the intrusion, tell us that Macbeth has seen his question concerning Banquo's issue answered as he did not wish it answered. But suddenly the "sight" fades, as is indicated in the text by the exclamation "What!" Being gone, the argument begins. Was the sight real or imaginary? The question "Is this so?" comes from a mind writhing in agony. The malign witch affirms it to be verity and immediately the witches, too, vanish. "Where are they? Gone?" Whereupon Lennox, who has come with the king to the door of the witches' house, is summoned and questioned. Did he see anything? Lennox twice affirms that he did not; whereupon with a groan, now knowing himself to be a slave to that which is not, Macbeth expresses the final judgment of the play:

> Infected be the air whereon they ride
> And damn'd all those that trust them.

Macbeth has been damned by his imagination for he will still trust them.

Thus has the Oxford question as to the reality of the effects of the imagination been woven into the texture of the play by showing Macbeth discussing in three different scenes the reality of what he imagines he has seen. The arguments constitute a progression showing how "fortis imaginatio generat casum," for the imagination creates fear, and each fear a greater one, according to the Senecan maxim, "Things bad begun make strong themselves by ill" (III, ii, 55).

The dramatist has been at pains to lead his audience to appreciate the power of the human imagination by carefully chosen gradations. Macbeth's imagination can shake him while yet only a murderous purpose. It can unnerve him by the vision of an unreal dagger. It can paralyze him with fear by the image of Banquo's gory corpse. It can deceive him by horrid apparitions. It can even picture to him that "horrible sight," the line of the future Scottish kings descended from Banquo. At what point in this progression are we to admit an objective reality? Here opinions have and will continue to differ. Every investigator may satisfy himself where the line is to be drawn, but he never has satisfied others. Shall we say they are all real? Or shall we assign all to the imagination? The dramatist strove to make the latter alternative easy for all to whom it is a welcome thought; but left all free to find a limit short of this if they please. The audience at the Globe Theater may take ghosts, devils, apparitions, and sights for verity, but some at Hampton Court and most modern playgoers will not.

When Gervinus says, "Shakespeare's spirit world signifies nothing but the visible embodiment of the images conjured up by a lively fancy," he is speaking to a modern audience in a modern world. The world of King James was very different, and no such convenient generalization is possible in reference to it. But one has only to look and see that Shakespeare wrote his plays with a view to their differing appeal to minds of differing calibers. This it is which has enabled these plays to endure the transformation of popular thought which has since taken place. Ben Jonson foresaw this when he said that his friend was "for all time."

But if King James is to see this play, the important question which at once arises is: What will be his attitude toward the witches, demons, specters, and sights with which the play is peopled? The answer is both interesting and unexpected; for strange as it may seem to those who have not looked into the matter, King James, too, was by this time skeptical concerning the witches of whom in his early years he had written so learnedly in his *Daemonologie*. So we may expect that Shakespeare, when writing a play for his king which exhibits the mighty power of the imagination, will venture to invite the king to take a more rational view concerning witches and necromancy by showing him what strange things the human imagination can do to us.

NOTES

1. The "Discovery of Witchcraft," in his *Amenities of Literature*.

2. New Orleans, 1887, pp. 15–16; reprinted in *The Prototype of Hamlet* (New York, 1890), pp. 54–55.

3. "Shakespeare meant the judicious to take the Ghost [of Banquo] for an hallucination, but knew that the bulk of the audience would take it for a reality." A. C. Bradley, *Shakespearean Tragedy* (1904), p. 493.

"The language and the imagery which he [Shakespeare] employed [in *Macbeth*] were such that each hearer could interpret according to his condition or temperament." Margaret Lucy, *Shakespeare and the Supernatural* (1904).

Shakespeare "distinctly leaves open the question whether these preternatural appearances [in *Macbeth*] are not in fact subjective visions." H. J. Bridges, *Our Fellow Shakespeare* (1916), p. 165.

"To his own generation one of the most amazing things about Shakespeare must have been his power to appeal to the 'generalty' and the 'judicious' at one and the same time." Dover Wilson, Introduction to the 1929 ed. of Lavater, p. xxvii.

4. On April 20, 1611, that notorious scalawag Simon Forman saw *Macbeth* performed at the Globe Theater, and when he reached home he opened his Holinshed to help him to remember what he had seen, and wrote out a description of the play in which he called the sisters "3 women feiries or nimphes," thus evidencing his adhesion to the third hypothesis of Holinshed. One would not expect a professional magician to accept the Sisters' deeds as imaginary, but it is worth noting that he saw nothing on the stage to indicate that they were "goddesses of destiny."

5. This correspondence may be traced throughout the play. Many thinkers have discovered this secret. Coleridge expressed it in his Bristol Lectures of 1813: "They [the witches] lead evil minds from evil to evil, and have the power of tempting those who have been the tempters of themselves." The latest statement of it which I have seen is found in Prof. Morozov's lecture, delivered at the Shakespeare Conference in Moscow in April, 1942: "Macbeth killed Duncan not because they [the weird sisters] had come into his life; they came into his life because he wanted to kill Duncan." *Shakespeare Association Bulletin*, Vol. XVIII, p. 57.

6. This paraphrase uses definitions found in the *Oxford English Dictionary*. Reference is made to the following numbered definitions: thought, 4d; fantastical, 1; single state of man; function, 2; smothered, 3; surmise, 5.

⎯⎯ ⎯⎯ ⎯⎯

1951—Harold C. Goddard.
"Macbeth," from *The Meaning of Shakespeare*

Harold Goddard (1878-1950) was professor of English at Swarthmore College and the University of Chicago. He is the author of *Studies in New England Transcendentalism* (1908) and *The Meaning of Shakespeare* (1951), the latter published posthumously.

> Man is probably nearer the essential truth in his superstitions than in his science.
>
>   HENRY DAVID THOREAU

I

In spite of the intimate links between *Hamlet* and *Othello*, if there were no external evidence to the contrary a case could be made for the view that Macbeth was the tragedy to come next after *Hamlet*, just as a case can be made for the view that *Macbeth* preceded rather than followed *King Lear*. In the former instance I have conformed to the nearly unanimous opinion of scholars. In the latter, more doubtful one I reverse the more generally accepted sequence and take up *Macbeth* before *King Lear*.

Macbeth and *King Lear* were so nearly contemporary that the question of their exact dates is not of overwhelming importance. It is psychological development, not chronology, that counts. And the two are not the same. We frequently go back in going forward. There are eddies in the stream. Ascent and descent are not continuous. We may go down temporarily in climbing a mountain. The child often resembles a grandparent more than he does either father or mother, and there is a similar alternation of generations in the world of art. Because one work is full of echoes of another does not prove that it must have immediately succeeded it. The likeness of *Macbeth* to *Hamlet* is no obstacle to the belief that *Othello* came between them, nor that of *King Lear* to *Othello* to the possibility that *Macbeth* may have intervened.

But somehow the idea that *King Lear* was written before *Macbeth* seems to involve more than this. It is a bit like thinking that *The Brothers Karamazov* was written before *Crime and Punishment*. The analogy is not a casual one. *Macbeth*, like *Crime and Punishment*, is a study of evil through a study of murder. Each is its author's most rapid, concentrated, terrific, and possibly sublime work. Each is a prolonged nightmare lifted into the realm of art. *King Lear* and *The Brothers Karamazov* are also studies of evil; but if they sound no lower depths, they do climb to greater heights than *Macbeth* and *Crime and Punishment*. All four fight through again the old war between light and darkness. But in *Macbeth* and *Crime and Punishment* we have "night's predominance," as Shakespeare phrases it, and the light is that of a star or two in the blackness, while in *King Lear* and *The Brothers Karamazov* the stars are morning stars and there is dawn on the horizon. I know how preposterous this will sound to those who consider *King Lear* the pessimistic masterpiece of the ages.

II

If it be true that all art aspires to the state of music, the opening of *Macbeth* approximates perfection. The contention of the elements and the battles of men are the themes of the witches' colloquy. But their lines are more overture than scene, and the drama has a second opening in the account given by the wounded Sergeant of Macbeth's conquest of the rebels. The passage is like a smear of blood across the first page of the play. The double opening defines precisely what we are to expect: a work dedicated not to the supernatural nor to blood but to the relation between the two. (The modern reader who is afraid of the word "supernatural" may substitute "unconscious.") Passion means originally the capacity to be affected by external agents. In this sense *Macbeth* is a play about human passion.

It is significant that the witches choose for their fatal encounter with Macbeth not the hour of battle but the moment

When the hurlyburly's done.

War plows the soil. Who wins is not what counts. It is what seeds are planted

When the battle's lost and won

that determines the future. Only that future can determine who did win. The phrase might well be written lost-and-won. Already in *Much Ado about Nothing* and *All's Well That Ends Well* (not to mention the Histories) Shakespeare had touched on the aftereffects of war on character. Men who have been valiant on the battlefield can come home to act like cads or criminals in time of peace.

The account of Macbeth's disemboweling of Macdonwald is one of the goriest things in Shakespeare. "Fie, savage, fie!" we are tempted to cry, remembering Hector. But

O valiant cousin! worthy gentleman!

is the way Duncan greets the bloody story. As a concordance will show, Bernard Shaw himself takes no greater delight than the gentle Shakespeare in using the word "gentleman" with devastating sarcasm.

Let each man render me his bloody hand . . .
Gentlemen all,

says Antony to the assassins of Caesar, conscious of his irony as Duncan was not.

. . . this dead butcher and his fiend-like queen

is the way Malcolm, with the finality of an epitaph, sums up this worthy gentleman and his wife in the last speech of the play. It is fitting that it should open with an example of his butchery. Macbeth, murderer of Duncan, and Macbeth, tyrant of Scotland, are implicit in Macbeth, slaughterer of Macdonwald. Yet there was a time, we feel, when Macbeth may have been gentle.

The opening scene and the closing act of *Macbeth* are given to war; the rest of the first act and the second to murder; the third and fourth to tyranny—with further murder. The play leaves us with the feeling that offensive war, crime, and tyranny are merely different faces of the same monster. Tyranny is just war catching its breath. Under it the preponderance of power is so markedly on one side that open violence is no longer necessary. The Enemy is now the subjects. If the fragmentary passages describing Scotland under Macbeth are assembled, they read like a documented account of life in the countries subjugated by the "strong" men of the twentieth century. With its remote setting and ancient superstitions, *Macbeth* to a superficial mind may seem dated. On the contrary few of Shakespeare's plays speak more directly to our time.

III

How did Shakespeare have the audacity to center a tragedy around a murderer and tyrant, a man so different in his appeal to our sympathies from a Romeo, a Brutus, or a Hamlet? He had done something of the sort before in *Richard III*, but Richard is more nearly a melodramatic and theatrical than a strictly tragic success. Doubts remain in many minds whether such a creature could ever have existed. But Macbeth is at bottom any man of noble intentions who gives way to his appetites. And who at one time or another has not been that man? Who, looking back over his life, cannot perceive some moral catastrophe that he escaped by inches? Or did not escape. *Macbeth* reveals how close we who thought ourselves safe may be to the precipice. Few readers, however, feel any such kinship with Macbeth as they do with Hamlet. We do not expect to be tempted to murder; but we do know what it is to have a divided soul. Yet Hamlet and Macbeth are imaginative brothers. The difference is that Macbeth begins more or less where Hamlet left off.

Now might I do it pat, now he is praying,

says the latter, meditating the death of the King,

And now I'll do 't. And so he goes to heaven;
And so am I reveng'd. *That would be scann'd.*

Strange things I have in head, that will to hand,
Which must be acted *ere they may be scann'd,*

says Macbeth, plotting the destruction of the Macduffs. The two couplets seem written to match each other. Yet Hamlet had to go down only a corridor or so from the praying King to commit a deed, the killing of Polonius, of which Macbeth's couplet is a perfect characterization.

My strange and self-abuse,

says Macbeth, unstrung at the sight of Banquo's ghost,

Is the initiate fear that wants hard use:
We are yet but young in deed.

Deeds, he divines, are the only opiates for fears, but their defect as a remedy is the fact that the dose must be increased with an alarming rapidity.

O, from this time forth,

cried Hamlet, shamed at the sight of the efficient Fortinbras,

My thoughts be bloody, or be nothing worth!

The Macbeth-in-Hamlet meant *deeds*, but there was enough of the original Hamlet still left in him to keep it "thoughts." But bloody thoughts are the seed of bloody deeds, and Macbeth, with the very accent of the Fortinbras soliloquy, says, without Hamlet's equivocation,

> from this moment
> The very firstlings of my heart shall be
> The firstlings of my hand.

The harvest of this creed is of course a complete atrophy of heart.

> The time has been my senses would have cool'd
> To hear a night-shriek,

he says when that atrophy has overtaken him,

> and my fell of hair
> Would at a dismal treatise rouse and stir
> As life were in't.

That is Macbeth gazing back, as it were, into his Hamletian past ("Angels and ministers of grace defend us!"), quite as Hamlet looks forward into his Macbethian future. In that sense the rest was not silence.

Hamlet is to Macbeth somewhat as the Ghost is to the Witches. Revenge, or ambition, in its inception may have a lofty, even a majestic countenance; but when it has "coupled hell" and become crime, it grows increasingly foul and sordid. We love and admire Hamlet so much at the beginning that we tend to forget that he is as hot-blooded as the earlier Macbeth when he kills Polonius and the King, cold-blooded as the later Macbeth or Iago when he sends Rosencrantz and Guildenstern to death. If in *Othello* we can trace fragments of a divided Hamlet transmigrated into Desdemona and Iago, in *Macbeth* an undivided Hamlet keeps straight onward and downward in Macbeth himself. The murderer of Duncan inherits Hamlet's sensibility, his nervous irritability, his hysterical passion, his extraordinary gifts of visualization and imaginative expression; and under the instigating influence of his wife the "rashness" and "indiscretion" of the later Hamlet are progressively translated into a succession of mad acts.

It is this perhaps that explains the main technical peculiarity of *Macbeth*, its brevity. It is so short that not a few have thought that what has come down to us is just the abbreviated stage version of a much longer play. As it stands, it has no "beginning" in the Aristotelian sense, scarcely even a "middle." It is mostly "end." The hero has already been tempted before the opening of the action. We do not know how long he has been turning the murder over in his mind before he broaches the matter to his wife, in a decisive scene which is recapitulated in half a dozen lines near the end of Act I and which occurred before Macbeth encountered the Weird Sisters. This is exactly the way Dostoyevski manages it in *Crime and Punishment*, where Raskolnikov is represented as having lain for days on his bed "thinking" before the story actually opens, and we learn only retrospectively of his meeting the previous winter with the officer and student in the tavern who echo his innermost guilty thoughts and consolidate his fatal impulse precisely as the Weird Sisters do Macbeth's. If the novelist abstains from attempting a detailed account of the period when the crime was being incubated, is it any wonder that the dramatist does, especially when he has already accomplished something resembling this seemingly impossible dramatic representation of inaction in the first two acts of *Hamlet*? Why repeat it? When we consider *Macbeth* as a separate work of art, what its author did or didn't do in another work has of course nothing to do with it. But when we consider the plays, and especially the Tragedies, as chapters of a greater whole, it has everything to do with it. What may be a disadvantage, or even a flaw, from the point of view of the man witnessing *Macbeth* for the first time in the theater may be anything but that to a reader of all the Tragedies in order. And the truth of the statement is in no wise diminished if we hold that Shakespeare himself was largely unconscious of the psychic relationship of his plays.

Viewed in the context of his other works, *Macbeth* is Shakespeare's Descent into Hell. And since it is his *Inferno*, it is appropriate that the terrestrial and celestial parts of his universe should figure in it slightly.

Explorations of the underworld have been an unfailing feature of the world's supreme poetry. From the Greek myths and Homer, to go no farther back or further afield, through the Greek dramatists and the theological-religious visions of Dante and Milton, on to the symbolic poems and prophecies of Blake and the psychological-religious novels of Dostoyevski, we meet wide variations on a theme that remains basically the same. All versions of it, we are at last in a position to recognize, are attempts to represent the psychic as distinguished from the physical world. The difference in nomenclature should not blind us to the identity of subject. We could salvage vast tracts of what is held to be the obsolete wisdom of the world if we would recognize that fact. Wisdom does not become obsolete.

IV

Yet there is a historical criticism which thinks Shakespeare was pandering to the superstitions of his audience in *Macbeth* and following a stage tradition rather than life in his study of the criminal nature. Professor Stoll, for instance, in his *Shakespeare Studies* devotes a long chapter, "The Criminals," to proving that Shakespeare's tragic evildoers are not "the real thing." If we seek the real thing we will find it rather, he says, in what science has discovered about the criminal, and what realistic literature, following in its footsteps, has portrayed, in the last century or two. "Men are neither good nor evil," says Professor Stoll, quoting Balzac. "In Nature," he goes on (no longer quoting), "the good and the bad, the healthy and the degenerate, are inextricably interwoven, are one. It was quite another atmosphere that Shakespeare breathed, an atmosphere charged with the dualism of the Middle Ages and earlier times. Good and evil then were as the poles asunder." "The web of our life is of a mingled yarn, good and ill together"; says Shakespeare, "our virtues would be proud, if our faults whipped them not; and our crimes would despair, if they were not cherished by our virtues." Professor Stoll's idea of the modern attitude exactly, down to the very metaphor! It is a Lord in *All's Well That Ends Well* speaking, but there is *Measure for Measure* with its "write good angel on the devil's horn" to show how completely Shakespeare agreed with him. And not one of his greater plays—including even *King Lear*, in which good and evil are indeed fiercely contrasted—but shows the same. Yet it was "quite another atmosphere that Shakespeare breathed." In that case, he did not make his plays out of the surrounding atmosphere.

Professor Stoll cites numerous near-contemporary examples (in which jockeys, gypsies, horse thieves, and pirates figure) to prove not merely the unrepentant but the carefree mood of the "real" criminal after his crime, in contrast with that of the Elizabethan stage offender. "After the crime they go on a lark, play cards with the family, or take a nap," he tells us. "How shallow and obsequious of us," he continues, "to bow to Shakespeare and almost all the choice and master spirits in drama and fiction up to the present age, in their opinion that though there is joy in our hearts when we engage in works of justice and mercy there is no joy in the heart of the miser as he hoards or in the heart of the murderer as he kills! Do we do good because, despite all, we love it, but they evil because they hate it? We ourselves know better." How almost all the choice and master spirits in drama and fiction up to our own more enlightened age happened to agree in their common blindness to notorious fact in this matter is not explained, but among the more modern and less deluded authorities that are cited against Aeschylus, Shakespeare, and Molière are such men as Sudermann, Pinero, and Henry Arthur Jones. Tolstoy is cited too, but he, as Professor Stoll admits, slipped back into the classic error in *The Power of Darkness*.

However that may be, I see no evidence that Shakespeare was unacquainted with either the lighthearted or the callous type of criminal. Autolycus is as carefree a pickpocket as anyone could ask for. Pistol, granted the caricature in his case, is admirably true to the supposedly "modern" criminal type; while it would be hard in all the literature of the nineteenth and twentieth centuries to match the self-possessed Barnardine in *Measure for Measure*, who, as we have seen, coolly upsets all plans for his execution by simply refusing to accommodate the prison authorities. And if anyone thinks these instances edge too near to farce, there are John of Lancaster, who commits his supreme treachery without an inkling, apparently, of its depravity, and Cloten, who goes to his most unspeakable crime in precisely the spirit which Professor Stoll so exhaustively documents. Iago says his plotting gives him so much pleasure that he forgets the passage of time, and even Hamlet—Iago–Hamlet—murders Polonius almost casually, refers to his corpse as if it were a sack of meal, and later comes home from his callous dispatch to death of his old school-fellows, Rosencrantz and Guildenstern, to exchange quibbles, however gravely, with the gravediggers—without a single apparent touch of remorse. The Duke of Cornwall, it is plainly hinted, did not intend to let his turning of the aged King Lear into the storm interfere in the slightest degree with a comfortable evening indoors at home. And the list could easily be extended. The discovery that criminals—many of them—can be carefree before, during, and after the crime may be one of the glories of scientific criminology but it would have been no news to Shakespeare.

Professor Stoll's modern instances are unassailable as far as they go, but what he fails to note is exactly what Shakespeare is so careful to observe: that there are criminals and criminals. As usual, he will not be seduced into too easy generalization or classification, and, instead of presenting us with a "criminal type," gives us every variety of offender against the law. His hired assassins, even when they speak only a few lines, are individualized, and, when there are several of them together, one is often of the carefree sort while one will hesitate and tremble. Professor Stoll's admission in passing that in *comedy* the earlier drama approximates what he calls the facts about the criminal nature is fatal to his argument. For in that case the practice in tragedy of Shakespeare and the other choice and master spirits was obviously not the result of ignorance but of something distinctive about the *tragic* criminal.

What that something is, the difference between Macbeth and Lady Macbeth makes plain, for the husband, not the wife, is the truly tragic figure, and the play is rightly entitled *Macbeth*, not *The Macbeths*. Professor Stoll's own criminological data suggest just this distinction. He quotes penological authorities to show that the sleep of criminals is not disturbed by uneasy dreams and that signs of repentance, remorse, or despair are seldom to be detected in them. In one group of four hundred murderers such signs were found in only three, and in another group of seven hundred criminals only 3.4 percent "showed signs of repentance or appeared at all moved in recounting their misdeeds." That that exceptional 3.4 percent were specimens of what Nietzsche calls the "pale criminal" and included probably the only ones capable of exciting tragic interest Professor Stoll does *not* go on to say. Imaginative literature is not criminology, and, except incidentally or for purposes of contrast, has no interest in portraying primitive, brutal, or moronic types. When rich or noble natures display atavistic traits or slip back into atavistic conduct, as do Hamlet and Othello, those traits begin to assume tragic interest, for tragedy has to do with men possessing the capacity to become gods who, momentarily at least, become devils. The normal man has little in common with these murderers of Professor Stoll's who slay their victims as unconcernedly as an old hand in a slaughterhouse kills cattle. But the normal man, in his lesser degree, *is* Orestes, Macbeth, and Raskolnikov. Such characters tell us, not how the ordinary run of criminals react, but how Aeschylus and Shakespeare and Dostoyevski would have felt, if they had themselves fallen into crime. They are the 3 percent of the 3 percent.

Professor Stoll derides especially the idea that criminals are obsessed with the horror of their deeds before they commit them: "Who sins thus, against the grain?" Or immediately after: "Instead of hearing, like the Scottish thane and the English king, ominous voices," real criminals, he tells us, are likely, after a murder, to fall asleep on the spot, or at least to sleep better afterward. And he cites Raskolnikov in *Crime and Punishment* as one of his examples—a most unfortunate one for his argument, for if ever a man was depicted as both sinning against the grain and being punished *instantly* for his deed it is Raskolnikov. Turn to the text. In the first chapter the murderer-to-be characterizes the crime he is to commit—which he can bring himself to refer to only as *that*—as hideous, loathsome, filthy, and disgusting, two of the four adjectives being identically Macbeth's. ("Temptations," says Professor Stoll, "are not hideous but beautiful." If he had said "fascinating," we could have agreed.) Yet Raskolnikov goes out to do the deed drawn by a power over which he *now* has no control—just as Macbeth was marshaled by the air-drawn dagger. And when does Dostoyevski show his murderer sleeping "better" after the murder? He goes home from it to one fearful nightmare after another, to sleep

> In the affliction of these terrible dreams
> That shake us nightly,

and to say, in effect, exactly as Shakespeare makes Macbeth say:

> Better be with the dead,
> Whom we, to gain our peace, have sent to peace,
> Than on the torture of the mind to lie
> In restless ecstasy.

"Crime and punishment," says Emerson, "grow out of one stem.... All infractions of love and equity in our social relations are speedily punished. They are punished by fear. . . . Commit a crime, and the earth is made of glass. Commit a crime, and it seems as if a coat of snow fell on the ground, such as reveals in the woods the track of every partridge and fox and squirrel and mole." Was Emerson, too, an Elizabethan? On the contrary, like Shakespeare and Dostoyevski, he was not a "fool of time."

Shakespeare's play and Dostoyevski's novel are both dedicated to the proof of Emerson's proposition. Different as are the literary traditions from which they stem, opposite in many respects as are the techniques of drama and fiction, point by point, detail by detail, Shakespeare's and Dostoyevski's treatments of the criminal heart and mind correspond. It is one of the most impressive analogies in all literature: an overwhelming demonstration that genius is independent of time. "Psychologically he was for the age correct," says Professor Stoll of Shakespeare. As if the soul altered from age to age, and was busy, about A.D. 1600, conforming to the conventions of the Elizabethan stage! "In that day when men still believed in diabolical possession," he begins. As if Job and Aeschylus, Dante and the Gospels were obsolete! The fact that the ignorant of all ages have believed in diabolical possession in a superstitious sense is no reason for blinding our eyes to the fact that the imaginative geniuses of all ages have also believed in it in another and profounder sense. And so, too, of the prodigies in the sky and elsewhere that accompany murder in Shakespeare and the Elizabethan drama. "Through it all," says Professor Stoll, "runs the notion that the moment of sin and the manner of the sinner are something prodigious and beyond the bounds of nature, as indeed they appear to be in the person of many a famous actor who saws the air in old paintings and prints." Professor Stoll in that sentence comes perilously close to saying that the moment of sin is *not* prodigious. The possibility that these supposedly astronomical and other portents may be psychical rather than physical phenomena—waking nightmares projected on shapes of the natural world that seem expressly molded to receive them—he does not appear to have taken into account. (Not to suggest thereby that they are just subjective.)

V

Deeds of violence that come exclusively out of the brute in man have no tragic significance and take their place in human memory with the convulsions of nature and the struggle to survive of the lower orders of life. But when a man of imagination—by which I mean a man in whom the image of God is distinct—stoops to crime, instantly transcendental powers rush to the scene as if fearful lest this single deed shift the moral center of gravity of the universe, as a finger may tip an immense boulder that is in delicate equilibrium. Macbeth and Lady Macbeth (as she was at the outset) seem created to stress this distinction. "A little water clears us of this deed," is her reaction to the murder of Duncan.

Will all great Neptune's ocean wash this blood
Clean from my hand? No, this my hand will rather
The multitudinous seas incarnadine,
Making the green one red,

is his. One wonders whether the supremacy of the moral imagination over the material universe was ever more tremendously expressed than in those four lines. In them, space is, as it were, forever put in its place. When Lady Macbeth, in the end, attains the same insight that is Macbeth's instantly—"all the perfumes of Arabia will not sweeten this little hand"—she does not pass, it is to be noted, to the second part of the generalization. It is this defect in imagination that makes her, if a more pathetic, a less tragic figure than her husband.

The medieval mind, in the tradition of mythology, represented the tragic conflict, which our irreligious age is likely to think of as just a strife between opposing impulses, as a struggle between devils and angels for the possession of man's soul. Devils and angels are out of fashion. But it is not the nomenclature that counts, and the soundness of the ancient conception is being confirmed, under another terminology, in the researches of psychology into the unconscious mind.

Now the unconscious, whatever else or more it may be, is an accumulation of the human and prehuman psychic tendencies of life on the planet, and the unconscious of any individual is a reservoir that contains latently the experience of all his ancestors. This potential inheritance is naturally an inextricable mixture of good and evil. Hence whenever the threshold of consciousness is sufficiently lowered to permit an influx of the unconscious, a terrific tension arises between forces pulling the individual in different or opposite directions. Samuel Butler has given classic expression to this struggle in *Life and Habit*:

It is one against legion when a creature tries to differ from his own past selves. He must yield or die if he wants to differ widely, so as to lack natural instincts, such as hunger or thirst, or not to gratify them. . . . His past selves are living in unruly hordes within him at this moment and overmastering him. "Do this, this, this, which we too have done, and found our profit in it," cry the souls of his forefathers within him. Faint are the far ones, coming and going as the sound of bells wafted on to a high mountain; loud and clear are the near ones, urgent as an alarm of fire. "Withhold," cry some. "Go on boldly," cry others. "Me, me, me, revert hitherward, my descendant," shouts one as it were from some high vantage-ground over the heads of the clamorous multitude. "Nay, but me, me, me," echoes another; and our former selves fight within us and wrangle for our possession. Have we not here what is commonly called an *internal tumult*, when dead pleasures and pains tug within us hither and thither? Then may the battle be decided by what people are pleased to call our own experience. Our own indeed!

This passage makes clear why an unmediated polarity is a distinguishing mark of the unconscious and suggests a biological reason for the Delphic character of all true oracles. Every sentence, declares Thoreau, has two sides: "One faces the world, but the other is infinite and confronts the gods." An oracular utterance is merely an extreme form of such a sentence, an incarnation in microcosmic form of the duality Butler depicts. In choosing between its worldly or infernal and its unworldly or celestial meaning, the individual without realizing it recruits an army, the good or bad impulses and acts of millions who have gone before him. Dreams too—many of them—have this ambiguous character and without violence to their imagery can often be taken in contradictory senses. And tragic irony always can. But so hidden may be the second meaning that it requires the future to reveal it, as it may take a second or several readings to uncover it in the printed play.

VI

From end to end, *Macbeth* is packed with these Delphic effects as is no other work of Shakespeare's: words, acts, and situations which may be interpreted or taken in two ways at the peril of the chooser and which in the aggregate produce an overwhelming conviction that behind the visible world lies another world, immeasurably wider and deeper, on its relation to which human destiny turns. As a face now reveals and now conceals the life behind it, so the visible world now hides this other world as does a wall, now opens on it as does a door. In either case it is *there*—there not as a matter of philosophical speculation or of theological tradition or hypothesis, but there as a matter of psychic fact.

Scholars who dismiss the supernatural elements in *Macbeth* as stage convention or condescension to popular superstition stamp themselves as hopelessly insensitive not merely to poetry but to sincerity. Not only the plot and characters of the play, which are up to a certain point the author's inventions, but its music, imagery, and atmosphere—effects only partly under his conscious control—unite in giving the impression of mighty and inscrutable forces behind human life. Only one convinced of the reality of these forces could conceivably have imparted such an overwhelming sense of their presence. Neither could a mere stage contrivance have exercised the influence *Macbeth* has over the imaginations of later poets: Milton, Blake, the Keats of *Hyperion*, Emily Brontë, to name no others. Each sees the poet's vocation, as Shakespeare did in *Macbeth*, as an attempt to reclaim a dark region of the soul. "Shine inward," is the blind Milton's prayer to Celestial Light, "there plant eyes." "To open the immortal Eyes of Man inwards," says Blake, is his great task. "To see as a god sees," cries Keats,

and take the depth
Of things as nimbly as the outward eye
Can size and shape pervade.

Macbeth is a milestone in man's exploration of precisely this "depth of things" which our age calls the unconscious. The very phrase "depth psychology" has been used to differentiate the psychology of the unconscious from shallower attempts to understand the mind.

The more obviously Janus-like passages in *Macbeth*, where the surface meaning is contradicted from below, have often been pointed out. The double intention of the three prophecies concerning the invulnerability of Macduff, Birnam Wood, and the progeny of Banquo no one could miss. These, to be sure, have their theatrical aspect. But they have universal undertones and overtones. Many examples of dramatic irony in the play, too, are familiar: Macbeth's "Fail not our feast," with Banquo's prophetic reply, "My lord, I will not"; the entrance of Macbeth the moment after Duncan has asserted that treachery cannot be read in the face; the appearance of Lady Macbeth just as Macbeth is lamenting his lack of a spur to the murder; Macbeth's words to the murderer outside the window concerning the blood of Banquo that stains his face:

'Tis better thee without than he within,

a line that fairly gleams and undulates with protean meanings. Following one another in uninterrupted succession these things ultimately produce the conviction that there is something deep in life with power to reverse all its surface indications, as if its undercurrent set in just the opposite direction from the movement on its surface.

Take the famous knocking in the scene following the murder of Duncan.

I hear a knocking
At the south entry,

says Lady Macbeth. "Here's a knocking, indeed!" exclaims the Porter (who has been carousing till the second cock) and goes on to fancy himself the porter of hell gate.

Whence is that knocking?
How is 't with me, when every noise appalls me?

cries Macbeth. It is the same knocking—Macduff and Lennox come to arouse the Porter at the gate—but the sound might just as well be in three separate universes for all it has in common to the three listeners. Lady Macbeth hears it with her senses only; the Porter (dragged out of a dream perhaps) with a slightly drunken comic fancy; Macbeth with the tragic imagination. The sensitive reader hears it differently with each. How shall the man in the theater hear it? Here is a poetical effect beyond the capacity of the stage.

And yet it might be managed better there than it generally is. At such performances of the play at least as I remember, the knocking is heard from the first as a clearly audible noise. This is an obvious mistake. What Macbeth hears is not Macduff and Lennox trying to awaken the Porter, but all the powers of hell and heaven knocking simultaneously at his heart. If the auditor is to feel it with Macbeth, he must hear it with him. His ear and heart, that is, must detect it before his mind. He must hear the sound in Macbeth's listening attitude, in the awe on his face, before the physical sound reaches his ear. He, like Macbeth, must be in doubt as to whether he has heard or only imagined. And so the stage sound should begin below the auditory threshold and mount in a gradual crescendo until it becomes indubitably the pounding at the gate, which, with the dissipation of doubt, brings Macbeth back to earth.

Wake Duncan with thy knocking! I would thou couldst!

He is at the gate of hell indeed. But still outside. Repentance is yet possible. The cue for the Porter's speech, which follows immediately, is as perfect as if it had been given by thought-transference. And yet the authenticity of the Porter scene has been doubted!

"Is the king stirring, worthy thane?" Macduff inquires when the gate has finally been opened and after Macbeth has returned. "Not yet," replies Macbeth, and what a shudder the future reads into those two words!

"This is the door," says Macbeth. Four words, this time, instead of two, and as ordinary ones as there are in the language. Yet, as Macbeth utters them, they seem whispered back at him in a voice no longer his own, from the very bottom of the universe. How shall an actor get this effect? He cannot. It transcends the theater as certainly as it does not transcend the imagination of the sensitive reader.

Does Lady Macbeth faint, or only pretend to faint, following the discovery of the murder? The point has been much debated. Everything she says or does in this scene is necessarily pretense. She is compelled by the situation to ape the symptoms of fear. But the acting by her body of an assumed fear is the surest way of opening a channel to the genuine fear she is trying to hide. As in the case of Hamlet's antic disposition, the counterfeit on the surface elicits the true from below.

I will not do 't,

cries Coriolanus when his mother begs him to go through the motions of obeisance to the people,

Lest I surcease to honour mine own truth,
And by my body's action teach my mind
A most inherent baseness.

The psychology here is the same, except that Lady Macbeth does what Coriolanus declares he will not do. Feinting becomes fainting. By sheer willpower (plus a stimulant) Lady Macbeth has held the unconscious out. Now its inundation begins. The end is the sleepwalking scene—and suicide.

At the beginning of the third act Macbeth plans the murder of Banquo. He tries to convince the two cutthroats he has picked for the deed that their ill fortunes in the past were not due to him, as they thought, but to Banquo. His mind is so confused, however, that not only can he not keep track of the passage of time ("Was it not yesterday we spoke together?"), but he mixes hopelessly these men's supposed grievances against Banquo in the past with his own fears of him at present and in the future:

Are you so gospell'd
To pray for this good man and *for his issue,*
Whose heavy hand hath bow'd you to the grave
And beggar'd yours for ever?

It is the descendants of Banquo, not the children of the murderers, he is worrying over. And so of the fierce passage about the dogs that follows. Again, it is of himself, not of them, he is speaking, unawares.

What beast was 't, then,
That made you break this enterprise to me?

Lady Macbeth had asked long before. At last Macbeth realizes that he is indeed slipping below even "the worst rank of manhood" to a bestial level of "demi-wolves" and "hounds." Of insects, even! as the most horrifying, and yet pathetic, line in the play reveals in the next scene:

O, full of scorpions is my mind, dear wife!

And so, when he cries to the two he is suborning, "Your spirits shine through you," we know the spirits he glimpses behind them are the same "black agents" to which he has sold himself. Indeed, so closely does he identify himself with these men and the deed they are to commit for him that he tells them no less than four times in a dozen lines that he will be with them presently again: "I will advise you"; "[I will] acquaint you"; "I'll come to you anon"; "I'll call upon you straight."

As the third scene of the third act opens, a third murderer has just joined the other two where they wait at twilight to waylay the unsuspecting Banquo and Fleance. The next twenty-two lines make one of the most eerie passages in Shakespeare. Who is this Third Murderer? Macbeth himself? As all students of the play know, this explanation of the mystery was suggested long ago, and the idea gains a certain plausibility when we notice that Macbeth has prepared what might well serve as an alibi to cover a secret absence from the palace.

> Let every man be master of his time
> Till seven at night,

he declares to his lords, just after Banquo leaves for his ride,

> to make society
> The sweeter welcome, we will keep ourself
> Till supper-time alone; while then, God be with you!

and the point has added force when we recall that Portia (Bassanio's Portia) and Imogen covered absences from home that they did not wish noted, in just the same way. How easily, too, Macbeth could have hidden his identity—with darkness and fear to help him further to disguise disguise.

> Come, seeling night,
> Scarf up the tender eye of pitiful day,
> And with thy bloody and invisible hand
> Cancel and tear to pieces that great bond
> Which keeps me pale!

"That great bond" is generally taken as referring to the promise of the Weird Sisters to Banquo, but it might also at the same time refer to the great bond of light which by day holds all good things in harmony but keeps pale the criminal who fears it until night tears it to pieces.

But I do not intend to defend the view that Macbeth was the Third Murderer—or that he was not.[1] I wish rather to call attention to a remarkable fact concerning the response of readers to this question. Over the years I have called the attention of hundreds to it, most of whom had never heard of it before. It seems to exercise a peculiar fascination and to set even ordinarily casual readers to scanning the text with the minutest attention. And to what conclusion do they come? With a small group no one can predict. But with numbers sufficient to permit the law of averages to apply, the results have an almost scientific consistency. After allowing for a small minority that remains in doubt, about half are convinced that Macbeth was the Third Murderer and the other half are either unconvinced or frankly think the hypothesis far-fetched or absurd.

But if the idea that Macbeth was the Third Murderer never entered Shakespeare's head, by what autonomous action of language does the text take on a meaning to the contrary that convinces nearly half of the play's readers? And not only convinces them, but, on the whole, convinces them for the same reasons. That without any basis hundreds should be deluded *in the same way* is unthinkable. But why, then, it will be asked, did not Shakespeare make his intention plain?—a question that reveals a peculiar insensitivity to poetry. What the poet wanted, evidently, was not to make a bald identification of the two men but to produce precisely the effect which as a matter of fact the text does produce on sensitive but unanalytic readers, the feeling, namely, that there is something strange and spectral about the Third Murderer as, unexpected and unannounced, he appears at this remote spot where

The west yet glimmers with some streaks of day.

Utter darkness is imminent. Now is the time when the last streaks of day in Macbeth's nature are about to fade out forever—and here is the place. Whether he is present or absent in the flesh, it is here and now that he steps through the door above which is written "Abandon all hope, ye who enter." The author must convince us that virtually, if not literally, it is Macbeth who commits the murder. By letting us unconsciously see things simultaneously from two angles, he creates, as sight with two eyes does in the physical world, the true illusion of another dimension, in this case an illusion that annihilates space.

Macbeth's body—who knows?—may have been shut up in his chamber at the palace. But where was the man himself—his ambition, his fear, his straining inner vision, his will? They were so utterly with the hired instruments of that will that we can almost imagine them capable of incarnating themselves in a spectral body and projecting themselves as an apparition to the other two. And who killed Banquo? Is it the cat's paw that pulls the chestnuts from the fire, or he who holds the cat and guides the paw? So here. And we must be made to feel it—whatever we think. It is the poet's duty to bring the spirit of Macbeth to life on the scene. He does.[2]

How he does it is worth pausing a moment to notice—in so far as anything so subtle can be analyzed—for it reveals in miniature the secret of his power over our imaginations throughout the play.

The Third Murderer speaks six times. All but one of his speeches—and that one is but two lines and a half—are brief, one of one word only, and one of two. And every one of these speeches either has something in it to remind us of Macbeth, or might have been spoken by him, or both.

1. When the First Murderer, disturbed, asks who bade him join them, his Delphic answer is:

Macbeth.

2. He is the first to hear the approaching Banquo:

Hark! I hear horses.

The horse, *that on which we ride*, as we have noted elsewhere, is one of the oldest symbols of the unconscious, and that this very symbol is in a highly activated state in Macbeth's mind Shakespeare has been careful to note from his "pity, like a naked new-born babe, striding the blast," and "heaven's cherubin, hors'd upon the sightless couriers of the air" onward. Later, when messengers bring word of Macduff's flight to England, Macbeth's imaginative ear evidently catches the galloping of their horses before it rises above the threshold of consciousness and he translates it into supernatural terms:

> *Macb.*: Saw you the Weird Sisters?
> *Lennox*: No, my lord.
> *Macb.*: Came they not by you?
> *Lennox*: No, indeed, my lord.
> *Macb.*: Infected be the air whereon they ride,
> And damn'd all those that trust them! I did hear
> The galloping of horse: who was 't came by?
> *Lennox*: 'Tis two or three, my lord, that bring you word
> Macduff is fled to England.

The Weird Sisters could not have been far off, either, when Banquo was murdered. It is interesting, to say the least, that it is the Third Murderer who first hears the horses. Whoever he is, he is like Macbeth in being sensitive to sound. He and Macbeth, it might be said, hear ear to ear.

3. The Third Murderer's next speech is his longest. To the First Murderer's "His horses go about," he replies:

> Almost a mile; but he does usually—
> So all men do—from hence to th' palace gate
> Make it their walk.

Dashes, in place of the more usual commas, help bring out what is plainly a slip of the tongue on the Third Murderer's part. He has begun to reveal what in the circumstances is a suspicious familiarity with Banquo's habits, when, realizing his mistake, he hurriedly tries to cover it with his plainly parenthetical "so all men do" and his consequently necessary substitution of "their" for "his." But Macbeth does much the same thing just before the murder of Duncan is discovered:

> *Lennox*: Goes the king hence today?
> *Macb.*: He does—he did appoint so.

"He does usually—so all men do." "He does—he did appoint so." Such an echo sounds almost as if it came from the same voice. Only someone like Macbeth in combined impulsiveness and quick repentance of impulsiveness could have spoken the Third Murderer's words.

4. The fourth speech confirms the third:

> 'Tis he.

He is the first to recognize Banquo.

5. "Who did strike out the light?" Who *did*? Is it possible that one of the cutthroats is quite willing to kill a man but balks at the murder of a child? We do not know. But it does not need the King's "Give me some light!" in *Hamlet* or Othello's

> Put out the light, and then put out the light,

to make us aware of a second meaning in this simple question. It was the question that Macbeth must never have ceased to ask himself as he went on down into utter darkness.

6. "There's but one down; the son is fled." The Third Murderer is more perturbed than the others at the escape of Fleance. When at the beginning of the next scene Macbeth learns from the First Murderer of the death of the father and the flight of the son, he cries:

> Then comes my fit again. I had else been perfect,
> Whole as the marble, founded as the rock,
> As broad and general as the casing air:
> But now I am cabin'd, cribb'd, confin'd, bound in
> To saucy doubts and fears.

It is mainly on this speech that those who hold absurd the idea that Macbeth was the Third Murderer rest their case, proof, they say, that the news of Fleance's escape came to him as a surprise. But others think the lines have the same marks of insincerity combined with unconscious truth as those in which Macbeth pretended to be surprised and horrified at the death of Duncan.

All this about the Third Murderer will be particularly abhorrent to "realists," who would bring everything to the bar of the senses, and logicians, whose fundamental axiom is that a thing cannot both be and not be at the same time.[3] One wonders if they never had a dream in which one of the actors both was and was not a character from so-called "real" life. Anything that can happen in a dream can happen in poetry. Indeed this scene in which Banquo dies seems one of the most remarkable confirmations in Shakespeare of Nietzsche's main thesis in *The Birth of Tragedy*, that dreams and the drama come out of a common root. When an audience gathers in a theater, they come, if the play is worthy of the theater's great tradition, not to behold a transcript of the same old daylight life, but to dream together. In his bed a man dreaming is cut off from all social life. In the theater he is dreaming one dream with his fellows.

VII

From his encounter with the ghost of Banquo at the banquet, Macbeth, too deep in blood to turn back, repairs at the beginning of Act 4 to the Witches' cavern, bent on extorting the truth about the future, however bad, from these "filthy hags," as he calls them in self-torture. Which raises the question we have intentionally postponed: Who are the Weird Sisters? The Fates? Just three old women? Or something between the two?

Their own reference to "our masters" would rule out the idea that they are The Fates or The Norns, if nothing else did. Bradley declares without qualification: "There is not a syllable in *Macbeth* to imply that they are anything but women." But certainly almost every syllable of the play that has to do with them implies that, whatever they are, they are in intimate contact with that dark Underworld with the existence of which the play is centrally concerned. "In accordance with the popular ideas," Bradley goes on to say, "they have received from evil spirits certain supernatural powers," to control the weather, for example, to become invisible, to foresee the future, and so on. So when we behold them actually doing these things in the play it makes little difference whether we consider them supernatural beings themselves or women who have sold their souls to supernatural beings. The impression in either case is the same: that of demi-creatures, agents and procurers of those powers that, when men's wills falter, pull them down out of their freedom as the earth does the body of a bird whose wings have failed.

At the outset there is something mysterious and wonderful about the Witches, but they grow progressively more noisome and disgusting as Macbeth yields to them. Such is ever the relation of temptation to sin. The poet has shown us various earlier stages of moral disintegration in Henry IV, Henry V, Brutus,

Hamlet, and others. Here is the same thing carried immeasurably further. It is as if man's integrity, once having begun to split up, tends to divide further and further, like the process of organic growth reversed. The Witches, representing this process, resemble fragments of those who, having taken and failed the human test, would revenge themselves on those who are trying to pass it by dragging them back to chaos. "They met me in the day of success!" It is easier to fall than to fly, to destroy than to create, to become like matter than to become like light. Whoever enlists on the side of destruction becomes in that sense an agent of fate.

The ingredients of the Witches' caldron confirm this conception of them. Those ingredients are things that in mythology and superstition, in the old natural philosophy and in our own ancestral consciousness, are associated with the darkest and cruelest elements of human nature: things voracious like the shark, sinister like the bat, poisonous like the adder, or ravenous like the wolf—and of these only fragments, preferably their most noxious or loathsome parts, the tooth, the scale, the sting, the maw, the gall, the entrails. To this predominantly animal brew are added a few vegetable elements, like hemlock and yew, suggestive of death and the grave, and a few reputedly subhuman ones from Turk or Tartar. A baboon's blood cools the whole.

Here Shakespeare is merely reiterating in intensified symbolic form what he has said from the beginning about unregulated appetite and passion. Here, recompounded into a sort of infernal quintessence, is the worst in the spirits of such men as Cardinal Pandulph and Cardinal Beaufort, of Don John and John of Lancaster, of Thersites and Iago. It is as if human nature, which never developed a special gland for the secretion of venom, tends when it degenerates to turn every organ—hand, lip, and brain—into such a gland. The whole body exudes malice and spite of life. The Witches are embodiments of this death-force. Women? Of course—and who has not seen and turned away in horror from just this malevolence in some shrunken old crone? And yet not women—under-women who have regressed beyond the distinctions of sex.

> You should be women,
> And yet your beards forbid me to interpret
> That you are so.

How fitting, after man has done his utmost through war to bring disorder, that the cause of still further dissipation toward chaos should pass, when war closes, into the hands of these wizened hags, the natural representatives of the metaphysically female role of matter in the universe! Earth we think of as clean and beautiful, but spirit gone back to matter is, in all senses, another matter. It is then something miasmic and rotten. "Lilies that fester smell far worse than weeds." It is not just the battlefield covered with things torn and mangled. It is the battlefield after the stench and the putrefaction have set in. The Witches in *Macbeth* are perhaps the completest antitypes to peace in Shakespeare.

The play presents explicitly the relation of Macbeth to the Witches. It leaves implicit Lady Macbeth's relation to them, which is all the more interesting on that account. They do not need to accost her on any blasted heath. She herself invites them into her heart.

Hie thee hither,

she cries to her husband when she has read his letter,

That I may pour my spirits in thine ear.

But who are her spirits? We do not have to wait long to know. A messenger enters with word that "the King comes here to-night." Whereupon Lady Macbeth, in a passage that is the very prophecy and counterpart of the caldron scene, summons her spirits, the murdering ministers that wait on nature's mischief—a very definition of the Weird Sisters—calling on them to unsex her, to cram her with cruelty from top to toe, to turn her milk to gall. That ought to be enough. But Shakespeare makes the connection even more concrete. In planning the murder of Duncan, it is Lady Macbeth who, Circe-like, suggests that Duncan's chamberlains be transformed to beasts by wine and the guilt for the King's death laid at their door:

> When in *swinish* sleep
> Their drenched natures lie as in a death,
> What cannot you and I perform upon
> The unguarded Duncan?

It is this cowardly stratagem which finally convinces Macbeth that the enterprise is safe, and which leads, when the murder is discovered, to the unpremeditated death of the chamberlains at Macbeth's hands.

> *First Witch*: Where hast thou been, sister?
> *Second Witch*: Killing *swine*.

The Second Witch and Lady Macbeth are about the same business. Who can question who poured the suggestion into Lady Macbeth's ear, and helped Macbeth to execute it later? It is the Adam and Eve story over again, with the Witches in the role of the Serpent. Yet these same Witches are powerless over those who do not meet them halfway:

Third Witch: Sister, where thou?
First Witch: A sailor's wife had chestnuts in her lap,
And munch'd, and munch'd, and munch'd. "Give me," quoth I.
"Aroint thee, witch!" the rump-fed ronyon cries.

The Witch is impotent under the exorcism, and swears to try her luck in revenge
on the woman's sailor husband. So little, Shakespeare thus makes plain, is there
any fatalism involved in the proximity of the Weird Sisters where a resolute will
resists. Fire is hot. And fire is fascinating to a child. If the child goes too near
the fire, he will be burned. We may call it fate if we will. It is in that conditional
sense only that there is any fatalism in *Macbeth*.

VIII

The end of the story is mainly an account of how these two once human
beings pass into that subhuman realm of disintegration where the Witches are at
home. One is pushed into the abyss as it were by her memories. The other leaps
into it fanatically, as if embracing it. Her fall is primarily pitiful; his, fearful.

Because, before the deed, Lady Macbeth suffered from defect of imagination
and excess of propensity to act, her punishment, in compensation, takes the form
of being pursued, as by furies, by her memories, by the facts of the past. "How
easy is it, then!" she had said. "What's done cannot be undone," she says now.
Formerly she scorned her husband for his moments of abstraction:

Be not lost
So poorly in your thoughts.

Now she is not only lost but buried in her own, abstracted to the point of
somnambulism.

Come, thick night,
And pall thee in the dunnest smoke of hell,

she had prayed on the verge of the first murder. "Hell is murky!" she mutters in
the sleepwalking scene. Her prayer is answered. She is there. She has a light with
her continually in a vain attempt to shut out the images that follow one another
in perpetual succession. The blood runs from the old man's body unendingly.
She washes her hands over and over. Such a circle is madness. Lady Macbeth is
caught in it. She prefers death.

Because Macbeth saw the horror in advance and shrank from action, yet let
himself be enticed on into it, only to wish his crime undone the moment he
had committed it, his punishment takes the form of a fury of deeds. He meets
anywhere, in full daylight, the specters that at first came to him only by twilight

or at night. If hers is a retrospective and nocturnal, his is a diurnal and dramatic nightmare. If she is transported to an underworld, he transforms his own life into hell. It becomes an alternation of fear and fury. His perpetual reassurance to himself that he cannot know fear is a measure of the fear he feels. As his hand once dyed the world red, his heart now paints it a sickly white. "Cream-fac'd loon! . . . lily-liver'd boy . . . linen cheeks . . . whey-face." These are not so much descriptions of what he sees as projections of what he feels. "Hang those that talk of fear" might be his command for his own death. Now he would have his armor put on, now pulled off. The two moods follow each other with lightning-like rapidity.

> I pull in resolution.
> . . . Arm, arm, and out! . . .
> I 'gin to be aweary of the sun,
> . . . Blow, wind! come, wrack!
> At least we'll die with harness on our back.

These oscillations in less than a dozen lines. And between the fear and the fury, moments of blank apathy culminating, when Lady Macbeth's death is announced, in the famous

> To-morrow, and to-morrow, and to-morrow,

the *ne plus ultra* in English words of the meaninglessness of life—

> a tale
> Told by an idiot, full of sound and fury,
> Signifying nothing.

This is Hamlet's sterile promontory, his foul and pestilent congregation of vapors, his quintessence of dust, carried to their nadir. The kingdom Macbeth's ambition has conquered turns out to be a limbo of blank idiocy.

Of Macbeth's physical bravery at the end too much has been made, for it is mainly desperation. There are other things that help him retain our sympathy more than that.

> They have tied me to a stake; I cannot fly,
> But, bear-like, I must fight the course.

That might well be the memory of some bear-baiting Shakespeare witnessed as a boy. And another touch pierces even deeper. When Macduff finally confronts the object of his revenge, crying, "Turn, hell-hound, turn!" Macbeth exclaims:

Of all men else I have avoided thee.
But get thee back; my soul is too much charg'd
With blood of thine already.

It is his sole confession of remorse. But like one star in the blackness it is the
brighter on that account.

IX

The fourth act of *Macbeth* has been accused of sagging. It has even been
pronounced "tedious." After the concentration of the first three acts on the
two central characters, a fourth act which omits both of them except for its
first scene is bound to fall off somewhat in interest. Yet the long passage in
which Malcolm tests Macduff, to make certain that he is not a hidden agent
of Macbeth, is just one more variation of the mousetrap situation in *Hamlet*,
with echoes of the casket theme from *The Merchant of Venice* and a touch, in
reverse, of the temptation scene from *Othello*. If a passage with such patterns
behind it is found wanting in dramatic tension, it is surely more the actors' or
reader's fault than Shakespeare's. In it Malcolm reveals on a smaller scale some
of the most engaging traits of Hamlet: something of the same modesty, wisdom,
circumspection, and poetic insight, the same tendency to dramatize himself, to
pass himself off for less than he is, to lie low and play psychological games on
others, but without a trace of Hamlet's antic disposition. He speaks in this scene
mainly about evil, but in doing so his vocabulary manages to be full of such words
as angels, grace, child, snow, lamb, milk. If we know Shakespeare, we know what
this means. The man's imagination is contradicting his intellect. His metaphors
are giving away the deeper truth. He speaks of himself as "a weak poor innocent
lamb," yet proceeds a few lines later to assert that he is so full of

All the particulars of vice so grafted,
That, when they shall be open'd, black Macbeth
Will seem as pure as snow,[4] and the poor state
Esteem him as a lamb, being compar'd
With my confineless harms.

The projection on Macbeth of the attributes of snow and of the lamb need not
deceive us as to whose they really are.

Nay, had I power, I should
Pour the sweet milk of concord into hell.

This is a sort of inverted or celestial irony. Malcolm thinks he is stigmatizing
himself as the undying enemy of peace, but over his head the words are a
prophecy that, when he comes to the throne, his love of peace will assuage the

infernal state to which Scotland has been reduced under Macbeth. At the sight of Macduff's genuine grief Malcolm is convinced of his integrity and abjures the "taints and blames" he has just laid on himself as bait. In his retraction, however, he does not claim for himself "the king-becoming graces" he previously listed as his deficiencies, but we more than suspect that he possesses something of every one of them. The mere fact that he is able to give us the most nearly perfect picture in Shakespeare of the ideal king is in itself significant. He seems to have inherited the gentleness of his father along with a greater valor. The outlook for Scotland under him is bright.

X

At the end of the interview between Malcolm and Macduff comes the passage describing the heavenly gifts and graces of the English king (Edward the Confessor), particularly his power to cure "the evil" by royal touch. Historical scholarship tells us that here Shakespeare turns aside from his play to pay a compliment to King James. Doubtless he does pay such a compliment. But that he turns aside to do it is not so certain. Here, to begin with, is the most effective of contrasts between the English king and the Scottish tyrant. More than that. Here is explicitly announced the contra-theme to the main subject of the play. That subject is human traffic with infernal spirits. But King Edward—though "how he solicits heaven, Himself best knows"—has the capacity to become the agent of celestial powers, can use spiritual force to heal rather than to destroy, is an instrument not of darkness but of light. Nothing could be less of a digression than this passage. Without it, and without various little touches throughout the play that support what it says, the play would be a different thing. It is one thing to believe in infernal spirits alone, quite another to believe in both infernal and celestial ones.

Our age speaks of its own spiritual unrest, thinks it permissible to believe in spiritual influences and tendencies, but holds it rank superstition to believe in spirits. It wants the adjective without the noun. The absurdity of this position was long ago demonstrated once for all by Socrates in the *Apology*:

> Did ever man, Meletus, believe in the existence of human things, and not human beings? . . . Did ever any man believe in horsemanship, and not in horses? or in flute-playing, and not in flute-players? No, my friend; I will answer to you and to the court, as you refuse to answer for yourself. There is no man who ever did. But now please to answer the next question: *Can a man believe in spiritual and divine agencies, and not in spirits or demigods?*

And Meletus, driven to the wall, admits, "He can not."

Where there is a gravitational pull, there must be a mass of matter pulling. Where there is illumination, there must be something emitting light. Where there is attribute, there must be substance. Over thousands of years the habits of the human imagination in this matter have never deviated. Socrates and Shakespeare are obedient to them. Those habits, we may be certain, have not been altered by the materialisms and rationalisms of a few generations of the nineteenth and twentieth centuries. During those generations it became fashionable to believe that things psychical are a sort of product or secretion of the brain. Faced suddenly with psychic reality itself, as it has been in two world wars, this unheroic philosophy now cries out in consternation with Macbeth:

> The time has been,
> That, when the brains were out, the man would die,
> And there an end; but now they rise again
> With twenty mortal murders on their crowns
> And push us from our stools. This is more strange
> Than such a murder is.

It is indeed, and from end to end the play is saturated with this strangeness. We put it down with the ineradicable conviction that the instruments of darkness of which it tells are real. It has exposed the sensitive imagination to an experience which otherwise only personal indulgence in cruelty might impart.

There are some human consciousnesses, says John Cowper Powys,

> who are tempted to give themselves up to a pleasure in cruelty; but if they knew the unspeakable ghastliness of the reality they are thus creating for themselves, they would stop dead, *there* where they stand, with a shiver of paralyzed self-loathing. That such cruelty is suicidal from a human stand-point, they know well. They know the ordinary human hell they are preparing for themselves. What they don't seem to know is the far worse cosmic Terror they are bringing down upon them. Insanity, that's what it is; not merely human insanity, but unutterable, unspeakable, *nonhuman insanity*. Sometimes in dreams of the night people who have been deliberately cruel get a glimpse of what they have done, and *what companions they have now got.*
>
> The psychology of cruelty is a strange thing. The cruel person says to himself: "I have got beyond human law and human feeling. All is now permitted me, if I can but harden my heart." Little does he know! Better had he never been born *than have gone where he has gone* and attached to himself the ghastliness of the abyss that now clings to him. The "Hell" of the mediaeval imagination is a poetical joke compared with what he is on the way to experience—crying indeed "upon the mountains to cover

him and the floods to overwhelm him"! Horror is a very peculiar and a very appalling thing; and those who have peeped through the cosmic chink into the Horror-Dance of the abyss would sooner henceforth hold their hands in a candle-flame and burn them to the bone, than give themselves up to deliberate cruelty.

This is precisely the Horror encountered at death by Kurtz, the European who reverted to African savagery, in Conrad's *Heart of Darkness*. It is the Horror of which Henry James gives more than a glimpse in *The Turn of the Screw*.

XI

But now at the end comes the strangest and most paradoxical fact about this play. And the loveliest. If *Macbeth* is Shakespeare's Descent into Hell, it is also his spring myth. This picture of blackness is framed in light, placed, we might almost say, against a background of verdure.

Shakespeare announces this theme, however faintly, in the first pages of the play. The bleeding Sergeant brings word that peace has been made with the rebels but that fresh war at the same moment has broken out with Norway. So storms, he says, sometimes come from the east where the sun rises, or discomfort from spring which promises comfort. Since word is immediately brought that Macbeth has averted the new threat with a second victory, we dismiss the Sergeant's metaphor from mind, not noticing how much better it fits the play as a whole than the minor incidents to which he applies it. For what is the tyranny of Macbeth between the reigns of Duncan and Malcolm but winter come back after the promise of spring only to be overcome in turn by spring itself? For, however delayed, spring always wins. So Malcolm and Macduff subdue the tyrant and Scotland looks forward to a dispensation of peace. Thus does a figure from its first page impart to the play its underlying pattern.

All this, however well it fits, might seem like making too much out of a metaphor thrown out so casually, if we did not know Shakespeare's habit of announcing important themes in the opening lines of his plays, and if, in this case, he had not so strikingly confirmed at the end what he hints at in the beginning. I refer to the coming of Birnam Wood to Dunsinane. When each of Malcolm's soldiers hews down a branch and bears it before him, it is only in a manner of speaking that the forest moves. But it does move in another and lovelier sense. The legend Shakespeare makes use of is a myth of the coming of spring. "The legend of the moving forest originated in the German religious custom of May-festivals, or summer welcomings, and . . . King Grunenwald is originally a winter giant whose dominion ceases when the May feast begins and the greenwood draws near."

War is winter. Peace is spring. Were ever symbols more inevitable than these, especially in the religion and poetry of northern peoples? Winter is a giant. Spring, in comparison, is a maiden. How powerless she seems in his presence! But because the sun is on her side and moves in every root and bud she undermines the sway of the tyrant. She has great allies. And so does peace in this play. The Old Man, for instance, who talks with Ross outside the castle and bids him farewell in those Desdemona-like words:

> God's benison go with you; and with those
> That would make good of bad, and friends of foes;

the Doctor who says at the sight of Lady Macbeth,

> More needs she the divine than the physician.
> God, God forgive us all!

the Waiting-Gentlewoman who bids him, "Good-night, good doctor"; little Macduff; the pious King Edward. These, and others, play no conspicuous part in the story. Yet perhaps Shakespeare is implying that it is only by the collaboration of thousands like them, whose contributions singly may seem as insignificant as single grassblades do to spring, that war, like winter, can be overcome.

NOTES

1. Those interested may find the main arguments pro and con summarized in the Variorum Edition.

2. He does something similar in the scene where Hamlet visits Ophelia in her closet. See my article, "In Ophelia's Closet," in *The Yale Review*, Vol. XXXV, No. 3 (spring, 1946). These interpretations tend to confirm each other.

3. This suggests a very real dilemma in the theater where obviously the actor who plays Macbeth either must or must not play the Third Murderer. More proof perhaps that Shakespeare transcends the stage. Yet something of the effect that the reader gets can surely be suggested in the acted scene, which should be a challenge to a stage director of poetic perception.

4. Notice the echo of the casket theme from *The Merchant of Venice* in that "open'd," and of *Othello* in that "black" and "snow."

1958—Francis Fergusson. "Macbeth," from *Shakespeare: The Pattern in His Carpet*

Francis Fergusson (1904-1986) was a literary scholar and a professor at Princeton University and Rutgers University. He was the author of *Trope and Allegory: Themes Common to Dane and Shakespeare* (1977), *Shakespeare:*

Macbeth was written in 1605–1606, very near *King Lear*, when Shakespeare was at the height of his power. Many critics regard it as the greatest of the tragedies. It is easy to agree with them while one is under its spell.

The story, the main characters, and the dark setting in eleventh-century Scotland, are derived from Holinshed's *Chronicles*. Shakespeare combined the story of Macbeth with that of Donwald's murder of King Duffe, to suit his poetic purpose. He was not trying to write a history, and he knew no doubt that Holinshed's account of that remote time was itself a mixture of fact and legend. But the story had a topical interest: James of Scotland, who had ascended the English throne in 1603, was supposed to be a descendant of the Banquo of the play. It is probable that Shakespeare wrote it for performance at James's court; certainly it would have had special interest for the King. As a young man, James had written his *Daemonologie*, an attempt to get at the truth in the popular superstitions about witches. As a learned amateur theologian, he would have appreciated the fine points in the philosophy of evil underlying the play. As a ruler, he would have watched the career of Macbeth, murderous usurper of the Scottish throne, with fascination. One can trace all of these elements in *Macbeth*; but for us, and for all ages, it lives as the most terrible murder story ever written, and as a poem which haunts the imagination like music.

It is the shortest and most concentrated of the tragedies, and Shakespeare gets it under way with more than his usual speed. The brief appearance of the Witches (Act I, scene 1) suggests that unnatural powers are abroad, seeking Macbeth; their childish doggerel, "Fair is foul, and foul is fair," tells us that things are not what they seem in Scotland. Good old King Duncan with his sons and attendants enters to meet the "bleeding Captain" who has news of a great battle (scene 2); and Duncan also finds that things are not what they seem. "Doubtful it stood," says the gasping Captain, of the battle, "as two spent swimmers, that do cling together, / And choke their art." The battle is between the Scots under their generals Macbeth and Banquo, and the invading Norwegians allied with the Scottish traitor, the Thane of Cawdor. The Scots seem to be winning; then losing: "So from that spring, whence comfort seemed to come, / Discomfort swells." The Captain faints before he can finish his story, but Ross appears to let us know that the Scots were victorious at last, mainly because of Macbeth's demoniac fighting, and that Cawdor is dead. King Duncan decides to reward Macbeth with the traitor's title—and that too sounds sinister and ambiguous, though poor old Duncan meant it so well.

The effect of these two scenes is to focus interest on Scotland, now threatened with mysterious dangers. As in all of Shakespeare's plays about kings, the fate of the monarchy underlies the action: *Macbeth* will not end until the monarchy

is firmly established again. But in this play, more than in any other, Shakespeare
is interested in evil itself: the way men feel its pull, the ways it may affect the
individual and society. In these opening scenes he builds in our imagination the
dark and deceptive atmosphere, the "world of the play," which affects all of the
characters. He shows how their motives are hasty and irrational: even Duncan,
who is so good, is caught in this drive. He overdoes his rewards to Macbeth; soon
he will be racing to Macbeth's castle, supposedly to receive hospitality and honor,
actually to meet his death.

But it is when we meet Macbeth (scene 3) that the action of the play begins
to take on its full power. He and Banquo, leaving the field of battle, meet the
Witches, who have been expecting them; and Macbeth's first line echoes the
Witches' chant of scene 1: "So fair and foul a day I have not seen." Macbeth
is not only the protagonist, he is also the character who sees most deeply into
what is going on. It has often been pointed out that he is both a powerful and
ambitious warrior, and a suffering poet and seer. Perhaps Shakespeare thought
of him as one of the Celtic Scots, a distant cousin of the Welsh Glendower, who
was also fighter, bard, and magician in one. It is Macbeth's subtle and fertile
imagination that makes him so susceptible to temptation; but it also gives him
his appalling insight into his own human passion and torment. In the sequence
of his monologues in Act I we watch the murderous motivation grow; we can see
how it looks from inside—in its own nightmarish light—and also in the sober
light of Macbeth's reason.

When the Witches tell him (Act I, scene 3) that he will be Thane of Cawdor,
and then King, they feed the secret dream he had shared only with his Lady.
When Ross greets him as Thane of Cawdor, he is caught up—"rapt," as Banquo
notices—in a vision of supreme power:

> Two truths are told,
> As happy prologues to the swelling act
> Of the imperial theme.

But he knows, in a moment, that the Witches' truth is double-edged:

> This supernatural soliciting
> Cannot be ill, cannot be good.

And he sees, with dismay, that it has overpowered him:

> . . . why do I yield to that suggestion,
> Whose horrid image doth unfix my hair,
> And make my seated heart knock at my ribs,
> Against the use of nature?

He is alternating between his vision of murder as absolute power, and his vision of the same murder as reason and common-sense reveal it. In this paradoxical experience, he concludes, "Nothing is / But what is not."

In the very next scene (scene 4) he learns that Duncan will spend the night at his castle; and now it seems all but certain that fate or hidden powers have decreed that he shall have the crown by murder. When he joins his lady, and she tells him (Act I, scene 5):

> Thy letters have transported me beyond
> This ignorant present, and I feel now
> The future in the instant

their dream of power seems more real to them than time itself, with its pedestrian facts. But Macbeth recovers even from that. In his great monologue on the brink (Act I, scene 7), the sense of reality, and time, is back; he is "on this bank and shoal of time," and cannot "jump the life to come." He sees exactly what Duncan's murder will mean:

> He's here in double trust:
> First, as I am his kinsman, and his subject,
> Strong both against the deed; then, as his host,
> Who should against the murderer shut the door,
> Not bear the knife myself.

Worse than simple slaughter, the murder is treachery of the deepest kind, which Shakespeare (like Dante) regarded as the deathliest sin, for it cuts the root of all trust, without which no human relationship is possible. Macbeth sees that it will violate the feeling of all humanity: "Pity, like a naked newborn babe . . . Shall blow the horrid deed in every eye, / That tears shall drown the wind." In this sober light, that of reason and experience, he sees the murder as the impossible stunt it is:

> I have no spur
> To prick the sides of my intent, but only
> Vaulting ambition, which o'erleaps itself,
> And falls on th'other—

But at that moment Lady Macbeth finds him.

Lady Macbeth lacks her husband's double vision, but she is an equally profound image of a human spirit in the grip of evil. When Lady Macbeth gets the news (Act I, scene 5) she is as "rapt" as Macbeth, and she too knows that what she wants to do is evil and will not bear the light of day and reason. But she is not appalled, perhaps because she will not perform the butchery directly, but through her husband. Moreover, she can protect herself from the physical horror by rationalizing the corpse as a mere "picture" or "painted devil." Her willful and doctrinaire heartlessness gives us our sharpest sense of human slaughter; but Lady Macbeth herself can repress all natural feeling until it returns, in the sleepwalking scene, to mock her.

Neither of the Macbeths could perform the murder alone. But they are united in a deep, if unregenerate, love; and as a team they feel omnipotent. "This night's great business," says Lady Macbeth, when her husband first joins her (Act I, scene 5), "shall to all our nights and days to come/ Give solely sovereign sway and masterdom." When Macbeth loses this power drive, she gives it to him again; and, sustained by her will, he can say,

> I am settled, and bend up
> Each corporal agent to this terrible feat.
> Away, and mock the time with fairest show.
> False face must hide what the false heart doth know.

Those lines sum up very briefly the themes of concealment, of trying to outwit or "mock" time, and of the murder as an unnatural tour de force. So ends Act I.

No one can miss the excitement of the offstage murder (Act II, scene 2) as reported first by Lady Macbeth, with her glassy self-command, and then by Macbeth, grotesquely helpless after his "feat." But the murder makes a crucial stage in the movement of the play. It is a good idea to pause a moment, to see how Shakespeare reveals this turning point from several points of view.

First there is the Porter who comes (Act II, scene 3) to answer the knocking that frightened the Macbeths. He is resentful at being waked up with a hangover, and he lets three imaginary sinners into hell before he opens the real door to the real knockers. His imaginary sinners were all familiar types. The farmer raises the price when crops are scarce, and absurdly hangs himself when they are abundant. The equivocator is one of the Jesuits who were intriguing against the government; they believed it right to equivocate in defense of their persecuted religion, i.e., "for God's sake." The tailor has stolen cloth from his customer's already tight French-style breeches. All three absurdly try to outwit evil by evil means, and are thus brothers-under-the-skin of Macbeth.

When the Porter at last lets in Macduff and Lennox he plays a final variation on his farcical theme. He makes them wait while he recounts his adventure with drink, "an equivocator with lechery." He had wrestled with drink, and after an even and dubious struggle, has "cast him." His drunkenness is grossly physical, but it reminds us of the Macbeths' more terrible inebriation and their even contest with it. Some readers, including even Coleridge, have found the Porter too coarse for their taste. But Shakespeare knew that a deep motive affects the whole being, including the body and its functions. Having shown the insane drive of evil in the high moral imagination of Macbeth, he now reveals it in the most homely, lewd, and farcical analogies. Moreover he wants his audience to recover, for a moment, from the excitement of the murder, and reflect that all Scotland is now entering the gates of hell.

The lords summoned by the clanging of the bell are at first too bewildered to think. But Macbeth, while they eye him, and while he maintains his pretense of innocence, is realizing his plight in all its hopelessness. Everything he says has a double meaning, which the audience can understand (Act II, scene 3):

> Had I but died an hour before this chance,
> I had lived a blessed time; for from this instant
> There's nothing serious in mortality.
> All is but toys.

That ostensibly expresses the grief of host, kinsman, and subject; but we hear in it his real despair. When Macduff asks him why he killed the grooms, instead of saving them for questioning, he replies:

> Th' expedition of my violent love
> Outrun the pauser, reason.

He is trying to say that the expedition (or hastiness) of his love for Duncan got ahead of his reason, which would have told him to pause. But here again his insight betrays him: we know that it was the violent love of Lady Macbeth that outran his reason at the crucial moment. And we know that ever since the Witches tempted him with their equivocations he has been trying to outrun his own reason.

Anyone who has tried to wink at his own reason, when hurrying into some minor misdeed, can recognize the accuracy of this phrase, "to outrun the pauser, reason." Shakespeare knew all about this motive, in the commonest human experience; that is why Macbeth gets under our skin still. He understood it also in the light of the philosophy he had inherited from the Middle Ages. Reason was supposed to be God's gift to man, which, if obeyed, could reveal to him nature and nature's order, in the individual soul, in society, and even in the cosmos. Macbeth is therefore trying to violate his own nature, the basis of human society, and the divine order in the stars. He cannot succeed; his reason will be with him however fast he travels. At this moment in the play he senses the fact that this unwinnable race is all he has to look forward to.

When the lords recover from their first shock, they too begin to realize what Duncan's murder will mean to them. I have pointed out that during Act I everyone feels the deceptive and unnatural atmosphere in Scotland; and that though Duncan and his nobles do nothing criminal, they too find themselves hurrying like Macbeth, puzzled by the ambiguous meaning of events. Now they enter the hell created by Macbeth, as though Lady Macbeth's "blanket of the dark" covered the earth. Ross, in his talk with the Old Man (Act II, scene 4), builds the scene in our imaginations:

> Thou seest the heavens, as troubled with man's act,
> Threatens his bloody stage: by th' clock 'tis day,
> And yet dark night strangles the travelling lamp.
> Is't night's predominance, or the day's shame,
> That darkness does the face of earth entomb,
> When living light should kiss it?
>   *Old Man.* 'Tis unnatural,
> Even like the deed that's done.

This imagery of blood and darkness prevails until the end of Act IV, when Ross, Malcolm, and Macduff at last glimpse "living light" again. And the loss of natural time, which we know in the orderly sequence of day and night, is suggested in many ways. Scholars have pointed out that we cannot tell how long the action takes—months or years; they might have added that Shakespeare wanted precisely that effect. Like Dante, he sees hell as outside time. The Macbeths feel that, in the phrases I have quoted above. We are made to feel it in many echoing images, and in the rhythm of the action, which sometimes seems lightning-swift, sometimes nightmare-slow, getting nowhere.

The experience of Macbeth and his Lady is, of course, the center of the play. But it is revealed to us in its wider meanings through two complementary themes, that of the Witches, who start the whole action, and that of Ross, Malcolm, and Macduff, who find their way out of the Scottish hell and end Macbeth's career.

The Witches as actually written by Shakespeare are only the three Weird Sisters; Hecate is a late addition by Middleton. With Hecate out of the way, the dramatic and poetic style of the Witch scenes is consistent. And in the light of recent studies we can understand how Shakespeare saw them as stage figures.

He found the Witches and their equivocal prophecies in Holinshed, but developed them according to the popular lore of the time. The Renaissance knew a bewildering variety of witches and magicians, creatures of Latin legend, Norse mythology, and the folklore of northern Europe. We cannot tell whether Shakespeare "believed" in any of this; but we can see that he used it in the play to make the Witches actable, and recognizable to his audience, and at the same time to suggest, behind them, further unseen powers of evil.

When the Witches first appear (Act I, scene 1) we gather that they have been summoned by their Familiars: "I come, Graymalkin"; "Paddock calls." Familiars were minor evil spirits who took possession of old women or other susceptible types, thus making them "witches." Witches had to obey their Familiars, but received in return some power to do mischief themselves, to travel by air, and to sail in sieves. Shakespeare apparently did not show the Familiars onstage, since they are not mentioned in the cast or in stage directions; their presence is indicated only by what the Witches say and by offstage cries and whines. According to folklore, Graymalkin is a cat, Paddock a toad, urchin, or "hedgepig," and Harpier an owl. Through their Familiars the Witches are associated with supernatural powers, the Norns (the Fates of Norse mythology), or Satan himself. But they are not themselves supernatural. They are old women, seduced and thwarted by the spirits they adore and serve.

As old women crazily inspired by evil, the Witches are extremely actable, and far more uncanny than they would be under gauze, with a spooky green light on them. Their appetite for mischief is infinite, but what they can accomplish in that line is limited. The first Witch yearns in vain (Act I, scene 3) to sink the homecoming Pilot's ship, but she can only torment him:

> Weary sev'nights, nine times nine,
> Shall he dwindle, peak, and pine.
> Though his bark cannot be lost,
> Yet it shall be tempest-tossed.

In these lines we hear the teasing whine of one who is herself teased. We hear it more piercingly in the half-truths with which the Witches tempt Macbeth. Unable to ruin him directly, they must tease him into ruining himself. They crave to subject him to the frustrations they suffer, much as Iago craves to subject Othello to the envy and hatred which possess him. There is humor in Shakespeare's conception of the Witches: with their mocking nursery-rhymes, they are queer childish images of Macbeth's terrible futility.

The Witches' charms and incantations are traditional magic. In their final scene (Act IV, scene 1) all that they do is significant at showing their bond with evil. They appear, as before, in response to the mew, the whine, and the cry of their Familiars; but thereafter they deal with their "masters"—probably more potent spirits. The apparitions they show Macbeth, in the form of bodies or parts of bodies, are "necromancy," supposedly the best kind of prophecy. They show in this scene the utmost their "art" can accomplish, stirring the cauldron, making their circles, and adding the ingredients according to the recipes of classical demonology.

They are treating Macbeth with new respect because they know that Macbeth himself now has status in hell. Like Faust, Macbeth has "mine eternal jewel / Given to the common enemy of man." Moreover he has seen that he has probably sold his soul in vain, for Banquo rose from the dead to plague him (Act III, scene 4) and Banquo's son escaped for all his efforts. That point—the banquet

scene and its aftermath—marks the climax and turning point in Macbeth's
action. He has no hope of winning, nor can he turn back:

> I am in blood
> Stepped in so far, that should I wade no more,
> Returning were as tedious as go o'er—

the dreariest version of his nightmare race. Now (after the banquet scene), he is
"bent to know / By the worst means the worst," and he commands the Witches
to show it to him even though "destruction sicken."

The Witches are his to command; yet they contrive to play with him a little
longer. The apparitions are arranged in such a way as to make him hope, then
despair, then hope again. Then they finish him off in triumph: "Show! / Show! /
Show! / Show his eyes, and grieve his heart. / Come like shadows, so depart."

The apparitions refer in their ambiguous way to Macbeth's fate as it actually
overtakes him in Act V. They also suggest the nature of Macbeth's crimes, the
judgment of God upon them, and the return of the pretty world once he is
gone. They are announced by thunder, a sign of the voice of God since the most
ancient times. Macbeth half understands that himself; he wants to "tell pale-
hearted fear it lies; / And sleep in spite of thunder." The Armed Head means
Macbeth himself (whose head is cut off in the end) and Macduff, who kills him.
The Bloody Child also means Macduff, of course; and it is a reminder of Lady
Macbeth's babe (Act I, scene 7) whose boneless gums she is prepared to pluck
from her nipple to dash its brains out; and Macbeth's "pity, like a naked, newborn
babe" whom he was about to violate by murder. Shakespeare often uses children
as the most touching and natural symbol of new life and hope; in this scene
they suggest both what Macbeth was trying to kill, and his ultimate failure. The
"Child, crowned, with a tree in his hand," carries all these meanings. He means
Banquo's issue; the tree is the genealogical tree of the Scottish kings all the way
down to James. The tree also means Birnam Wood, and as such gives Macbeth
false hope. And the leafy tree is a symbol as old, and as universal, as thunder,
for the springtime renewal of life itself. It occurs in countless primitive festivals
which mark the death of Old Man Winter and the joyful birth of his successor.
Shakespeare was familiar with it, as the Maypole, in the spring festivals all over
England. It is still used in country districts.

These visions reveal what is going on in Macbeth's suffering, perceptive mind
and spirit, and they are connected with the imagery of his monologues. In this
respect they are like the premonitions of disaster that Shakespeare so often
grants to his tragic protagonists in the fourth act of the tragedy. But by means of
the Witches he gives them a kind of objective reality: behind them we can make
out the whole ordered world of Shakespeare's tradition, violated by Macbeth, and
now returning in triumph.

The Witches disappear as the endless procession of Kings begins, to the sound of hautboys, and we never see them again. Macbeth returns with a bump to present reality, and instantly hears "the galloping of horse," the windy sound of the losing race which is all he has to look forward to. We do not see him again until the final sequences in Dunsinane (Act V).

The rest of Act IV and much of Act V are dominated by Malcolm, Macduff, and Ross, who reverse the hellish course of events and end Macbeth's career. What Malcolm and his friends do is obviously essential to the whole plot, and equally important in revealing the meaning Shakespeare saw in the story. But the great scene in England (Act IV, scene 3), when they resolve to act, has puzzled some readers.

During the first three acts Macbeth's enemies have little to say for themselves; Macbeth is literally "getting away with murder." The darkness closes over them, and they are afraid to move. Ross sums up this situation when he tries (Act IV, scene 2) to explain to Lady Macduff why her husband has fled to England:

> I dare not speak much further,
> But cruel are the times, when we are traitors,
> And do not know ourselves; when we hold rumor
> From what we fear, yet know not what we fear,
> But float upon a wild and violent sea
> Each way and move.

When no man can trust himself, or anyone else, all are in a sense "traitors," no matter what they do. That is the plight of Malcolm and Macduff when we meet them in exile at the English court (Act IV, scene 3). The scene is in three movements: first, the painful dialogue between Malcolm and Macduff; second, the interlude with the English Doctor; and finally, the sequence with Ross, who brings the news of Lady Macduff's murder, after which they unite and take action.

The first movement of the scene, in which Malcolm and Macduff try in vain to find some basis for mutual trust, often seems too long, and is, therefore, usually cut in production. Malcolm's false confession, that he has more lust, avarice, and treachery than Macbeth himself, is taken from Holinshed. It is, of course, a piece of philosophizing about evil: lust is the lightest of sins, avarice more dangerous, but only treachery (Macbeth's sin) is beyond all remedy. The verse of this sequence lacks the visionary intensity of the rest of the play. The movement is slow, like that of careful, tentative thinking. And we are likely to feel that the classification of sins, when made so explicit, is rather stiff and old-fashioned. And yet Shakespeare had his dramatic intention in writing the scene in just this way. Malcolm and Macduff, in England, are free from the rush of immediate danger, but they do not "know themselves." They are in a kind of vacuum; time seems hardly to move at all; they resort to thought in their search for a way out. But they fail: Malcolm cannot trust Macduff, who left his wife and child, and Macduff, after Malcolm disavows his confession, sadly remarks, "Such welcome and unwelcome things at once / 'Tis hard to reconcile," echoing the "fair is foul" theme with which the whole play started.

At that point the Doctor appears, and we learn that the English King, Edward the Confessor, is about to cure, by his touch, a disease which resists the Doctor's medical arts. According to an old legend the English kings inherited the miraculous gift of healing scrofula, "the King's evil," and James I, though skeptical, still "touched" for this disease. This scene also is often cut in production, and some critics think Shakespeare put it in at the last minute to flatter James. However that may be, it seems to be an essential part of Shakespeare's design. The Doctor foreshadows the Doctor (Act V, scene 1) who remarks of the sleepwalking Lady Macbeth, "More needs she the divine than the physician." King Edward may remind us of "the gracious Duncan," who glimpsed the clear evening sky just before entering Macbeth's dark castle. In this scene the interlude serves to remind us, not only that "sundry blessings hang about [Edward's] throne, / That speak him full of grace," but also of the healthful world of nature which is still there, behind the nightmare. And it suggests that Malcolm and Macduff can never return to that reality by their own reason or their own efforts: some outside help is needed, some "grace of God."

The third movement of the scene, which begins with Ross's entrance, shows how the three exiles at last receive this grace. "Good God, betimes remove / The means that makes us strangers," says Malcolm, when he recognizes Ross. His prayer defines the motive of all three exiles. But the prayer is not granted until they face the worst: the news of the slaughter of Lady Macduff and her children, which convicts them all of a share in Macbeth's guilt. Only then can they recognize themselves, and then each other, as they really are in the real world. Their way is clear at last; they find the faith to put their cause to the ordeal of battle; and in Malcolm's final words we already hear the healthy throb of military music:

> This tune goes manly.
> Come go we to the King, our power is ready,
> Our lack is nothing but our leave. Macbeth
> Is ripe for shaking, and the powers above
> Put on their instruments. Receive what cheer you may,
> The night is long that never finds the day.

Shakespeare apparently planned this scene (like so much of *Macbeth*) in accordance with medieval theories of evil and its cure through the grace of

God. But he presents it all in terms of Malcolm's and Macduff's experience. They are lost, and they cannot think their way out. But when they accept that fact, the scene changes. The faith they get in each other and in their cause is, in the last analysis, as mysterious, as irrational, as Macbeth's evil drive; but such a suprarational act of faith is the only cure for the terrible uncertainty which has paralyzed them. The swift movement of the play starts again; the theme of striving beyond reason, now interpreted as an act of faith, resounds in a major key. Throughout the fifth act we are aware of the armies with their drums and trumpets converging on Dunsinane. When they triumph, all the ambiguous omens reveal their literal truth and their natural explanations; the nightmare dissolves, and the daylight world of reason and common sense comes back.

In the last act, however, the deepest images are those of Macbeth and his lady. Through the clear, but sympathetic, eyes of the Doctor and the Nurse we watch Lady Macbeth walking in her sleep. Is she fully human, or a puppet of her visions? As she reenacts the murder of Duncan, then of Banquo, she repeats her formulas for suppressing the horror, but now they no longer work. "Oh, oh, oh!" she sighs, smelling the blood: "The heart is sorely charged," says the Doctor. In her nightgown, alone, she would look less like the power-mad woman of Act I than like a little girl lost in the dark.

Macbeth has also become a kind of puppet, but a dangerous one. Caithness reports (Act V, scene 2):

Some say he's mad; others, that lesser hate him,
Do call it valiant fury, but for certain
He cannot buckle his distempered cause
Within the belt of rule.

As Macbeth tries in vain to rule his country and his fate, we see him as a mechanical monster: his pestered senses recoil; he is a dwarfish thief in a giant's robe: he sags with doubt or shakes with fear. At the end his head comes in on a pole, looking, I suppose, like Lady Macbeth's painted devil that scares the eye of childhood. But even here, in the last few hours, Macbeth's insight does not leave him. Out of the knowledge it gives him come some of the saddest melodies ever written:

My way of life
Is fallen into the sear, the yellow leaf,
And that which should accompany old age,
As honour, love, obedience, troops of friends,
I must not look to have; but in their stead
Curses, not loud but deep, mouth-honour, breath,
Which the poor heart would feign deny, and dare not.

These lines express the same vision which Macbeth got just after Duncan's murder, that for him, henceforth, "there's nothing serious in mortality." *Macbeth* is the most unified of Shakespeare's tragedies; the whole meaning of the play resounds in all of the verse. If one listens to that music, there is little need for scholarly explanations.

—⁓〰⁓— —⁓〰⁓— —⁓〰⁓—

1959—L. C. Knights. "Macbeth: A Lust for Power," from *Some Shakespearean Themes*

L. C. Knights (1906–1997), an English critic, is probably most famous for his essay "How Many Children Had Lady Macbeth?" in which he attacked what he considered the excessively character-based criticism propounded by writers such as A. C. Bradley. But the essay below, which discusses Macbeth's hunger for power, is sometimes regarded as the more profound.

Macbeth defines a particular kind of evil—the evil that results from a lust for power. The defining, as in all the tragedies, is in strictly poetic and dramatic terms. It is certainly not an abstract formulation, but lies rather in the drawing out of necessary consequences and implications of that lust both in the external and the spiritual worlds. Its meaning, therefore, is revealed in the expansion and unfolding of what lies within the initial evil, in terms of direct human experience. The logic is not formal but experiential, and demands from us, if we are to test its validity and feel its force, a fulness of imaginative response and a closeness of realization, in which both sensation and feeling become modes of understanding. Only when intellect, emotion, and a kind of direct sensory awareness work together can we enter fully into that exploratory and defining process.

In other words, the essential structure of *Macbeth*, as of the other tragedies, is to be sought in the poetry. That of course is easily said; what it means is something that can only be grasped in relation to specific instances or not grasped at all. We may take as an example Macbeth's "aside" when he has been greeted as Thane of Cawdor.

> This supernatural soliciting
> Cannot be ill; cannot be good:—
> If ill, why hath it given me earnest of success,
> Commencing in a truth? I am Thane of Cawdor:
> If good, why do I yield to that suggestion
> Whose horrid image doth unfix my hair,

And make my seated heart knock at my ribs,
Against the use of nature? Present fears
Are less than horrible imaginings.
My thought, whose murder yet is but fantastical,
Shakes so my single state of man,
That function is smother'd in surmise,
And nothing is, but what is not. (1.3.130–42)

This is temptation, presented with concrete force. Even if we attend only to
the revelation of Macbeth's spiritual state, our recognition of the body—the
very feel—of the experience, is a response to the poetry, to such things as the
sickening seesaw rhythm ("Cannot be ill; cannot be good") changing to the
rhythm of the pounding heart, the overriding of grammar ("My thought, whose
murder yet is but fantastical") as thought is revealed in the very process of
formation, and so on. But the poetry makes further claims, and if we attend to
them we find that the words do not only point inward to the presumed state of
Macbeth's mind but, as it were, outward to the play as a whole. The equivocal
nature of temptation, the commerce with phantoms consequent upon false
choice, the resulting sense of unreality ("nothing is, but what is not"), which has
yet such power to "smother" vital function, the unnaturalness of evil ("against the
use of nature"), and the relation between disintegration in the individual ("my
single state of man") and disorder in the larger social organism—all these are
major themes of the play which are mirrored in the speech under consideration.
They emerge as themes because they are what the poetry—reinforced by action
and symbolism—again and again insists on. And the interrelations we are forced
to make take us outside the speeches of the protagonist to the poetry of the play
as a whole. That "smother'd," for example, takes us forward not only to Lady
Macbeth's "blanket of the dark" but to such things as Ross's choric comment after
the murder of Duncan:

                    by th' clock 'tis day,
And yet dark night strangles the travelling lamp.
Is't night's predominance, or the day's shame,
That darkness does the face of earth entomb,
When living light should kiss it? (2.4.6–10)

In none of the tragedies is there anything superfluous, but it is perhaps
Macbeth that gives the keenest impression of economy. The action moves directly
and quickly to the crisis, and from the crisis to the full working out of plot and
theme. The pattern is far easier to grasp than that of *Lear*. The main theme of the
reversal of values is given out simply and clearly in the first scene—"Fair is foul,
and foul is fair"; and with it are associated premonitions of the conflict, disorder

and moral darkness into which Macbeth will plunge himself. Well before the end of the first act we are in possession not only of the positive values against which the Macbeth evil will be defined but of the related aspects of that evil, which is simultaneously felt as a strained and unnatural perversion of the will, an obfuscation of the clear light of reason, a principle of disorder (both in the "single state of man" and in his wider social relations), and a pursuit of illusions. All these impressions, which as the play proceeds assume the status of organizing ideas, are produced by the interaction of all the resources of poetic drama—action, contrast, statement, implication, imagery and allusion. Thus the sense of the unnaturalness of evil is evoked not only by repeated explicit references ("nature's mischief," "nature seems dead," "'Tis unnatural, even like the deed that's done," and so on) but by the expression of unnatural sentiments and an unnatural violence of tone in such things as Lady Macbeth's invocation of the "spirits" who will "unsex" her, and her affirmation that she would murder the babe at her breast if she had sworn to do it. So too the theme of the false appearances inseparable from evil, of deceit recoiling on the deceiver, is not only the subject of explicit comment

—And be these juggling fiends no more believ'd,
That palter with us in a double sense— (5.8.19–20)

it is embodied in the action, so that Macbeth's despairing recognition of mere "mouth-honour" among his remaining followers (5.3.27) echoes ironically his wife's advice to "look like th' innocent flower, But be the serpent under't" (1.5.64–65) and the hypocritical play of the welcoming of Duncan; and it is reinforced by—or indeed one with—the evoked sense of equivocation and evasiveness associated with the witches, and the cloud of uncertainty that settles on Scotland during Macbeth's despotism. It is fitting that the final movement of the reversal that takes place in the last act should open with the command of Malcolm to the camouflaged soldiers, "Your leavy screens throw down, And show like those you are" (5.6.1–2).

II

The assurance of *Macbeth* has behind it, is indeed based on, a deeply imagined resolution of perplexities inherent in any full exposure to life. Freedom from the tyranny of time and illusion is finally related, at the deepest levels of consciousness, to the central affirmations of the spirit; and conversely, the obsessed awareness of time without meaning, like the subjection of mind to appearance, is revealed not simply as consequential on false choice but as intrinsic to it: for "the eye altering alters all." There is a similar assurance in the use of "nature," in that aspect of the play's imaginative structure that impels us to say not merely that Macbeth's crime is unnatural (i.e., inhuman) but that the values against which evil is defined are in some sense grounded in nature. To suggest how this is so, to relate the insights operative here to those already touched on, it is necessary to step back from the play and to see it in the wider context of Shakespeare's development as a whole. Although in recent years much has been written about the meanings of nature in Shakespeare and his contemporaries, there is still need for further clarification of the perceptions controlling the use of this elusive, indispensable and pregnant word.

In Shakespeare's poetic thought we find two apparently contradictory intuitions regarding man's relation to the created world existing independently of human choice and will. Nature and human values are felt as intimately related, and at the same time as antagonistic.

They are related in two ways. Shakespeare, like almost all poets, uses natural imagery to evoke and define qualities that are humanly valuable, indeed indispensable to any full humanity:

> She that herself will sliver and disbranch
> From her material sap, perforce must wither
> And come to deadly use.

>   For his bounty,
> There was no winter in't; an autumn 'twas
> That grew the more by reaping.

These are striking instances, but in even apparently casual metaphors and similes—"my love is all as boundless as the sea," "and she in thee Calls back the lovely April of her prime," "as dear to me as are the ruddy drops that visit my sad heart"—it seems that we have to do with a relationship more intimate than that of mere resemblance: the mind has in some sense *found itself* in nature; for, as Leone Vivante says of Shakespeare's images of budding and of morning, "the grace of things in their birth and their first purity would not be perceived, if it were not *first* a quality of our mental synthesis which is revealed in and through them." This is indeed a truth of general application; Blake's Tiger, Herbert's Flower, Marvell's Garden (in the poems of those names), and Wordsworth's

>   uncertain heaven, received
> Into the bosom of the steady lake,
>   (*The Prelude*, 5.387–88)

all imply a basic kinship of human and nonhuman life: mind would be less truly itself if it were not deeply responsive to images such as these. The correspondences between mind and natural forms and natural processes is attested by common speech as well as by the poets. Just as it is with peculiar rightness that George Herbert can say, "And now in age I bud again," or that Marvell can speak of "a green thought in a green shade," so images of budding, growing, harvesting, of night, dawn and day, of seasons and weathers, of climates and landscapes, are integral to the speech in which we ourselves feel after inner experience.

> La Nature est un temple où de vivants piliers
> Laissent parfois sortir de confuses paroles;
> L'homme y passe à travers des forêts de symboles
> Qui l'observent avec des regards familiers.

In Shakespeare there is no attempt to explain the working of these *regards familiers*; but the mere fact that his plays and poems are full of these more-than-analogies implies that psychic life is at home in nature.

But even if we leave aside the difficult question of natural symbolism, there is no doubt that wherever Shakespeare envisages a fully human way of life he thinks of it as closely related to the wider setting of organic growth, as indeed, in a quite concrete and practical way, directly based on man's dealings with the earth that nourishes him. It is of course in *The Winter's Tale* that we are most explicitly aware of nature as a powerful controlling presence—a presence moreover not vaguely felt but specifically rendered in the great pastoral scene with its many reminders of seasonal activities, humble in themselves but translucent to the great myths. But Shakespeare's vision of the intimate relationship between man and nature, of nature as the necessary basis and, under certain conditions, the pattern for civilization, goes back to the period before the final plays and before the tragedies. It is expressed in the beautiful but strangely neglected speech of Burgundy, in *King Henry V*, when he urges peace.

>   let it not disgrace me
> If I demand before this royal view,
> Why that the naked, poor, and mangled Peace,
> Dear nurse of arts, plenties, and joyful births,
> Should not in this best garden of the world,
> Our fertile France, put up her lovely visage?
> Alas! she hath from France too long been chas'd,
> And all her husbandry doth lie on heaps,
> Corrupting in its own fertility.
> Her vine, the merry cheerer of the heart,
> Unpruned dies; her hedges even-pleach'd
> Like prisoners wildly overgrown with hair,
> Put forth disorder'd twigs; her fallow leas
> The darnel, hemlock and rank fumitory
> Doth root upon, while that the coulter rusts
> That should deracinate such savagery;

The even mead, that erst brought sweetly forth
The freckled cowslip, burnet, and green clover,
Wanting the scythe, all uncorrected, rank,
Conceives by idleness, and nothing teems
But hateful docks, rough thistles, kecksies, burrs,
Losing both beauty and utility.
And as our vineyards, fallows, meads, and hedges,
Defective in their natures, grow to wildness,
Even so our houses and ourselves and children
Have lost, or do not learn for want of time,
The sciences that should become our country,
But grow like savages, as soldiers will
That nothing do but meditate on blood,
To swearing and stern looks, defus'd attire,
And every thing that seems unnatural. (5.2.31–62)

There is here an imaginative vision that transcends the simple sequence of the argument. After the preliminary invocation of peace the passage is built on a simple inversion: uncultivated nature ("corrupting in its own fertility"—a phrase that Milton must have remembered) is compared to disorderly or uncultivated human life, which in turn is compared to "wild" or "savage" nature. But what we have to deal with is something more complex than a simple comparison which is then given again with the terms reversed; Burgundy is throughout expressing a sense of the interrelationship—a two-way traffic—between man and nature. Natural fertility ("our fertile France") is the necessary precondition not only of life at the biological level but of the highest reaches of manmade civilization—the "arts" and "sciences" (both of which can be interpreted in the widest sense); whilst at the same time, since peace is the nurse not only of these but of all that comes to birth, of the very fertility on which the whole range of human activity depends, and since it is man who *makes* peace, man is responsible for nature. The alternative to peace is "wildness" in both man and nature, and for man to tame that wildness in himself is a process analogous to taming what is given in external nature. So much is stated or directly suggested: what is not quite explicit but imaginatively present, adding life and vibrancy to the flat prose-meaning to which I have reduced the poetry, is the vision of peace. Conceived throughout as a wholesome *activity*—"laying" hedges, ploughing, and so on are taken as representative examples—it is a state in which arts and sciences and daily beauty and utility are conceived both as end and as condition of the fertility on which all alike depend. Behind the image of life and nature run wild for lack of human care is the implied ideal of natural force tended and integrated into a truly human civilization. And the inclusive "Peace," teeming with human activity, is the "natural" end of the "joyful births": it is the alternative "wildness" that is "unnatural."

But if Burgundy's speech, looking forward as it does to *The Winter's Tale*, represents an important element in Shakespeare's imaginative vision of man and nature, there is also another, its polar opposite, of which a brief reminder will serve. If nature is bounty she is also decay; she is the ally of chance in "untrimming" "every fair" (Sonnet 18); it is the same sky that indifferently "cheers" and "checks" both men and flowers (Sonnet 15). Worse still, if nature as the world of organic growth and decay is indifferent to human needs, as instinct and appetite ("blood") she can be positively hostile to the life of the spirit. And between "natural law" as traditionally understood (i.e., reason) and the law of nature by which, as Falstaff lightly remarked, the young dace is a bait for the old pike, there is an absolute distinction.

All this Shakespeare knew well enough, and in *King Lear*, addressing himself to the question of man's place in nature, and with a full view of all the potential evil in man as part of nature, he magnificently reaffirmed the autonomy of the spirit. Yet in Shakespeare's poetic thought the idea of relationship to nature seems as integral as the idea of the fundamental difference between the two realms. The question we are forced to ask, therefore, is, If human nature is not entirely at home in the world of nature, if in some essential ways it is set over against nature, how can mind find itself in nature, as there is such abundant testimony that it does? How is it that in *Macbeth* (to be specific) essential distinctions of good and evil, belonging to the inner world, can be defined in imagery of the outer world of nature, defined moreover in such a way that the imaginative correspondence goes far beyond the use of selected analogies and implies a symbolic equivalence—indeed a relationship—between what is "natural" for man and what is "natural" in the simplest and widest sense of the word?

We are led back once more to *King Lear*, to one scene in particular where we first become conscious of a change in direction of the imaginative current of the play, as though a slight but unmistakable breeze were announcing that a tide, still at the ebb, is about to turn. In the opening scenes of act 4 the worst is still to come; both Gloucester and Lear have still to reach the lowest point of their despair. But Gloucester, we know, is in the care of Edgar, and in the fourth scene, immediately after we have been told of Lear's purgatorial shame, Cordelia enters, "with drum and colours," seeking her father.

> *Cordelia*: Alack! 'tis he: why, he was met even now
> As mad as the vex'd sea; singing aloud;
> Crown'd with rank fumiter and furrow-weeds,
> With hardocks, hemlock, nettles, cuckoo-flowers,
> Darnel, and all the idle weeds that grow

In our sustaining corn. A century sent forth;
Search every acre in the high-grown field,
And bring him to our eye. [*Exit* AN OFFICER.]
       What can man's wisdom
In the restoring his bereaved sense?
He that helps him take all my outward worth.
    Doctor: There is means, madam;
Our foster-nurse of nature is repose,
The which he lacks; that to provoke in him,
Are many simples operative, whose power
Will close the eye of anguish.
    Cordelia: All bless'd secrets,
All you unpublish'd virtues of the earth,
Spring with my tears! be aidant and remediate
In the good man's distress! Seek, seek for him,
Lest his ungovern'd rage dissolve the life
That wants the means to lead it. (4.4.1–20)

What is remarkable here is the particular quality of the awareness of nature that lies behind and informs the poetry. Lear's "ungovern'd rage" is compared, as before, to elemental fury ("as mad as the vex'd sea"), and his mock crown is fittingly made up of "idle weeds," astonishingly present in the clogged movement of the lines that list them. Yet co-present with these—and given emphasis by the lift and smooth sweep of the verse—is "our sustaining corn"; and the same earth bears the medicinal plants that foster restoring sleep ("balm of hurt minds, great nature's second course"). Nature, then, is contemplated in both its aspects, as that which preserves and as that which impedes, encroaches on or rises in turmoil against man's specifically human activities; and it is contemplated with a peculiar serenity. It is of course contemplated from the standpoint of Cordelia; and her qualities—those particularly that lie behind this serenity—have been explicitly and beautifully evoked in the immediately preceding scene. The law of her nature, it is clear, is quite other than the law of nature to which Goneril and Regan abandon themselves:—

      it seem'd she was a queen
Over her passion; who, most rebel-like,
Sought to be king o'er her. (4.3.14–16)

Yet there is nothing rigid in this self-control. She is mov'd, though "not to a rage"; and we feel it fitting that one so far removed from all that is merely natural should yet attract to herself images and associations from the world of nature,

>   patience and sorrow strove
> Who should express her goodliest. You have seen
> Sunshine and rain at once; her smiles and tears
> Were like, a better way, (4.3.18–20)

just as it is perfectly in keeping that religious associations—"There she shook the holy water from her heavenly eyes" (4.3.30–31)—should almost immediately blend with those of "sunshine and rain at once". What we are given in the poetry is a sure and sensitive poise, and it is Cordelia's integrity—her tenderness, as we have seen, at one with her strength—that explains her full and ready responsiveness. It is because she is fully human—though there are also potent suggestions of divine grace—that she is "natural" in a different sense from that intended in Edmund's philosophy. Her sense of the bounty of nature (of "our sustaining corn" as well as of the "rank fumiter and furrow-weeds") lies behind her invocation,—

>   All bless'd secrets,
> All you unpublish'd virtues of the earth,
> Spring with my tears! be aidant and remediate
> In the good man's distress!

But it is because of her love and pity ("the good man" is the erring Lear) that she can invoke so whole-heartedly the "unpublish'd virtues of the earth"—can invoke them moreover not simply as allies from a different realm, but with a suggestion of kinship and intimacy that almost equates their working with the power of outgoing and healing life that lies deep in the soul. It is in this sense that Cordelia "redeems nature from the general curse Which twain have brought her to" (4.4.207–8).

It is this complex resolution of feeling, issuing in new insight, that lies behind the use of "nature" in *Macbeth*. Since the insight stems from a mode of being and is inseparable from it, it cannot be summed up in a formula. But in matters of this kind simple formulations have their uses, if only as a way of ensuring that necessary complexity has not, in the course of argument, degenerated into mere verbal complication, or that mountains are not being made out of molehills. Shakespeare, then, does not say that "nature, however inscrutable, is basically beneficent"; he does not say that there is "in nature a core of tenderness, which lies even deeper than pride or cruelty". He says—though it takes the whole of *King Lear* to say it adequately—that nature *per se* is something quite other than human nature, and that it cannot properly be conceived in human terms; that its humanly relevant quality only exists in relation to a particular human outlook and standpoint; and that what that quality is depends on the standpoint from which the relation is established. "Nature-as-beneficent" is a concept that only has meaning for the good man—or at all events for the man who admits the imperatives of his own humanity. Perhaps it is easier to grasp this in relation to the world—the given "nature"—of inner experience. The mind ("that ocean, where each kind does straight its own resemblance find") contains within itself elements corresponding to nonhuman life—Blake's tiger and lamb. So long as these natural forces are not integrated by the specifically human principle they are, or are likely to become, chaotic and destructive. Given that principle, they may be sublimated and transformed, but they are not disowned: they are freely accepted as the natural sources of life and power. So too with the external world of nature: it is only the man who recognizes his own humanity, and that of others, as something essentially other than a product of the natural world, who is really open to nature; neither fascinated nor afraid, he can respond creatively to its creativeness, and, paradoxically, find in nature a symbol for all that is natural in the other sense—that is, most truly human. It is, I think, some such perception as this, attained in *King Lear*, that lies behind and validates the elaborate and imaginatively powerful analogy between the human order and the order of nature in *Macbeth*.

III

There is no vague "philosophy of nature" in *Macbeth*. The nature against which the "unnaturalness" of the Macbeth evil is defined and judged is human nature; and essential characteristics of that nature—its capacity for and intimate dependence on relationship—are powerfully evoked throughout the play. In act 3, scene 4 Macbeth, overcome by his vision of Banquo's ghost, glances back to a time when murder was common, to what will later be known as the Hobbesian state of nature.

> Blood hath been shed ere now, i' th' olden time,
> Ere humane statute purg'd the gentle weal;
> Ay, and since too, murthers have been perform'd
> Too terrible for the ear: the time has been,
> That, when the brains were out, the man would die,
> And there an end; but now, they rise again,
> With twenty mortal murthers on their crowns,
> And push us from our stools. This is more strange
> Than such a murther is. (3.4.74–82)

This is a more profound version of the origins of society than is suggested by the notion of contract or expediency. What "purges" the supposed mere multitude and makes it into a "gentle" commonweal is a decree greater than any law in which it may be embodied, for it is what is dictated by the very fact of being human; if you accept your humanity then you can't murder with impunity. Nor is this simply a matter of judicial punishment: the murdered man "rises" again, in you. Killing may be common in wild nature, but it is not natural to man as man; it is a violation of his essential humanity. When Lady Macbeth describes her husband as "too full o' the milk of human kindness" she intends to be disparaging, as Goneril does when she speaks of Albany's "milky gentleness" or calls him a "milk-liver'd man" (*King Lear*, 1.4.351; 4.2.50). But what the phrase also says is that human kindness is natural to man as man, and, like his mother's milk, nourishes his manhood. When Malcolm accuses himself of imaginary crimes, and in so doing reflects the evil that Macbeth has brought on Scotland, the climax is,

> Nay, had I power, I should
> Pour the sweet milk of concord into Hell,
> Uproar the universal peace, confound
> All unity in earth. (4.3.97–100)

"Concord," "peace," "unity"—these are *active* words, signifying not a mere absence of disagreeables, a mere deliverance from "continual fear, and danger of violent death," but the condition of positive human living. We learn little about a play by making lists of words, but it is a significant fact that *Macbeth* contains a very large number of words expressing the varied relations of life (not only "cousin," "children," "servants," "guest," "host," but "thanks," "payment," "service," "loyalty," "duties"), and that these sometimes, as in act 1 scenes 4 and 6, seem to be dwelt on with a special insistence. At the end of the play, when Macbeth thinks of what he has lost, it is not "honour, wealth and ease in waning age" (*Lucrece*, 1. 142) but

> that which should accompany old age,
> As honour, love, obedience, troops of friends, (5.3.24–25)

An awareness of those "holy cords" which, though they may be severed, are "too intrince"—too intimately intertwined—"to unloose" (*King Lear*, 2.2.75–76), is integral to the imaginative structure of *Macbeth*. That the man who breaks the bonds that tie him to other men, who "pours the sweet milk of concord into Hell," is at the same time violating his own nature and thwarting his own deepest needs, is something that the play dwells on with a special insistence.

Now as we have seen in relation to *King Lear* it is only when the essential needs and characteristics of human nature are given an absolute, unconditional priority, that nature in its widest sense can be invoked as an order underlying, invigorating, and in a certain sense offering a pattern for, human nature. So too in *Macbeth*. In Macbeth's apocalyptic soliloquy before the murder, the "Pity" that dominates the chaotic natural forces and rides the whirlwind appears as a new-born babe—an offspring of humanity, naked, vulnerable, and powerful. It is, we may say, because of the symbol of the babe, and all it stands for, that Shakespeare can invoke the powers of nature and associate them, as Professor Wilson Knight shows that he does, with all that is opposed to, and finally victorious over, the powers of destruction.

It is in the scene of Duncan's entry into Macbeth's castle (1.6.)—"a perfect contrast in microcosm to the Macbeth evil"—that we are most vividly aware of the energies of untaught nature in significant relation to the human order. The scene is set for full dramatic effect between Lady Macbeth's invocation of the powers of darkness ("The raven himself is hoarse, that croaks the fatal entrance") and Macbeth's final resolution, and Duncan's courtesy underlines the irony. But the contrast is not confined to the situation. The suggestion of a sweet fresh air, the pleased contemplation of the birds that build and breed, affect us first as sensory contrasts to the smothering oppression ("Come, thick Night") so recently evoked; but like the images of darkness and disorder the presented scene is inseparable from the values it embodies and defines.

> This guest of summer,
> The temple-haunting martlet, does approve,
> By his lov'd mansionry, that the heaven's breath
> Smells wooingly here: no jutty, frieze,
> Buttress, nor coign of vantage, but this bird
> Hath made his pendent bed, and procreant cradle:
> Where they most breed and haunt, I have observ'd
> The air is delicate.

What we are contemplating here is a natural and wholesome *order*, of which the equivalent in the human sphere is to be found in those mutualities of loyalty, trust and liking that Macbeth proposes to violate. And it is an order that is at one with the life it fosters. The opening lines of the scene, in short, are not only beautiful in themselves, they form an image of life delighting in life. It is in terms of destructive and self-destructive energies that Macbeth's power lust is defined; and it is from the "life" images of the play, which range from the temple-haunting martlets to Macduff's "babes," his "pretty ones," and include all the scattered references to man's natural goods—sleep and food and fellowship—that we take our bearings in the apprehension of evil.

IV

In the great soliloquy of 1.7. Macbeth tries to provide himself with prudential reasons for not committing murder:—

> But in these cases,
> We still have judgment here; that we but teach
> Bloody instructions, which, being taught, return
> To plague th'inventor.

But the attempt at a cool calculation of consequences (already at odds with the nervous rhythm and the taut muscular force of the imagery of the opening lines) almost immediately gives way to an appalling vision of judgment.

> Besides, this Duncan
> Hath borne his faculties so meek, hath been
> So clear in his great office, that his virtues
> Will plead like angels, trumpet-tongu'd, against
> The deep damnation of his taking-off.

These lines have of course behind them the traditional conception of the Day of Judgment, and it is nothing less than the nature of judgment that the play reveals. Just as, in Spinoza's words "blessedness is not the reward of virtue but virtue itself," so the deep damnation of this play is revealed in the intrinsic qualities of an evil deliberately willed and persisted in. It is revealed above all as a defection from life and reality.

> So that in vent'ring ill we leave to be
> The things we are for that which we expect;
> And this ambitious foul infirmity,
> In having much, torments us with defect
> Of that we have: so then we do neglect
>   The things we have, and, all for want of wit,
>   Make something nothing by augmenting it.

So Shakespeare had written in *The Rape of Lucrece* (148–54), where lust—a type sin, "including all foul harms" (199)—was defined as the urge to possess something that in the experience inevitably proves mere loss, an overreaching into insubstantiality and negation. In *Macbeth* the positives so securely established—the assured intimation of "the things we [sc., truly] are"—throw into relief, and so sharply define, the defection that occupies the forefront of the play. It is this that makes the play's irony so deeply significant—the irony of making "something nothing by augmenting it," that is, in Banquo's phrase, "by seeking to augment it" (2.1.27); and that central irony of losing in gaining—for Macbeth, like Tarquin, is "A captive victor that hath lost in gain" (*Lucrece*, 730)—lies behind all the often noted dramatic ironies that multiply as the play proceeds. Fear and disorder erupt into the specious security and apparent order that temporarily succeed the murder of Duncan. "Things bad begun" attempt to "make strong themselves by ill," yet each further step is as "tedious" (Macbeth's word) and self-frustrating as the last. And the concomitant of the outer disorder and inner disintegration (with both of which Macbeth identifies himself in the great invocation of chaos in 4.1.) is something that appears to the observer as the betrayal of life to automatism, and within Macbeth's own consciousness as a deepening sense of the loss of significance. It is a radical failure of the human to inhabit his proper world of creative activity. A brief examination of these two related aspects of that failure will conclude our examination of the play's philosophy.

We touch for the last time on the question of "nature." Early in the play we are told of "the merciless Macdonwald" that he is "worthy to be a rebel,"

> for to that
> The multiplying villainies of nature
> Do swarm upon him. (1.2.9–12)

Now nature, we have seen, is a power that can be invoked in the service of what is essentially right and wholesome on the sole condition that "human kindness" is recognized as an absolute. Nature by itself, however, is clearly a submoral world, and to "Night's black agents" (3.2.53) in the outer world correspond, within,

> the cursed thoughts that nature
> Gives way to in repose. (2.1.8–9)

Man, the inhabitant of two worlds, is free to choose; but if, disregarding the "compunctious visitings of Nature," he chooses "Nature's mischief" (1.5.45, 50), his freedom is impaired. He has "untied the winds" (4.1.52), and the powers of nature enter the human sphere as autonomous agents: in the language of the play, the "villainies of nature" "swarm upon him" as a more or less passive host.

The explanation of this phrase thus involves us in a consideration of one of the main structural lines of the play, where to the creative energy of good—enlisting and controlling nature's powers—is opposed the automatism of evil. To listen to the witches, it is suggested, is like eating "the insane root, that takes the reason prisoner" (1.3.84–85); for Macbeth, in the moment of temptation, "function," or intellectual activity, is "smother'd in surmise"; and everywhere the imagery of darkness suggests not only the absence or withdrawal of light but—"light thickens"—the presence of something positively oppressive and impeding. Both Macbeth and his wife wilfully blind themselves ("Come, thick Night," "Come, seeling Night"), and to the extent that they surrender the characteristically human power of intellectual and moral discernment they themselves become the "prey" of "Night's black agents," of the powers they have deliberately invoked.

Automatism is perhaps most obvious in Lady Macbeth's sleepwalking, with its obsessed reliving of the past, but Macbeth also is shown as forfeiting his human freedom and spontaneity. If one ultimate aspect of evil is revealed in Macbeth's invocation of chaos, in his determination to be answered,

> though the treasure
> Of Nature's germens tumble all together,
> Even till destruction sicken,

another is suggested by the banal repetitions of the witches' incantations, the almost mechanical beat in which their charms are "wound up." And just as the widespreading confusion (enacted on the "metaphysical" plane) is reflected in the particular action, so Macbeth's terror-stricken advance in evil is tuned to that monotonous beat. "One feels," says W. C. Curry, "that in proportion as the good in him diminishes, his liberty of free choice is determined more and more by evil inclination and that he cannot choose the better course. Hence we speak of destiny or fate, as if it were some external force or moral order, compelling him against his will to certain destruction." Most readers have felt that after the initial crime there is something compulsive in Macbeth's murders; and at the end, for all his "valiant fury," he is certainly not a free agent. He is like a bear tied to a stake, he says; but it is not only the besieging army that hems him in; he is imprisoned in the world he has made.

It is from within that world that, prompted by the news of his wife's suicide, he speaks his last great speech.

> She should have died hereafter:
> There would have been a time for such a word.—
> To-morrow, and to-morrow, and to-morrow,
> Creeps in this petty pace from day to day,
> To the last syllable of recorded time;
> And all our yesterdays have lighted fools
> The way to dusty death. Out, out, brief candle!
> Life's but a walking shadow; a poor player,
> That struts and frets his hour upon the stage,
> And then is heard no more: it is a tale
> Told by an idiot, full of sound and fury,
> Signifying nothing. (5.5.17–28)

His wife's death, it has often been observed, means nothing to him. Commentators have been exercised to determine the precise meaning of the words with which he greets it—"She should have died hereafter" ("She would have died sometime," or, "Her death should have been deferred to a more peaceable hour"); but the point of the line lies in its ambiguity. Macbeth is groping for meanings, trying to conceive a time when he might have met such a situation with something more than indifference, when death itself might have had a significance it cannot have in the world of mere meaningless repetition that he goes on to evoke. As a final irony this *is* the world where when a thing is done it is merely—"alms for oblivion"—done with, because it is a world devoid of significant relations.

Clearly then we have in this play an answer to Shakespeare's earlier questionings about time's power, as we have also a resolution of his earlier preoccupation with the power of illusion and false appearance. Macbeth *has betrayed himself* to the equivocal and the illusory. So too time appears to him as meaningless repetition because he has turned his back on, has indeed attempted violence on, those values that alone give significance to duration, that in a certain sense make time, for "without the meaning there is no time." He has directed his will to evil, towards something that of its very nature makes for chaos and the abnegation of meaning. The solid natural goods—ranging from food and sleep to the varied mutualities of friendship, service, love—are witnesses to the central paradox of evil, that however terrible its power it can only lead to "nothing."

In the lines,

> it is a tale
> Told by an idiot, full of sound and fury,
> Signifying nothing,

there is combined the apparent force—the sound and fury—and the essential meaninglessness. For Macbeth, now, though in a different sense from when he used the phrase, "nothing is, but what is not."

But the play's last word is not, of course, about evil.

> What's more to do,
> Which would be planted newly with the time,—
> As calling home our exil'd friends abroad,
> That fled the snares of watchful tyranny;
> Producing forth the cruel ministers
> Of this dead butcher, and his fiend-like Queen,
> Who, as 'tis thought, by self and violent hands
> Took off her life;—this, and what needful else
> That calls upon us, by the grace of Grace,
> We will perform in measure, time, and place.

It is a fitting close for a play in which moral law has been made present to us not as convention or command but as the law of life itself, as that which makes for life, and through which alone man can ground himself on, and therefore in his measure know, reality.

1976—John Berryman. "Notes on *Macbeth*," from *The Freedom of the Poet*

John Berryman (1914–1972) was one of the most important American poets of his generation, author of such volumes of poetry as *Homage to Mistress Bradstreet* and *77 Dream Songs*. He also wrote a small number of critical essays.

We might approach the characters of Lady Macbeth and Macbeth through one of her observations about him in her soliloquy (i. 5. 21–2):

> what thou wouldst highly,
> That wouldst thou holily . . .

Here is a remark unlike any ever made by an actual human being since the beginning of speech—as unlike life as a great work of music is unlike anyone's humming. Its *subject* is life, but the means is high art, *just as* the means—the true means—of "Take the Fool away" was. What is Shakespeare telling us, through Lady Macbeth, about Macbeth and about herself? Macbeth is ambitious, but an idealist. Now Lady Macbeth is ambitious also, as the whole soliloquy sufficiently shows. But the tone of contempt in "holily"—extraordinary word!—tells us that she not only possesses no such double nature herself but complains of it in him. Lady Macbeth's character—about which so much has been written—is very simple. She is unscrupulous, but short-winded. No doubts beset her, except about the steadfastness of her accomplice. Single-natured, she is even willing to lose the nature she has ("unsex me here") in order to accomplish her purpose. But, nihilistic, she has no staying power. Macbeth stays the course. By Act III she has already ceased to matter, weary, plunging toward insanity and suicide. The nature was shallow from the beginning, with its confidence that "A little water clears us of this deed"; only ambition mobilizes it, and only the horror of guilt can deepen it. There are just enough touches of sensibility—her analysis of her husband, and "Had he not resembled / My father as he slept I had done't"—to make her seem lifelike.

Lady Macbeth, in short, has no idea of what she is getting into. Now the reason she is conceived in this way, of course, is that she may throw a contrasting light on her husband, who is double-natured, heroic, uncertainly wicked, both loyal and faithless, meditative and violent, and does know what he is getting into. This knowledge of his is the real burden of the great soliloquy in i. 7:

> If it were done when 'tis done, then 'twere well
> It were done quickly;

The first "done" here means "finished," and the lines that follow show that what Macbeth has in mind is far deeper and more savage than any mere not-getting-away-with-the-murder, so to speak. Macbeth believes in "justice," and is afraid of teaching his own assassin (later) what to do; and he believes in eternal life, punishment, and would like to *skip it* ("jump the life to come"). He *believes*; his wife believes in nothing except her own ambition and her own guilt. He is also given to us as "brave," and "deserving" to be so called, and "worthy," and "frank," and he is full of scruples. But he has another nature. He is envious, ambitious, and hypocritical (the reasons he gives his wife, at i. 7. 31ff., for not proceeding are quite different from the reasons he has just given himself). Therefore, he can be tempted. Shakespeare holds the balance exquisitely even between supernatural *solicitation* to evil (original) and supernatural *encouragement* to evil (secondary), as in Macbeth's line to the apparitional dagger:

> Thou marshall'st me the way that I was going . . .

Holding the balance even is really to ask: does it matter? Does it matter, that is, whether man falls in with temptation or just falls? The world is certainly full of temptations, whether created by nature or by the underworld of man's nature.

This duality of Macbeth is what makes the play possible; it also accounts for the ambiguity, the mystery, that characterizes the play throughout. But it only partly accounts for his hold upon the audience's or reader's sympathy. This is primarily a response to the imagination with which his creator has endowed Macbeth. His imagination mediates between his two natures, expressing and accounting for both, and projecting itself also into the future, in a way inaccessible to Lady Macbeth. One minute before she is bleating about "A little water," he has said:

> Will all great Neptune's ocean wash this blood
> Clean from my hand? No, this my hand will rather
> The multitudinous seas incarnadine.
> Making the green one red.

His mysterious brooding has scarcely a parallel elsewhere even in Shakespeare's work. Increasingly, as the play advances, its antithetical subjects are cruelty and his own suffering; hand in hand these move, until the universe seems to consist of nothing else. There is nothing in *Macbeth* so intolerable as the last act of *Othello*, but no other Shakespearean tragedy is so desolate, and this desolation is conveyed to us through the fantastic imagination of its hero.

—·/\/\·—   —·/\/\·—   —·/\/\·—

1986—William Empson.
"Macbeth," from *Essays on Shakespeare*

William Empson (1906–1984) was a professor at Cambridge University and the University of Sheffield, a poet, and one of the finest literary critics of his time. His *Seven Types of Ambiguity* (1930), a study of the meanings of poetry, is a classic of modern literary criticism. It was followed by *Some Versions of Pastoral* (1935) and *The Structure of Complex Words* (1951). In *Milton's God* (1961) Empson engaged in a vehement attack on Puritanism. His poetry *Poems* (1935) and *The Gathering Storm* (1940) was noted for its wit and metaphysical conceits. A collected edition of his poems appeared in 1955. William Empson was knighted in 1979.

J. Dover Wilson's arguments, in his edition of the play (1947), for an early revision by Shakespeare himself, designed to shorten it for a Court performance, seem to me valuable but untrue. Valuable, that is, because they draw attention to points you do not easily notice otherwise, and untrue because these points add to the dramatic effect when noticed: it is therefore unnecessary to suppose they are confusions due to revision.

All this is separate from the generally accepted opinion, not questioned either by Dover Wilson or myself, that the scenes and passages involving Hecate were added by Shakespeare especially to please James I. Admittedly, if that is so, it makes an unusually short play even shorter; and many critics have used that as an argument for believing in substantial cuts. I don't mean to deny the possibility, but don't feel that much can be built on it. In any case, the play gives great opportunities for trick staging with the witches (they always had a resinous white smoke, says Dover Wilson, but didn't start flying on wires till after Ariel had done it in *The Tempest*; a year or two later, on his dating, than Middleton's first vulgarisation of *Macbeth* in 1610); it was probably altered a little whenever it was done with new machinery. It doesn't seem likely that the audience would complain of being given short measure, and surely that would be the only practical objection to a short text.

However, if I may chatter about my prejudices at once, so as to help the reader's work of judging my whole position, I do feel sympathetic to a theory which would put the first draft of the play earlier. *Macbeth* is now generally put later than *Lear*, but it seems much more satisfactory to have *Lear* at the end of the main tragic series; as a matter, that is, of the development of Shakespeare's thought and feeling, and this seems to me a stronger argument than the one from style which has also been plausibly advanced. You then have some kind of breakdown after *Lear*, rather accidentally recorded in *Timon*, and then a recovery which always remained in some important way partial, so that after this recovery he always felt somehow above his characters, even in *Antony and Cleopatra* never again really part of them. He could have fallen back on an old style, presumably, merely because it suited the case in hand; but what you are really trying to envisage is an entire development under heavy pressure. However, this kind of thing only makes me want to put *Macbeth* before *Lear* and after *Othello*; I don't see that there is a strong argument, either from style or development, to help Dover Wilson in trying to put the first draft of the play considerably earlier.

On his general thesis, that many Shakespeare plays bear marks of repeated revision, I feel less inclined to prattle about the psychology of the Bard; it is a delightful occupation, but the guesses are so liable to cancel one another out. One would think he had neither the time nor the inclination for revising, but the more you make him careless about his old work the more possible it seems that he threw away the perfect first version of *Macbeth* just to get through one Court performance quick enough. What does seem to me incredible is that the Company would allow him to do it; the decision rested with them, and it was not at all in their interest. They made their money out of the public performances, and only needed the Court for protection; at least this is commonly accepted, though perhaps one could argue that James was paying much more than Elizabeth had done (the evidence given by Harbage, for instance, seems to deal mainly with Elizabeth): but anyway the public performances were still important to them. The Globe audience was going to demand to see a play all the more after it had been honoured by performance at Court, and that audience would demand the full text—they wouldn't even know what the Court cuts had been. Dover Wilson describes many other details of procedure, but he never I think explains exactly how a full Shakespeare text so often got lost after a performance at Court; and for that matter why, if the surviving bits of *Measure for Measure* had to be dragged up to full length by a hack for the public stages after this process, the same did not have to be done for *Macbeth* too. One can hardly suppose it was left for Middleton four years later; these fighting little theatres were on a repertory basis. I presume he means they all got too drunk to carry the text home (though not their individual parts in some cases); a plausible theory, because James does seem to have gone in for tossing the drink around; but surely somebody could have been sent home with the full text, even if they had risked bringing it with them. There were plenty of servants about; one wouldn't think the actors were mingling with the throng very much anyway; surely they could manage to get drunk without losing the most important bit of property they had brought. They were rather property-minded characters. You can imagine it happening once, but there would be a good deal of fuss about not letting it happen again.

The only standard argument for putting *Macbeth* later than *Lear* seems to be the Porter's joke about equivocation, which is held to be a direct reference, beyond doubt, to the trial of the leading Jesuit Garnet from the end of March 1606 onwards (that is, none of the other arguments seem to me decisive). One cannot simply reply that the joke was added when it was topical, because it fits in with so major a cry as Macbeth saying "I now begin / To doubt the equivocation of the fiend", let alone minor phrases which merely echo the story; they cannot all have been added later, because that assumes a dramatist who didn't know what he was writing about to start with. However, I think it is dangerous in this process of dating to neglect the element of luck; in fact it seems fair to be rather superstitious about the luck of a man of genius, in such matters, because he can feel somehow what is going to become "topical". Obviously the idea that equivocation is important and harmful and above all protean did not simply become discovered at the trial of Garnet; it would be as plausible to say that the trial went off as it did because that was felt (these state trials of course were as elaborately prepared beforehand as any in recent history). The echoes of the Shakespeare play in other people's plays, usually called in evidence, come very soon after the trial—while it was topical; provokingly soon if you want to argue that Shakespeare had rushed out his masterpiece in between. Indeed the current theory, as I understand, makes him not merely write it but prepare it for a Court performance (with elaborate business presumably) between May and early August of 1606; surely that amount of pace is too hot. And on the other hand none of these echoes come early enough to support the pre-equivocation draft of 1602 posited by Dover Wilson. I think Shakespeare simply got in first with this topic, in 1605, and did not have to add anything to make it look startlingly topical in its second year. It was already about what was really happening; for that matter, I should think it just comfortably predated the actual Gunpowder Plot affair.

By the way, Dover Wilson's argument that the prattle of the child Macduff must be a later insertion intended as a reference to the Garnet trial (because he says a traitor means one who "swears and lies") does seem to me absurd. The argument is that the child uses the word in a different sense from that of Ross, who has just said it, so the effect is artificial and can't have been in the first draft; but obviously children often do do that. This seemed to need fitting in here, but I wish to avoid fussing about trivialities; probably no one would deny that there may have been cuts and insertions by Shakespeare. The very specific proposals of Dover Wilson about what was cut are what I want to examine here.

In the first place, he feels that the murder of Duncan comes too quickly, or anyway abnormally quickly; the hesitation of Macbeth is a key dramatic effect which in most plays would be given space. This is true, but the whole point about

Macbeth is that he is hurried into an ill-considered action, or that he refuses to consider it himself: "let not light see"—"the eye wink at the hand"—"which must be acted ere they may be scanned"; the play is crowded with such phrases, and its prevailing darkness is a symbol of his refusal to see the consequences of his actions. These consequences are to be long drawn out, but the choice of killing Duncan is to be shown as the effect of two or three shocks close together. Dover Wilson proposes whole scenes to be added before the murder of Duncan, and I think this would not merely be less "exciting" but off the point of the play. A. C. Bradley, to be sure, has said this already, but I don't think he recognised enough the "psychology" as the contemporary audience would see it, which was rather what we now call "existentialist". Problems about free will, which are raised particularly sharply by prophetic witches, were much in the air, and also the idea of the speed with which the self-blinded soul could be damned. One might perhaps imagine that Shakespeare cut down his first version to get the right effect, but that he really intended the effect, and wasn't merely pushed into it by a Court performance, seems hard to doubt.

Some remarks by Dover Wilson on the state of mind of Macbeth, which only bear indirectly on the question of cuts, had better be looked at next. Murderous thoughts, we are told, first come to him, not before the play nor yet on hearing the prophecy, but on hearing that he has become Thane of Cawdor so that half of the prophecy has been fulfilled. The temptation fills him with horror: "the symptoms would be meaningless" unless he were "an innocent spirit reeling under an utterly unforeseen attack". This first assault of the Tempter is viewed in moral terms, and Macbeth repels it as such, but the idea continues to "mine unseen". When Duncan appoints Malcolm his heir, though the deed seems as terrible as ever, Macbeth "has moved appreciably nearer to it". I should have thought he clearly plans to do it: the words are:

> Stars, hide your fires;
> Let not light see my black and deep desires:
> The eye wink at the hand: yet let that be
> Which the eye fears, when it is done, to see.

The chief thought here, surely, as in all these habitual metaphors of darkness, is that Macbeth wants somehow to get away from or hoodwink his consciousness and self-knowledge and do the deed without knowing it. His first meeting with his wife helps forward this process, as Dover Wilson agrees. But by the stage of the I.vii soliloquy ("if it were done . . .") he has reached "a new stage of his disease"; he is thinking not morally but purely from self-interest, says Dover Wilson. Yet "the voice of the good angel can still be heard by us, though not by Macbeth, speaking through the poetry which reveals his subconscious mind". (A. C. Bradley ought to be given credit here, I think.) The proof that his objections are now only prudential is that those are the only ones he makes to his wife (but they are the only ones he *dares* make) and this is why he is won over by her plan to hide the murder—though obviously open to suspicion, it gives him "the talisman his soul craves", an *appearance* of safety (so far from that, it seems to me, what wins him over is her reckless courage). After the murder he has no morality but only bad dreams of being assassinated, which drive him on from crime to crime (but it is the suppressed feeling of guilt, surely, which emerges as neurotic fear—that is how he is "possessed", if you regard him as possessed).

All this discussion about when he is thinking "morally" seems to me to ignore the central fact that there are two moral systems in view, even though one of them is firmly called a bad system. When the witches lead off with "fair is foul and foul is fair" they are wicked; but when Macbeth says their soliciting "cannot be good, cannot be ill" he is in real doubt; and the first soliloquy of Lady Macbeth is presented as a quite laborious and earnest inversion of moral values. The Machiavellian or the Ambitious Man has his moral struggles no less than the Christian or the loyal feudalist, and what prevents Macbeth from confessing his scruples to his wife is a genuine moral shame.

> Thou wouldst be great,
> Art not without ambition, but without
> The illness should attend it; what thou wouldst highly
> That thou wouldst holily,

and so on, is not meant merely as obvious moral paradox from the author but as real moral blame from the deluded speaker; a man *should* be ambitious and *should* have the "illness" required for success in that line of effort; it is good to will highly, and slavish to will "holily". The inversion of moral values is sketched as an actual system of belief, and given strength by being tied to the supreme virtue of courage. Of course it is presented as both wicked and fallacious, but also as a thing that some people feel. (Dover Wilson indeed makes this point himself, by saying that she regards the private murder as a glorious act, just as Macbeth does killing in battle. But Macbeth is involved in this puzzle too, as is rubbed in by the irony of "nothing affeared of what thyself didst make, strange images of death".) There is a good deal of truth, in fact, in the Victorian joke that the Macbeths commit the murder as a painful duty. Indeed they never seem to regard royalty as a source of pleasure at all. Lady Macbeth regards the crown as an "ornament", a satisfaction to pride; and Macbeth says in so many words, "I have no spur / To prick the sides of my intent, but only / Vaulting ambition, which o'er-leaps itself." Unless you regard this moral paradox as already obvious, given from the start, it is natural to feel that the characters are practically unmotivated and must have been explained in early passages which are now cut.

The great question "How many children had Lady Macbeth?" had better be fitted in here. The question cannot be regarded as merely farcical, as one might say, "Who wants children anyhow?" Macbeth is far more concerned to found a royal line than to be King himself; he howls on and on against the threat that his descendants will be supplanted by Banquo's. When Lady Macbeth says she would kill her child she is felt to be ridiculous as well as devilish, because without a child the main purpose would be defeated. But the murdered or the helpless child comes echoing back into the play all through (as Cleanth Brooks pointed out); it is the one thing strong enough to defeat Macbeth and the whole philosophy he has adopted. In the story, however, we are left in doubt whether the Macbeths have any children; it would be symbolically appropriate if they hadn't, but Macbeth's talk would be absurd unless they have, as perhaps it is; and there the matter is left. It is the only crux in the play, I think, which need be regarded as a radical dramatic ambiguity.

The first of Dover Wilson's arguments for a cut scene is what he calls the "ambiguity" of Banquo. A. C. Bradley remarked that only Banquo knew what the witches had told Macbeth, and by keeping silent after the murder, though suspicious in soliloquy, he "yielded to evil". Dover Wilson says that this "shows Bradley at his weakest", because Shakespeare could not possibly have intended to show to James I the supposed founder of his line as a criminal. Besides, James believed in the Divine Right of Kings, even of usurpers once legally crowned, and would have thought Banquo's behaviour merely correct. Exactly; the King would find nothing to complain about, and other persons in the audience could look at the character in other ways—surely this second point of Dover Wilson destroys his previous argument that a scene has been cut. Besides, if James was the person to whom Banquo needed justifying, it is absurd to suppose that the scene justifying him was cut out precisely to suit performance before James.

It seems to me, in any case, that all the lords are meant to be "ambiguous", in the quite flat vague sense that we feel any of them may be playing his own game during this period of confusion, though we never get it clear. "Cruel are the times, when we are traitors, and do not know ourselves"—the point could hardly be rubbed in more firmly, with even the child Macduff prattling about whether his father is a traitor too. It is not merely a literary effect; it is what people really do feel in times of civil war, and Shakespeare had a practical and lasting fear of civil war. The witches say it is "fog" in the first scene, and fog it remains not only in Macbeth's mind but in all the nobles'; we are given two sheer scenes (II.iv and III.vi) of suspicious gossip between persons hardly worth naming, to intensify the thing merely. Ross in the first of these scenes is clearly telling lies to Old Man. Old Man tells a prodigious story about what the birds did on the night Duncan was murdered, so Ross says on that night Duncan's horses turned wild in nature and began kicking their stalls down. "'Tis said they ate each other" says eager Old Man, and Ross says "They did so, to the amazement of my eyes / That looked upon it. Here comes the good Macduff." Surely even a very superstitious audience would realise that he has waited to see how much Old Man will swallow; he is "spreading alarm and despondency". But this isn't meant to reduce the magic of the play to farce; the idea is that a fog of evil really has got abroad, and as likely as not did produce prodigies; the fact that Ross is telling lies about them only makes it all worse. In short, I believe that the various muddles which have occupied the minds of critics (the kind of thing which allowed the Victorian Libby to produce a rather impressive argument that Ross was the villain all through) were deliberately planned to keep the audience guessing but fogged.

On this basis, I think, we can advance with tolerable firmness upon the baffling confusions about the previous Thane of Cawdor. At the beginning of the play messengers arrive from two battlefields; they speak obscurely, but we learn that Cawdor was assisting the King of Norway, who was at the southern battlefield. We then see Macbeth returning from the northern battlefield; he is met by Ross and Angus, who are sent to tell him he has been given the thaneship of Cawdor, and he has never heard of the treachery of Cawdor; Angus says he doesn't know whether Cawdor "was combined / With those of Norway, or did line the rebel / With hidden help and vantage"; and Ross says nothing about it, though he was the messenger from the south in the previous scene. Dover Wilson points out that the prophecy of the witches, that Macbeth will become Thane of Cawdor, "loses half its virtue" if Macbeth has just been fighting Cawdor and knows he is a traitor; but anyhow the audience must be meant to gather that he doesn't know it. "The real explanation", says Dover Wilson (thus I think giving an example of what he calls "Bradley at his weakest", the treatment of a play as a historical document) is that Cawdor had *secretly* helped both the Norwegian invader and the Scotch rebel lord; so this must have been said plainly in one of the cut lines. This rule that secrets have to be said plainly, one is tempted to observe, would lighten the work of the historian if properly carried out. But the historian has still got to worry about how Macbeth managed to fight two decisive battles, practically on the same day, in both Fife and Inverness, north and south of east Scotland and more than a hundred miles apart. The messengers came in almost simultaneously; of course he could conceivably have done it by moving as fast as the messengers—a horse relay system has to be envisaged, though we see him returning from the battle on foot. But there is nothing in the deliberately confused scene I.ii to convince a practical listener that Macbeth went to a new battlefield; so far from that, as soon as he had finished with the rebels (we are told, I.ii.30, by the messenger from the northern battlefield) he and Banquo began to fight the invaders; then Ross comes in from the southern battlefield and never mentions Macbeth, though he uses the peculiar term "Bellona's bridegroom" which practically all commentators assume to mean Macbeth in person. Duncan, to whom these things are told, expresses no interest whatever in the conduct of the campaigns but only attends to the passing phrase about the traitorship of Cawdor, adding that Macbeth shall succeed him. This need not make Duncan look weak; he is dealing with the only immediate essential point. It is only reasonable to suppose that the Norwegians, holding the sea and fully informed by the traitor, would attack at two points at once. I hope I do not appear subtle here; I am trying to follow what the first audiences would make of it. They were very much better-trained than I am on picking up the spoken word; they also thought very keenly, after succeeding in hearing words, along their own lines of military and political strategy. They would certainly notice that Duncan never examines the case of Cawdor, and is only told of Cawdor's confession by his child Malcolm, who may easily have been lied to. I do not mean that there is a story about Cawdor to be dug out of the Shakespeare text, only that the fate of the previous Thane of Cawdor (from the point of view of the first listeners) was already made a baffling and fateful thing before Macbeth began to howl out "And therefore Cawdor shall sleep no more, Macbeth shall sleep no more." In fact, everybody feels this; it is the poetry of the thing. All Macbeth's inheritance is appalling; here he inherits from a man who, in spite of a circle of contradictory gossip, remains baffling and is assumed to need no trial. The smashing irony of "There's no art / To find the mind's construction in the face . . . O worthiest cousin" is transferred obviously by Duncan from Cawdor to Macbeth as soon as Macbeth enters. We do not have to worry about Cawdor; he is presumed to be in the usual fog. But his name does sound like Fate in the play, merely because Macbeth has got to be the same kind of thing all over again. Perhaps it is tedious to say something so obvious; but editors who try to tidy the play really do need to be told the obvious. So far from being a cut version of a tidy historical play now unfortunately lost, it is a rather massive effort, very consistently carried out, to convey the immense confusion in which these historical events actually occur.

Various minor arguments are often produced for believing in cuts, for example the large number of incomplete lines. It seems to me that they merely give a more dramatic and vigorous rhythm. The most extreme case of this uneasiness in the editorial ear is "Toad, that under cold stone," which practically every editor since Pope has wanted to tinker with because it "doesn't scan", whereas of course it is a wonderfully powerful sound effect. However, Dover Wilson is not particularly guilty here; and one cannot blame his ear for feeling that there is something peculiar about the beginning of the play—the whole second scene is pretty close to turgid rant. I think it was needed, however hard it may be to stomach, just to get enough pace at the beginning; the audience has to be thrown into a wild and whirling situation right away. Has to be, that is, if you are going to get to the murder of Duncan very quickly; certainly, if you are going to put in a lot of extra scenes before it, you will want a different beginning, but to argue from one to the other is only to argue in a circle. The same applies to the complaints of editors about the "abruptness" of scene iv, the way Duncan weeps for joy over the loyalty of Macbeth, dooms himself by making Malcolm his heir, and arranges an immediate death by inviting himself to Macbeth's castle, actually in three consecutive sentences. Surely it is absurd to say that this masterly piece of compression cannot have been intended, merely *because* it is so compressed. You might as well say that Wagner must have composed the first draft of his music for a single flute, because he cannot have intended to be so noisy. As to the arguments that the audience needs to be told where Macbeth's castle is before Duncan says "from hence to Inverness", so that an earlier passage must have been cut—the audience are told it in the next sentence; as soon as their interest in the subject has been aroused. As to the arguments that the appearance of a third murderer for Banquo, and Macduff's desertion of his wife and family, are puzzling and therefore must have been prepared for in earlier passages now cut—of course, they are *meant* to seem puzzling; they are part of the general atmosphere of fog and suspicion.

Dover Wilson speaks with great confidence about a passage in Malcolm's curious scene of self-accusation:

Nay, had I power, I should
Pour the sweet milk of concord into hell,

and so on. "That here we have an instance of re-writing after the completion of the original dialogue cannot, I think, be denied", he says, and the reason is that the passage is aimed at pleasing James; instead of following Holinshed and accusing himself of falsehood, he accuses himself of contentiousness, "a strange vice and expressed in strangely modern terms", says Dover Wilson (oddly), but this would please James who was a pacifist. The change was made "because Shakespeare had come to know more of his royal master's mind in the interval". This seems to me a really remarkable case of arguing in a circle. Dover Wilson himself suggests that Shakespeare went to Edinburgh in 1602 or so and wrote the first draft of the play there specifically to curry favour with a possible future King of England; if this is true, it seems quite unnecessary to suppose he had to learn a rather prominent fact about the mind of James four years later. In any case, the mind of Shakespeare himself can reasonably be considered when we wonder why he wrote something down. He thought civil war a real and horrible danger, and he was right in fearing it would come; we need not suppose he was lying to flatter the King when he says it here. And he hardly alters the Holinshed moral anecdote at all, from this point of view; he merely illustrates it. The objection to lying in kings is that by lying they make people quarrel; you don't want a child's copybook rule against lying here, you want to relate the harmfulness of lying to the appalling scene before you; and that is all he does. Surely it is absurd for Dover Wilson to call this a case where revision "cannot be denied".

However, his major thesis does not turn on these dubious minor points; it raises two important questions, and many people will feel it to give them probable and reasonable answers. He maintains that the full play of *Macbeth* gave a much more prolonged struggle between Macbeth and his wife, in which things that now seem baffling to a careful reader, if not to an audience, were given intelligible preparation. I do not want to treat this as absurd; in fact it seems rather wilful to argue, as I am now doing, that the first part of the play was intended to be as thin and confused as so many critics have found the existing text. On the other hand, since we cannot recover these lost scenes if there were any, it does seem at least tolerably useful to show that we can get along without them; and I think that to answer the two questions on that basis (chiefly, of course, by collecting previous opinions) improves or restores the play a good deal.

The first main argument is that Lady Macbeth, in her second soliloquy and her first two conversations with her husband, repeatedly says or appears to say that she is going to kill Duncan herself; but then without further explanation it turns out that both she and Macbeth assume Macbeth is going to do it. It does seem likely that this change of plan would at least have been mentioned. By the way, what seems to me a more immediate argument for some cut in I.vii is that she makes Macbeth change his mind so ridiculously quickly; he says with apparently settled conviction "We will proceed no further in this business", and within thirty lines he is merely asking for a good plan. The answer here, surely, is that all poetic drama uses poetry as a substitute for repetition of arguments and "sleeping on" a problem and such like; the convention feels natural because it is clearly what the stage requires—the characters talk so powerfully that the story can move forward. In real life the Macbeths would argue for half the night, but the audience is actually presented with the morning after a few minutes of action. Here you might possibly invent some arrangement about the time, but the same device is used later in the play with no break at all; the banquet at which Banquo's ghost appears leads us on to dawn in a few minutes, and this seems a natural consequence of the brief exhausted worrying of the Macbeth couple after dismissing their guests. These conventions of course have been much discussed, and they are not questioned here by Dover Wilson. I wanted to remark that we should only accept Elizabethan conventions if they are in a sense natural, that is, such as modern actors and producers can make an audience accept. It is off the point to list "the Elizabethan conventions", as some critics have done; because the Elizabethans did not formulate such things and rather imagined they were free from them. In the case of Lady Macbeth, we can say that the mere force of her two speeches is enough to prevent Macbeth from looking too ridiculous; but also that, even if it isn't, the main point of the story is that he let himself be hurried into a wrong decision.

The second main argument, from the same scene, is that she scolds him because, though unwilling to do the murder now that "time" and "place . . .

adhere", he had been willing to promise he would do it when he needn't act, and she finds this a typical mark of cowardice. It seems obvious to deduce that the promise was made before the battle, therefore of course before the meeting with the witches; but Dover Wilson maintains that this would spoil the whole shock of their prophecy. He therefore argues that Macbeth must have visited his wife after seeing the witches and before reporting to the King on his conduct in the battle; a scene has therefore been cut. But a definite geography can be fitted together; Macbeth has been fighting near the east coast, because the Norwegian invader could throw in fresh troops when the rebel was defeated; he walks westwards to the King's headquarters to report; and his wife is in his castle at Inverness, a day's ride to the west again. He has a positive duty to report to the King before going to her. Surely this kind of point was firm in the Elizabethan mind, however foggy everything else was made. (Even if you are determined to have him gallop between the two battlefields instead of staying at one of them, he still has an obligation to report before he goes home.) In this scene with his wife, now lost, says Dover Wilson, he must have sworn he would kill Duncan when occasion arose, and she in her turn must have insisted, probably using her now misplaced invocation to the "spirits that / tend on mortal thoughts", that she would do it herself. In our text "I.v", jammed together from bits of the lost scenes, she is still assuming she will do it herself; and the change of plan by which Macbeth does it, says Dover Wilson,

> ought by all dramatic rights to be explained to the audience. This was originally done, I suggest, by means of a further dialogue between husband and wife, preceded perhaps by a scene in which, going into the bedroom knife in hand, she cannot bring herself to do it.

So three whole scenes are to be added before we finish with Duncan. The first objection, I think, must be that this painstaking treatment would throw away the whole impression of "fog" which has been established at the start; the impression, that is, of a fatal decision made hurriedly in confusion. The play that Dover Wilson is imagining, or rather not imagining, would be like a "debate" by Racine. Also I do not see why, in the first of these lost scenes, Lady Macbeth insisted that *she* would kill Duncan, if the whole point of the scene was to make *him* swear he would do it. Also the arguments keep on being drawn from our existing text as though it were the original text, though that is what is being denied; if Lady Macbeth *didn't* say she would kill Duncan as late as our "I.v" (because her remarks to that effect have been dragged in from an earlier scene) then you can't require further scenes which presume that she *did* say it. However, this amount of confusion might be justified. What does seem clear is that the play supposed by Dover Wilson would not do what *Macbeth* does. I suspect he would have two jealous hell-hounds, each of them greedy to be first at the kill. In any case, he would not have an atmosphere of wincing and horrified determination, in which a crucial decision is scrambled through hurriedly and confusedly.

Before reaching this bold theory, Dover Wilson recalls various older suggestions about why Lady Macbeth says Macbeth had broached the enterprise before:

> (1) on psychological grounds as a bold lie or as an exaggeration, based on his letter to her, and (2) on technical grounds, as an "episodic intensification" like the allusion to Lady Macbeth's children, or as a piece of dramatic legerdemain resorted to in order to stress at this juncture the less admirable side of Macbeth's character. The trouble with this last explanation, in some ways the most plausible of the four, is that as no spectator or reader apparently observed the point until 1865, it can hardly have been intended to stress anything.

But surely it can add to the atmosphere without the critics arguing about it first; both the actors and the audience are always doing a great deal of "interpretation" which doesn't get written down. I am anxious not to ignore these partial ways of swallowing the effect, without which it would no doubt have long been felt as obtrusively confused. Instead of that it feels like a fierce strain on your attention, intelligible somehow but intensely far from common life—new factors keep being thrown in. To that extent it should I think be called a "dramatic ambiguity"; but all the same I think the text here is meant to yield one straightforward story about what happened.

If we take "I.vii" as it stands, surely we have to believe that Macbeth *did* broach the enterprise to his wife before the battle and before meeting the witches, and before the play; what is more, we have to feel that this belated piece of news about Macbeth is credible on the spot, though it comes as a dramatic surprise. Lady Macbeth goes on to hint that he was half drunk at the time. At least, I am not sure that her metaphor in itself need carry much weight, but an actor could easily emphasise the lines so as to make it prominent:

Was the hope drunk
Wherein you dressed yourself? Hath it slept since
And wakes it now, to look so green and pale . . .

It is not hard to believe that she could drink with him till he talked rashly; she boasts very soon after that she drank the grooms under the table and was only made bold by it. The argument against believing in this previous conversation, according to Dover Wilson, is that the first witch scene, "depicts the terror of Macbeth's soul when the idea of murder *first* comes to him", and the first speech of his wife "makes it clear that so far he has refused to entertain any but honourable thoughts". As to the second point, she only makes clear that he has been deciding against the murder; how can she know all this, about how much he wants to do it, and fears to do it, if they have never mentioned the subject to each other? No doubt in real life she could, but surely the dramatic impression is that this kind of topic is practically the small talk of the Macbeth household. As to the first point, which I agree is stronger and must be answered by imposing a greater dramatic strain, it is a commonplace that Macbeth and Banquo react quite differently to the witches. Banquo is needed in the scene as the innocent mind, which accepts the prophecy about himself as merely a statement about the future; Macbeth, because he already has murder in view, immediately accepts *his* part of the prophecy as a kind of order that he must bring it about. What horrifies him so much is that the witches appear as an externalisation of his secret, guilty daydreams; partly he feels exposed; but even worse he feels that the imaginary world has become real and must now be acted upon. The reaction is immediate; the sequence is:

> *3. Witch.* All hail, Macbeth! that shalt be king hereafter.
> *Banquo.* Good sir, why do you start, and seem to fear
> Things that do sound so fair?

and almost his first words alone call it "this supernatural *soliciting*"; whereas so far from tempting him to act, they have if anything told him that there is no need for action; he is sure to become King. This actually occurs to him a few lines later ("If chance will have me king, why chance may crown me, / Without my stir"), and he seems to throw the idea aside till Duncan appoints Malcolm his next heir. Then it comes back to him strongly, but he has already begun to waver away from it again by the time he meets his wife. Incidentally, the phrase "my thought, whose murder yet is but fantastical" does not sound to me as if the thought first came into his mind a few moments ago; the point is rather "in spite of hearing the witches just now, my thought is *still* only imaginary; the fatal decision has still not been taken". Surely none of it sounds like a man who has never thought of such a thing before. Bradley makes most of the points along this line, and I feel Dover Wilson ought to have done more to recognise them. But he might still say that they are the "weak side" of Bradley, deductions in the study which are ineffective on the stage. I do not agree, though no doubt the effect depends largely on the actor and the production. We are not meant, probably, to decide in the first witch scene that Macbeth has already discussed the murder; but we are meant to be in a position to reflect, when his wife brings out her accusation, "after all, he didn't act like a man to whom the idea was new, such as Banquo, and he has gone on wavering ever since; she is probably exaggerating, but they probably have talked about it before".

This seems to me an important point, because if accepted it would clear up a lot of muddling about the idea of Fate, which has become almost habitual in critical writing on *Macbeth*. Shakespeare I think always uses the word with a fairly clear suggestion that it stands for an excuse, and for his audience it was at best a learned classical idea, not one that they couldn't avoid taking seriously. The dramatic trick, in the structure of the first Act of *Macbeth*, is that the audience is put through what appears to be an experience of Fate but is then expected to think more sensibly. The audience is anyway expected to be frightened by the witches, and during the first meeting of Macbeth with the witches the audience might as it were be stampeded into the immediately plausible theory of Dover Wilson, that Macbeth had an innocent mind before now but has at once been forced into a damnable intention by a supernatural power. But afterwards, listening to Lady Macbeth, and no longer frightened by the witches, they are to recover their theology; they should think "Yes, after all, a witch *couldn't* have made him do it, unless he had weakened his own will before." "Compare the case of Banquo", they could go on; and this line of thought was not difficult for them, because they had assumed Macbeth to be wicked before they came; their chief engagement in the witch scenes would be from puzzles about the limitations of the powers of devils and the free will of man. That the self-blinded soul would fall fast when pushed by witches would still be a natural expectation, fulfilled by the dramatic structure. I don't say that a modern producer could easily recover this movement of thought, but it does prevent what I have just called "a dramatic trick" from being a mere cheat.

The strongest modern attack on *Macbeth* was made by Robert Bridges, whose central charge was this:

> It would not be untrue to the facts as Shakespeare presents them to precede the drama with a scene in which Macbeth and Lady Macbeth should in Machiavellian composure deliberate together upon the murder of Duncan, but plainly such a scene would destroy the drama.

A simple distinction is needed here; to act such a scene would destroy the sequence of feelings which the audience is meant to go through, but to believe that it happened doesn't destroy the drama, in fact the audience are meant to have come round to that (apart from the "composure") by the end of the first Act. A certain amount of surprise is quite usual in plays; what Bridges seems to have felt is the old Puritanical objection to all plays, that they don't tell all the truth all the time.

Macbeth's first meeting with his wife in the play (end of I.v) requires good acting. He is gravely shaken by the thought of guilt but has still not decided to incur it. He leaves it to her to raise the topic at all. She can see just what he is feeling, and begins at once to twist him into action. She pretends that the indecision and conscience in his face are merely the outward marks of a savage determination; let him hide them, and there will be no more trouble. It is too much effort for him to start to unwind this misunderstanding; he merely says it will have to be discussed later. But meanwhile his wife, who knows he is going to say this, has cut the ground from under him by implying that *she* is going to do the murder, so he needn't worry about it again. She does not however say this in so many words, and no doubt assumes that he will not be able to leave her carrying all the burden. The words are framed with a grim and triumphant ambiguity, as is obvious at once, but one does not easily notice that the ambiguity carries this twist of personal argument as well:

> He that's coming
> Must be provided for; and you shall put
> This night's great business into my dispatch,
> Which shall to all our nights and days to come
> Give solely sovereign sway and masterdom.

The whole thrill of the first phrase is that it means "I have to do my housework next; I have to get ready a grand dinner-party; don't you worry, you have only to keep your face straight" as well as "somebody has to plan how to kill the guest"; but neither idea says quite positively that she will do the killing. It is true, of course, that her soliloquy just before has prayed for cruelty enough to use a knife, which she rightly fears she may not have; but this is a matter of preparing enough determination for her share in the murder, not of saying she is determined to reject the help of her husband. The balance of the thing seems to me to be kept just right.[1]

The next great scene between them is in I.vii, after Macbeth has said "We will proceed no further in this business." She has to rally all her powers, makes a variety of accusations against him for *not* being ready to do it, and says she would have killed her baby *if* she had sworn to kill it as Macbeth has sworn to kill Duncan; she never says that *she* has sworn to kill Duncan. But there is again the obscure threat against him, very hard for him to stand up against, that perhaps if he refuses he will only be thrusting the work upon *her*. Macbeth's first words when he yields are "If *we* should fail" and from then on they both assume they will work together. Finally in II.ii, after making the chamberlains drunk and leaving the daggers beside them, she remarks that she thought of doing it herself before Macbeth came, but found she couldn't; she had already planned for him to come, and has only to ring a bell to bring him.

This seems to me a consistent story, not leaving any need for three extra scenes that would destroy the pace; hard to get across in the acting, no doubt, but that need not astonish us. The curious thing, rather typical of the combination of grasp of mind with wilfulness in Dover Wilson, is that he admits nearly all of it himself. It is agreed that Macbeth's mind has been "rendered temptable by previous dalliance of that fancy with ambitious thoughts"; it is agreed that, by offering to do the murder, his wife "leads him unconsciously forward by removing from his path the terror that immediately confronts him". Perhaps it is unnecessary to answer at such length a theory to which its propounder, very fairly, has already given the essential answers.

II

It struck me that this essay seemed rather too confident, so I turned to a work of attractive confidence and vigour by J. M. Robertson, *Literary Detection* (1931), concerned to prove that a great variety of hands mangled the play of *Macbeth* incessantly from its first drafting by Kyd; very depressing to read, naturally. The great days of Disintegration are over, but the subject cannot be ignored; I noticed G. B. Harrison recently (*Shakespeare's Tragedies*, 1951) saying that the collaborator must have written such things as

Thoughts speculative their unsure hopes relate,
But certain issue strokes must arbitrate.

We need not pretend it is good, but I think that Shakespeare, a peaceable man, was usually embarrassed when he had to write something particularly soldierly; it is rather the same even with Fortinbras. Also one cannot call the theatrical effect bad; these laboured confusing patches somehow add to the wild foggy background. We cannot say they are certainly not Shakespeare's because they aren't in "his style".

The main argument for disintegration is from "tags" or repeated phrases, and the results seem valuable in showing what a large common stock the Elizabethans could draw upon. Robertson assumes that a "tag" could not be repeated unless deliberately, and uses such phrases as "Shakespeare does not go about picking from Kyd in general". I think he often echoed Kyd, but without noticing it, and would only have been mildly interested if you had told him so. The fact that what amounts to "Give me the daggers" is said by a woman in both *Soliman and Perseda* and *Arden of Faversham* seems worth knowing as part of the mental background of the audience (for instance, it shows they would not find Lady Macbeth incredible); but we need not think Shakespeare would avoid repeating it. Indeed a dramatist who worked under such a taboo would have to become very eccentric. We might go so far as to deduce that Shakespeare did not despise the Kyd part of his background.

Many of the objections of Robertson seem to me worth answering but in no need of so startling an answer; for example, "the man who can see nothing absurd in the blood-boltered Sergeant ploughing his gory way from Fife up to Forres, ahead of the mounted nobles, is capable of any bluff" (since it is about

150 miles). But it is enough to assume there were two battles, with Macbeth and the Sergeant at the near one; a natural presumption from the two messengers—I don't deny that a line or two making it clearer may have got cut. The "aside" of Macbeth at the end of "I.iv", announcing his treachery to the King in Council, is absurd in itself and "the couplets are utterly out of place in an aside"—a good point, but it isn't meant to be an "aside"; it is a soliloquy on the apron-stage after the Council scene is over. "Shakespeare never brought the primary exposition of Macbeth's growth of purpose to clearness because he was hampered by a composite recast of an old play." But there is a positive merit in having his growth of purpose a mystery which only gradually clears. "The juggling cauldron stuff is extraneous to the very idea of Fate", therefore can't be Shakespeare's; "what the play needed, for him, in that kind, was just the really thrilling sense of 'Fate and metaphysical aid'". The devil, in short, ought to be presented as a gentleman; I think Shakespeare hadn't got all this respect for Fate, and would regard the sordidness of the witches as a traditional and proper thing to show about them.

The undue refinement in this last case is perhaps a natural result of no longer believing in the witches; I agree that they can't be seen in their original proportions by a modern audience. But I think a certain wincing away from the play causes many of Robertson's other objections, as in the sustained argument that the Porter's scene cannot be Shakespeare's. Middleton's *Blurt Master-Constable* makes the servant of a prostitute say "I am porter in Hell", so Middleton wrote it. But the familiarity of the idea was no objection to it; the audience would only see the point more readily. And the idea is not merely to provide "comic relief", which Robertson easily shows wasn't always required. The idea is that the servants regarded the victory and the visit of the King as an occasion for a gaudy night; only their masters regarded it as an occasion to enter Hell.

The repeated use of theatrical couplets at the ends of the scenes appeared particularly vulgar to Robertson, and he throws out a number of them which seem to me to sum up the thought of the play particularly vividly, such as

> The eye wink at the hand; yet let that be
> Which the eye fears, when it is done, to see.

and even "Hover through the fog and filthy air" is called a "vacuous tag-line", though it establishes from the start the theme of fog that Robertson always ignores. Even the central lines

> But cruel are the times, when we are traitors
> And do not know ourselves, when we hold rumour
> From what we fear, yet know not what we fear,
> But float upon a wild and violent sea,
> Each way, and move

are said to be certainly not Shakespeare's because they have "no sense". Here one must lose patience, I think; no one who had experienced civil war could say it had no sense. I find I take *know ourselves* to mean chiefly "ourselves know", as with a comma between the words, but "know the right name for our actions, and therefore in some degree our own natures" is also prominent; *hold rumour* could be like "hold parley with", be ready to entertain such a rumour, or simply "hold onto it" by believing it; the compactness is rather strained but surely not unlike Shakespeare. I still feel strongly what I said about *move* here in my *Ambiguity* (end of Chap. II) but the passage is still very good even if you regard it as incomplete or are determined to emend "move" to "none".

Robertson takes "Before my body / I throw my warlike shield" as admittedly intolerable, known even by its defenders to be very bad; he jeers at E. K. Chambers for saying one could not deny it to Shakespeare merely on grounds of style, and says "Chambers does not distinguish between the sense of style and the sense of sense". This case seems worth attention, because I suspect the trouble is merely that the critics don't see the point. "I will not yield" and so on, says Macbeth,

> Though Birnam Wood *be* come to Dunsinane,
> And thou opposed, *being* of no woman born,
> Yet I will try the last; before my body
> I throw my warlike *shield*. Lay on, Macduff,
> And damned be he that first cries "hold, enough".

The argument is "*although* the protections promised by the witches have failed me, *yet* I will try the bodily protection which is all I have left"; once you notice this idea, surely, you have nothing to grumble about.

NOTE
1. As to the much discussed problem about whether Lady Macbeth "really" faints, it seems to me quite invisible; she probably wouldn't know herself. She is only keeping going by an effort of will, and she can see that this is a good time to stop the effort.

1987—Harold Bloom. "Introduction," from *Macbeth* (Bloom's Modern Critical Interpretations series)

Harold Bloom (1930–) is Sterling Professor of the Humanities at Yale University. He has edited many anthologies of literature and literary criticism and is the author of more than 30 books, including *The Western Canon* and *Shakespeare: The Invention of the Human*.

Critics remark endlessly about two aspects of *Macbeth*, its obsession with "time," and its invariable recourse to metaphors of the stage, almost on the scale of *Hamlet*. *Macbeth*, my personal favorite among Shakespeare's dramas, always has seemed to me to be set in a Gnostic cosmos, though certainly Shakespeare's own vision is by no means Gnostic in spirit. Gnosticism always manifests a great horror of time, since time will show that one is nothing in oneself, and that one's ambition to be everything in oneself is only an imitation of the Demiurge, the maker of this ruined world.

Why does Shakespeare give us the theatrical trope throughout *Macbeth*, in a universe that is the *kenoma*, the cosmological emptiness of the Gnostic seers? In *Hamlet*, the trope is appropriate, since Claudius governs a play-act kingdom. Clearly, we confront a more desperate theatricality in *Macbeth*, where the cosmos, and not just the kingdom, is an apocalyptic stage, even as it is in *King Lear*. Macbeth's obsession with time is the actor's obsession, and the director's, rather than the poet-playwright's. It is the fear of saying the wrong thing at the wrong time, thus ruining the illusion, which is that one is anything at all.

What always remains troublingly sympathetic about Macbeth is partly that he represents our own Oedipal ambitions, and partly that his opposition to true nature is Faustian. Brutally murderous, Macbeth nevertheless is profoundly and engagingly imaginative. He is a visionary Jacobean hero-villain, but unlike Richard III, Iago, and Edmund, and unlike the hero-villains of Webster and Tourneur (Bosola, Flamineo, Ludovico, Vindice), Macbeth takes no pride or pleasure in limning his night-piece and finding it his best. Partly that is because he does not and cannot limn it wholly by himself anyway. Both the supernatural and the natural play a very large part—the witches throughout, and the legitimately natural, almost genealogical revenge of Birnam Wood coming to Dunsinane.

These interventions, demonic and retributive, mean that Macbeth never can get anything quite right, and he is always too cursed with imagination not to know it. Macbeth, far from being the author of that greatest of all night-pieces, *Macbeth*, is merely the object of the drama's force, so much a part of its terrible nature that he needs to augment his crimes steadily just so as to prolong himself in time.

Macbeth's originality as a representation is what makes him so shockingly more interesting than anyone else in the play. This is not just to repeat the commonsense notion that literary evil is much more fascinating than literary good; Lady Macbeth after all is considerably less absorbing for us than her husband is. Nor is it even the consequence of what Howard Felperin terms Macbeth's "literary modernity," his constant re-invention of his own nature, his inability to take that nature for granted. Why are the other male characters in *Macbeth* so gray, so difficult to distinguish from one another in character or personality? Shakespeare wastes little labor in portraying even Duncan and Banquo, let alone Macduff, Malcolm, and Donalbain. As for Lennox, Ross, Menteth, Angus, Cathness—you could not tell these players apart even if a scorecard were provided. The dramatist grants high individuality only to Macbeth, and by doing so makes us confront what it is that we find so attractive in this very bloody villain.

I surmise that Macbeth is so dreadfully interesting because it is his intense *inwardness* that always goes bad, and indeed keeps getting worse down to the very end. His is an inversion of that biblical dualism set forth by Jeremiah the prophet, in which we are taught the injustice of outwardness and the potential morality of our inwardness, which demands justice against the outside world. As a Shakespearean representation, Macbeth empties out inwardness without making it any less interesting; we cannot understand either his nihilism or his imaginative force if we rely upon a superior moral stance in relation to him. That moral stance is not available to us, not just because our own ambitions are perpetually murderous, but primarily because we *are* interesting to ourselves for precisely the reasons that Macbeth is interesting to us. And what makes us interesting to ourselves is that we have learned to see ourselves as we see Macbeth.

He has taught us that we are more interesting to ourselves than others can be precisely because their inwardness is not available to us. If cognitively we have learned disinterestedness from Hamlet, or learned that we can love only those who do not seem to need our love, then cognitively we have learned a dangerously attractive solipsism from Macbeth. Hamlet and Falstaff are not solipsists, for wit demands both other selves and a world external to the self. Macbeth is neither a wit nor a Counter-Machiavel, like Hamlet and Falstaff, nor a Machiavel, like Edmund and Iago. He neither writes with words nor with the other characters. He simply murders what is outward to himself, and at the end is not even certain that Lady Macbeth was not outward to himself. He remains so original a representation of the simultaneous necessity and disaster of a constantly augmenting inwardness that we have not caught up with him yet. Perhaps his greatest horror for us is his brooding conviction that there is sense in everything, which means that he is totally over-determined even as he tries so murderously to make himself into something new.

II

Macbeth, even in the somewhat uncertain form that we have it, is a ruthlessly economical drama, marked by a continuous eloquence astonishing even for Shakespeare. It cannot be an accident that it is the last of the four supreme tragedies, following *Hamlet*, *Othello*, and *Lear*. Shakespeare surpasses even those plays here in maintaining a continuous pitch of tragic intensity, in making everything overwhelmingly dark with meaning. Early on, Macbeth states the ethos of his drama:

My thought, whose murther yet is but fantastical,
Shakes so my single state of man that function
Is smother'd in surmise, and nothing is
But what is not.

Murder is the center, and will not cease to perplex Macbeth, for whom its ontological status, as it were, has been twisted askew:

The time has been,
That when the brains were out, the man would die,
And there an end; but now they rise again
With twenty mortal murthers on their crowns,
And push us from our stools. This is more strange
Than such a murther is.

Everything that Macbeth speaks in the course of the drama leads into its most famous and most powerful speech, as fierce a Gnostic declaration as exists in our language:

To-morrow, and to-morrow, and to-morrow,
Creeps in this petty pace from day to day,
To the last syllable of recorded time;
And all our yesterdays have lighted fools
The way to dusty death. Out, out, brief candle!
Life's but a walking shadow, a poor player,
That struts and frets his hour upon the stage,
And then is heard no more. It is a tale
Told by an idiot, full of sound and fury,
Signifying nothing.

The dramatist, according to Macbeth, is the Demiurge, who destroys all meaning whatsoever. But his nihilistic play, featuring life as hero-villain, is so badly acted in its most crucial part that the petty pace of fallen time is only accentuated. Macbeth therefore ends in total consciousness that he has been thrown into the cosmological emptiness:

I gin to be a-weary of the sun,
And wish th' estate o' th' world were now undone.

Mysticism, according to an ancient formulation, fails and then becomes apocalyptic. The apocalyptic fails, and then becomes Gnosticism. Gnosticism, having no hopes for or in this life, necessarily cannot fail. Macbeth, at the close, cannot fail, because he has murdered all hope and all meaning. What he has not murdered is only interest, our interest, our own deep investment in our own inwardness, at all costs, at every cost. Bloody tyrant though he be, Macbeth remains the unsurpassed representation of imagination gone beyond limits, into the abyss of our emptiness.

1991—Thomas McAlindon. From "Macbeth," in *Shakespeare's Tragic Cosmos*

Thomas McAlindon (1932–) is a senior lecturer in English at the University of Hull, England. He has written critical studies on topics ranging from Greek and medieval romance to the poetry of Yeats, but his main interest is in Renaissance drama. He is the author of *Shakespeare minus "Theory"* (2004), *Shakespeare's Tudor History: A Study of Henry IV, Parts 1 and 2* (2001), and *Doctor Faustus: Divine in Show* (1994).

Even though the text overtly invites us to do so, nothing might seem more reductive than to consider Macbeth as a tragedy of ambition. The meaning of Macbeth's ambition, however, is complex, being deeply enmeshed in Shakespeare's conception of microcosmic and macrocosmic nature, so that it reaches out to engage in a significant relationship with everything else in the play. In this respect Shakespeare is developing a conception of ambition which was systematically and explicitly articulated in Marlowe's *Tamburlaine the Great*, where the hero, a 'fiery thirster after sovereignty' (Part I,II.vi.31), justifies his ambition and its attendant violence by an appeal to the dynamics of Nature:

> Nature, that fram'd us of four elements,
> Warring within our breasts for regiment
> Doth teach us all to have aspiring minds. (Part I,II.vii.18–20)[1]

Thus 'martial' Tamburlaine is identified throughout with the element of fire, at once the 'noblest' and most 'aspiring' as well as the most destructive of the elements. Zenocrate is the Venus whose tears moderate his violence, his marriage to her being analogous to the concordant discord of Nature herself. Her death unleashes all the destructiveness in his nature, so that he ends his career with the burning of Babylon and dies as the victim of a fiery fever.[2]

The character of Macbeth and the whole atmosphere in which he moves set Shakespeare's tragedy at a vast remove from Marlowe's. But in addition to the common subject of an ambitious usurper, and the shared Renaissance sense that ambition can be a noble virtue or a deadly vice, the two plays have an underlying philosophical affinity that must have been readily perceptible to Renaissance audiences.

Macbeth's ambition is a desire not so much for power and wealth as for 'greatness'. It proceeds from a restless striving which he himself scarcely understands and which compels him to 'o'erleap' all obstacles of person, time, and place so as to win, as tokens of his transcendent worth, golden opinions and the golden round. It is a form of desire made manifest not only in martial valour but also in a powerful imagination which obliterates the achievements and satisfactions of the present with its bewitching delineations of future deeds. It makes him yearn always for 'more' (I.iii.70), drives him to 'do and . . . do and . . . do' (line 10), makes him vault beyond great and greater to 'the greatest' (line 117). But counterbalancing this compulsion towards striving and strife is Macbeth's 'milk of human kindness' (I.v.14), signifying the impulse which binds him to others in affectionate partnership; thus before his tragic transformation he is a man loved (I.vi.29; IV.iii.13) as well as admired by all. Emblematised as he stands shoulder to shoulder with Banquo in defence of a just social order, this union of contrary impulses is already on the point of collapse at the beginning of the play; and its collapse is Macbeth's and his country's tragedy. Critics have rightly pointed out that although *Macbeth* is the shortest of Shakespeare's tragedies, it has some claim to being 'the most complex and subtle in its statement'.[3] Many, too, have pointed out the characterisation of its criminal hero has a strange ambivalence which is reflected in a ubiquitous sense of doubleness. That the play's subtle complexities are generated by its dualistic outlook is generally acknowledged; what remains to be emphasised is that its dualistic character emanates from a particular construction of reality which Shakespeare absorbed from his own culture.

Perhaps more than any of the other tragedies, *Macbeth* dramatises a struggle between the forces of unity and disunity. Without opening up the debated question as to what extent it is a tragedy tailored to please King James, one can reasonably detect in this emphasis a discreet nod in the direction of James's title—in which he himself took pride—as the prince of peace and union. The emphasis can be seen in the characterisation of Duncan as a conscientious ruler who leaves fighting to those of his nobility who relish it, rewards them generously for their endeavours, and seeks to bind them all to him and to each other in a gracious and fruitful mutuality.[4] Although the order which Duncan represents is a feudal order, Shakespeare naturalises, validates, and interprets it not by the discourse of hierarchy but by that of contrarious unity. Some three years before *Macbeth*, Middleton and Dekker celebrated James's coronation and progress through the city of London with an 'entertainment' which actually personifies the Four Elements and shows them joining hands in a renunciation of their 'natural desire / To combat each with other'—symbolising an end to the dissensions which afflicted English society at the close of Elizabeth's reign.[5] So too Shakespeare delineates the essential significance of Duncan's character in the superb passage where he and Banquo evoke an image of nature's opposites, both elemental and sexual, joyfully united in a procreant harmony (I.vi.1–10). To argue that *Macbeth* deploys the 'naive', 'geriatric', unequivocal discourse of a metaphysically sanctioned absolutism, and that this hierarchical discourse is mischievously negated at every point by a double-vision discourse that reflects the deconstructive energies and indeterminacies of language (a subversive process which Shakespeare himself was by implication unaware of) is entirely unacceptable.[6] As even this purportedly 'naive' and 'geriatric' passage suggests, the double vision of the play is manifestly the product of its controlling discourse: the harmonious order jointly imagined by Duncan and Banquo accommodates hierarchy, but it is essentially a loving partnership of nature's opposites; and the poetry no less than the dramatic context makes clear that this contrarious, 'pendent' order is as fragile and vulnerable as it is fruitful.

Evil is regularly referred to in the most orthodox manner in *Macbeth* as unnatural, on the assumption that whatsoever is natural is good. But this simple conception of nature is assimilated to a more comprehensive view which acknowledges 'nature's mischief' (I.v.50) no less than its bounty (III.i.97), compunction (I.v.4), and love. The fate of Macduff's nest and its abandoned 'birds', pitilessly destroyed 'At one fell swoop' by Macbeth's 'Hell-kite' (IV. iii.216–19), stands in diptychal relation to the Duncan–Banquo passage on the temple-haunting martlet and correlates with numerous imagistic echoes of nature's dark ferocity. This natural ferocity is intimately associated with demonic evil and with the attempt of the fallen angels (IV.iii.22) to undo the work of the Creator; many in Shakespeare's audience would no doubt have recalled standard Christian doctrine to the effect that the strife of the elements in the world and in humankind was a consequence of the Adamic fall.[7] But the demonic supernaturalism of the play functions more as intensification than as explanation: it adds horror, mystery, and awe to the extraordinary spectacle of cruel violence erupting in the 'gentle weal' and its most 'worthy gentleman'. The most important insight furnished by the play is that the equivocating witches and the malignant spirits that tend on mortal thoughts are potent precisely because they are in tune with the bewildering doubleness of the natural order.

NOTES

1. Text in Christopher Marlowe, *The Plays*, ed. Roma Gill (London: Oxford University Press, 1971).

2. See my *English Renaissance Tragedy* (London: Macmillan; Vancouver: University of British Columbia Press, 1986), pp. 92–9.

3. John Russell Brown, 'Afterword', in *Focus on 'Macbeth'*, ed. Brown (London: Routledge, 1982), p. 249.

4. Cf. Peter Hall, 'Directing *Macbeth*: an Interview with John Russell Brown,' in *Focus on 'Macbeth'*, ed. Brown. Duncan is very gracious and courteous, but also adroit and in control; anything but senile (pp. 234–5).

5. See p. 259, n. 13. James's peaceful reign unites not only the Four Elements but also the Four Kingdoms (England, Scotland, Wales, Ireland)—'by Brute divided, but by . . . [James] alone . . . again united and made one' (pp. 225–6). Hindsight might point to the Gunpowder Plot (1605) as one of many historical ironies bearing on the idealisation of James's gift for unity and peace. But Middleton's pointed (and characteristic) emphasis on the naturalness of conflict deflects such criticism.

6. Malcolm Evans, *Signifying Nothing: Truth's True Contents and Shakespeare's Text* (Brighton: Harvester Press, 1986), pp. 113–20. For a comparable attempt to show that *Macbeth* contradicts its own 'conservative ideology', see Alan Sinfield, '*Macbeth*: History, Ideology and Intellectuals', *CQ* 28 (1986), 63–77. This 'oppositional analysis' of the play (reading it 'against the grain') is designed 'to expose, rather than to promote, State ideologies'—the promotion of such ideologies being a fault of both Shakespeare and his conservative and liberal critics. The analysis leads to the conclusion that although Macbeth is 'certainly . . . a murderer and an oppressive ruler . . . he is but one version of the Absolutist ruler, not the polar opposite' of Duncan and Malcolm. Sinfield adds that 'by conventional standards, the present essay is perverse' (pp. 70, 74–5).

7. Thomas Aquinas, *Summa Theologica*, I–II, qq. 82, 85; Alain de Lille, *The Plaint of Nature*, prose 3, metre 5, prose 8, Pierre de La Primaudaye, *The French Academie*, pp. 418 (I.xi), 528 (I.ixv); Milton, *Paradise Lost*, VII.192ff., X.640ff.

1996—Harold Bloom. "Introduction," from *Macbeth* (Bloom's Notes series)

Macbeth ought to be the least sympathetic of Shakespeare's hero-villains. He is a murderer of old men, women, and children, and has a particular obsession with overcoming time by murdering the future: hence his failed attempt to kill Fleance, and his successful slaughter of Macduff's children. And yet the playgoer and the reader cannot resist identifying with the imagination of Macbeth. A great killing-machine, Macbeth has few attributes beyond imagination to recommend him, and that imagination itself is anything but benign. Yet it is open to the powers of the air and of the night: occult, mediumlike, prophetic, and moral at least in part, it must be the most singular imagination in all of Shakespeare's plays. And yet it has great limitations; it is not much allied to Macbeth's far more ordinary, indeed inadequate intellectual powers. Its autonomy, together with its desperate strength, is what destroys all of Macbeth's victims, and at last Macbeth himself. Imagination or "fantasy" is an equivocal term in the Renaissance, where it can mean both poetic furor, a personal replacement for divine inspiration, and a loss-in-reality, perhaps as a consequence of such a displacement of sacred by secular.

Shakespeare has no single position in regard to the fantasy-making power, whether in *Macbeth* or in *A Midsummer Night's Dream* or *The Tempest*. Yet all these are visionary dramas, and in some sense pragmatically exalt imagination even as they question it. But *Macbeth* is a tragedy, and a visionary tragedy is a strange genre. Like Hamlet, Othello, and Lear, Macbeth is a tragic protagonist, and yet like Claudius, Iago, and Edmund, Macbeth is a villain, indeed a monster of murderousness far surpassing the others. We find it difficult, as we read or watch a performance of *Macbeth*, to think of its protagonist as a criminal dictator, a small-scale Hitler or Stalin, and yet he is pragmatically just that. I do not think that Macbeth's wistful scruples, his nostalgias and regrets, draw us to him; he is never in any danger of collapsing back into the innocence he rarely ceases to crave. The reader and playgoer needs to ask: "Why, even in despite of myself, do I identify with Macbeth, down to the very end?" It cannot be that Macbeth's desires and ambitions essentially are our own; even if the Oedipal desire to slay the father (the good King Duncan) is universal. Even if we are all would-be usurpers, most of us presumably do not desire to terrorize our societies. The appeal of Macbeth, hardly to be resisted, seems to me at the heart of Shakespeare's concerns in this great domestic tragedy of blood.

Macbeth's imagination is at once his greatest strength and his destructive weakness, yet it does not provoke an ambivalence in us. We thrill to its poetic, expressionistic strength, whatever its consequences. Shakespeare, on some level, may be making a critique of his own imagination, which has much in common with Macbeth's, and yet the play is anything but a condemnation of the Macbethian imagination. Indeed, as Macbeth increasingly becomes outraged by the equivocal nature of the occult promises that have been made to him, his sense of being outraged contaminates us, so that we come to share in his outrage. He becomes our paradigm of confounded expectations, and we are moved by him as we are moved by Captain Ahab, who in Melville's *Moby-Dick* plays the role of an American Macbeth. Ahab is not a murderer, and yet his obsessive hunt for *Moby-Dick* destroys the *Pequod* and its entire crew, except for the storytelling Ishmael. Melville modeled Ahab's imagination upon Macbeth's, and a close comparison of Ahab and Macbeth is capable of illuminating both figures. Like Ahab, Macbeth is made into a monomaniac by his compulsive imagination, though killing King Duncan has little in common with the vain attempt to kill the White Whale, who has maimed poor Ahab. Still, like Ahab, Macbeth attempts to strike through the mask of natural appearances in order to uncover the malign principles that, at least in part, would seem to govern the universe. The cosmos, both in Shakespeare's play and in Melville's prose-epic, seems to have resulted from a creation that was also a fall. Both Macbeth and Ahab are central and appropriate to their universes; their imaginings of disaster bring about fresh disasters, and their battles against their own sense of having been outraged by supernatural forces bring about cataclysmic disorders, both for themselves and nearly everyone else about them.

The comparison between Macbeth and his descendant Ahab has its limits. Ahab's guilt is only that of an instrument; he leads his crew to destruction, but he himself is neither a tyrant nor a usurper. Macbeth, a far greater figure than Shakespeare's Richard III or his Claudius, nevertheless is in their tradition: he is a plotter and an assassin. And yet he has sublimity; an authentic tragic grandeur touches and transfigures him. That difference arises again from the nature and power of his prophetic imagination, which is far too strong for every other faculty in him to battle. Macbeth's mind, character, affections are all helpless when confronted by the strength and prevalence of his fantasy, which does his thinking, judging, and feeling for him. Before he scarcely is conscious of a desire, wish, or ambition, the image of the accomplished deed already dominates him, long before the act is performed. Macbeth sees, sometimes quite literally, the phantasmagoria of the future. He is an involuntary visionary, and there is something baffling about his ambition to become king. What do he and Lady Macbeth wish to do with their royal status and power, once they have it? An evening with King and Queen Macbeth at court is an affair apocalyptically dismal: the frightened Thanes brood as to just who will be murdered next, and the graciousness of their hostess seems adequately represented by her famous dismissal to stay not upon the order of their going, but go! Whether the Macbeths still hope for progeny is ambiguous, as is the question of whether they have had children who then died, but they seem to share a dread of futurity. Macbeth's horror of time, often remarked by his critics, has a crucial relation to his uncanniest aspect, transcending fantasy, because he seems to sense a realm free of time yet at least as much a nightmare as his time-obsessed existence. Something in Macbeth really is most at home in the world of the witches and of Hecate. Against the positive transcendence of Hamlet's charismatic personality, Shakespeare set the negative transcendence of Macbeth's hag-ridden nature. And yet a negative transcendence remains a transcendence; there are no flights of angels to herald the end of Macbeth, but there is the occult breakthrough that persuades us, at last, that the time is free.

MACBETH
IN THE TWENTY-FIRST CENTURY
❧

Criticism of *Macbeth* in the early years of the twenty-first century continues to be widely varied, with some critics examining aesthetic issues and others elaborating on the newer perspectives brought forth in the late twentieth century. One trend in recent criticism has been to explore *Macbeth's* appeal to and affect on its audience from Shakespeare's time until now. Other critics have turned again to matters of historical and literary tradition. Michael Hays's essay "*Macbeth*: Loyal Stewards and Royal Succession" discusses the play within the context of medieval romance, in terms of both the characters and the narrative materials. Hays maintains that Macbeth, Banquo, and Macduff are chivalric knights engaged in military and political struggles all centering around matters of kingship, while Lady Macbeth serves briefly as an evil version of the courtly lady. With respect to the narrative, Hays sees *Macbeth* as following a motif of exile and return, whereby Macbeth's reign of chaos is replaced by the return of Malcolm, the legitimate and worthy heir to the throne.

Another fine essay, Alexander Leggatt's "*Macbeth*: A Deed Without a Name," identifies yet another important tension in the text, namely that the act of murder itself is unfixed and unnameable. Though Macbeth's killing of Duncan is unambiguous, Leggatt demonstrates that there is no actual naming of the deed but, rather, a series of indirect references, which can be described as architectural metaphors, such as the violation of Duncan's body as a temple, "the spring, the head, the fountain of your blood," and the duplicitous expression of horror on Lady Macbeth's part as she exclaims, "What! In our house!" Likewise, Leggatt points out that "this concealment of agency becomes one of the key effects of the play," beginning with the witches' riddling statements, through the Porter's inability to remember the name of the fourth devil, and to the broken marriage bond between Macbeth and his wife as a result of their murderous collusion.

2003—Michael L. Hays.
"*Macbeth*: Loyal Stewards and Royal Succession,"
from *Shakespearean Tragedy as Chivalric Romance*

Michael L. Hays (1940-) is a Shakespearean scholar. He is the author of *The Public and Performance: Essays in the History of French and German Theater, 1871–1900* (1981), editor of *Critical Conditions: Regarding the Historical Moment* (1992), and editor of *Melodrama: The Cultural Emergence of a Genre* (1996).

[. . .]

III

The influence of chivalric romance is evident in the delineation of the major characters, all of whom are represented as knights or ladies. Of these, I consider Macbeth and Macduff at length because both engage in single combats affecting Scottish rule and serve as stewards to their kings; Banquo and Malcolm in brief, Banquo as a foil to Macbeth, Malcolm as a knight in his own right and as heir.

Shakespeare delineates Macbeth early and late as a knight of surpassing prowess in battle, especially in single combat. But imagery and allusions color his conduct as less than chivalrous and his character as less than morally or religiously correct. In describing the first battle, the wounded Sergeant emphasizes Macbeth's ferocity unrestrained by the customs or methods of chivalric combat.

> For brave *Macbeth* (well hee deserves that Name)
> Disdayning Fortune, with his brandisht Steele,
> Which smoak'd with bloody execution
> (Like Valours Minion) carv'd out his passage,
> Till hee fac'd the Slave:
> Which nev'r shooke hands, nor bad farwell to him,
> Till he unseam'd him from the Nave to th' Chops,
> And fix'd his Head upon our Battlements. (I,ii,16–23)

Macbeth disdains "Fortune" and relies on his abilities to fight Macdonwald. With his sword dealing "bloody execution," he "carv'd out his passage" through rebel troops as if they were, in today's slang, so much "dead meat." Confronting Macdonwald, Macbeth omits the courtesies of chivalric combat between knights; he "nev'r shooke hands, nor bad farwell to him." The combat suggests both murder and mutilation. One blow to the rebel leader "unseam'd him from the Nave to th' Chops"; a second decapitated him, whereupon Macbeth "fix'd his Head upon our Battlements" (I,ii,23). The power of his first stroke typifies the strength of chivalric heroes; the decapitation of the second typifies the knight's proof of victory over traitors or other evil-doers in chivalric romance. But the manner of the first blow—an upward thrust, rather than a downward slash—was characteristic of swordstrokes by Roman soldiers, not chivalric knights. The subtle association here prepares for the later, more explicit identification of Macbeth with Roman soldiers when Macduff declares him the champion without peer from "all the Legions / Of horrid Hell" (IV,iii,55–56). From the start, Shakespeare limns Macbeth as a militarily able but morally ambiguous knight.

The Sergeant's description of the second battle emphasizes Macbeth, like his counterparts in chivalric romance, engaging and killing large numbers of soldiers.

So they [Macbeth and Banquo] doubly redoubled stroakes upon the Foe:
Except they meant to bathe in reeking Wounds,
Or memorize another *Golgotha*,
I cannot tell (I,ii,37–41).

These hyperboles resemble those of romance. As a knight of renowned prowess, Macbeth should be in the thick of battle. Thus, later, Macduff knows where to find him in the siege of Dunsinane; "There thou should'st be, / By this great clatter, one of greatest note / Seemes bruited" (V,vii,20–22). Macbeth's increased efforts result in widespread bloodshed and carnage, as if he meant "to bathe in reeking Wounds." It is entirely in his character as a knight that Macbeth later represents his multiple murders in a similar way when he says to Lady Macbeth, "I am in blood / Stept in so farre, that should I wade no more, / Returning were as tedious as go ore" (III,iv,136–138). That the carnage should "memorize another *Golgotha*," however, adds another allusion with both Roman and Christian associations.

All of Macbeth's reported deeds are performed in feudal service to his king. But a knight owes his loyalty and service to others, especially his beloved. The conflict of these loyalties and the services which they require determine the action in many romances.[21] And so it is in *Macbeth*. Thus, Macbeth confronts a conflict between his loyalties to his king and to his wife. No sooner has he persuaded himself that good reasons argue against his assassinating Duncan and that he lacks a "Spurre / To pricke the sides of my intent" (I,vii,25–26) to become king by killing him than Lady Macbeth[22] enters—yet another entrance of intense dramatic irony. When he demurs from murder, she scolds him. She impugns his love for her—"From this time, / Such I account thy loue" (I,vii,38–39)—, questions his bravery and his courage, and discredits his honor. Although the play lacks a fully developed love story, it does not lack its central motive of a lady's approval won by a knight's performance of brave deeds. These attacks lead to Macbeth's irritable but sensible response: "Prythee peace: / I dare do all that may become a man, / Who dares no [do] more, is none" (45–47). Lady Macbeth, undeterred by his reply, attacks his virility and challenges his obligation as a knight to perform deeds in accord with sworn words. The conflict between loyalties is clear: to keep his word to her, Macbeth must break his vow of allegiance to Duncan.

Macbeth's decision to murder Duncan transmutes him into a false steward. Duncan honors him as the chief defender of Scotland in repulsing invasion and defeating insurrection. Macbeth responds with the appropriate sentiments of feudal fidelity of a knight to his king. But, after the witches enchant him and his wife entices him, he acts on her advice to conceal his true intentions and give the appearance of loyalty. So he becomes a false steward, an ambitious knight planning, deciding on, and committing regicide; then murdering others to punish disaffection or defeat the future, with disastrous consequences for Scotland.

Banquo and Macduff are also delineated as knights. The Sergeant reports that Banquo was as involved as Macbeth in the bloodshed and slaughter of the battle against forces led by "the Norweyan Lord." After the Sergeant breaks off, Rosse enters and reports, among other matters, a single combat between Sweno and Macduff. The "selfe-comparisons" (I,ii,55) suggest the boasts made by champions in chivalric romance before they engage in single combat to decide political or religious issues.[24] The courtesy of this formality signals Macduff's chivalric conduct as a knight in single combat, both here and in his confrontation with Macbeth, which begins with the "selfe-comparisons" of his untimely birth and his challenge to Macbeth to yield. In the Court Scene, Macduff thinks of his country as a fallen companion-at-arms and, like the knight he is, urges Malcolm to "Bestride our downfall Birthdome" (IV,iii,4). In the later combat, he knows that Macbeth is to be found in the thick of battle when he seeks to avenge the murder of his family.

Proofs of their martial prowess define both Banquo and Macduff less than proofs of their loyalty to the rightful king, Banquo is an obvious foil to Macbeth, as his explicit statement of allegiance to Duncan shows. When Macbeth suggests that his support will "make Honor" (II,i,26) for him, Banquo replies,

> So I lose none,
> In seeking to augment it, but still keepe
> My Bosome franchis'd, and Allegeance cleare,
> I shall be counsail'd. (26–29)

Banquo's silence after the murder is inexplicable. He speaks no words which accord with what the audience knows of him and what he knows: the witches' prophecies, the events required to fulfill them, and the murder of Duncan in

Macbeth's castle. His silence may be a fulfillment of the sort of advice Macbeth considers for himself, then rejects: "If Chance will have me King, / Why Chance may Crowne me, / Without my stirre" (I,iii,143–144). Or his later assertion that he stands "In the great Hand of God . . . and thence, / Against the undivulg'd pretence . . . / Of Treasonous Malice" (II,iii,136–138) may be taken as a strong statement which clears James's legendary ancestor of everything but obtuseness. And his silence permits the play to go on.

Macduff is shown to be closer to the throne than any other character in the play. If Banquo is honorable by his professions of allegiance to the king, Macduff is the more so in actively serving him, adhering to the line of succession, and placing the country's interests ahead of his own. In all of his actions, large and small, Macduff aligns himself with Duncan and Malcolm, and alienates himself from Macbeth. In the discovery scene, for example, he enters the castle to wake the king and discovers him slain. He gives the news to Malcolm and Donalbain. He questions Macbeth why he slew the guards. He agrees with Banquo's opposition to treason. In later scenes, he acts the patriot to the line of succession and to his country, even at personal cost. He indicates his refusal to attend Macbeth's coronation and insinuates his suspicions about his rule (II,iv). He is reported to have avoided Macbeth's feast (III,iv) and to have rebuffed Macbeth's request for his services in preparation for war (III,vi). He goes to England to urge Malcolm's return to overthrow Macbeth. Tested by Malcolm, he proves himself loyal and, overcoming his grief at the murder of his family, swears vengeance against Macbeth (IV,iii). In the final act, he seeks and confronts Macbeth, defeats him offstage, and re-appears with his head on his sword. After his entry, he is the first to hail Malcolm as king. Throughout, he is a foil to Macbeth as a knight serviceable to his king, loyal to the throne, and devoted to his country—all points shown throughout the play and stressed in the Court Scene.

Malcolm is subtly delineated as a knight. Identifying the Sergeant as the one who "fought / 'Gainst my Captivitie" (I,ii,4–5), he suggests his presence at and likely participation in the battle against Macdonwald. In the Court Scene, he declares his intent to engage Macbeth in single combat—a point not heretofore noted, so far as I know—and implies a self-regard as the capable chivalric champion of his people.

But he is shown mainly as son and heir. In responding to Duncan's questions, Malcolm shows himself to be obedient and deferential to a revered father and king (I,ii,iv). In the confusion after the disclosure of Duncan's murder, Donalbain speaks first, to ask "What is amisse?" (II,iii,97); when he has a direct answer from Macduff, Malcolm asks the pertinent question which no one else has thought to ask: "O, by whom?" (100). Malcolm's and Donalbain's asides to each other indicate their suspicions and their sense of danger. They prudently elect to escape by separate flights to England and Ireland; Malcolm does not reappear until much later and Donalbain never. However, Macbeth's digression on Duncan's sons, perhaps the most awkward of the several interruptions which delay Banquo's ride from court, reminds the audience of them:

> We heare our bloody Cozens are bestow'd
> In England, and in Ireland, not confessing
> Their cruell Parricide, filling their hearers
> With strange invention. But of that to-morrow. (III,i,30–33)

Some time thereafter, Lennox and an anonymous lord represent Macbeth's story of their patricide and report that Malcolm "is receyv'd / Of the most Pious *Edward*, with such grace, / That the malevolence of Fortune nothing / Takes from his high respect" (III,vi,26–29). Malcolm's benevolent reception resembles that which exiled heroes in chivalric romances typically receive from rulers when they arrive in foreign lands. Expecting Macduff to keep his distance from Macbeth, Lennox and the lord pray that

> Some holy Angell
> Flye to the Court of England, and unfold
> His Message ere he come, that a swift blessing
> May soone return to this our suffering Country,
> Under a hand accurs'd. (III,vi,45–49)

And Malcolm does receive such a message before Macduff's arrival. The prophecies and the corresponding figures of the armed head, the bloody baby, and the crowned child anticipate the return of Malcolm and Macduff (IV,i). The Court Scene shows Malcolm establishing his qualifications for rule by successfully testing Macduff and converting his grief to anger so that Macduff's vengeance may serve political purposes as well as give personal satisfaction (IV,iii). The final act shows the execution of Malcolm's plan and justifies the "Haile King of Scotland" (V,ix,24), which Macduff is the first to give. Until the Court Scene, all of these reminders give Malcolm a presence throughout the middle part of the play which belies his absence from the stage. They emphasize the compulsion making exile necessary and indicate the return to follow. At the same time, they show the careers of Malcolm and Macduff converging, and focus our interest on their meeting in England.

[. . .]

VII

Macbeth has often been regarded as a "statement of evil";[37] it is not. The truth of this claim extends only so far as the figure of Macbeth himself, a part of the play, a significant part of the play, but not the whole. *Macbeth* could not be clearer; it dramatizes the triumph of a good credibly limned over an evil indelibly delineated in this tragedy more than in any of Shakespeare's other major tragedies.

But the triumph is defined by romance, and in this sense, *Macbeth* is, as I have termed Shakespeare's major tragedies, a tragic romance. Whatever Macbeth is able to gain by regicide, he loses in the restoration of the successor to the Scottish throne. Shakespeare represented at some length and in great detail the usurper as false steward to his king and country, and used the recurrent metaphors of giant, thief, and dwarf from chivalric romance to color him; these taints render judgment on Macbeth. At the same time, Shakespeare devoted great care and rare energy to dramatizing Malcolm, especially in the Court Scene, as the capable, sanctified, and effective successor to his father. His entire career traces the well-known exile-and-return motif of chivalric romance. The restoration, the return leg of this motif, is decided in general by a just and holy war, a major concern of writers of chivalric romance; in specific, by a single combat, which is a feature of romance rather than life and, certainly, as we have seen, not of Shakespeare's sources.

In none of his other major tragedies, except possibly *King Lear*, is Shakespeare at such pains to win our respect, if not our sympathy, for the protagonist's successor. Malcolm has lost a father and a country. But Shakespeare gives him neither the time in the immediate aftermath of the assassination nor the opportunity in the time thereafter to express his grief. Shakespeare chose not to show Malcolm grieving, but he did not show him to be heartless. On the contrary, Malcolm refers to his grief on two occasions: one, when he speaks of his "strong sorrow [not yet] / Upon the foot of motion" and, two, the echoes of this line, when he urges an indulgence of sadness (IV,iii,1–2) and calls the campaign against Macbeth "our great Revenge". These remarks are not much for those who want more. But Malcolm, who is a son, is also a king-to-be; he acts according to what must be done for the future, and what must be done is military and political, not emotional and personal.

Of course, sympathy for Macduff is easy, and readers often take the easy way here. One reason is that, roughly speaking, Malcolm appeals to our minds, Macduff to our hearts. Malcolm's public obligations and his calculations to discharge them are less moving than his indicated but unseen sorrows, far less than Macduff's expressed griefs. However shocking his family's slaughter and however moving his response to the news of their deaths, Macduff is not the hero, not even the cynosure, in the Court Scene or at the end of the play. It cannot be overlooked that he acquiesces in Malcolm's self-imputed voluptuousness and avarice, evils which he regards as more manageable than malicious. Nor can it be ignored that Malcolm out-smarts and out-maneuvers him throughout the scene. And Macduff acknowledges as much; he is the first to salute Malcolm as king; "Haile King for so thou art" (V,ix,20). We must do no less. Otherwise, we refuse to accept the judgment of the play which is built into its language, its imagery, its motifs, and its structures—all of which reflect or resonate the influence of chivalric romance.

A reason for disciplining our responses to the meaning of *Macbeth* is its thematic emphasis on the stability of rule, not least in orderly succession from one ruler to the next, and the relationships between kings and stewards. To make more of Macduff than of Malcolm, by enhancing the one or diminishing the other, defies the play. It resists the fact that the political disaster befalling Scotland results from Macbeth's overstepping the limits of his position. It runs counter to the subordinate position of knights to kings in a feudal state, which Shakespeare and his audience assumed and, for the most part, celebrated.[38] It thus imposes modern notions—neo-Romantic or new-historical—to overturn or transvalue a political order different from, if not antithetical to, ours.

These political considerations require us to respect, at least for the purpose of appreciation, a concomitant set of personal qualities and associated virtues assumed by *Macbeth* and the Court Scene. Malcolm's "modest Wisedome"— what we should understand as circumspection—is Holinshed's "mean virtue betwixt these two extremities" of Duncan's benign naïveté and Macbeth's malign suspiciousness. This circumspection prevents Malcolm from placing an "absolute Trust" in his followers or from having an "absolute feare" of them; it is the very quality which underlies his test of Macduff. Malcolm assumes no correlation, direct or inverse, between appearance and reality, or between them and loyalty and treachery, and consequently, no absolutes in human affairs. He bases this "modest Wisedome," in turn, on his knowledge that the potentiality for evil exists in all men, is enlarged by the power and opportunity to exercise it, and requires "God above/[to] Deale between thee and me" (120–121). Malcolm's self-accusations, his catalogue of vices, at once reveal his knowledge of this potentiality and taint him with it. His retraction convinces because his knowledge and circumspection imply the self-control to be as virtuous as he claims himself to be. The retraction is the more convincing because it is, in one sense, unnecessary. Shakespeare's Malcolm, unlike Holinshed's, does not need Macduff to assist him in the campaign. The effect of the confirmation clears Malcolm of the taint of his self-slanders and coronates his personal qualities.

Malcolm's personal qualities have, as the drift of the test of Macduff's patriotism suggests, political consequences, mainly stability. The first is obvious; Malcolm's rule will be as benign as his father's, but in lacking his father's naïveté, Malcolm will be less prone to betrayal. For if Malcolm were merely as good as his father and in the same ways and no other, he would be as liable to treachery also. The result would be periodic cycles of political order and chaos. By improving on his father in the way in which he does, Malcolm promises a rule that is a linear progression of growth and bounty. Thus, Malcolm breaks the cycle, and "the time is free" (V,viii,55).

The tragedy of *Macbeth* is a tragedy confined to the fortunes of one man within a complex political, religious, and social structure in which the individual finds his proper rewards in the full execution of the functions appropriate to his place in that structure. Macbeth's tragedy results from an informed decision to adopt a course of action which deludes him that he can disrupt and destroy that structure and yet attain his ends. Before his death, Macbeth recognizes his disastrous choice and its disastrous personal consequences: "that which should accompany Old-Age, / As Honor, Love, Obedience, Troopes of Friends, / I must not looke to have" (V,iii,24–26). His recognition reasserts some, but not all, of the social values threatened by his unrestrained exercise of personal ones. This reassertion, based on the protagonist's acquisition of self-knowledge, contributes much of the satisfaction which tragedy gives. For the career of the tragic protagonist is a process of educating him to the audience's social values. It thus affirms them. As the protagonist's tragic course of action suggests man's imperfect nature, so his acquisition of self-knowledge implies the possibility of his perfectibility. This is the tragic vision.

But the tragic vision is not necessarily confined to the protagonist. It is certainly not confined to Macbeth. For in the Court Scene, Malcolm is shown to possess the tragic vision that, although man is capable of great evil through sin, he is also capable of great good through self-discipline. The terror of Macbeth's career and what pity there is, if any, at his death are different measures of a sense of social and personal waste. Perhaps the verdict rendered by Malcolm on the deaths of Macbeth and Lady Macbeth—"this dead Butcher, and his Fiend-like Queene" (V,ix,35)—marks the triumph and the promise of the tragic vision so fully developed in him, the king succeeding. The return of this exiled hero who has proven his worth is, in *Macbeth*, good cause for the celebration attending it—an ending which is all romance, like the play itself.

NOTES

21. The obvious parallel of the potentially tragic conflict between divided loyalties to one's king and to one's beloved is Lancelot's in Malory's *Le Morte D'Arthur*.

22. Lady Macbeth also resembles the three witches, who, in part, resemble the witches of folk-lore and romance. In Chaucer's "Wife of Bath's Tale," witches appear in an out-of-the-way place, guide the questing knight, and vanish.

24. Taylor Culbert, "The Single Combat in Medieval Heroic Narrative" (Diss. University of Michigan, 1957), 84–87, 134–136.

37. Knights, 29.

38. We should remember, too, that Shakespeare, as a member of the King's Men under James, and, before, as a member of the Lord Chamberlain's Men under the queen, would likely be sympathetic to the royal view of relationships with the nobility.

    39. *Macbeth*, 9th edn., Arden Shakespeare (London: Methuen, 1962), 10,
n. 55.
    40. "Preface to *Macbeth*," *More Prefaces to Shakespeare*, ed. Edward M. Moore
(Princeton: Princeton University Press, 1974), 62, n. 2.

——————— ——————— ———————

2005—Alexander Leggatt. "*Macbeth*: A Deed Without a Name," from *Shakespeare's Tragedies: Violation and Identity*

Alexander Leggatt recently retired as professor of English at the
University of Toronto's University College. An award-winning teacher
and theater critic, he is the author of *King Lear* (2004), *Introduction to
English Renaissance Comedy* (1999), and *English Stage Comedy, 1490–1990:
Five Centuries of a Genre* (1998).

INTERPRETING A MURDER

We have seen that acts of violation unsettle the identities of both the victims and
the perpetrators. Chiron and Demetrius are reduced to Rape and Murder. The
loss of Cressida's identity is bound up with, and in part created by, the instability
of Troilus. Othello, re-making Desdemona, undoes himself; and Lear, trying
to turn Cordelia into nothing, becomes nothing himself. Sometimes the lost
identity is in play with a new one that can be named: Hamlet's madness, taking
over Hamlet; the cunning whore of Venice, taking over Desdemona; Diomed's
Cressida. But the new identity is often nameless: a figure like your father, he
that was Othello, the thing that looks like Lear. It all goes back to "This was thy
daughter" and beyond that to "My name was Don Andrea." We have also seen that
the identities of the acts themselves become unsettled. Romeo's killing Tybalt and
his breaking into the Capulet tomb color, and are colored by, the consummation
of his marriage with Juliet. Lavinia's rape and her marriage shadow each other;
so do Desdemona's murder and her wedding night. In *Macbeth* there seems to
be no question about Duncan's identity, or Macbeth's, and when Macbeth kills
Duncan there seems to be no ambiguity about the act. There are many ways to
describe it, all images of violation. However, beneath these descriptions—and
this is the first note struck when the murder is discovered—is the idea that the
act is unnameable. This time it is not the perpetrator or the victim but the act
itself whose identity is unfixed.

    The murder, like the rape of Lavinia, takes place offstage. We never see
the body; but in the moments that follow its discovery, the characters, led by
Macduff, try to do what Lavinia's family has to do: find words for what has

happened. Macduff's first reaction is a generalized shock, in a single word that, like Lear's "never," can only repeat itself as though there is nothing more to say. He goes on to declare the failure of thought (like the "thoughts beyond the reaches of our souls" [I.iv.56] the Ghost triggers in *Hamlet*) and the failure of language: "O horror! horror! horror! / Tongue nor heart cannot conceive, nor name thee!" (II.iii.64–65). In *Titus*, *Hamlet* and *Othello* looking, like speaking, is a way to fix reality. Macduff warns Macbeth and Lennox that the murder does to sight what it does to thought and language: "Approach the chamber, and destroy your sight / With a new Gorgon!" (II.iii.72–73).

In between, he has found an image to embody his sense of violation. There is after all a way to name it and a way to describe it:

> Most sacrilegious Murther hath broke ope
> The Lord's anointed temple, and stole thence
> The life o'th'building! (II.iii.68–70)

As Lavinia's body is for Aaron a rifled treasury (I.i.631) and her rape is like an enemy breaking into a city, so the temple of Duncan's body, the body of an anointed king, has been broken into. Speaking to Malcolm and Donalbain, Macduff finds an image in family terms: "The spring, the head, the fountain of your blood / Is stopp'd; the very source of it is stopp'd" (II.iii.98–99). Othello saw Desdemona's body as the spring that gave him life; Duncan was that for his sons, and now, with the spring stopped, it is though their own lives will dry up. Blocked parenthood is, as we shall see, an obsessive theme in the play. Duncan's murder is the death of a king, the death of a father, the stopping of life itself.

But these images of violation alternate with moments when meaning seems to break down. Calling the sleepers to awake, Macduff talks as though what has happened is not the ultimate crime but the ultimate judgment:

>   up, up, and see
> The great doom's image!—Malcolm! Banquo!
> As from your graves rise up, and walk like sprites,
> To countenance this horror! (II.iii.78–81)

Lady Macbeth calls the bell "a hideous trumpet" (II.iii.82), and Banquo's "when we have our naked frailties hid" (II.iii.126) recalls naked souls rising from their graves in a Doomsday painting.[1] Hamlet's father breaking out of his grave, the disturbance of domestic peace when Brabantio is roused from his bed—these images are now expanded, both in language and in action, as half-dressed people, alarmed and bewildered, fill the stage. As in *King Lear* the first murder and the Last Judgment seem conflated, so here the horror of this one crime and the horror of ultimate judgment—the judgment Macbeth told himself he was prepared to

risk (I.vii.1–7)—become one. The meaning of Duncan's murder expands beyond
the kingdom and the family to become the essence of all crime, and crime itself,
in a breakdown of meaning, infiltrates the idea of judgment.

In the midst of his own struggle to say what has happened, Macduff tells
Macbeth and Lennox, "Do not bid me speak: / See, and then speak yourselves"
(II.iii.73–74). Macbeth echoes Macduff's sense of ultimate ruin—"renown, and
grace, is dead; / The wine of life is drawn" (II.iii.94–95)—but goes on to strike
a slightly false note: "Here lay Duncan, / His silver skin lac'd with his golden
blood" (II.iii.111–12). There is a touch of Marcus here, covering the physical
horror in ersatz beauty.[2] Lady Macbeth's "What! in our house?" (II.iii.88) seems
false in the other direction, in its apparent banality; though in its own way it is
telling. Her earlier line, "The doors are open" (II.ii.5) establishes the conditions
for murder: as for Macduff a temple has been violated, for Lady Macbeth a
threshold is crossed, a house no longer affords protection. The difference is that
she opened those doors herself. It is the perpetrators who have the greatest
difficulty finding words for the deed; Macbeth overdecorates, Lady Macbeth
under-reacts while revealing more than she intends to.

There is also some difficulty about naming the doers of the deed. Malcolm's
reaction to the news raises the question of agency, and seems designed to start a
revenge action: "O! by whom?" Lennox's reply is guarded: "Those of his chamber,
as it seem'd, had done't" (II.iii.100–1). "As it seem'd" keeps the question open,
as does Macbeth's revelation that he killed the grooms, putting them beyond
interrogation. Left alone, Malcolm and Donalbain suspect everybody—"Let's
not consort with them" (II.iii.135) and decide to flee the country. For a while
the deed seems to lack a doer. Then in the following scenes, suspicion spreads,
as agentless as the murder itself. There is no detective work, no handkerchief to
give a clue, no equivalent of Lavinia writing in the sand. Macduff is apprehensive
about the new reign, Banquo suspects the truth, but keeps his thoughts to himself,
and by III.vi the roundabout sarcasm of Lennox accuses Macbeth without quite
using the words. It is as though agency has been suspended. The horror of the
murder is clear, and has many dimensions; part of its horror is that it seems to
float free of the actions and the knowledge of particular people.

Throughout *Macbeth*, the language dwells obsessively on unnameable deeds;
and these deeds are done by unnameable agents. The question of identity shifts
into the question of agency. "Who's there?" becomes "who did this?" In most
cases we can give an answer, or think we can. But when we look for the answers
given in the play, we find its language slides and dissolves. Language itself is
now in the condition of Lavinia after the rape: something terrible has happened,
but it cannot say what it was, or who did it. When Hamlet denies responsibility
for the death of Polonius—"Hamlet does it not, Hamlet denies it" (V.ii.232) he
names himself twice, and the denial is an implicit self-accusation. There is no
such clarity in the language of *Macbeth*.

THINGS UNNAMEABLE

Long before the murder itself, a curious vagueness about who is doing what pervades the language of the play. It is clear that Duncan's generals are fighting an invasion and a rebellion, but the messengers' reports that give details are oddly murky. The Captain, describing Macbeth's confrontation with Macdonwald, declares that Macbeth

> carv'd out his passage,
> Till he fac'd the slave;
> Which ne'er shook hands, nor bade farewell to him,
> Till he unseam'd him from the nave to th' chops,
> And fix'd his head upon our battlements. (I.ii.19–23)

Who did the killing? The antecedent of "which" seems to be "the slave," Macdonwald; the antecedents of "he" and "him" in the next line are ambiguous. By the end of the passage it is evidently Macbeth who has killed Macdonwald, but the initial effect is of an action in which we cannot distinguish the actors. This concealment of agency becomes one of the key effects of the play. The narrative confusion continues when Macbeth confronts either the King of Norway or the traitor Cawdor in hand-to-hand combat, and at first it is not clear which one he is fighting. Again there is a problem of antecedents; Macbeth "Confronted him with self-comparisons" (I.ii.56), but who is "him"? "Rebellious" in the next line suggests Cawdor. But in the following scene confusion is worse confounded when Macbeth seems to know nothing of Cawdor's treachery.[3]

The riddling language of the witches participates in—and since they begin the play may be said to trigger—the general uncertainty. Their paradoxes can be decoded: "When the battle's lost and won" (I.i.4) and "Lesser than Macbeth, and greater" (I.iii.65) are riddles that do not require an Oedipus to solve them. "Fair is foul, and foul is fair" (I.i.11) is a simple moral inversion, and when Macbeth echoes it in his first line, "So foul and fair a day I have not seen" (I.iii.38) he turns it into another fairly easy riddle. But the cumulative effect is that, just as the body turns against itself in Lear, so words are set to fight each other, even cancel each other out. Macbeth's first line disturbs us not by the particular riddle it poses but by the way it shows him participating in this general self-canceling of language. It is an effect we have seen before: this is and is not Cressida, I think my wife be honest, and think she is not.[4] Words are "As two spent swimmers, that do cling together / And choke their art" (I.ii.8–9).

Choking suggests the swimmers will drown. The next stage after self-cancellation is that words disappear, as the witches do. In their charm "Thrice to thine, and thrice to mine" (I.iii.35) we cannot tell what they are talking about. There, a word seems missing; when they describe their action in the cauldron scene as "A deed without a name" (IV.i.49) a word is deliberately erased. At times, like the Ghost in *Hamlet*, they are silent under questioning, as they are with Banquo in their first encounter; they speak only to Macbeth. Then they reverse themselves, speaking only to Banquo; when Macbeth wants to hear more their response to his repeated questions is silence. On "Speak, I charge you" (I.iii.78) they vanish, as the Ghost did on a similar command.

Like Lavinia and the Ghost, the witches provoke the question, "what are you?" (I.iii.47). A puzzle about their identity is built into the text. In the Folio speech headings they are identified only by number; in its stage directions they are witches, and for convenience I have adopted the general practice of calling them that. But that word is used only once in the play's dialogue (I.iii.6). Elsewhere they are (with variations) weird sisters; that is what they call themselves (I.iii.32). (The adjective derives from the Old English word for fate or destiny.) In earlier versions of the story their identities are shifting and uncertain: they are variously wildly dressed women, goddesses of destiny, nymphs or fairies, women of striking beauty, demons in the form of women.[5] Banquo's questions are like the questioning of the Ghost in *Hamlet*, alternatives tried out against silence:

> What are these,
> So wither'd and so wild in their attire,
> That look not like th'inhabitants o' th' earth,
> And yet are on't? Live you? Or are you aught
> That man may question? You seem to understand me,
> By each at once her choppy finger laying
> Upon her skinny lips: you should be women,
> And yet your beards forbid me to interpret
> That you are so. (I.iii.39–47)

Of the earth or not, alive or not, questionable or not, women or not: they inhabit a series of border zones, with something nameable on one side of the border and something unnameable on the other. Bombarded with questions, they say nothing about themselves, replying only with riddling statements about their questioners. The mystery deepens in the cauldron scene, when they refer to "our masters" (IV.i.63) and these masters turn out to be apparitions who rise at the witches' bidding. Who in fact are the masters, the witches or the spirits? And what are those spirits?

This sense of an encounter with the unknowable touches even the Porter scene. The Porter brings solid reality into the murky world of the play: jokes about drink, sex and urine; stock comedy about tailors, farmers and equivocators. But the Porter, having invoked Beelzebub, cannot remember "th' other devil's name" (II.iii.8). His three imaginary visitants are followed by an unknown fourth. The Porter gets no further than "What are you?" (II.iii.18), then breaks off his routine. What, not who: in a play that follows with almost comic rigor the old storytelling rule of three, the introduction of a fourth is a brief glimpse beyond the border into something truly unknown, and unknowable—unless the fourth visitant is Macduff, who appears at this point as a totally new character and who has, we shall see, his own uncanniness.

The suppression of agency, the self-canceling of language, encounters with the unnameable—all these come to a head around the murder of Duncan. Macbeth and Lady Macbeth compulsively use the passive voice to talk about the murder, concealing their own agency in the act as Troilus suppresses agency in his warning to Cressida, "something may be done that we will not" (IV.iv.93). "He that's coming / Must be provided for" (I.v.65–66); "If it were done, when 'tis done, then 'twere well / It were done quickly" (I.vii.1–2); "I go, and it is done" (II.i.62). Not only does the deed have no doer, it has no name. "Provided for" conflates murder with hospitality in a remark that heard out of context would be perfectly innocent. Elsewhere the deed is "it": the word applied compulsively to a character, the Ghost, in *Hamlet* is here applied just as compulsively to an act. Lady Macbeth's strong impulse to drive her husband to murder meets an equally strong counterforce in her refusal to say what she actually means:

> what thou wouldst highly
> That wouldst thou holily; wouldst not play false,
> And yet wouldst wrongly win; thou'dst have, great Glamis,
> That which cries, 'Thus thou must do,' if thou have it;
> And that which rather thou dost fear to do,
> Than wishest should be undone. (I.v.20–25)

While she accuses her husband of fear, her own fear of the words that will name the deed drives her into a series of desperate evasions.

Macbeth's incomplete sentence "And falls on th' other—" (I.vii.28) anticipates his inability to say "Amen," the word that gives closure. The grooms have asked for blessing, and a murderer cannot complete that thought. As we shall see, part of Macbeth's horror is that the murder itself remains forever unfinished, and the failure of his language to give closure is a warning of that larger failure. It is practically a physical blockage: "'Amen' / Stuck in my throat" (II.ii.31–32). Cordelia feels love pressing her tongue down; eventually she is strangled. So is Desdemona. Lavinia loses her tongue. Macduff's tongue fails him (II.iii.64–65). But Macbeth's problem is with the word itself, which blocks the passage that would utter it. Elsewhere language is ambiguous. Lady Macbeth's "All our service, / In every point twice done, and then done double" (I.vi.14–15) conceals a wicked pun on "double" as treacherous, and leads to Macbeth's "He's here in double trust" (I.vii.12), where the pun seems no longer under the speaker's control but built into the language. "My thought, whose murther yet is but fantastical" (I.iii–139) is equivocation of another kind. Macbeth speaks the forbidden word for once, but while admitting he is thinking of murder he also suggests that thought itself is murdered, as if to suppress the word it is in the act of speaking. Words destroy each other: "This supernatural soliciting / Cannot be ill; cannot be good" (I.iii.130–31) leaves nothing but a blank; so does "nothing is, but what is not" (I.iii.142). The self-canceling of identity in Iago's "I am not what I am" is extended to action and finally to existence itself.

UNMAKING MACBETH

The disconnection and internal conflict that affect language also affect the body—or, more precisely, the language that imagines the body. Tarquin in *Lucrece* is in some ways an early study for Macbeth, but in one respect he is radically different. The components of his being work together: "His drumming heart cheers up his burning eye, / His eye commends the leading to his hand" (435–36). Macbeth commands,

> Stars, hide your fires!
> Let not light see my black and deep desires;
> The eye wink at the hand; yet let that be,
> Which the eye fears, when it is done, to see. (I.iv.50–53)

The disconnection of eye and hand recalls Cressida's disconnection of eye and heart (I.ii.285–86). While Tarquin is active, Macbeth characteristically retreats to "let that be" and "when it is done." He also calls for a disconnection between the act and the external world that might see it, as he will later ask the earth not to hear his footsteps (II.i.56–58). More startlingly, Lady Macbeth commands "That my keen knife see not the wound it makes" (I.v.52). Since it is the knife (not Lady Macbeth) that does the killing it must be a sentient being, and she wants it blocked from the sight of its own deed.

As language turns against itself, so does the body. Macbeth feels an internal disruption that recalls *King Lear*:

> why do I yield to that suggestion
> Whose horrid image doth unfix my hair,
> And make my seated heart knock at my ribs,
> Against the use of nature? (I.iii.134–37)

We have seen that those who do acts of violation undo themselves. Othello and Lear lose their names. Macbeth never loses his name; but he seems to lose contact with his own body. He looks at his own hands and, like Lear, fails to recognize them:

> What hands are here? Ha! they pluck out mine eyes.
> Will all great Neptune's ocean wash this blood
> Clean from my hand? No, this my hand will rather
> The multitudinous seas incarnadine
> Making the green one red. (II.ii.58–62)

In the first line the echoes of *Lear* work backwards, from the reunion with Cordelia to the blinding of Gloucester, as Macbeth's own hands, initially unfamiliar, seem to turn against him and Duncan's blood becomes his own. He called for darkness so that he could kill Duncan, and tried to conceal the deed in language so that he could not see it. Now, in killing Duncan he has blinded himself; except that he can still see the blood with terrible clarity, and it runs out of control as his hands did. Titus and Lear saw the sea flooding the land; Macbeth sees his own guilt flooding the sea. The world outside the private consciousness, which he and Lady Macbeth asked to hear nothing and see nothing of the murder, now registers nothing else. As Macbeth is internally disconnected, the border between himself and the life outside himself breaks; the thoughts he has tried to suppress now confront him everywhere he looks. And that border, dividing "me" from "not me," is the border that defines identity.

Far from being silent and unknowing, the outside world sends back disembodied voices, like the calls of "Graymalkin" and "Paddock" (I.i.8–9) the witches hear. Macbeth hears something as he leaves Duncan's chamber (II. ii.14–17); we never know what. In the chamber he hears a voice cry "Sleep no more!" but to Lady Macbeth's question "Who was it that thus cried?" (II.ii.34, 43) there is no answer. We seem to be in a kind of anti-drama without actors in which things are done, but no one does them, things are said but no one says them. Macbeth projects himself into an allegorical play where it is "withered Murther," not Macbeth himself, who walks the stage "thus with his stealthy pace" (II.i.52–54) towards the exit that stands for Duncan's chamber.[6] "Thus" implies Macbeth is walking as he speaks the line. His direction has been set by the unseen dagger: "Thou marshall'st me the way that I was going" (II.i.42). It is not the killer who guides the dagger but the dagger that guides the killer. Even Macbeth's evasions are out of his control, for they recoil on him as statements of truth. He is indeed withered murder: like Chiron and Demetrius in their roles as Rape and Murder, he is becoming his own crime; through the rest of the play we will see him wither and, like Goneril, come to deadly use.

That he lets a dagger lead him is a sign that his own will is suspended. Lady Macbeth complains that when circumstances were wrong for the deed he was willing to make them right: now they are right, "That their fitness now / Does unmake you" (I.vii.53–54). She sees his refusal to act as an unmaking of his being. But for Macbeth it is action itself that unmakes him: "To know my deed, 'twere best not know myself" (II.ii.72). It is not just that "to live with what he has done, he must erase his knowledge of himself";[7] in declaring that consciousness of the deed and consciousness of himself cannot exist together, he suggests that he and the deed cannot exist together. Instead of a character expressing himself in action, this action cancels a character. This was the fate of Tarquin: "So that in vent'ring ill we leave to be / The things we are" (148–49); it was the fate of Othello when he turned against Desdemona, of Lear when he turned against Cordelia.

HAUNTED BY MACBETH

The deed Macbeth tried to imagine as beyond his will or agency is now beyond his control. He has said, "I go, and it is done" (II.i.62). Lady Macbeth assures him, "what's done is done" (III.ii.12). In the sleepwalking scene this becomes "What's done cannot be undone" (V.i.64); finality has become entrapment. While the deed is done in the sense of committed quite early in the play, it is not done in the sense of finished.[8] Macbeth's fantasy that his hand would turn the sea red finds an equivalent in reality when the darkness he and Lady Macbeth have called for becomes literal in the outside world, as the light–dark reversal of *Romeo and Juliet* finally affects Verona: "by th' clock 'tis day, / And yet dark night strangles the travelling lamp" (II.iv.6–7). Others besides Macbeth have heard strange voices in the night (II.iii.55–62). As Macbeth's tyranny advances, Scotland itself becomes a wilderness of crying voices. At first we know who is crying: "Each new morn, / New widows howl, new orphans cry" (IV.iii.4–5). But eventually the source ceases to matter: "sighs, and groans, and shrieks that rent the air / Are made, not marked" (IV.iii.168–69). The passive voice has returned, and with it the horror of being no longer able to feel horror, no longer wanting to know who is crying.

In a crude way Macbeth has invaded other lives and other houses: "There's not a one of them, but in his house / I keep a servant fee'd" (III.iv.130–31). But he has invaded other lives more insidiously than that. The Lord who speaks with Lennox describes the present condition of Scotland by contrasting it with what he hopes for:

> we may again
> Give to our tables meat, sleep to our nights,
> Free from our feasts and banquets bloody knives,
> Do faithful homage, and receive free honours,
> All which we pine for now. (III.vi.33–37)

He is describing Macbeth's own condition: insomnia, lack of true fealty, feasts turned to horror. Scotland suffers not just because of Macbeth but along with him. The border between the private consciousness and the outside world, holding firm in Hamlet's distinction between the world as it seemed to him and the world as it really was, has become alarmingly porous. We may recall the way Lavinia's ordeal shadows the entire world of *Titus Andronicus*.

It is not just that physical violence has spread. The mental conditions that helped to breed that violence have also spread. Chief of these is the undoing of identity. *Troilus and Cressida* showed a world of unstable identities, theatrically centering on Cressida. *Macbeth* shows a similar world, not just theatrically centering on Macbeth but created by him. Macbeth, to know his deed, could not know himself; Rosse complains, "cruel are the times, when we are traitors, / And do not know ourselves" (IV.ii.18–19). Scotland is in the same condition, "Almost afraid to know itself" (IV.iii.165). Mass slaughter means identities no longer matter: "the dead man's knell / Is there scarce ask'd for who" (IV.iii.70–71). This is the horror of the death camp, of nameless bodies bulldozed into mass graves. Anonymity shows in small ways, in the recurring effect of unknown messengers entering. When Rosse arrives in England Malcolm does not at first recognize him (IV.iii.160). The messenger who warns Lady Macduff begins, "I am not to you known" (IV.ii.64). A more terrible non-recognition is Lady Macduff's question of the murderers, "What are these faces[?]" (IV.ii.78). She is looking at things that resemble the human face; but what are they really?

The deceptive appearance of loyalty and hospitality the Macbeths have presented to Duncan makes appearance itself seem untrustworthy. This mistrust shapes Malcolm's treatment of Macduff in IV.iii. The appearance of virtue, so powerful when Desdemona walked on stage and Othello's suspicions fell away, has now been rendered inoperative: "Though all things foul would wear the brows of grace, / Yet Grace must still look so" (IV.iii.23–24). Grace has no choice but to look like itself, but it is so easily imitated its appearance means nothing. Yet Malcolm finds a way of turning deception against itself. He paints a false portrait of himself as evil, to see if Macduff has a breaking point, if there is a degree of evil he will not tolerate. The experiment works, but it is a near thing. Macduff is willing to accept lust and avarice on a grand scale, and though Malcolm's unswearing of his own detraction finally restores confidence between the two men it leaves Macduff silent at first, then confused: "Such welcome and unwelcome things at once, / 'Tis hard to reconcile" (IV.iii.138–39). There is a touch of Macbeth-like equivocation here: Malcolm cannot be ill, cannot be good. Macduff speaks, however, not of contradiction but of reconciliation; and he calls reconciliation hard, not impossible.

RESISTING MACBETH

Up to a point, Macbeth's consciousness has spread outward and infected the world. Paradoxically, this sign of his power is also a sign of his failure. He has not closed off Duncan's murder with the act itself, as he wanted to; the act has taken on a life of its own, carrying him and everyone else along with it. In the scene in England Malcolm uses Macbeth's own instruments, equivocation and deception, against him. In another image of the body turning against itself (and with an echo of Hamlet forcing Claudius to drink his own poison) Macbeth has declared,

> this even-handed Justice
> Commends th'ingredience of our poison'd chalice
> To our own lips. (I.vii.10–12)

In the second half of the play Macbeth's actions both spread beyond him and turn against him.

We see this in the murder of Banquo. It seems a mirror image of the killing of Duncan. Banquo expresses duty and loyalty to his king, as Macbeth did (III.i.15–18) but we know his thoughts too are otherwise; this time, however, it is the king who after an exchange of courtesies kills the subject. Speaking to his wife Macbeth uses the old language, the passive voice that conceals agency: "there shall be done / A deed of dreadful note" (III.ii.43–44). Murder thrives on anonymity, and the hired killers are simply "those men" (III.i.45). (At a similar point Richard III hired Tyrrel, who hired Forrest and Dighton. They had names.) Macbeth has again called on darkness to cover the murder, keeping the killers nameless and unseen; but this time darkness works against him. When the third murderer asks "Who did strike out the light?" and the first replies, "Was't not the way?" (III.iii.19), it is clear there has been a blunder, and in the darkness Fleance escapes.

Banquo returns, like Hamlet's father, not as a disembodied ghost but as a walking corpse, covered with blood like Duncan, but not, this time, decently offstage to be described in decorative language. Like the ruined Lavinia, the blind Gloucester and the dead Cordelia, he is there on stage, and Macbeth has to look at him. The horror is focused by the fact that only Macbeth can see him, and sharpened for the audience by the fact that we can see him too. We could not literally see the copulating bodies Othello saw; but we have no such protection here. Breaking out of the grave like Hamlet's father, Banquo frustrates Macbeth's need for an ending:

> the time has been,
> That, when the brains were out, the man would die,
> And there an end. . . . (III.ii.77–79)

We might have thought Banquo's appearance at the banquet was dramatic enough, and need not be repeated. But as the Ghost reappears unexpectedly in Gertrude's closet, Banquo reappears unexpectedly in the cauldron scene to gloat over the procession of his descendants. This is another way in which Banquo denies closure: he has a son, whom Macbeth fails to kill, and the first of his descendants to appear leads Macbeth to cry in protest, "Thou art too like the spirit of Banquo: down!" (IV.i.112). The cry of "down!" is Macbeth's vain attempt to stop the future.

If he cannot stop the future, perhaps he can gain a kind of control by knowing it. For that he turns to the witches. Up to a point they mimic the mental world he created in order to murder Duncan. In a grotesque literalizing of his images of the disconnected body, their brew consists of dismembered body parts: eye, toe, tongue, liver, gall, finger—nothing is put in whole. The riddling ambiguity of the last two prophecies (none of woman born can harm him, he cannot be vanquished till Birnam Wood comes to Dunsinane) reflects Macbeth's own equivocation, his own tendency to hide the truth in language. Yet the first prophecy is a plain and valid warning: "beware Macduff" (IV.i.71). Its speaker, an armed head, suggests a warrior in battle, and (being only a head) foreshadows Macbeth's fate. It is the second apparition, whom the witches describe as "More potent than the first" (IV.i.76), who begins the equivocation. But while the words offer lying hope, the pictures, like the armed head, offer hidden warnings. The second, a bloody child, suggests violent, unnatural birth, the hidden meaning of "none of woman born" (IV.i.80). The third, holding a tree in its hand, shows how the trick of Birnam Wood will be done. The first two apparitions address Macbeth by name, three times; the third does not use his name. The effect is that as the future they foreshadow draws inexorably nearer, Macbeth's identity fades.

Whatever power the witches represent acts as the Porter says drink acts on the drinker: it "equivocates him in a sleep, and, giving him the lie, leaves him" (II.iii.35–37). As in the cauldron scene the two deceptive prophecies are grounded in the first prophecy's simple truth, in the subsequent action equivocations unravel into plain meaning—Macduff was born by Caesarean section, Malcolm and his soldiers carry boughs in their hands—leaving Macbeth nowhere to hide. Malcolm's command, "Now, near enough: your leavy screens throw down, / And show like those you are" (V.vi.1–2) signals a return to reality and an end to deception, even the deception he himself has practiced.

The countermovement establishes values that work against Macbeth's evil. The survival of Fleance, and the show of eight kings, confirm the fertility with which Banquo has been associated since he asked the witches which of the seeds of time would grow (I.iii.58–59) and saw the "pendent bed, and procreant cradle" where martlets "breed and haunt" (I.vi.8–9) even on Macbeth's castle. The majesty and sheer continuity of the show of kings, horrifying to Macbeth, proclaim the survival of the order his killing of Duncan violated. As he saw his own hands plucking out his eyes, now he finds himself blinded by the sight of majesty: "Thy crown does sear mine eye-balls" (IV.i.113). Young Macduff seems at first a cynical child, a fit inhabitant of the world Macbeth has created: there are enough liars and swearers to hang up the honest men, if his mother does not weep he will quickly have a new father. But though Lady Macduff has unequivocally called her husband a traitor (IV.ii.44–45)—which he is, to his family—when the murderer repeats the charge the boy cries, "Thou liest, thou shag-hair'd villain!" (IV.ii.82). Loyalty is one of the values Macbeth has violated; with an echo of Desdemona's denial of Othello's crime and Cordelia's "No cause, no cause," the boy's loyalty to his father wipes out his father's disloyalty to him.

The King of England is a kind of anti-Macbeth, healing his subjects with a touch of his hand, able to pass the gift to his successors, having "a heavenly gift of prophecy" (IV.iii.143–56). Macbeth has no successors, he is the plaything of devilish prophecies, and his hands are not exactly healing. At the end of the play, Malcolm's announcement that Thanes will now be Earls suggests a new language for a new era, and an Anglicizing of Scotland, with an implied hope that he will rule as the English king does. His declaration, "Cousins, I hope the days are near at hand, / That chambers will be safe" (IV.iv.1–2) counters the horror of violated space that has run through the play. "Cousins" restores the language of relationship, a language Malcolm uses constantly:

> You, worthy uncle,
> Shall, with my cousin, your right noble son,
> Lead our first battle. . . . (V.vi.2–4)

Malcolm brings back to Scotland some of the values Macbeth has violated.

ENEMY ACTION

So far, the play seems to be generating images of restoration and healing like those we thought were at work in the final scenes of *Titus*. But Malcolm's order "Show like those you are" (V.vi.2) contains that treacherous word, "like," the word that unsettled the identity of the Ghost in *Hamlet* even as it seemed to confirm it. Equivocation, the medium of the witches and of Macbeth himself, is still with us. Repeating an effect we have seen in *Titus*, *Hamlet* and *Lear*, Scotland is restored through an invasion by a traditional enemy, England. Macbeth makes some play with this: his taunt "Then fly, false Thanes, / And mingle with the English epicures" (V.iii.7–8) shows his contempt for the effete and decadent south. Malcolm's declaration that from now on Thanes will be Earls may make us wonder if he has come to save Scotland or to abolish it. The saintly English King remains offstage; England is represented onstage by Old Siward, whose refusal to mourn the death of his son has some of the inhumanity, the denial of relationship, we see in Macbeth. Malcolm politely refuses to accept it (V.ix.12–19), but we are left with a question: is the force coming in from the south all that different from the force it is dislodging?[9] In the opening scenes, with loyal generals fighting rebels, it was Macbeth and Banquo, fighting on the side of right, who seemed to "memorize another Golgotha" (I.ii.41), equating them with the killers of Christ. Is there similar ambiguity here?

Malcolm does not kill Macbeth; that is a task for Macduff, a more ambivalent figure. Macduff's first appearance in the play follows immediately upon the murder of Duncan; before that, we had no inkling of his existence. It is as though the murder itself has called him into being. Macbeth has created his own nemesis, with a name eerily like his own.[10] This similarity, as in the case of Edmund and Edgar, is a clue to a mirror-effect. Macduff is in some respects unnatural, like the man he kills.[11] His desertion of his family preserves him to help save Scotland, but it still registers as a betrayal. His wife calls him a traitor (IV.ii.3–4, 44–45) and complains "He wants the natural touch" (IV.ii.9). His disloyalty leaves his son in a Macbeth-like contradiction: "Father'd he is, and yet he's fatherless" (IV.ii.27). It fuels Malcolm's suspicion: "Why in that rawness left you wife and child . . . Without leave-taking?" (IV.iii.26–28). Hearing of the slaughter, Macduff himself turns quickly from blaming heaven's desertion to blaming his own:

> Did Heaven look on,
> And would not take their part? Sinful Macduff!
> They were all struck for thee. (IV.iii.223–25)

When he declares that if anyone else kills Macbeth, "My wife and children's ghosts will haunt me still" (V.vii.16) it seems one haunted man is about to be killed by another.

While each man has in a sense made himself unnatural, Macduff, "from his mother's womb / Untimely ripp'd" (V.viii.15–16), was unnatural in his very birth. He speaks of his birth as the Macbeths speak of the murder, in the passive voice that conceals agency, making it an act that cannot be fully imagined—and with good reason. The language stresses the violation of the natural time of childbirth, and the damage to his mother's body. Caesarean section in this period was fatal to the mother; Macduff killed his mother by being born. The language-trick of the prophecy makes Macduff an uncanny contradiction: he is alive, but he was never born. The second apparition, the bloody child, conflates his own birth and his child's death. Though Macduff comes with the party of healing and restoration, there is something in him that comes from Macbeth's territory. As Othello must kill himself, Macbeth must be killed by something like himself. It is the ultimate consequence of the disappearance of the border that separates the self from the other.

MURDER, SEX AND GENDER

As a child, a husband and a father, Macduff is unnatural, and through his association with marriage, birth and parenthood, he takes us back for a closer look at the couple who kill Duncan. A central paradox of the play is that the murderers who try to keep their deed without a name and without an agent reveal themselves in the process with a detailed intimacy that makes this arguably one of the closest examinations of private life in English drama. It matters first of all that they are a couple. More is at stake here than the violation of kingship, loyalty and the host–guest relationship. The sexual preoccupations of earlier tragedies may seem at first to have little place in this play. But Macduff's violent origin adds to the blood of murder the blood of childbirth, and the other blood, the blood of the marriage bed that figures so prominently in *Romeo and Juliet* and *Othello* is, as we shall see, not so far away. Asserting his virtue, Malcolm declares he is a virgin, and a man who has not killed is a virgin.[12] That may be why his final dismissal of "this dead butcher, and his fiend-like Queen" (V.ix.35) has such an odd double effect: we see its theoretical justice, yet it seems chilling and priggish. The virginal Malcolm, "Unknown to woman" (IV.iii.126), cannot know what has passed between Macbeth and Lady Macbeth; he does not know them as we have. He has neither committed murder nor made love.

Though sexuality does not touch the language of violence in this play as pervasively as it does in *Romeo and Juliet* and *Troilus and Cressida*, it is there. Fortune is Macdonwald's whore, Macbeth is Valour's minion and Bellona's bridegroom (I.ii.14–15, 19, 55). The evil that seems to be in the air is also touched with the sexual. Banquo's prayer, "Restrain in me the cursed thoughts that nature / Gives way to in repose!" (II.i.8–9) suggests the Compline Hymn,[13] a charm against nocturnal emissions in which good Christian men try to protect themselves from succubi: "Tread under foot our ghostly foe, / That no pollution we may know." Macbeth and his wife regularly use forms of the verb "do" for murder, and, threatening the sailor whose wife refused her chestnuts, the first witch uses it without (at first) an apparent meaning: "I'll do, I'll do, and I'll do" (I.iii.10). But elsewhere in Shakespeare "to do" is to copulate,[14] and when the witch has found her victim, "I'll drain him dry as hay" (I.iii.18). That will finish his relations with the wife who has offended her.[15]

Sex and gender are key issues for Macbeth and his wife, and they intertwine. Romeo, Troilus and Lear felt their gender roles, their identities as men, destabilized. They feared and resisted the woman in themselves. The instability of gender affects both parties here. Which is the lord, and which is the lady? Lady Macbeth's telltale reference to "my battlements" (I.v.40) suggests she owns the castle. She accuses her husband of being "too full o'th'milk of human kindness" (I.v.17). When she urges him to come home "That I may pour my spirits in thine ear" (I.v.26) it sounds as though she is going to impregnate him as Mary was impregnated. Elsewhere in Shakespeare "spirit" can mean penis or semen.[16] In the next line "chastise with the valour of my tongue" (I.v.27) attributes what is conventionally a male virtue to what is (just as conventionally) a woman's weapon.

Her most powerful effort is to turn something like Lear's curse on Goneril's body against her own. This takes her beyond simple gender reversal, into a new sense of what it means for her to be a woman. In asking to be unsexed she is not just calling for sterility:

> Come, you Spirits
> That tend on mortal thoughts, unsex me here,
> And fill me, from the crown to the toe, top-full
> Of direst cruelty! make thick my blood,
> Stop up th'access and passage to remorse. . . . (I.v.40–44)

Remembering the sexual meaning of "spirit," she is asking, paradoxically, to be both unsexed and impregnated. She wants the spirits to fill her body, but in the process to block its passages. She is not asking for a male body, but for a female body that once the spirits have done their work will be impregnable, because it is already pregnant. Thickened blood recalls the curdled milk to which the Ghost compares its poisoned blood (I.v.68–70), and anticipates the thickening light of Macbeth's invocation of darkness (III.ii.50). Pregnant with cruelty (otherwise what milk would she have in a childless marriage?) she will breastfeed accordingly: "Come to my woman's breasts, / And take my milk for gall, you murth'ring ministers" (I.v.47–48). The ministers will either turn her milk to gall, or suckle on the gall that is her milk, or both.[17]

When she imagines—and not just imagines, remembers—breastfeeding a human infant, she turns the image around in what sounds like a denial of the nurturing capacity of her own body, a denial more shocking because it draws not on a latent inhumanity but on a genuine memory of maternal love:

> I have given suck, and know
> How tender 'tis to love the babe that milks me:
> I would, when it was smiling in my face,
> Have pluck'd my nipple from his boneless gums,
> And dash'd the brains out, had I so sworn
> As you have done to this. (I.vii.54–59)[18]

Promise-keeping is a male virtue, a warrior's virtue. Hector went to battle against the pleas of his family because he had promised the Greeks, and one of the most stinging battlefield taunts in *Coriolanus* is "I do hate thee / Worse than a promise-breaker" (I.viii.1–2). Macbeth has promised; and men, his wife argues, should keep their promises even if it means killing a child; she would. But if promise-keeping is a male virtue, she describes it in an image drawn from an experience only a woman can have. The bearded witches may inhabit a gender twilight zone, but Lady Macbeth is a woman. There is nothing that in Shakespeare's theatre would remind us of the male body beneath the costume; that is a trick for the comedies. Asking to be unsexed, she is asking not to be turned into a man, not even (as we might at first think) to be made asexual. She wants her sexuality transformed while remaining that of a woman. Language gives her no way to formulate this, and so she falls back on the negative, self-canceling word "unsex." The result is perhaps the most extraordinary of the attacks on the female body we have seen throughout these plays, an attack she conducts herself as she asks to be impregnated with cruelty and to breastfeed with gall, and talks of killing an infant she herself is nursing, and loves, as an act of integrity. The body is still female, but the values it exemplifies belong to a gender that, like the murder, has no name.

She wants Macbeth to be a man; but they have to debate what that means. To his protest, "I dare do all that may become a man; / Who dares do more, is none" she replies, "When you durst do it, then you were a man" (I.vii.46–49). Is it manly to kill, or manly not to kill? The issue as Lady Macbeth frames it is not man versus woman but man versus beast: "What beast was't then, / That made you break this enterprise to me?" (I.v.47–48). This cuts off the possibility that the restraint Macbeth wants to show is a female virtue and therefore a human one (it was the woman in Hector who wanted to end the war); she tries to present it as subhuman. But because this is a scene between a man and a woman, the question of gender is implicitly in play; and the notion of maleness becomes unstable as they give contradictory readings of it. As part of his mirroring of Macbeth, Macduff is similarly challenged. When he hears of the slaughter of his family, Malcolm tells him, "Dispute it like a man" and he replies "I shall do so; / But I must also feel it as a man" (IV.iii.220–21). Malcolm plays something like Lady Macbeth's role, seeing violent action as manly; Macduff, breaking convention, sees passionate grief as manly. A few lines later he will revert to stock thinking—"O! I could play the woman with my mine eyes" (IV.iii.230)—but just for a moment he extends, as Macbeth has tried to do, the idea of what it is to be a man. He needs a period of simple grief, which Malcolm, who wants him to turn straight to anger, does not seem to understand. Malcolm is a virgin, and has no children.

Lady Macbeth tries to transform her gender into something unnameable, while remaining sexually a woman; Macbeth and Macduff in different ways try, if not to work against gender, at least to rethink the gender stereotypes they are offered. Romeo and Troilus, challenged to act like men, do not question what that means. Macbeth and Macduff do. But if Macbeth is prepared to question gender, his sex, like his wife's, remains constant. Her challenge to him to be a man cannot be separated from the fact that this is a childless marriage. Since Lady Macbeth has breastfed, she must have had at least one child (the number does not matter), as her historical equivalent did from a previous marriage.[19] Here we enter into a set of questions, like the questions around Othello's wedding night, that the play provokes but does not directly answer. Did the Macbeths have children, who died? Daughters, whom they discount? Did Lady Macbeth have children only by another man? In the latter case, it would appear that the problem lies with Macbeth, not with her, and an implicit taunt in "I have given suck" might be, "It's not my fault that we can't have children." Is Macbeth impotent, or potent but sterile? Or was Lady Macbeth's body damaged in childbirth?[20] None of these questions can be answered directly, and we may think that Shakespeare's art has trapped us once again into taking his characters as real and prying into their private lives. Yet Macbeth makes one assumption that is worth noting: he accepts without question the implication of the witches' address to Banquo as "greater" and "happier" than himself (I.iii.65–66): because Banquo's issue will succeed, that means his will not (III.i.60–63), though logically the future could leave room for both. Whatever medical speculations we may entertain, the point is that Macbeth sees himself as without issue. It is a condition, if not of his body, at least of his mind; at that level the witches have sterilized him as the first witch sterilized the sailor.

It is at that level, the mind and the imagination, that the sexuality in this play operates most powerfully. All we know about the Macbeths in bed is that neither of them can sleep properly. For the play's purpose the key event in their sex life is the murder of Duncan. Lady Macbeth's invocation of the spirits is at one level a masturbatory fantasy that arouses her sexuality even as it transforms it. She prepares Macbeth for the deed by challenging his manhood. The act itself, that seems for a while to have no identity, has in fact a double one, a linking of killing and sexual consummation that recalls *Romeo and Juliet* and *Othello*. The Porter's lecture on drink provides a gloss on Macbeth's hesitation to kill:

> Lechery, Sir, it provokes, and unprovokes: it provokes the desire, but it
> takes away the performance. Therefore, much drink may be said to be an
> equivocator with lechery: it makes him, and it mars him; it sets him on,
> and it takes him off, it persuades him, and disheartens him; makes him
> stand to, and not stand to. . . . (II.iii.29–35)

The self-canceling of language becomes the body's own self-canceling, transposing into a different key Lady Macbeth's rebukes to her husband for having the desire but not the performance, and her accusation that the fitness of the occasion has unmade him. She asks him, "Was the hope drunk, / Wherein you dress'd yourself?" and continues, "From this time / Such I account thy love" (I.vii.35–39). Making the killing a test of his love as well as of his manhood, she challenges him sexually: is he too drunk on equivocation to do the deed?

Macbeth imagines withered murder moving "with Tarquin's ravishing strides" (II.i.55), making the killing of Duncan (who like Lucrece is in bed) a displaced sexual act.[21] In *Titus Andronicus* we have seen rape conflated with marriage. The Macbeth marriage as we have seen it has been about one thing: killing Duncan. In the early scenes that is all they ever talk about. It is by killing Duncan that Macbeth consummates his marriage. The blood on the bed makes this a wedding night, and when he emerges from the chamber Lady Macbeth addresses him for the first time as "my husband!" (II.ii.13).[22] The couple is then disturbed as Troilus and Cressida were after a night of sex (IV.ii.36–45) by a knocking at the door. Shakespeare kept Romeo's killing of Tybalt separate from his taking of Juliet's virginity, even as he allowed an interplay between them. Here killing and consummating are folded into one, and we begin to realize why naming the deed is so difficult.

Naming the perpetrator has also been difficult. If we see the deed as the consummation of Macbeth and Lady Macbeth's marriage, then we can say that the doer of the deed is not Macbeth or Lady Macbeth but the marriage itself. The sheer difficulty, the straining of the normal sense of agency, involved in putting it that way suggests why the agent is so hard to identify, why the characters so often retreat to the passive voice. But if we can think in these terms, we can see a link with other plays in which the agent of violation unravels, undone by the deed itself.

Macbeth kills Duncan; there is blood on the bed. To that extent the consummation succeeds. But as Romeo and Juliet saw in their consummation only death, a death they not only accepted but desired, so the Macbeths breed no new life. The difference is that Romeo and Juliet, wanting only to "die" together, have no interest in the future; but the Macbeths do. Resolved on the deed, Macbeth tells his wife, "Bring forth men-children only!" (I.vii.73), as though once he has done it she will conceive at last. But Rosse's tribute to his conduct on the battlefield, "Nothing afeard of what thyself didst make, / Strange images of death" (I.iii.96–97), suggests that Macbeth as procreator can only make one thing. The result of the consummation is not a new-born babe, naked or bloody, but a dead old man, and by the end of the play Macbeth is killing children. When the murderer taunts Macduff's son, "What, you egg!" (IV.ii.82), the killing seems to extend earlier than birth. Scotland has become an infertile body in which life dies before it can be born. The consummation has failed and it seems—the reservation is important—that the marriage fails along with it, the agent undone, as were Othello and Lear, by the deed it committed.

PORTRAIT OF A MARRIAGE

Other marriages in the tragedies we have examined—Lavinia and Bassianus, Juliet and Romeo, Desdemona and Othello—are brief and end violently. Violence is the heart of the Macbeths' marriage, its consummation. But it is the central event in a long story, not the culmination of a brief one. Unlike the other couples they are established when the play begins, and we have glimpses of a shared history. Their marriage also undergoes not a quick, violent end, a wedding night that is also a death, but a slow unraveling through time. Once consummated, it falls apart for reasons Cressida would understand: things won are done. The Macbeths are like a couple who were brought together by sex and draw apart when their sex life fades, or whose only mutual interest was their children, and who draw apart when the children leave home. They end the play as far apart as Troilus and Cressida, in contrast to the close final relationships of other couples, sexual and familial: Romeo and Juliet, Othello and Desdemona, Titus and Lavinia, Lear and Cordelia. The murder of Duncan broke the bonds of loyalty, severed the ties of king and subject, father and son, disconnected words from their meanings, and one sense from another. Now it seems to have broken the marriage bond of the couple who perpetrated it, as though the violent consummation of their marriage at once fulfilled it and destroyed it.

Yet, just as there is an Othello who can say, "That's he that was Othello; here I am" and a Lear who can say "This is not Lear," so to say that the marriage of Macbeth and Lady Macbeth is simply finished may not be the whole truth. We need to take account, first of all, of the uncanny strength of their relationship as we see it in the early scenes. Their initial bonding is remarkable. Lady Macbeth first enters reading aloud a letter from her husband, and the inseparable blending of his words and her voice melds them together. Even before he arrives she addresses him urgently, in the second person, as though he were on stage with her. They both, in different scenes, call for the coming of darkness (I.iv.50–51, I.v.50–54): their minds operate together, over a great distance, as Romeo's and Juliet's do after Romeo's banishment.

After the murder that bond seems to be broken. There are overtones of sexual disappointment in Lady Macbeth's "Nought's had, all's spent, / Where our desire is got without content" (III.ii.4–5).[23] She complains, as Portia and Lady Percy did, that her husband is keeping alone, not sharing his griefs with her (III.ii.8–9). His attempt to open out to her, "O! full of scorpions is my mind, dear wife!" (III.ii.36) involves a split in language between a natural endearment that now sounds incongruous and an image of private torment. He has told her about the air-drawn dagger, and she sounds skeptical about it (III.iv.61–62); but the most striking dramatization of the split between them is that he can see Banquo and she cannot. The more urgently he tells her to look—"Pr'ythee, see there! / Behold! look! lo!" (III.iv.67–68)—the clearer it becomes that she cannot see as he does: "You look but on a stool" (III.iv.67). Theatrically the authority belongs to Macbeth; it is part of the play's horror that we have begun to see with his eyes, to sense what it is like to *be* Macbeth. In the process, Lady Macbeth draws away from him, and from us; she has only one more appearance, and they are never seen together again. He misreads her inability to see the ghost as courage in not reacting to it, and pays tribute: "You make me strange / Even to the disposition that I owe" (III.iv.111–12). The wording of the tribute implies two kinds of estrangement: setting his fear against her courage, he feels estranged from himself; but there is also a suggestion of his growing estrangement from her. Simply put, they no longer understand each other.

Yet he is also, up to a point, drawing on her. He begins to play something like her old role, urging her to put on false courtesy to Banquo as she urged him to deceive Duncan (III.ii.29–35) and challenging the murderers' sense of their own manhood (III.i.90–102). Playing her role, he both makes her redundant and shows how much he has learned from her. He hides from her his intention to kill Banquo, saying in effect, I can do this without you. Yet he still needs other voices to encourage him, to tell him to be "bloody, bold, and resolute" (IV.i.79), and so he turns to the witches. Their instruction to him to say nothing to the apparitions, only listen to them (IV.i.69–70, 89), shows how unlike his new source of courage is to his old one. Even when they were in conflict, Lady Macbeth was always prepared to hear him out before she counterattacked. Now he is dealing with strange powers whose relation to him is unclear, and there is no real dialogue. In the process we sense anew how much he needed her, and how much he has lost in his estrangement from her.

For all his vacillations she could steady him enough to make him do the deed. Now he alternates between flat despair and reckless defiance, going in a few lines from "I have liv'd long enough" to "I'll fight, till from my bones my flesh be hack'd" (V.iii.22, 32). Menteth describes Macbeth as a man radically at war with himself: "all that is within him does condemn / Itself, for being there" (V.ii.24–25). The self-canceling of language now becomes the self-canceling of Macbeth himself as he goes alone into a private hell—whose effect, paradoxically, is so public that even a minor character viewing him from a distance can see what is happening. Lady Macbeth could urge him to action, to a sense of himself, and to concealment. In the banquet scene she tried to stop him from going to pieces in public and when she failed did her best to cover for him; her influence gone, going to pieces in public becomes his mode of life, and he is totally exposed to his enemies. The more alone he is, the more we feel his original dependence on her.

She too is alone, but in the strange border country of the sleepwalking scene, in which she is asleep yet moving and speaking, she carries on a one-sided conversation with him, a ghostly echo of their early relationship. In her first scene she talked to her absent husband as though he were there. Now she talks to him again. The difference is that this time he will not come on to the stage and join her. She talks to someone who cannot hear, and is heard by people she does not know are listening. The Gentlewoman reports, "Since his Majesty went into the field, I have seen her rise from her bed, throw her night-gown upon her, unlock her closet, take forth paper, fold it, write upon't, read it, afterwards seal it, and again return to bed; all this while in a most fast sleep" (V.i.4–8). We think back to that first letter, the sign of their bonding, whose words we heard. This is a letter, like Cressida's, whose words we never hear and whose purpose is unknown. Again language has disappeared. Is she writing to him or to herself? Is she writing over again the letter he wrote to her? In any case she has been doing this since he went to war; it is in some way an attempt to deal with his absence.

Her only relationship has been with him; she has no Nurse, no Pandarus, no Emilia. The Gentlewoman is a horrified watcher who can do nothing but watch; her mistress shows no awareness of her. Just once her imagination reaches out to another woman: "The Thane of Fife had a wife: where is she now?" (V.i.41–42). This is the one point where she strays beyond what we have seen of her early in the play, and the one killing she seems to think of with remorse. As Macbeth has drawn away from her, has she come to think of herself, for the first time, as a woman who might have links with other women?[24] Her death is marked by an offstage cry of women, as though there is a whole female community that mourns her, a community we have never seen or even known about. As though to highlight the separation of men and women, the cue for the cry is one of Macbeth's most masculine images, "We might have met them dareful, beard to beard, / And beat them backward home. What is that noise?" (V.v.6–7). He does not seem to recognize the sound of female voices.

Yet whatever unseen life that cry may suggest, Lady Macbeth has shown no awareness of it, any more than she does of the Gentlewoman. In the sleepwalking scene, the only time she is on stage with another woman, the only person she talks to is Macbeth. Most of her lines are explicitly addressed to him, and all of them could be. Like Lear's last conversation with Cordelia, it is one half of a dialogue with someone who does not respond, and it may be that lack of response that keeps drawing her back to him, refighting the old arguments, reissuing the old commands. Though she scrambles different murders together (V.ii.59–61), her memories center on the murder of Duncan, the night of their consummation, the blood on her own body she cannot wipe away. She ends with an attempt to restore their broken bonds, saying as Edgar says to Gloucester, "give me your hand," telling him their loss of virginity is forever, "What's done cannot be undone," and leading him off with the threefold command, "To bed, to bed, to bed" (V.ii.63–65) as though for another encounter, like Juliet and Cressida urging their lovers not to leave. Through all this she is in her nightgown, carrying a candle that evokes a bedchamber. It is their most intimate scene.[25]

Does he reach out to her as she does to him? It is the cry of women that leads him to observe how dead his senses are (V.v.9–15). He asks the Doctor about "your patient" (V.iii.37), not "my wife." But he does ask, and he seems to know without being told that her memory is her affliction (V.iii.40–45). When he asks the doctor if he can cure the kingdom (V.iii.50–56) he may simply be turning back to business; but the implied equation of her sickness and Scotland's (like the equation of Lavinia's violation and Rome's) makes a link between public and private life, Macbeth as king and Macbeth as husband. His first response to her death, "She should have died hereafter: / There would have been a time for such a word" (V.v.17–18), sounds like the indifference of a busy man. But the word "hereafter" triggers the word "to-morrow" and Macbeth's fullest, most terrible vision of the wasteland he now inhabits. By one reading, he has forgotten her already and turns to philosophizing and self-centered despair. By another and I think a truer one, "To-morrow and to-morrow and to-morrow" is a depth-charge of grief that goes off after a small delay. She is not mentioned in it because she is everywhere in it, pervading all its ideas. Elsewhere Macbeth's despair has indeed been focused on himself:

> I have liv'd long enough: my way of life
> Is fall'n into the sere, the yellow leaf;
> And that which should accompany old age,
> As honour, love, obedience, troops of friends,
> I must not look to have. . . . (V.iii.22–26)

Here and in his other moments of despair it is his own particular life that is ruined. In 'To-morrow and to-morrow and to-morrow' it is life itself. If we ask what makes the difference, the answer nearest to hand is that he has just heard of the death of Lady Macbeth.[26]

In her eagerness for the murder of Duncan Lady Macbeth urged time on so that it collapsed on itself:

> Thy letters have transported me beyond
> This ignorant present, and I feel now
> The future in the instant. (I.v.56–58)

For a brief moment, when a servant says "The King comes here tonight" and she replies "Thou'rt mad to say it" (I.v.31) Macbeth is already king in her mind, and she is shocked that a servant knows the secret. At this point, for her there is nothing but the future, as in the sleepwalking scene there is nothing but the past. Now that she has gone time resumes its normal course, trudging forward with no purpose at all:

To-morrow, and to-morrow, and to-morrow,
Creeps in this petty pace from day to day,
To the last syllable of recorded time;
And all our yesterdays have lighted fools
The way to dusty death. Out, out, brief candle!
Life's but a walking shadow; a poor player,
That struts and frets his hour upon the stage,
And then is heard no more: it is a tale
Told by an idiot, full of sound and fury,
Signifying nothing. (V.v.19–28)

Creation began with the Word; "the last syllable" implies that recorded time is a language; and language, unstable and self-destructive for so much of the play, will one day simply stop. When we look ahead we see universal death, and when we look behind we see more deaths, individual deaths. In the middle is the individual consciousness, the brief candle. Perhaps Lady Macbeth appears in the speech after all, the candle of the sleepwalking scene become the candle of her life, and Macbeth's, and (like the grave in *Hamlet*) anybody's.

Macbeth is in it too, a player who has done a lot of strutting and fretting in the last few scenes, whose part will end, like Hamlet's, in silence, not just because he has stopped speaking but because he is no longer heard. In his isolation Macbeth feels like an actor without an audience. The idea touched on in earlier plays, that we see ourselves only in the eyes of others, is taken deeper here. The actor exists only in the perception of the audience, and when there is no audience to hear him there is nothing of him left. At the personal level, Macbeth's speeches (and therefore Macbeth) have been meaningless without Lady Macbeth to hear and reply. Finally, he is not even an actor, with the freedom and the initiative an actor has to conduct his own performance. Everyone is a character in a story, with no existence outside the voice of the narrator; the story's language is meaningless noise, and the narrator is an idiot. But if life is a tale told by an idiot, who is the idiot? Iago mischievously imagined God as a peeping Tom; Macbeth's blasphemy cuts far deeper. With Lady Macbeth he took part in a dialogue, a drama, in which each had a voice. Now there is only one voice, neither hers nor his, but the voice of a cosmic idiot telling a story that means nothing.

UNSETTLING THE ENDING

At this point a messenger enters and Macbeth commands, "Thou com'st to use thy tongue; thy story quickly" (V.v.29). Life, we might think, goes on after all, as it does in *The Tempest* when Prospero, having imagined the vanishing of all life, turns with brisk energy to disposing of Caliban. Language resumes, and storytelling has an immediate purpose. But the story the messenger tells, that Birnam Wood is on the move, seems to make all action meaningless: "If this which he avouches does appear, / There is nor flying hence, nor tarrying here" (V.v.47–48). The messenger's tale may be colored after all by its existence in that other story, the tale told by an idiot.

It may even be that we take this awareness through the rest of the play. Perhaps, amid the triumph of good and Macbeth's own heroic resistance, including the last grand gesture when he frees himself from the prophecies and fights to the end, this vision of absurdity is never quite shaken. There are many local reasons for misgivings about the ending. Is Donalbain's absence, to which the dialogue calls our attention (V.ii.7–8), a sign of future trouble?[27] In Siward's inhuman stoicism, we have noted, there may be a touch of Macbeth. Malcolm ends as Duncan began, thanking his followers, and the repeated cries of 'Hail!' echo the witches.[28] We are back to the beginning of the play, and this is not reassuring. According to Naomi Conn Liebler, "Malcolm's and Macduff's combination of unusual birth, childlessness, and virginity suggest no potential for procreative renewal."[29]

But there may be misgivings that cut deeper than this. The play began with confused narrative and murky language. It steadied itself after the murder of Duncan—once done, that deed registers clearly as an act of horror—and the contrast between Macbeth's tyranny and the saintly English king gives a sharp moral clarity. Yet we never see that king, and the journey we take through the play is largely Macbeth's journey. "Nothing" is a key word in *King Lear*, but we can draw meaning and value out of Cordelia, even—we might say, particularly— in the agony caused by her death. But the last scenes of *Macbeth*, even more noisy and violent than the first since battles are now enacted, not just described, are shadowed by the possibility that all this sound and fury is a tale told by an idiot, signifying nothing. If we see it that way, and if we take it that this sense of absurdity comes into the play as Macbeth's reaction to the death of his wife, it may be a last grim tribute to the Macbeths and the power of their marriage.

We could never enter the mind of Lavinia; but as we have seen, her experience of being violated echoed in various ways through the play, which was haunted by her rape. The world of *Macbeth* is haunted by Duncan's murder in a similar way, but it is more deeply haunted still. There was no question of entering into the minds, if they had them, of Chiron and Demetrius, but the mood of post-coital exhaustion that hits the play might owe something to them. We do enter, with alarming intimacy, into the minds of Macbeth and Lady Macbeth, and into what we might call the mind of their marriage. Their attempt to deny agency is, ironically, part of a close examination of these particular agents. What looks like a noisy public play, beginning and ending with the clang of battle, has at its still, frightening center a murder in a domestic space, and turns out on closer inspection to be one of Shakespeare's most intimate dramas, his fullest examination of a marriage.

It is a marriage sealed in blood, linking it with *Romeo* and *Othello*, and with the conflation of marriage and rape in *Titus*. While Troilus and Cressida worked to undo each other, Macbeth and Lady Macbeth work together to undo not just Duncan's life but life itself—along with language and meaning. In the process they seem to become estranged from each other; but if we look more closely at the scenes in which they are most alone, we can see them reaching out to each other, as Titus tries to reach Lavinia across the gap of silence and Lear tries to reach Cordelia across the gap of death. In Lavinia we see, from outside, what it looks like to be the target of violation, and that is hard enough to take. The whole play struggles to cope with it. In Macbeth and Lady Macbeth we are taken, with terrible authority and conviction, into the minds of two people who have centered their life together on doing a deed of violation, we watch those minds infecting each other and the world, and in their destruction, greeted by other characters with easy satisfaction, something of us is destroyed—because they themselves have exemplified so powerfully the very human bond they have violated.

NOTES

1. See Arthur F. Kinney, *Lies Like Truth: Shakespeare, Macbeth, and the Cultural Moment* (Detroit: Wayne State University Press 2001), p. 200.

2. To Marion Lomax it sounds as though Duncan is wearing a masque costume: *Stage Images and Traditions: Shakespeare to Ford* (Cambridge: Cambridge University Press 1987), p. 57. Marjorie Garber points to the error in heraldry of placing metal against metal: *Coming of Age in Shakespeare* (London and New York: Methuen 1981), p. 107.

3. On the narrative confusion of the opening scenes, see Barbara Everett, *Young Hamlet: Essays on Shakespeare's Tragedies* (Oxford: Clarendon Press 1989), p. 99. There is a cinematic equivalent in Akira Kurosawa's *Throne of Blood* (1957) in the confusing journey of Washizu and Miki (the equivalents of Macbeth and Banquo) through the Cobweb Forest.

4. Lawrence Danson, *Tragic Alphabet: Shakespeare's Drama of Language* (New Haven and London: Yale University Press 1974), p. 123.

5. Geoffrey Bullough (ed.), *Narrative and Dramatic Sources of Shakespeare*, vol. 7 (London: Routledge and Kegan Paul; New York: Columbia University Press 1973), pp. 494–95, 495, 513, 519. Stephen Greenblatt writes of Shakespeare's witches, "it is . . . extremely difficult to specify what if anything they do, or even what, if anything, they are": "Shakespeare Bewitched," *Shakespeare and Cultural Traditions*, ed. Tetsuo Kishi, Roger Pringle and Stanley Wells (Newark: University of Delaware Press; London and Toronto: Associated University Presses 1994), p. 31.

6. Adrian Poole reads the passage in similar terms, and sees an equivalent effect in "if th'assassination / Could trammel up the consequence" (I.vii.2–3), where it is "assassination," not Macbeth, that does the deed: *Tragedy: Shakespeare and the Greek Example* (Oxford and New York: Basil Blackwell 1987), p. 46.

7. James L. Calderwood, *If It Were Done: Macbeth and Tragic Action* (Amherst: University of Massachusetts Press 1986), p. 39.

8. On the lack of finality in the play, see Stephen Booth, *King Lear, Macbeth, Indefinition, and Tragedy* (New Haven and London: Yale University Press 1983), pp. 93–94.

9. David Margolies, *Monsters of the Deep: Social Dissolution in Shakespeare's Tragedies* (Manchester and New York: Manchester University Press 1992), p. 102.

10. There is a similar effect in *Richard III*, where Richmond enters the play's consciousness for the first time when Richard becomes king; again the names are similar.

11. In the 1979 Thames television production, based on Trevor Nunn's 1976 stage production for the Royal Shakespeare Company, Macduff, after killing Macbeth, enters holding two daggers in his bloodstained hands, exactly as Macbeth did after killing Duncan.

12. See Chapter 2, n.12.

13. Arden note, p. 46.

14. Gordon Williams, *A Glossary of Shakespeare's Sexual Language* (London and Atlantic Highlands, NJ: Athone 1997), pp. 101–2.

15. Dennis Biggins, "Sexuality, Witchcraft, and Violence in *Macbeth*," *Shakespeare Studies*, 8 (1975), pp. 257–60.

16. Williams, *Glossary*, pp. 284–85.

17. This speech is examined in terms of Elizabethan medical theory by Jenijoy La Belle, "'A Strange Infirmity': Lady Macbeth's Amenorrhea," *Shakespeare Quarterly*, 31 (1980), pp. 381–86. The blocked passage implies a stopping of menstrual blood, and breast milk was menstrual blood turned white (382–83). A woman whose periods had stopped could, like the witches, grow a beard (384).

18. Holinshed's account of the manners of the Scots, taken from Hector Boece, includes the detail that Scottish women took breastfeeding as a serious responsibility and were particularly insistent on nursing their own children (Bullough, *Sources*, p. 506).

19. Bullough, *Sources*, p. 433.

20. In *Shakespeare: A Life* (Oxford: Oxford University Press 1998) Park Honan speculates that Anne Shakespeare's reproductive system was damaged when she had twins, and this would explain the subsequent childlessness of the marriage (p. 231).

21. On the sexual connotations of the murder, see Calderwood, *If It Were Done*, pp. 42–47, and Ralph Berry, *Tragic Instance: The Sequence of Shakespeare's Tragedies* (Newark: University of Delaware Press; London: Associated University Presses 1999), pp. 150–63. As Karen Bamford has pointed out to me, Macduff's reference to the Gorgon carries associations of rape: Medusa was transformed to a Gorgon after Neptune raped her.

22. Arthur Kirsch, *The Passions of Shakespeare's Tragic Heroes* (Charlottesville and London: University Press of Virginia 1990), p. 81.

23. Biggins, "Sexuality," pp. 260–61.

24. William Davenant's Restoration adaptation and Orson Welles' 1948 film both construct a relationship between Lady Macbeth and Lady Macduff, Davenant by writing new dialogue, Welles by having Lady Macduff reside in Macbeth's castle and reassigning speeches to create conversations between the women.

25. As Arthur F. Kinney points out, there is a public dimension to this scene: Lady Macbeth "in a nightdress, carrying a candle . . . enacts a popular shaming ritual for shrews, but one often employed also for witches" (*Lies Like Truth*, p. 171).

However, unlike the victim of an actual shaming ritual, Lady Macbeth has no awareness whatever of being watched and judged.

26. In Diana Leblanc's 1999 production at Stratford, Ontario Macbeth delivered the speech over the body of his wife, which had been brought on stage. The effect was moving, and of course settled the question of the speech's relation to her death. But it required new business that changed the effect of the text, and it may be more powerful to let the audience make the connection itself, making us responsible for it rather than having it forced on us.

27. Donald W. Forster, "*Macbeth's* War on Time," *English Literary Renaissance*, 16 (1986), p. 321. Roman Polanski's 1971 film version ends with Donalbain on his way to consult the witches.

28. Booth, *Indefinition*, pp. 91, 92.

29. *Shakespeare's Festive Tragedy: The Ritual Foundations of Genre* (London and New York: Routledge 1995), p. 222.

BIBLIOGRAPHY

Adelman, Janet. *Suffocating Mothers: Fantasies of Maternal Origin in Shakespeare's Plays, Hamlet to The Tempest.* London: Routledge, 1992.

Aitchison, Nicholas Boyter. *Macbeth: Man and Myth.* Stroud: Sutton, 1999.

Bartholomeusz, Dennis. *Macbeth and the Players.* New York: Cambridge University Press, 1969.

Berger, Harry, Jr. "The Early Scenes of *Macbeth*: Preface to a New Interpretation." *English Literary History* 47 (1980): 1–31.

Blits, Jan H. *The Insufficiency of Virtue: Macbeth and the Natural Order.* Lanham, Md.: Rowman & Littlefield, 1996.

Bloom, Harold. "Macbeth." In *Shakespeare and the Invention of the Human*, 516–545. New York: Riverhead Books, 1998.

———. *William Shakespeare's Macbeth.* Modern Critical Interpretations series, edited by Harold Bloom. New York: Chelsea House, 1987.

Booth, Stephen. "Macbeth, Aristotle, Definition, and Tragedy." In *"King Lear," "Macbeth," Indefinition, and Tragedy*, 81–118. New Haven and London: Yale University Press, 1983.

Bradshaw, Graham. *Shakespeare's Scepticism.* New York: St. Martin's Press, 1987.

Braunmuller, A. R., ed. *Macbeth.* Cambridge and New York: Cambridge University Press, 1997.

Brooks, Cleanth. "The Naked Babe and the Cloak of Manliness." In *The Well Wrought Urn: Studies in the Structure of Poetry.* New York: Harcourt, Brace Jovanovich, 1975.

Brown, John Russell, ed. *Focus on Macbeth.* Boston: Routledge & Kegan Paul Ltd., 1982.

———. "Macbeth." In *Shakespeare's Dramatic Style*, 160–191. London: Heinmann Educational Books Ltd., 1970.

Burnham, Douglas. "Language, Time and Politics in Shakespeare's *Macbeth*." In *Displaced Persons: Conditions of Exile in European Culture*, edited by Sharon Ouditt. Burlington, Vt: Ashgate Publishing Company, 2002.

Calderwood, James L. *If It Were Done: Macbeth and Tragic Action*. Amherst: The University of Massachusetts Press, 1986.

Carroll, William C., ed. *Macbeth: Texts and Contexts*. Boston: Bedford/St. Martin's, 1999.

Coursen, Herbert R. *Macbeth: A Guide to the Play*. Westport, Conn.: Greenwood Press, 1997.

Cowell, Andrew. *At Play in the Tavern: Signs, Coins, and Bodies in the Middle Ages*. Ann Arbor: The University of Michigan Press, 1999.

Craig, Leon Harold. *Of Philosophers and Kings: Political Philosophy in Shakespear's Macbeth and King Lear*. Toronto, Ont.; Buffalo, N.Y.: University of Toronto Press, 2001.

Curry, Walter Clyde. *Shakespeare's Philosophical Patterns*. Baton Rouge: Louisiana State University Press, 1959.

Davidson, Clifford. *The Primrose Way: A Study of Shakespeare's Macbeth*. Conesville, Iowa: John Westburg & Associates, 1970.

Elliott, G. R. *Dramatic Providence in 'Macbeth':* A Study of Shakespeare's Tragic Theme of Humanity and Grace. With a supplementary essay on *'King Lear'*. Westport, Conn., Greenwood Press, 1970.

Everett, Barbara. "Macbeth: Succeeding." In *Young Hamlet: Essays on Shakespeare's Tragedies*, 83–105. Oxford and New York: Oxford University Press, 1989.

Goddard, Harold. *The Meaning of Shakespeare*. Chicago: The University of Chicago Press, 1951.

Hawkins, Michael. "History, Politics and Macbeth." In *Focus on Macbeth*, 155–188. Boston: Routledge & Kegan Paul Ltd., 1982.

Heal, Felicity. *Hospitality in Modern England*. Oxford and New York: Oxford University Press, 1990.

Honigmann, E. A. J. "Macbeth: The Murderer as Victim." In *Shakespeare: Seven Tragedies: The dramatist's manipulation of response*, 54–76. London and Basingstoke: The Macmillan Press Ltd., 1976.

Huggett, Richard. *Supernatural on Stage: Ghosts and Superstitions of the Theatre*. New York: Taplinger Publishing Co., 1975.

Jacobi, Derek. "Macbeth." In *Players of Shakespeare 4: Further Essays in Shakespearean Performances by Players with the Royal Shakespeare Company*, edited by Robert Smallwood, 193–210. Cambridge: Cambridge University Press, 1998.

Jorgensen, Paul A. *Our Naked Frailties: Sensational Art and Meaning in Macbeth*. Berkeley: University of California Press, 1971.

Kliman, Bernice W. *Macbeth*. Manchester and New York: Manchester University Press, 2004.

Knight, G. Wilson. *The Imperial Theme*. London: Oxford University Press, 1931.

——— *The Wheel of Fire*. London; New York : Routledge, 2001.

Leggatt, Alexander, ed. *William Shakespeare's Macbeth: A Sourcebook*. London; New York: Routledge, 2006.

Levin, Harry. "Two Scenes from *Macbeth*." In *Shakespeare's Craft: Eight Lectures*, edited by Philip H. Highfill, Jr., 48–68. Carbondale: Southern Illinois University Press, 1982.

Long, Michael. *Macbeth*. Boston: Twayne Publishers, 1989.

Mack, Maynard, Jr. "The Voice in the Sword." In *Killing the King: Three Studies in Shakespeare's Tragic Structure*. New Haven and London: Yale University Press, 1973.

McElroy, Bernard. "*Macbeth*: The Torture of the Mind." In *Shakespeare's Mature Tragedies*, 206–237. Princeton: Princeton University Press, 1973.

Miola, Robert S. "Senecan Tyranny." In *Shakespeare the Classical Tragedy: The Influence of Seneca*, 92–121. Oxford and New York: Oxford University Press, 1992.

Mitchell, John Dietrich. *Macbeth Unjinxed*. Midland, Mich.: Northwood Institute Press, 1985.

Muir, Kenneth. *The Sources of Shakespeare's Plays*. London: Methuen, 1977.

Muir, Kenneth, and Philip Edwards. *Aspects of Macbeth: Articles Reprinted from Shakespeare Survey*. Cambridge; New York: Cambridge University Press, 1977.

Nicoll, Allardyce. *The Garrick Stage: Theatres and Audiences in the Eighteenth Century*, edited by Sybil Rosenfeld. Athens, Ga: University of Georgia Press, 1980.

——— *A History of Early 19th-Century Drama, 1800–1850*. Cambridge: Cambridge University Press, 1937.

——— *A History of Late 19th-Century Drama, 1850–1900*. Cambridge: Cambridge University Press, 1946.

Norbrook, David. "Macbeth and the Politics of Historiography." In *Politics of Discourse: The Literature of and History of Seventeenth-Century England*, edited by Kevin Sharpe and Steven N. Zwicker, 78–116. Berkeley: University of California Press, 1987.

Nostbakken, Faith. *Understanding Macbeth: A Student Casebook to Issues, Sources, and Historical Documents*. Westport, Conn.: Greenwood Press, 1997.

Palmer, Daryl W. *Hospitable Performances: Dramatic Genre and Cultural Practices in Early Modern England*. West Lafayette, Indiana: Purdue University Press, 1992. Cambridge and New York: Cambridge University Press, 2000.

Paul, Henry N. *The Royal Play of Macbeth*. New York: Macmillan, 1950.

Robinson, Henry Crabb. *The London Theatre 1811–1866. Selections from the Diary of Henry Crabb Robinson*, edited by Eluned Brow. London: Society for Theatre Research, 1971.

Rosenberg, Marvin. *The Masks of Macbeth*. Berkeley: University of California Press, 1978.

Rowe, Katherine. *"Humoral Knowledge and Liberal Cognition in Davenant's* Macbeth." In *Reading the Early Modern Passions: Essays in the Cultural History of Emotion*, edited by Gail Kern Paster, Katherine Rowe, and Mary Floyd-Wilson, 169–191. Philadelphia: University of Pennsylvania Press, 2004.

Sanders, Wilbur, and Howard Jacobson. "Macbeth: What's Done Is Done." In *Shakespeare's Magnanimity: Four Tragic Heroes, Their Friends and Families*, 57–94. New York: Oxford University Press, 1978.

Schoenbaum, S., ed. *Macbeth: Critical Essays*. New York: Garland, 1991.

Shaheen, Naseeb. *Biblical References in Shakespeare's Plays*. London: Associated University Presses, 1999.

Simpson, Matt. *A Man Forbid: A Reading of Shakespeare's Macbeth*. London: Greenwich Exchange, 2003.

Spencer, Christopher. *Davenant's Macbeth from the Yale Manuscript*. New Haven: Yale University Press, 1961.

Spurgeon, Caroline F. E. *Shakespeare's Imagery and What It Tells Us*. Cambridge: Cambridge University Press, 1935.

Stavisky, Aron Y. *Shakespeare and the Victorians*. Norman, Okla.: University of Oklahoma Press, 1969.

Styan, J. L. *The Shakespeare Revolution*. Cambridge: Cambridge University Press, 1977.

Wills, Garry. *Witches and Jesuits: Shakespeare's Macbeth*. Oxford and New York: Oxford University Press, 1995.

Wheeler, Thomas. *Macbeth: An Annotated Bibliography*. New York: Garland, 1990.

ACKNOWLEDGMENTS

❧

Twentieth Century

Quiller-Couch, Arthur. "Macbeth." In *Notes on Shakespeare's Workmanship*, 3–59. New York: Henry Holt and Company, 1917. © 1917 by Henry Holt and Company.

Knight, G. Wilson. "Macbeth and the Metaphysic of Evil." In *The Wheel of Fire*. London: Oxford University Press, 1930.

Brooks, Cleanth. "The Naked Babe and the Cloak of Manliness." In *The Well Wrought Urn: Studies in the Structure of Poetry*, 22–49. New York: Harcourt, Brace & World, Inc., 1975. © 1947 and renewed 1975 by Cleanth Brooks, reprinted by permission of Harcourt, Inc.

Paul, Henry N. "Macbeth's Imagination." In *The Royal Play of* Macbeth. New York: Macmillan, 1950. © 1948, 1950 by Henry N. Paul.

Goddard, Harold C. "Macbeth." In *The Meaning of Shakespeare*, 493–521. Chicago: The University of Chicago Press, 1951. © 1951 by The University of Chicago. Reprinted by permission.

Ferguson, Frances. "Macbeth." In *Shakespeare: The Figure in His Carpet*, 237–249. New York: Delacorte Press, 1970. © 1958 by Frances Ferguson. Reprinted by permission.

Knights, L. C. "Macbeth: A Lust for Power." In *Some Shakespearean Themes*. London: Chatto and Windus, 1959. © 1959 by L. C. Knights.

Berryman, John. "Notes on *Macbeth*." In *The Freedom of the Poet*. New York: Farrar, Straus & Giroux, 1976. Copyright © 1976 renewed 1993 by Kate Donahue. Reprinted by permission of Farrar, Straus and Giroux, LLC.

Empson, William. "Macbeth." In *Essays on Shakespeare*, edited by David Pirie. Cambridge: Cambridge University Press, 1986. © 1986 by William Empson. Reprinted with the permission of Cambridge University Press.

Harold Bloom. "Introduction." In *Macbeth*. Bloom's Modern Critical Interpretations series. New York: Chelsea House, 1987. © 1987 by Harold Bloom.

McAlindon, Thomas. "Macbeth." In *Shakespeare's Tragic Cosmos*, 197–202. Cambridge and New York: Cambridge University Press, 1991. © 1991 by

Cambridge University Press. Reprinted with the permission of Cambridge University Press.

Harold Bloom. "Introduction." In *Macbeth*. Bloom's Notes series. New York: Chelsea House, 1996. © 1996 by Harold Bloom.

Twenty-first Century

Hays, Michael L. "*Macbeth*: Loyal Stewards and Royal Succession." In *Shakespearean Tragedy as Chivalric Romance*, 98–129. Rochester, NY, and Suffolk, UK: Boydell & Brewer, LTd. 2003. © 2003 by Michael L. Hays.

Leggatt, Alexander. "*Macbeth*: A Deed Without a Name." In *Shakespeare's Tragedies: Violation and Identity*, 177–205. Cambridge and New York: Cambridge University Press, 2005. © 2005 by Alexander Leggatt. Reprinted with the permission of Cambridge University Press.

INDEX

❧